Y0-DYS-925

President and CEO	Mark R. Baker
Publisher	Thomas B. Haines
Editorial Director	Ian J. Twombly
Author	Thomas A. Horne
Managing Editor	Sarah Deener
Additional Writing and Editing	Mike Collins Stephen Coonts Dave Hirschman Machteld Smith Jill W. Tallman Julie Summers Walker
Research	David Jack Kenny
Copy Editor	Kristy O'Malley
Additional Editing	Julie Filucci
Proofreaders	Keith Backes Melissa Whitehouse
Designer	Michael Kline
Art Director	Jill C. Benton
Additional Design	Elizabeth Z. Jones Adrienne Rosone Leigh Walsh
Photographers	Mike Collins Mike Fizer Chris Rose David Tulis
Production	Sylvia Horne

ISBN 978-1-940603-13-1
Printed and bound in the United States of America
First edition, 2018

Published by: Aircraft Owners and Pilots Association
421 Aviation Way, Frederick, Maryland 21701
301-695-2000
www.aopa.org

Freedom to Fly

AOPA and the History of General Aviation in America

By Thomas A. Horne

Contents

Foreword

By Stephen Coonts

The dream of flight is ancient, probably as old as our species. At some time in the long-lost past our ancestors watched the birds, envied their freedom, and no doubt wondered how they sustained themselves in this invisible yet tangible substance called air. We do know that upon the invention of writing and paper, some of the great thinkers speculated about how man might learn to leave the ground and fly as the birds do. Experimenters tinkered with balloons filled with hot air, then hydrogen, and finally gliders—trying to figure out the physics and engineering principles that would make flight possible.

After the Wright brothers mounted an internal combustion engine on a glider and achieved powered flight at the dawn of the twentieth century, the dream began to soar. Still, early airplanes were expensive, flimsy toys that were exquisitely dangerous. And there was the problem of learning how to fly them. Personal aviation was the province of rich playboys and daredevils.

World War I stimulated quantum leaps in aviation technology. Thousands of young men learned to fly in the military. General aviation was born in the decades between the world wars. The general aviation airplanes of that era, which later acquired the appellation of "The Golden Age," are today antique treasures, cherished and coddled and taken to the skies on clear days without much wind.

Henry Ford, who used solid engineering and mass production to give the nation the Model T—an automobile within the financial reach of the growing middle class—also dreamed of flight for Everyman. Ford envisioned a sky full of personal airplanes. His design, dubbed the "Flying Flivver," wasn't much of an airplane, and his potential customers didn't know how to fly. The whole

THAT WE HERE IN AMERICA CAN LEARN TO FLY, GET A PILOT CERTIFICATE, OWN OR RENT AN AIRPLANE, AND FLY ALMOST ANYPLACE WE WISH WITH ONLY A FEW SENSIBLE EXCEPTIONS... **WELL, IT IS ONE OF THE GREAT PRIVILEGES OF BEING AN AMERICAN.**

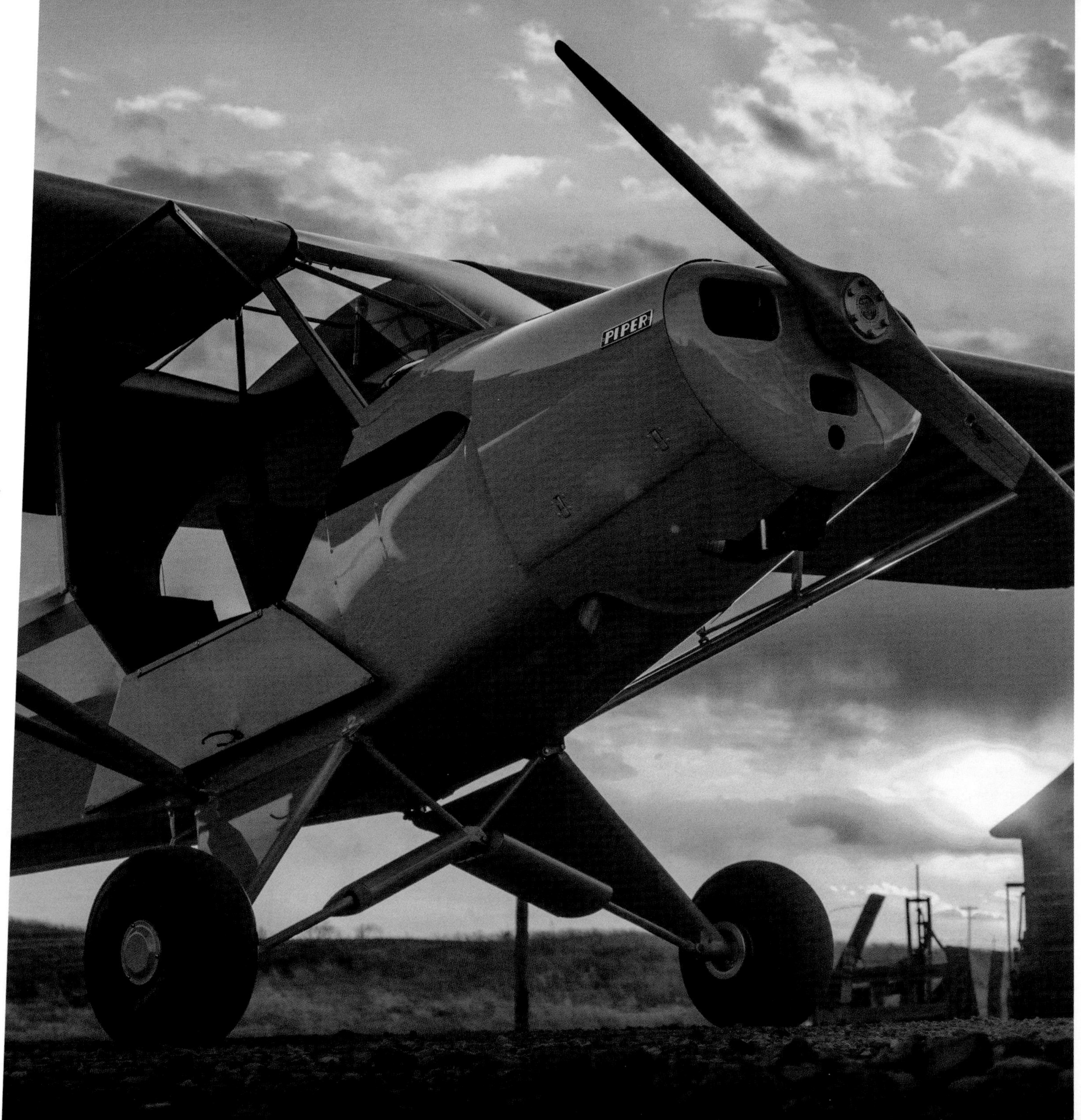

Nothing says general aviation like a little yellow Cub. Piper PA-18 Super Cub serial number one is a beautifully restored example of a classic aircraft that still flies—and inspires—today.

project was one of Ford's failures, decades ahead of its time.

In 1937, William T. Piper's J-3 Cub hit the market. The Cub was a real, honest-to-God, practical personal airplane within the financial reach of anyone willing to take instruction and who had a few extra dollars to devote to a new passion—one that could be flown from any reasonably flat, clear pasture. A natural progression from several predecessors, the Cub was an engineering triumph.

The design was so good the Cub morphed into an observation airplane during World War II. Nearly 20,000 Cubs were produced, most for the military market. Hundreds of thousands of young people learned to fly in a Cub. After the war all those pilots became an obvious market for talented designers and fledgling companies. The airplanes these aviation pioneers created are still with us today—Luscombes, Cessnas, Pipers, Stinsons, and many others.

Military and commercial aviation continued to evolve, but the dream of personal flight in one's own flying machine also grew as the middle class expanded exponentially in the decades after World War II. The dream is alive and well today, as the pages of this book will vividly prove.

Among the 40 or 50 different kinds of airplanes I have personally flown, from military jets to a large sample of light and medium twins, plus taildraggers and biplanes, the Cub remains my favorite. I owned one for about 15 years and regret the day I sold it (and recycled the money into another airplane).

Mine was a typical fabric-covered yellow Cub without an electrical system, made in 1946 (production ended in 1947), with no radio or navigation aids except a wet compass. It had been the recipient of an 85-horsepower engine somewhere along the way, one that had to be started by spinning the propeller by hand. It was basic aviation at its most elemental level.

The pilot sat in the rear seat of the small cockpit for weight-and-balance purposes. If there was a passenger, he or she sat in front, obscuring the pilot's view of the few instruments: the altimeter, airspeed indicator, and compass. The airplane had a tailwheel, sitting on what aviators call "conventional gear."

The takeoff drill was simple. Line up the Cub with the runway, usually grass, by looking out each side and ensuring there wasn't a deer, cow, or another airplane anywhere in the way. Advance the throttle to the stop while savoring the growl of that little engine, use the rudder to keep it going straight, lift the tail from the grass with the stick, and at a ridiculously low airspeed—about 40 miles per hour, as I recall—ease the stick back a trifle. Instantly the miracle of lift occurred without fuss or ceremony; the huge wing lifted the little airplane into the unstable air.

I always found that parting with the Earth sublime, as if I were an angel launching myself toward heaven.

That we here in America can learn to fly, get a pilot certificate, own or rent an airplane, and fly almost anyplace we wish with only a few sensible exceptions...well, it is one of the great privileges of being an American. Flight adds perspective to our lives. In no other country on the planet is general aviation less expensive or so reasonably regulated. In no other country is the dream of flight there waiting for anyone with a few extra dollars and the desire to take to the last great wilderness, the atmosphere that cloaks our planet.

Our freedom to fly didn't just happen. It has required intense political effort to preserve it as the nation urbanized and commercial aviation grew into a voracious Jabba-the-Hut giant. In this eightieth anniversary book by AOPA, an association of those who fly, you will learn of the triumphs and defeats through the years in the halls of Congress, state legislatures, and federal bureaucracies. Freedom is never free. Battles are never won or lost permanently, and they will continue as long as Americans like you and me are willing to fight to enjoy the magic and wonder of flight, for ourselves and future generations.

Enjoy this book, this paean to general aviation. Better yet, get out to the airport and go flying. And continue to support AOPA, which fights for all of us. Truly, we are stronger together.

I'll see you at the airport.

■ **STEPHEN COONTS** is a best-selling novelist, a former naval aviator, and a general aviation pilot.

Mark Baker, AOPA President and CEO

Introduction

Thank you for reading this book, a labor of love for those of us at AOPA who both look back with respect on our long and influential history and look forward with excitement about what the future means as we enjoy our freedom to fly.

I encouraged the creation of this book because sometimes we have to stop and look at where we've come from in order to understand where we are going. Think about it: five guys sitting around a table at Wings Field outside Philadelphia in 1939. Do you suppose they ever wondered, "Hmm...What's this going to look like in 80 years?" I think they would be surprised and proud of what we as a community have done. The freedom to fly they set out to protect that day is alive and well here in the twenty-first century.

This book is not just for today's members; this is also for pilots in the future and the people who will be leading this organization 20, 30, 40, and 50 years from now to understand that we took a pause—not a long pause, by the way—at our eightieth anniversary and captured it all.

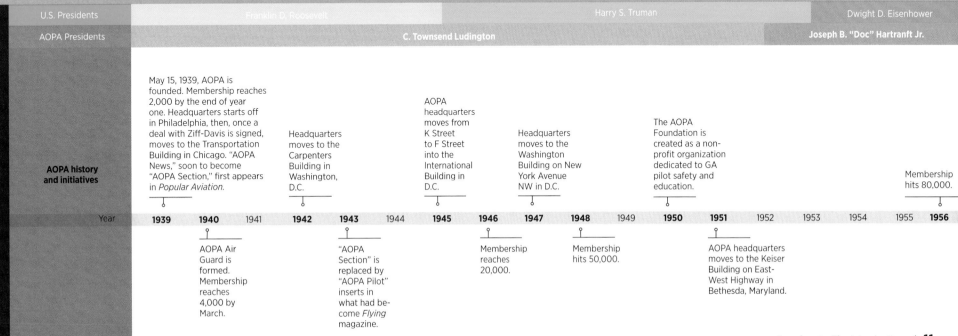

U.S. Presidents	Franklin D. Roosevelt (1939–1945); Harry S. Truman (1945–1953); Dwight D. Eisenhower (1953–)
AOPA Presidents	C. Townsend Ludington (1939–1952); Joseph B. "Doc" Hartranft Jr. (1952–)

AOPA history and initiatives

Year	
1939	May 15, 1939, AOPA is founded. Membership reaches 2,000 by the end of year one. Headquarters starts off in Philadelphia, then, once a deal with Ziff-Davis is signed, moves to the Transportation Building in Chicago. "AOPA News," soon to become "AOPA Section," first appears in *Popular Aviation.*
1940	AOPA Air Guard is formed. Membership reaches 4,000 by March.
1941	
1942	Headquarters moves to the Carpenters Building in Washington, D.C.
1943	"AOPA Section" is replaced by "AOPA Pilot" inserts in what had become *Flying* magazine.
1944	
1945	AOPA headquarters moves from K Street to F Street into the International Building in D.C.
1946	Membership reaches 20,000.
1947	Headquarters moves to the Washington Building on New York Avenue NW in D.C.
1948	Membership hits 50,000.
1949	
1950	The AOPA Foundation is created as a non-profit organization dedicated to GA pilot safety and education.
1951	AOPA headquarters moves to the Keiser Building on East-West Highway in Bethesda, Maryland.
1952	
1953	
1954	
1955	
1956	Membership hits 80,000.

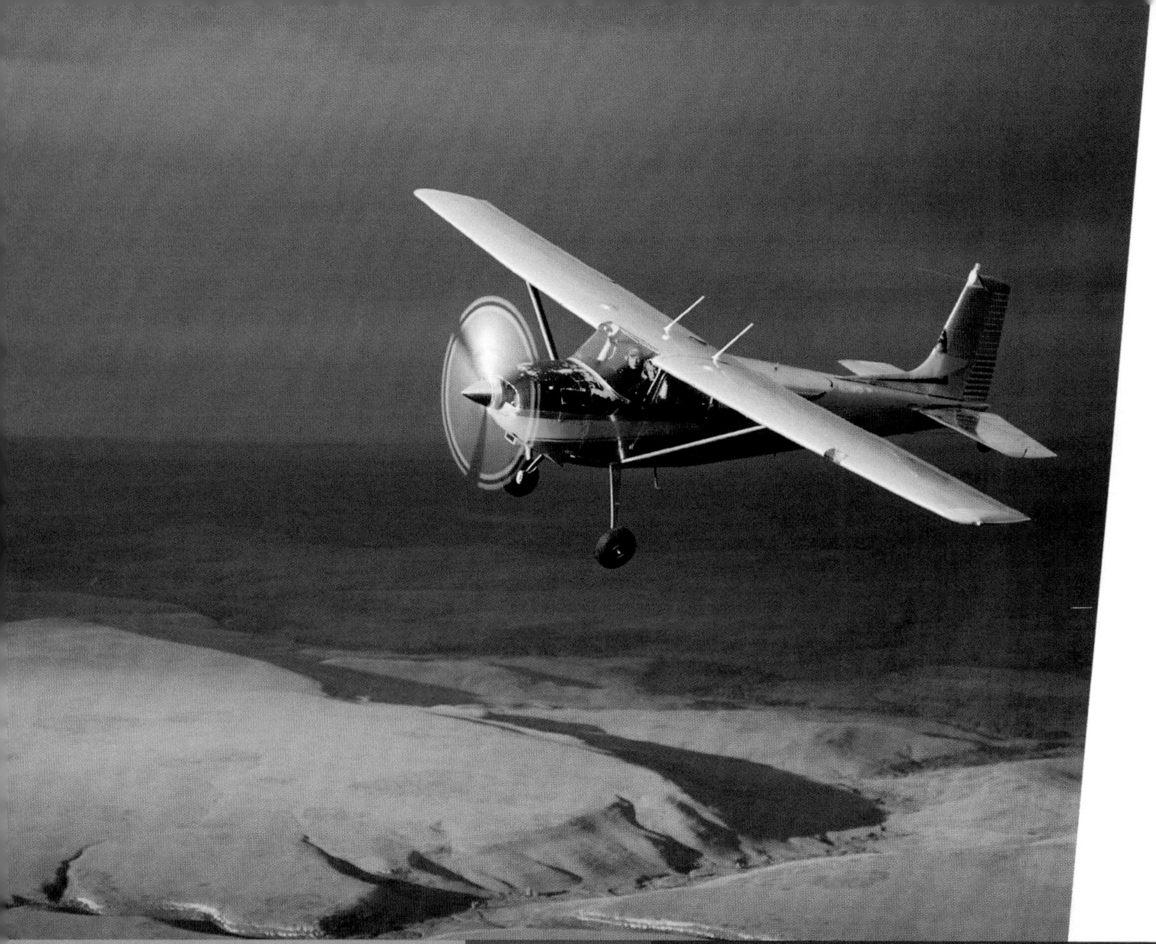

I believe that the richness of AOPA's story needs to be celebrated. It's really the members who have made the organization what it is today. The staff and leadership over the years have worked hard to create an organization full of useful benefits that people choose to belong to. Remember, this is not like union dues. People have a choice and we are grateful that so many have chosen to become members—and to stay members, often for decades at a time. I've met countless members who proudly share with me the date they joined, their member numbers, their pins. That's what I want to celebrate. That's a pride we need to share. As you read this book, I hope that pride comes through and that through these pages you can appreciate the role that general aviation and AOPA have played in our society over the past eight decades.

I've been a member of AOPA since I learned to fly in the 1970s. Like many others, I had a vague awareness of how the organization was started. But when I was given the opportunity—the responsibility—to lead this association in 2013, the first thing I did was read up on its history, because I wanted to understand what the founders were trying to do when they formed it as the winds of war were blowing

Dwight D. Eisenhower | John F. Kennedy | Lyndon B. Johnson | Richard M. Nixon | Gerald R. Ford

Joseph B. "Doc" Hartranft Jr.

1957 **1958** 1959 1960 **1961** **1962** 1963 1964 **1965** 1966 **1967** 1968 **1969** 1970 1971 **1972** 1973 1974 1975 1976 197

1958 — *AOPA Pilot* magazine makes its debut as an independent magazine with publication of the March 1958 issue.

1961 — The first *AOPA Airport Directory* is published, later known as *AOPA's Airports USA.*

1962 — International Council of Aircraft Owner and Pilot Associations, now IAOPA, started by Doc Hartranft and Victor Kayne.

1965 — Membership reaches 111,371. *AOPA Pilot* carries first aircraft and engine directory.

1967 — AOPA Foundation becomes AOPA Air Safety Foundation to reflect its work.

1969 — Membership grows to 148,000.

1972 — AOPA headquarters moves to the Air Rights Building on Wisconsin Avenue in Bethesda, Maryland.

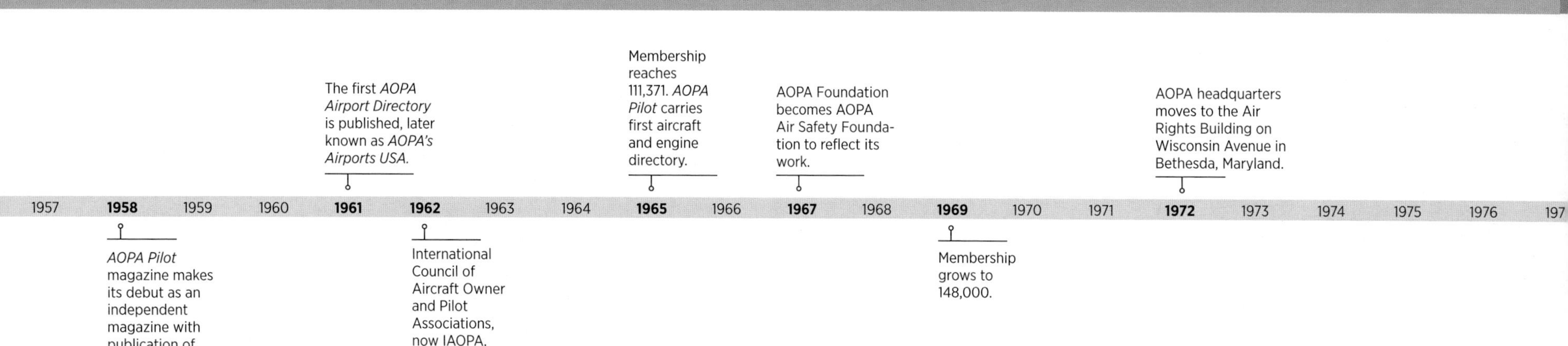

around the world. What was their intent, and were we as an organization upholding those principles that they held in such high regard?

I am pleased to see that we are upholding those principles and that AOPA is still true to its mission to protect the freedom to fly. As a result of this organization, general aviation in the United States is the envy of the world.

While we pause here to reflect on our past, we must constantly look to the future as the regulatory and economic challenges faced by pilots in other countries are constantly lapping at our shores. Our tireless vigilance allows general aviation to thrive here like nowhere else. You'll see that, page after page, as we outline how the organization overcame obstacle after obstacle to keep general aviation alive.

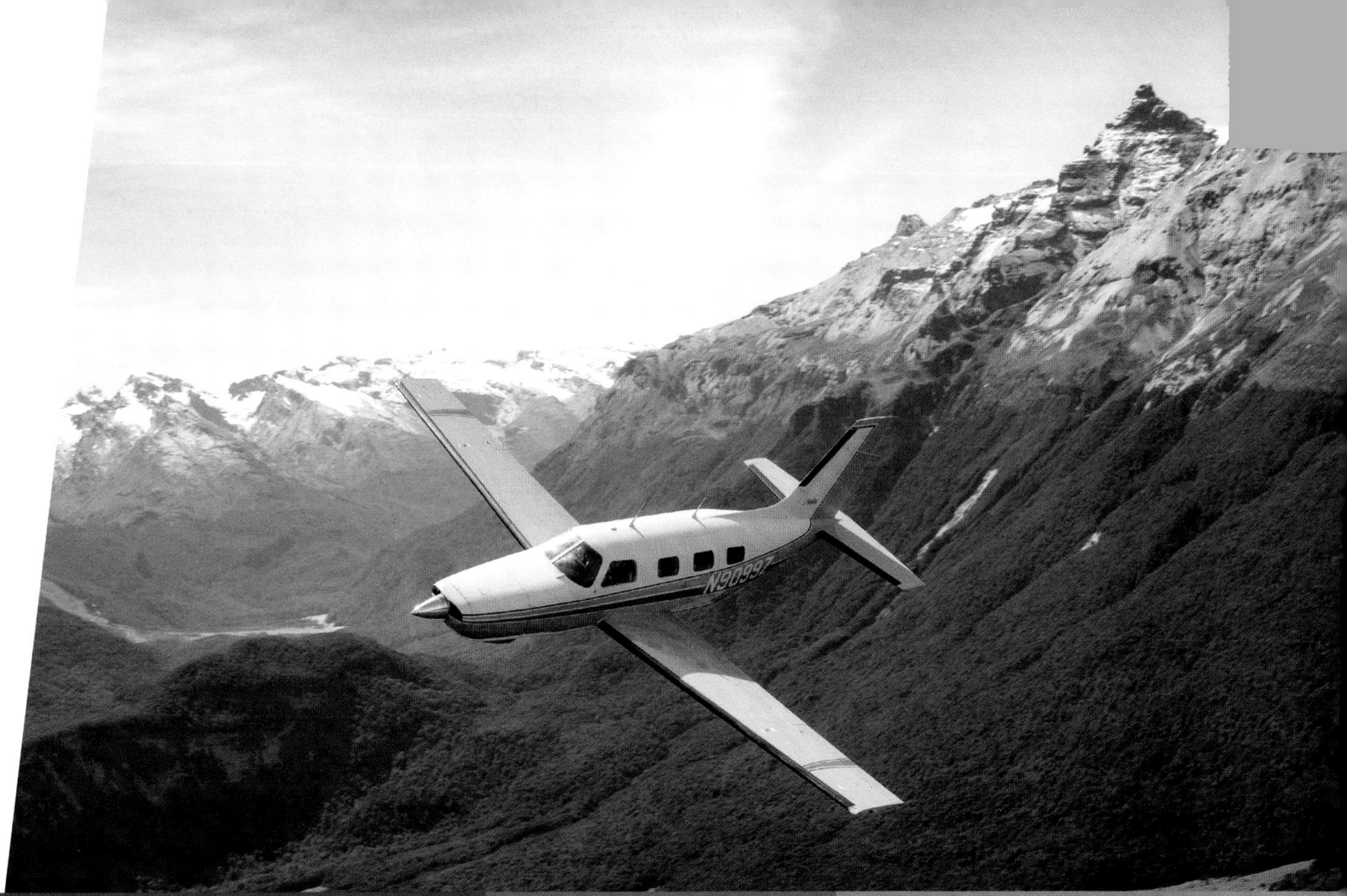

Jimmy Carter | Ronald Reagan | George H.W. Bush | Bill Clinton

John L. Baker | **Phil Boyer**

- **1978** Membership hits 220,000.
- **1979** Membership grows to 242,000.
- **1980** AOPA forms a Political Action Committee.
- 1981
- 1982
- **1983** In May, AOPA headquarters moves from Bethesda to Frederick, Maryland, at the Frederick Municipal Airport. Membership is up to 269,000.
- 1984
- **1985** Membership is at 258,000.
- 1986
- 1987
- 1988
- **1989** Membership reaches 301,000.
- 1990
- 1991
- **1992** Membership hits 303,000.
- **1993** AOPA Online is introduced on CompuServe.
- **1994** Project Pilot is launched to boost student pilot starts. General Aviation Revitalization Act (product liability reform legislation) is signed in August. Membership is up to 336,000.
- **1995** AOPA Online launches a comprehensive website in December.
- 1996
- **1997** AOPA Airport Support Network is launched. Membership reaches 341,000.

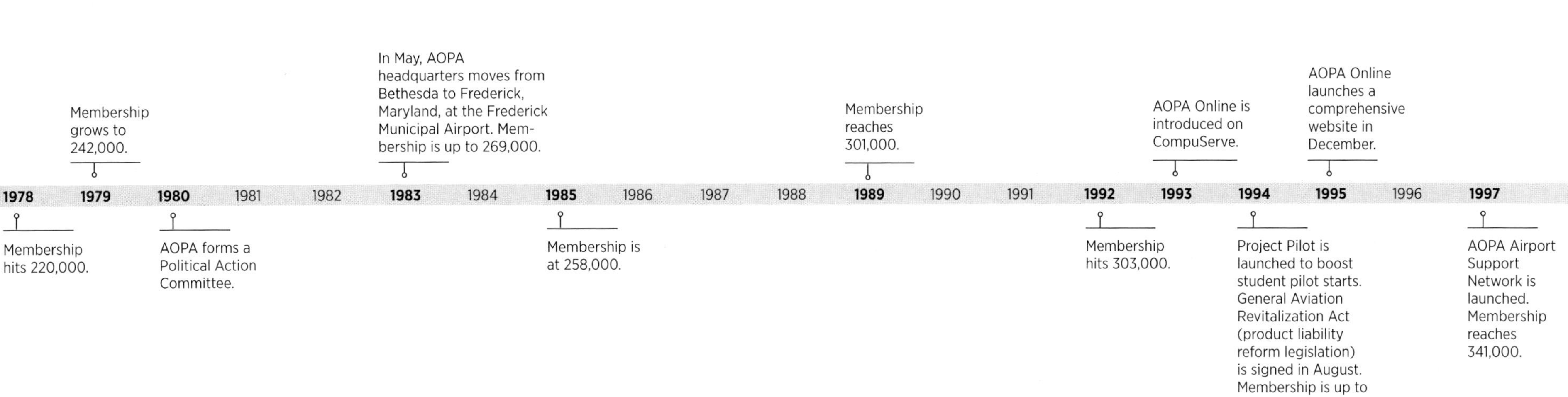

The story of AOPA's rich history dovetails with the growth of general aviation. AOPA's birth before World War II ensured our access to the skies during that turbulent time and proved the value of light airplanes and an engaged pilot population. That foundation served general aviation well when, after the war, the industry surged and airplanes became a part of society in a way the Wright brothers could never have imagined. Because of general aviation, we know what it is to have an unrivaled view of the world. The circular rainbows dancing on the edges of clouds, the morning light that bathes every scene in an almost magical glow, the welcome sight of home from 1,000 feet above—we are lucky to glimpse these views.

Today some 5,000 public airports and another 15,000 landing facilities of one sort or another support our fleet of nearly 200,000 aircraft and some 600,000 pilots. This didn't all just happen by itself. AOPA, with the support of its growing membership over the decades, nudged, cajoled, and led government and industry to understand the importance of this activity we call general aviation—the recreational and business use of personal aircraft. This freedom to fly is uniquely American, and it is that intertwined story of government, industry, and association that you will see on these pages. It could not happen anywhere else, but it did happen here—and this is how it happened.

Happy reading and blue skies,

Mark Baker, AOPA President and CEO

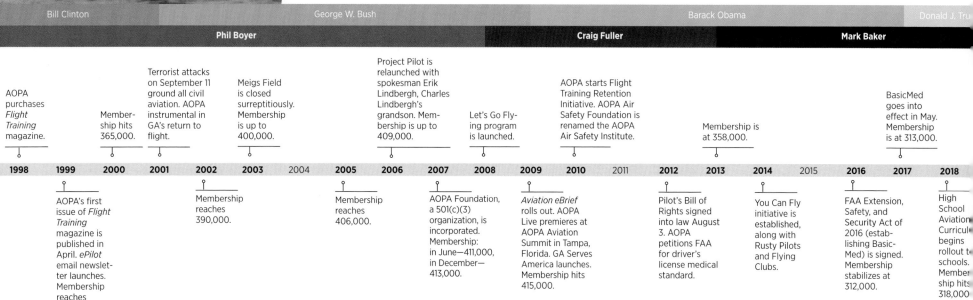

Bill Clinton | George W. Bush | Barack Obama | Donald J. Tru

Phil Boyer | **Craig Fuller** | **Mark Baker**

1998 AOPA purchases *Flight Training* magazine.

1999 AOPA's first issue of *Flight Training* magazine is published in April. *ePilot* email newsletter launches. Membership reaches 350,000.

2000 Membership hits 365,000.

2001 Terrorist attacks on September 11 ground all civil aviation. AOPA instrumental in GA's return to flight.

2002 Membership reaches 390,000.

2003 Meigs Field is closed surreptitiously. Membership is up to 400,000.

2004

2005 Membership reaches 406,000.

2006 Project Pilot is relaunched with spokesman Erik Lindbergh, Charles Lindbergh's grandson. Membership is up to 409,000.

2007 AOPA Foundation, a 501(c)(3) organization, is incorporated. Membership: in June—411,000, in December—413,000.

2008 Let's Go Flying program is launched.

2009 *Aviation eBrief* rolls out. AOPA Live premieres at AOPA Aviation Summit in Tampa, Florida. GA Serves America launches. Membership hits 415,000.

2010 AOPA starts Flight Training Retention Initiative. AOPA Air Safety Foundation is renamed the AOPA Air Safety Institute.

2011

2012 Pilot's Bill of Rights signed into law August 3. AOPA petitions FAA for driver's license medical standard.

2013 Membership is at 358,000.

2014 You Can Fly initiative is established, along with Rusty Pilots and Flying Clubs.

2015

2016 FAA Extension, Safety, and Security Act of 2016 (establishing BasicMed) is signed. Membership stabilizes at 312,000.

2017 BasicMed goes into effect in May. Membership is at 313,000.

2018 High School Aviation Curricul[um] begins rollout t[o] schools. Membership hits 318,000

1.

SETTING THE STAGE

Through the Great Depression, the passion for aviation thrived

Mention the 1930s and few will connect it with the growth of general aviation. Instead, the decade is firmly associated with the Great Depression. And for very good reasons. It was a pivotal event in U.S. history, and it spread around the world. What began as the stock market crash of October 29, 1929, led to a mass selloff of assets and a loss of confidence that curtailed purchasing, which in turn caused business failures and huge layoffs, a deflationary spiral, and mass bank runs and collapses as people attempted to withdraw their (uninsured) savings.

It took a while for the crisis to initially abate. The administration of President Herbert Hoover mounted a largely hapless effort to bring things under control. It wasn't until President Franklin D. Roosevelt's election in 1932 that anyone saw hope for recovery. The worst times were the mid-1930s, when unemployment reached 25 percent, half of all banks had closed, and some 2 million people were homeless. Debt soared, credit and spending power shrank, and loan defaults became the norm. Tariffs meant to protect American businesses from foreign competition instead brought price hikes. All this was quite a contrast to the "Roaring Twenties," when the U.S. economy had been the largest in the world, and unemployment ran at 5 percent.

America was quite different in the 1930s. Its population was 123 million (it's 327 million now, and counting), with one-third living in the New England states and more than half living in rural areas—some of which experienced a prolonged drought and subsequent "dust bowl" that forced 25 percent of the populations of Texas, Oklahoma, and Kansas to leave their homes. Only 27 percent of the total population had completed high school, and a mere 6 percent graduated from college. For those with jobs, the average income was $1,970 per year (that's about $28,900 in today's money). For those most heavily impacted by the Depression, there was no control over pricing, no unemployment insurance, no Social Security, no food stamps, no minimum wage, and no government programs to address these issues or to revitalize the economy. That began to change in the first 100 days of Roosevelt's first administration, with the initiation of an array of New Deal government programs.

It's only natural to wonder how civil aviation of any sort could manage to overcome gloom of such epic proportions. But overcome it did, largely because of its pervasive popular appeal as a cutting-edge technology, its

Orville and Wilbur Wright won the race to make the first controlled heavier-than-air flight but lost the "first-mover" advantage. Competitors including Glenn Curtiss (opposite below) rushed to enter the market during the years the Wrights spent improving their design and seeking military contracts.

symbol as a national source of pride, its pure entertainment value, its almost cult-like following—and, of course, its ability to distract from the Depression's hardships.

An irresistible attraction

The years leading up to the Great Depression had brought leaps forward in aviation. The Wright brothers had made the first truly public flight of their Model B Flyer near Le Mans, France, in 1908, in hopes of selling it to the French government. Other flights followed throughout Europe and then the United States, all attended by enthusiastic crowds wanting to see these much-publicized spectacles. Glenn Curtiss and Lincoln Beachey also put on flying shows.

The end of World War I produced a new breed of aviator: the barnstormer. Home from the fighting in Europe, without jobs and anxious to remain flying, pilots began traveling from town to town in Curtiss JN-4 Jennys. They offered rides for pay and eventually refined their loops and rolls into exhibitions, which they often performed in groups.

In some parts of the nation, aviation was still new and exhilarating, and if people on the ground stopped and pointed when an airplane flew overhead, the pilot could almost be guaranteed to make a few dollars if he landed in a farmer's field for a day or so.

Sometimes barnstormers worked with wing walkers—or they walked their own airplane's wings while another pilot flew the airplane. Sometimes they invited volunteers to jump out with parachutes. Those who flew in California frequently barnstormed in between gigs as stunt pilots in the burgeoning film industry.

CURTISS JN-4

The birth of general aviation

The Curtiss JN-4 Jenny, America's most significant aeronautical contribution to World War I, was used to train an estimated 95 percent of all U.S. and British pilots who flew in the conflict. To design his first tractor aircraft—all his previous products were pushers—Glenn Curtiss brought in B. Douglas Thomas, who had worked for both Avro and Sopwith Aviation Company in England. The JN-4D was powered by a 90-horsepower Curtiss OX-5 liquid-cooled V-8 engine.

After the war, Curtiss installed a 150-horsepower Hispano-Suiza engine and mail compartments on some JN-4Ds for the U.S. Air Mail Service. But pioneering airmail ships may be the smallest of the Jenny's postwar stories. Many of the more than 10,000 Jennys built became surplus following the armistice in 1918. The availability of relatively inexpensive war-surplus aircraft, combined with discharged Army pilots who wanted to continue flying, led to the launch of the barnstorming era—and the beginnings of general aviation as we know it today. Few commercially produced airplanes even existed at the time, and they were far more expensive than the returning pioneer airmen could afford.

Ready-to-fly Jennys that reportedly were sold for as little as $300 made aviation accessible—and encouraged a wide variety of aerial entrepreneurs. Clyde Edward Pangborn was one of them. He volunteered to fly for the Army Signal Corps and after the war with Ivan Gates formed the Gates Flying Circus. Pangborn became known as "Upside Down" because he would roll a Jenny onto its back and then glide inverted. Pangborn wasn't always behind the stick, however; a photo shows him falling in May 1920 while attempting to descend a ladder from a flying Jenny into an automobile at Coronado Beach, California. Daredevil wing walker Gladys Ingle would routinely move in flight from the wings of one Jenny to another.

Largely because of the barnstormers, the Jenny first popularized aviation and introduced flying to the American public. In addition to barnstorming aerobatics, the Jenny gave many Americans their first airplane ride. And while it probably was not their intention, the barnstormers kept aviation in the public eye as they introduced the nation to the potential for both private and commercial flying.

The barnstormers and mail pilots who survived went on to launch commercial aviation in this country. Some offered charter services and flight instruction. Others chose to compete for airmail contracts, establishing the first scheduled air carrier routes—which later were followed by the earliest passenger airlines.

U.S. Pilots in 1930 | **15,458** ▲

Roscoe Turner and Gilmore the lion flew together in NR3057 for about five years—each with his own custom-fitted parachute.

One of these barnstormers was Roscoe Turner. Turner had a talent for self-promotion from the beginning, calling his one-airplane show The Roscoe Turner Flying Circus and wearing costumes he designed himself: tunics, riding breeches, boots, and plenty of buttons and wings. Turner parlayed his notoriety into a succession of flying jobs, and eventually came up with the publicity stunt for which he's best remembered: He convinced the president of the Gilmore Oil Company to purchase a Lockheed Air Express and employ him as the pilot—and he offered to make every flight with a lion cub in the airplane, to capitalize on the company's lion trademark. The lion cub—named Gilmore, of course—flew with Turner until he outgrew the airplane. Turner earned the company lots of publicity by using the Lockheed to break cross-country records.

It wasn't just men at the controls, either. Bessie Coleman, an African-American woman from Texas, went to France to learn to fly, then put on shows in the United States. She died in 1926 when jammed flight controls caused her to be thrown from a spinning Jenny. Katherine Stinson, whose brother founded the Stinson Aircraft Company, became the first woman to perform a loop, then set numerous long-distance and aerobatic flying records and taught at the family's flying school.

Two large flying schools also opened—the Embry-Riddle Company (which eventually became Embry-Riddle School of Aviation) began in 1925 at Cincinnati's Lunken Airport,

Charles A. Lindbergh

Reluctant hero

Others had tried but Lucky Lindy made it so

Although the Wright brothers had demonstrated manned flight more than 20 years prior, it was not until a young Minnesota pilot flew nonstop in an aircraft without a windshield across the Atlantic Ocean that aviation became the world's newest fascination. "We'd been standing on our heads to get them to notice us but after Lindbergh, suddenly everyone wanted to fly," said Elinor Smith Sullivan in 1927. "After Lindbergh" was the flight of the *Spirit of St. Louis,* Charles A. Lindbergh's historic 33.5-hour flight from New York's Roosevelt Field to LeBourget Aerodrome outside Paris, on May 20 and 21, 1927.

Like Smith Sullivan, herself the youngest licensed pilot in the world at age 16 in 1927, Lindbergh and others had been testing the limits of the "aeroplane" for many years. Lindbergh had been flying since 1923, having previously been a wing walker, parachutist, and aircraft mechanic. Lindbergh soloed in May 1923 in a Curtiss Jenny he had bought for $500. He was a barnstormer, became a flight instructor, and was one of the first to fly mail across the country, providing the service on Air Mail Route #2, from St. Louis to Chicago. He graduated first in his class in the U.S. Army Air Service in 1925.

In 1919, two British aviators had flown from New Brunswick, Canada, to Ireland—prompting Augustus Post, the secretary of the Aero Club of America, to propose to New York hotelier Raymond Orteig the awarding of a prize for an American aviator to fly the transatlantic route nonstop. By 1924, several

Following his record-setting transatlantic flight, Charles Lindbergh flew extensively with his wife, Anne Morrow Lindbergh. The Lindberghs had this Lockheed Model 8 Sirius equipped with floats for an air route exploration trip to China.

attempts had been made, but none successfully. Orteig reinstated the prize in 1927, and 25-year-old Lindbergh commissioned Ryan Airlines (the lowest bidder) to build him a monoplane for $10,580.

Taking off from Roosevelt Field at 7:52 a.m., Lindbergh had 450 gallons of fuel aboard, stared at a blank black wall in front of him while seated in a wicker chair, and had no means of communication. The 3,600-mile flight took him 10,000 feet in the clouds and as low as 10 feet above waves on the ocean. When he landed at 10:22 p.m. outside Paris, he could not see the throngs of people waiting to greet him. More than 150,000 people swarmed the young pilot, and aviation was never the same.

"People were behaving as though Lindbergh had walked on water, not flown over it," biographer A. Scott Berg would write some 70 years later.

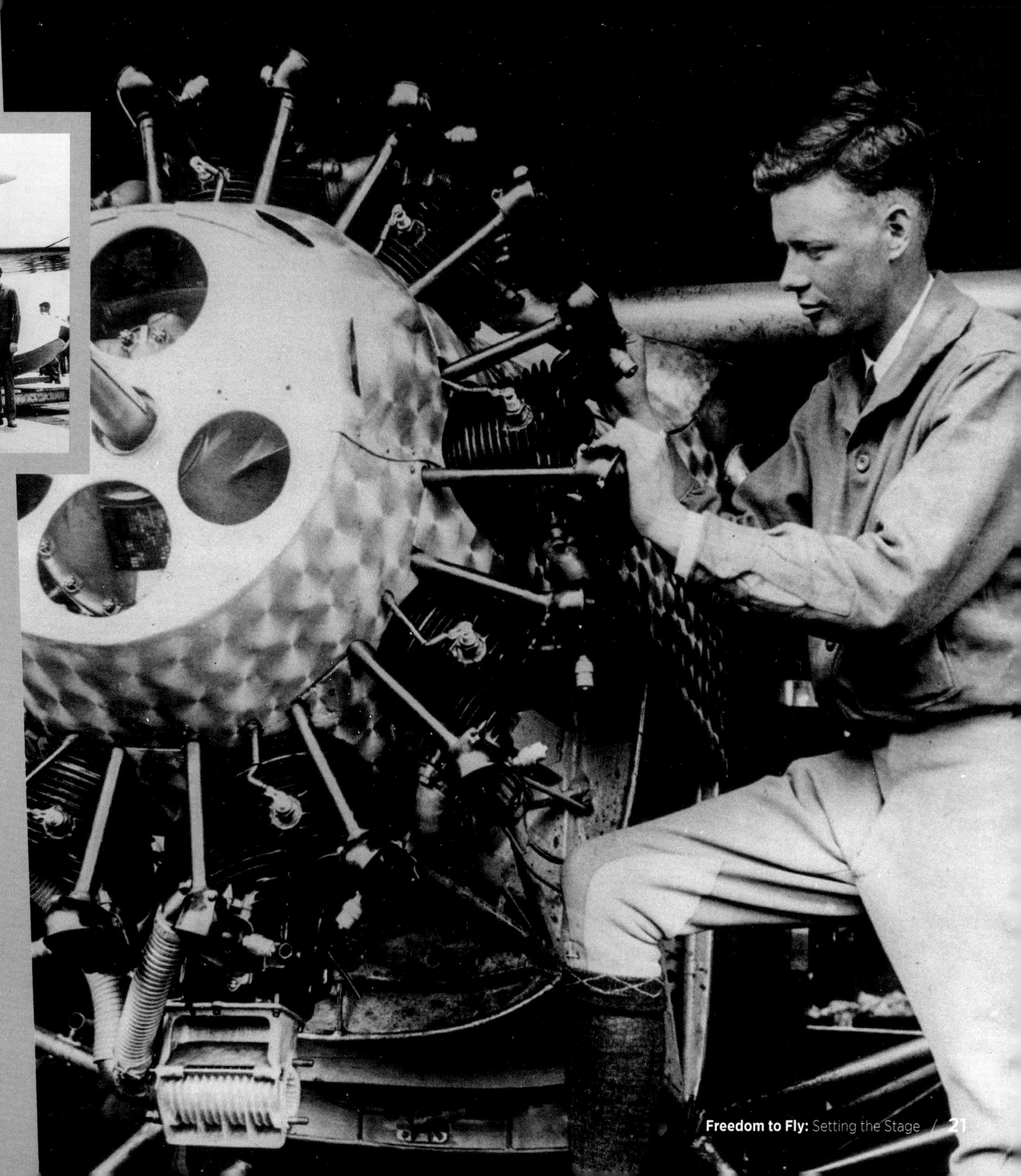

ERCO ERCOUPE

Rudder pedals? What rudder pedals?

Stalls and spins caused lots of fatal accidents in general aviation's early days, so in 1939 the stall- and spin-resistant Ercoupe was introduced. Designed by engineer Fred Weick and built by Erco, the Engineering and Research Corporation of Riverdale, Maryland, the two-seat Ercoupe had tricycle landing gear with trailing-link struts for better ground handling—revolutionary features at the time. These features alone all but did away with ground loops and hard landings. To prevent stalls and spins, the Ercoupe's up-elevator travel was limited to prevent the airplane from reaching stall angles of attack. The twin-boom, H-style vertical stabilizers were mounted away from the airplane's longitudinal axis so that the propeller's P-factor and torque effects wouldn't be as great at low airspeeds and high angles of attack.

Another interesting touch was the method of ground steering: The control yoke was used to steer, just like in a car. And the yoke was interconnected with the rudders to ensure coordinated flight. There were no rudder pedals in early Ercoupes because they weren't needed. A single brake pedal graced the floorboard in front of the pilot, another nod to automotive design. All these features added up to an airplane that was easy, safe, and fun to fly. The canopy halves even slid down so that you had the feeling of being in a flying convertible.

The first Ercoupes went on sale from 1939 to 1941, but World War II interrupted production, save for a few military versions—and a one-off model that used rockets for jet-assisted takeoffs! When production resumed in 1946, the model 415-C Ercoupe became a smash hit, with a whopping 4,309 of the 75-horsepower, Continental C-75-powered, 112-mph/96-knot airplanes delivered that year. Back then, Ercoupes sold for $2,600 and were even sold at Macy's department stores. But after that, sales went downhill.

The Ercoupe type certificate then went through a succession of owners, including the Forney Aircraft Company and Alon Inc. Finally, Mooney Airplane Company built a much-modified version of the Ercoupe—with a single vertical stabilizer. Today, Univair provides parts for the Ercoupe, but manufacturing ceased in 1974. Owing to their light weight (1,260-pound maximum takeoff weight) and limited speed envelope, lighter Ercoupes are popular as Light Sport aircraft and can sell for less than $20,000.

"THERE IS NO EXCUSE FOR AN AIRPLANE UNLESS IT WILL FLY FAST!"

—ROSCOE TURNER, AIR RACER

and in 1928 the Spartan School in Tulsa, Oklahoma. Both continue to this day, as Embry-Riddle Aeronautical University and Spartan College of Aeronautics and Technology, respectively.

In retrospect, Charles A. Lindbergh was the most well-known barnstormer. He learned to fly in 1923, performed stunts at county fairs, and gave 15-minute rides for $5. A stint in the U.S. Army Air Service came next, followed by time as an airmail pilot. After that he made the first nonstop, transatlantic flight from Long Island to Paris in 1927, winning a $25,000 prize put up by New York hotelier Raymond Orteig and becoming a worldwide sensation. His importance to the growing popularity of aviation can't be underestimated. He was the rock star of his day. He couldn't avoid attracting attention, had no privacy, and drew a media frenzy wherever he went.

Then there were the air races. If the 1920s were the decade of barnstorming, the 1930s had the National Air Races—a circuit with races at several locations. A number of noteworthy designs came out of the competition—the Gee Bee, the Laird Solution and Super Solution, the Caudron C.460, and the Seversky SEV-S2, to name a few. Winners of the races took home the Bendix or Thompson trophies. These races produced colorful pilot/showmen including Roscoe Turner. Other air-racing pilots went on to greater fame, such as James H. "Jimmy" Doolittle, Jacqueline Cochran, and Louise Thaden. Large crowds attended and followed the races, some of which were marred by fatal crashes. But apart from the spectacle of air racing, the short-lived sport also brought improvements in engine technology and aerodynamics. Winning speeds were as high as 282 mph by the end of the decade—this, from piston singles! Most were faster than the fighter planes of the day. And in 1935, entrepreneur Howard Hughes caught the world's attention by pushing his own design—the H-1 Special—to a landplane record of 352 mph.

Hughes' fame preceded the H-1 record. In 1930, another event attracted immense public interest in flying. It was *Hell's Angels,* the first movie to feature air-to-air footage of in-flight dogfighting. Set in World War I, the movie's biggest flying scene required 137 pilots to film. Hughes directed and produced, and flew as a pilot in the film, but suffered the first of his four airplane accidents in the process, fracturing his skull and requiring reconstructive facial surgery. In all, three pilots and a mechanic died during the filming. The movie was the biggest action film of its day, and it didn't hurt that it was also one of the first "talkies" with scenes in color, and featured the first major appearance of 18-year-old starlet Jean Harlow.

Howard Hughes not only designed the dogfight scenes in the first major "talking picture" about aviation, but directed them by radio from a spotter airplane—and crashed, suffering a skull fracture attempting a maneuver chief pilot Paul Mantz had rejected as too dangerous.

The Ford Trimotor, America's first successful multiengine airliner, was skinned in corrugated aluminum to increase rigidity and reduce cost.

Lean years

By the start of the 1930s, we had become an aviation-obsessed nation. Newspapers reported on anything to do with the smallest of flying achievements. Aviation-themed magazines were the rage, and kids of all ages consumed comic books featuring flying adventures. Children built and collected balsa-wood airplane models, formed clubs, and earned aviation merit badges in the Boy Scouts. And where there were airports, there were gawkers.

Others, however, weren't there for a vicarious experience. They were pilots, flying a growing number of newly designed general aviation airplanes. The Depression was a tough time, but not all were poverty-stricken. Far from it. Some prospered as owners of businesses, some thrived as professionals, some had inherited wealth, some made money in real estate and oil, as did those involved in products having inelastic demand—such as gasoline, or canned or frozen food. For savvy businessmen, the Depression presented opportunities. Low prices, low costs, and devalued capital meant it took less money to start a business. As for real estate, the Florida land boom of the 1920s—a speculative bubble that burst in the early 1930s—served as an example of how land and houses could be bought for a fraction of their original asking prices. Those able to wait it out were generously rewarded.

The number of airline passengers also reflected the increased public acceptance—and glamour—of air travel. In 1930, only 6,000 people in the United States had flown in a commercial airliner, most likely a Ford Trimotor. By 1934 there were 450,000 paying passengers. When Douglas' sleek-looking, all-metal, 21-seat DC-3 entered service in 1936, even more made reservations.

Anyone with a job in those days was a lucky man or woman, and knew it. Those with the means eagerly took to the air in their own airplanes. Others formed flying clubs, pooled their money, and shared both expenses and camaraderie.

But as the Depression wore on, growth of the pilot population slowed. In 1929, airman statistics showed there were just 9,215 pilots, and by 1932, that number had risen to 18,591. That number dipped as low as 13,949 in 1934, before climbing to 17,681 in 1937. These figures include pilots having either private or commercial pilot certificates.

Manufacturing increases

General aviation airplane manufacturing grew in the 1920s, and produced a number of memorable designs—the early Fleet, Curtiss, Stearman, and Travel Air singles among them. But it was in the 1930s that manufacturing experienced a notable expansion. This expansion produced the "big three" manufacturers that continue to this day: Piper, Cessna, and Beechcraft.

CESSNA AIRMASTER

A taste of things to come

Aeronautical engineer and future Cessna President Dwane Wallace designed the Cessna Airmaster—and the stylish, high-wing airplane pointed the way to the company's future growth and popularity. Its full cantilever wing (no strut) and radial engine would continue throughout the late 1940s and 1950s in more powerful, capable, and commercially successful designs such as the 190/195 Businessliner.

The Airmaster also marked the end of the line for Cessna's use of 1930s staples such as fabric covering, wood wings, and Warner engines. The company's future designs would be made of metal, were roomier and faster, and could carry heavier loads over longer distances.

Wallace, a nephew of company founder Clyde Cessna, went on to lead the Wichita-based company for 40 years, and his most lasting achievements would come as the company's top executive.

'Our favorite missing person'

Daring aviatrix captured the world's attention

Of all the personalities who emerged in aviation in its infancy, it is Amelia Earhart who continues to enthrall us: What happened to that daring girl who set off to circumnavigate the world? Since her first 10-minute ride with air racer Frank Hawks in Long Beach, California, Earhart said, "I knew I had to fly." And fly she did, becoming America's sweetheart (with a little extra push from eventual husband George P. Putnam, a publicist) by setting world records for altitude, distance, and daring. But it was her final flight—and its disappearance—that forever etches her in our memory.

Born in Atchison, Kansas, in 1897, Earhart was the daughter of a banker and socialite who had a troubled and tumultuous childhood because of her alcoholic father. Her mother, considered progressive because she allowed her daughters to dress like tomboys, would eventually help fund her oldest daughter's flying passion. In 1923 at the age of 26, Earhart was the sixteenth woman to be awarded a pilot's license. She became a sales rep for Kinner Aircraft, and *Cosmopolitan* magazine hired her to write columns about flying. She also became a visiting faculty member for Purdue University and a great friend of first lady Eleanor Roosevelt (whom Earhart took flying). This national exposure—and her daring record-setting flights—made her a darling of the pre-World War II era.

When she proposed a flight around the world in 1937, Putnam put his promotion engine to work and created a media frenzy. And when Earhart and navigator Fred Noonan took off from Miami, Florida, on June 1, the world was watching. After completing 22,000 miles of the 29,000-mile trip, Earhart and Noonan departed Lae Airfield in the South Pacific for Howland Island, the longest overwater portion of the flight.

The pair were supposed to communicate with the U.S. Coast Guard ship *Itasca*, but although the ship's crew could hear Earhart, she could not hear their transmissions. At 7:42 a.m. the *Itasca* received this transmission from Earhart: "We must be on you, but we cannot see you. Gas is running low." A search of 150,000 square miles in the Pacific—at $4 million the most costly and intensive search and rescue of the time—never revealed a crash site or what happened to the Lockheed Electra 10E and its crew.

"The mystery is part of what keeps us interested," said Tom Crouch, aeronautics curator at the National Air and Space Museum. "In part, we remember her because she's our favorite missing person."

Amelia Earhart was a pioneer in aviation, and she was also a champion for commercial aviation and women's rights.

Clyde Cessna crashed his first airplane 13 times before achieving a successful flight in June 1911—like other pioneers trying to simultaneously learn how to design aircraft and fly them.

Brothers Clarence Gilbert and Gordon Taylor owned the Taylor Brothers Aircraft Corporation of Rochester, New York, and made their "Chummy" high-wing monoplane in 1926. It didn't sell, and Gordon died in 1928 in the crash of a successor design. A Pennsylvania oilman, William T. Piper, invested $400 in Taylor Brothers and lured them into moving to a bigger factory in Bradford, Pennsylvania. In 1930 Taylor Brothers went bankrupt, Piper bought the assets for the grand sum of $761, and the renamed Taylor Aircraft Company began building the E–2 Taylor Cub. Taylor left the company in 1935, then Piper moved the company to Lock Haven, Pennsylvania, in 1937, where it became Piper Aircraft Corporation.

In spite of the Depression, Piper believed there was a market for a simple, two-seat single-engine airplane, and so began production of the iconic Piper Cub line. First came the J–2 Cub in 1936, which racked up 1,200 sales. Then came the immensely popular J–3 Cub, with almost 20,000 total sales. The company remained in the Piper family until 1969. By that time it was an unqualified success, with sales of thousands of piston single- and twin-engine airplanes. After that, it passed through a succession of owners and at one point operated four

TAYLOR E–2 CUB

Precursor to an icon

The Piper J–3 Cub is one of the most identifiable airplanes in the world. It ranks as the fifth-most-produced civilian aircraft, and with an average of more than 2,200 manufactured per year from 1938 to 1947, it had by far the highest annual rate. But Piper can't take all the credit. The E–2 Cub began the lightplane revolution.

Designed by Clarence Gilbert Taylor and certified in 1931, the E–2 was originally an open-cockpit high-wing monoplane with a squared-off tail and angular wing tips. Good engines could be hard to come by in the early days of aviation, and Taylor went through a few before selecting the Continental A-40. One early failed engine was a 20-horsepower Brownback "Tiger Kitten," hence the Cub nickname. The engine turned out to have more roar than bite, and could barely lift the airframe off the ground.

William T. Piper came into the airplane business almost by accident. According to Taylor's obituary in *The New York Times*, the Bradford, Pennsylvania, Chamber of Commerce invested $50,000 in the company and inserted Piper to represent its investment. Piper was a successful oilman, and his business experience helped to shape the company strategy early on. In fact, Piper is credited with insisting the airplane be affordable and easy to fly.

When Taylor's company succumbed to the Great Depression, Piper bought the assets. He moved the company to Lock Haven in 1937 after a fire in the Bradford plant. By that time, Taylor's company had designed and built the updated J–2, more or less a J–3 with a Continental A-40. The J–3 was Piper Aircraft's design, and improved on Taylor's earlier work.

Taylor was said to be bitter about the loss of his designs and vowed to beat Piper. Although Taylorcraft never matched Piper's output, it produced many successful designs still appreciated today.

Curtiss
AEROPLANE AND MOTOR WORKS
NC
CUB

BEECH MODEL 17 STAGGERWING

Don't be misled by that muscular radial engine on the nose. In every sense but the most literal, the Beech Model 17 Staggerwing created the category of corporate jet.

Fast? Better believe it. In the Golden Age of air racing, Staggerwings won the Texaco, Bendix, and Harmon trophies in their first four years of production. They set speed and altitude records and could cruise at more than 200 mph, performance that rivaled some of the front-line fighters of the day. Indeed, more than half of the 781 airframes built from 1933 to 1949 went to U.S. and Allied armed forces during World War II, filling their need for swift, reliable courier aircraft.

Comfortable? Their big bench seats accommodated five prosperous adults in the manner of the era's luxury cars. Targeting the same businessmen who bought the massive sedans built by Duesenberg, Marmon, and Cord, Walter Beech was not about to forfeit sales for a lack of creature comforts. Mobile air conditioning hadn't been invented, but the windows cranked up and down.

After the Travel Air Manufacturing Company he'd co-founded was absorbed

Operating historic aircraft isn't for the faint of heart—or wallet. The fact that about 200 Staggerwings are still airworthy is a testament to the loving care lavished upon them by owners eager and able to bear the expenses of maintaining a tube-and-fabric airframe, radial engine, and delicately rugged retractable landing gear. To the enthusiast, the cost of preserving aviation's past is an essential investment in its future.

The first Beechcraft defined a new category of aircraft

by Curtiss-Wright in 1929, Beech tried unsuccessfully to convince the new owners to explore the market for a cabin-class biplane. In 1932, he lined up the financial backing to go off on his own, taking engineer Ted Wells with him.

The prototype of Wells' clean-sheet design flew just seven months later: a fixed-gear, wood-and-fabric biplane available with engines of up to 710 horsepower and a maximum gross weight of 6,000 pounds.

Initial sales were slow, although the base price of $19,000—about $330,000 in 2018 dollars—seems like a bargain today. The 1935 redesign that combined retractable gear with a 225-horsepower Jacobs engine also reduced the price by more than half, and sales increased steadily until civilian production was redirected to the war effort. The last Staggerwing was delivered in 1949.

Contemporary pilots unfamiliar with its niche-creating history or pivotal role in establishing one of the world's most venerable manufacturers are well aware of another of its defining characteristics: The Staggerwing is consistently ranked among the most beautiful airplanes ever built. Park one on the ramp near a Citation or even a Learjet, and the biplane is where crowds will gather. That's one reason why more than a quarter of them are still with us 70 years after production ended, most in airworthy condition—although now flying for pleasure (of onlookers almost as much as their owners) instead of business.

611
PAN AMERICA
CLIPPER TABITHA MAY
PAA

DOUGLAS DC-3

The workhorse that made airlines viable

The first of 20 Douglas DC-2s ordered by Trans World Airlines made its maiden flight on May 11, 1934; a month later, the company had booked orders for 75 of the twin-engine monoplanes. Soon Donald Douglas was producing one aircraft every three days, for the growing airline industry as well as the U.S. Navy and U.S. Army Air Corps. But the 12-seat airplane was too small to fill American Airlines' need for a sleeper aircraft to serve its transcontinental route.

A two-hour long-distance phone call—that reportedly cost American's president, C.R. Smith, more than $300—finally convinced a reluctant Douglas to meet American's requirement with a modified DC-2. The Douglas Sleeper Transport—with a wider cabin, longer fuselage, and bigger wingspan—ended up being an almost completely new design; the DC-3 could sleep 14 or seat 21. When production ceased in 1947, the company had built approximately 10,600—most of them C-47s, and not counting those made under license in the Soviet Union and Japan. Power was provided by Wright Cyclone and Pratt & Whitney Twin Wasp radial engines of 1,000 to 1,200 horsepower each.

On June 25, 1936, American completed the DC-3's first commercial flight, from New York to Chicago. In late 1938, DC-3 service from Newark, New Jersey, to Glendale, California, was scheduled for 18 hours, 40 minutes, including refueling stops—although revolutionary at the time, modern jets now can cross the country nonstop in one-third the time. The twin-engine taildragger also made passenger airlines economically viable. "The DC-3 freed the airlines from complete dependence upon government mail pay," Smith said years later. "It was an airplane that could make money by just handling passengers."

The C-47 Skytrain and other military variants distinguished themselves in several Allied invasions during World War II. In the early darkness of D-Day, nearly 1,000 dropped paratroopers behind the beaches of Normandy, France. After the war, General Dwight D. Eisenhower said the C-47 was one of four weapons without which the war could not have been won. Postwar, they served in the Berlin Airlift, in Korea, and—in Vietnam—as the AC-47 Spooky gunship.

After World War II many found, or went back to, airline service, and DC-3s—some repowered with twin turboprops—remain in service today. The model also made its way into the general aviation fleet as business and, less often, personal aircraft; today several museums and other organizations operate them, and flight training in the DC-3 is available, as well.

Elrey Borge Jeppesen

Captain Jeppesen

The man who charted the world

Today's pilots know the name Jeppesen from charts and flight training products, but they might not realize all pilots owe a debt to the man who pioneered accurate aviation navigation aids.

When Elrey Borge Jeppesen was a mail pilot in the 1930s, aviators used Rand McNally road maps to help them find their way. But road maps were designed for people who never left the ground. Jeppesen began compiling notes about every airport he visited, highlighting landmarks, elevations of obstructions, and airport runway information.

When several of his pilot friends expressed interest in getting a copy of his notes, Jeppesen printed copies of the material and sold them for $10. He flew professionally for decades while producing charts on the side, but stopped flying for the airlines in 1954 to concentrate on the chart business. The business he founded in his basement still bears his name, but now Jeppesen, a subsidiary of the Boeing Company, provides navigational charting, digital data, information services, and training products for pilots around the world, and "Jepp charts" is a permanent addition to the pilot lexicon.

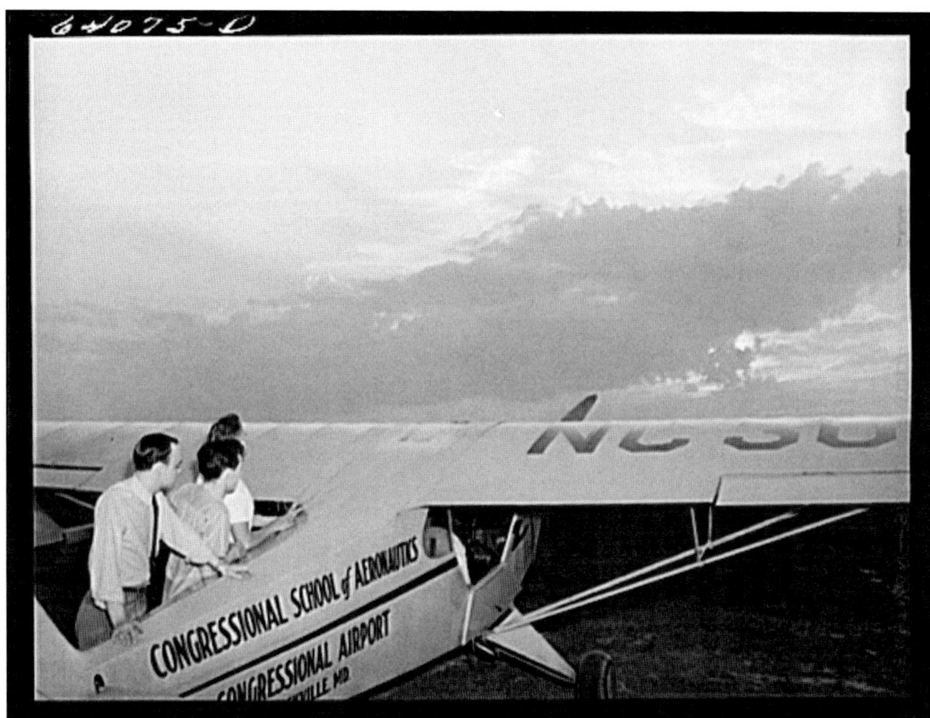

factories—in Lock Haven; Vero Beach, Florida; Lakeland, Florida; and Santa Maria, California.

The Travel Air Manufacturing Company of Wichita was started in 1925, and owned by partners Clyde Cessna, Lloyd Stearman, and Walter Beech. They built the Travel Air line, then merged with Curtiss-Wright in 1929. Eventually, all three partners left to form their own companies, with Walter Beech creating the Beech Aircraft Company with his wife, Olive Ann. Beech's first airplane, the Model 17 Staggerwing, became an instant hit—and so was the company's first twin, the Model 18 Twin Beech. What followed then was the Bonanza line, along with a largely exemplary production of other piston singles and twins, the King Air line of twin turboprops, and several business jets.

In 1927, Cessna formed the Cessna Aircraft Corporation, which produced the AW, CW-6, and DC-6 singles until 1931, when the company closed down for lack of business. The Depression had eased by 1934, and Cessna sold the company to his nephews Dwane and Dwight Wallace, who reopened the plant and resumed production. Cessna went back to farming, but Cessna the company went on to become a general aviation manufacturing powerhouse.

In those early days, the "Big Three" were all essentially family-owned enterprises. Today,

The Civilian Pilot Training Program operated at 1,132 colleges and universities and 1,460 flight schools. CPTP students are shown at Congressional Airport in Rockville, Maryland, in 1941, before the U.S. entered World War II (left).

all have gone through bewildering chains of ownership involving ever-larger corporations, and even foreign governments, with varying levels of commitment to general aviation. Some still look back with nostalgia to the formative years.

War clouds

By the latter half of the 1930s, productivity was increasing, unemployment was easing, and confidence was on a cautious upswing; gross domestic product rose 9 percent per year from 1933 to 1937. But by 1938, tensions in Europe prompted a growing conviction that the United States couldn't avoid becoming involved in another world war. Would we have the necessary number of warplanes and pilots to fight what was assumed would be a global conflict? With an Army Air Corps of just 1,500 airplanes and a force of 26,000 men, the answer was clearly "no." We needed more pilots and airplanes—and fast. General Henry H. "Hap" Arnold urged a program to train civilian pilots, and in December 1938, Roosevelt signed a law that established the Civilian Pilot Training Program (CPTP). After all, Great Britain, France, and, yes, Germany already had thinly veiled programs to teach civilians to fly in the military, so why not the United States?

The CPTP's aim was to train 20,000 college students annually, giving each of them 72 hours of ground school and 35 to 50 hours of flight instruction. Initially, there were to be 11 colleges and universities with their own designated training sites, but by 1941 there were 1,132 colleges and universities and 1,460 flight training schools in the CPTP. These were all privately operated flying schools at civilian airports all over the United States. Almost overnight, the Depression ended for these schools—as well as for the manufacturers

AERONCA C-2

A mile for a penny in the flying bathtub

Before the Cub, there was the Aeronca C-2. This simple, single-seat monoplane may just be the father of recreational flying in America. With a plywood seat and bare-bones instrumentation, the fabric-covered airplane sold for $1,495 when it was introduced in 1929. By mid-1930, the Great Depression had driven the price down to $1,245. The Aeronautical Corporation of America advertised operational costs lower than those of an automobile—including just one cent a mile for gas and oil—as well as docile handling characteristics that made flying accessible to the average person. The company (its name was formally shortened to Aeronca in 1941) sold 164 C-2s in 1930 and 1931, even as the Depression deepened.

Before the C-2, most aircraft were employed in some commercial role. But French-born Jean A. Roché, senior aeronautical engineer for the U.S. Army Air Service, designed the diminutive "Roché Original" as a personal aircraft. Working in Roché's garage, Roché and partner John Dohse assembled the airplane in their spare time and enlisted the help of colleague Harold Morehouse to outfit it with an engine. Aeronca bought production rights to what became the C-2 and modified it slightly for mass production.

The C-2 weighed 406 pounds empty, had a maximum gross weight of 700 pounds, and ran on a 26-horsepower engine. Instrumentation was basic; for early models, even the airspeed indicator was optional. Marketing for the little airplane boasted that it took off in 70 feet and landed at 30 mph. It was small, affordable, and easy to fly—ideal for novice fliers. Aeronca soon widened the fuselage for a two-seat C-3, and competitors flooded the market. The era of personal flying had begun.

James H. "Jimmy" Doolittle made a name for himself in air racing, setting numerous speed records in the 1925 Schneider Cup Race (lower left), and winning the 1931 Bendix Trophy in a Laird Super Solution (far left). Doolittle went on to lead the Tokyo Raid; he's shown here accepting a medal from the skipper of the *USS Hornet* before the raid (upper left). The medal, once given to a U.S. Navy officer by the Japanese, was wired to a bomb and returned "with interest."

"I AM NOT A VERY TIMID TYPE. IT'S VERY IMPORTANT TO SOME PEOPLE, BUT NOT TO ME. I HAVE A SIMPLE PHILOSOPHY: **WORRY ABOUT THOSE THINGS YOU CAN FIX. IF YOU CAN'T FIX IT, DON'T WORRY ABOUT IT; ACCEPT IT AND DO THE BEST YOU CAN."** —JAMES H. DOOLITTLE

James H. Doolittle

Racer to war hero

Before the war, Doolittle pushed limits

First outside loop, first instrument flight, first aeronautical engineering doctorate degree, multiple world speed records and air race victories, leader of the first U.S. air raid on Japan in World War II, medal of honor, lieutenant general, corporate leader, and best-selling author. James H. Doolittle was at the forefront of aviation during its most dynamic period in the 1920s and 1930s, and he stayed in the vanguard throughout its rapid technological advancements and worldwide industrialization in the 1940s.

Short and scrappy, Doolittle was born in 1896, spent his youth in Alaska, then moved with his family to Southern California where he became a competitive boxer, and he saw an airplane for the first time in 1910. He learned to fly in the U.S. Army during World War I and became a flight instructor, but didn't serve overseas.

He was a star on the air racing circuit in the 1920s and 1930s, winning national titles in radical, new, and dangerous aircraft designs such as the stubby Gee Bee R-1. In 1929, he made the first "blind flight," validating instrument flying techniques.

During World War II, he led the 16-airplane raid on Japan flying B-25s from the *USS Hornet*, a major morale boost for the United States, which was still reeling from the surprise attack at Pearl Harbor.

He continued to fly later in the war as a general in North Africa and Europe and implemented new, aggressive tactics that encouraged fighter pilots to break away from bombers and attack German airfields and ground targets. Previously, U.S. fighters had been ordered to stay with and protect U.S. bombers at all times.

Doolittle married Josephine "Jo" Daniels in 1917, and the title of his best-selling autobiography, *I Could Never Be So Lucky Again*, referred to meeting, falling in love with, and marrying her—not his flying exploits. He died in 1993 at age 96.

paid to supply training aircraft. These included thousands of Piper Cubs, Aeroncas, Taylorcrafts, Waco UPF-7s, and Meyers OTW biplanes.

The thousands of pilots trained in the CPTP would go on to be commissioned in the Army or Navy and sent for more specialized training at military airfields. Among them were astronaut and Senator John Glenn, World War II ace Richard Bong, and Senator George McGovern, to name a few. After the attack on Pearl Harbor, the name was changed to the War Training Service (WTS), used until the program ended in 1944. When all was said and done, it had trained more than 435,000 pilots.

The CPTP proved that government investment in Depression-era economic programs could also work to boost general aviation, and with immediate effect. Meanwhile, in the private sector, the general aviation pilot population steadily advanced. From 1937 to 1939, the number of pilots nearly doubled, from 17,681 to 33,706. By 1940, there were 69,729 pilots; in 1941 that number almost doubled, to 129,947.

And in Philadelphia, a group of lawyers, industrial executives, and a student at the University of Pennsylvania had joined up to represent general aviation's interests on what was rapidly becoming a complex political stage.

Louise Thaden

Speed racer

This Air Derby victor helped found The Ninety-Nines

Louise Thaden greets a crowd estimated at 18,000 after winning the heavy division of the first women's transcontinental Air Derby in 1929.

Few women pilots achieved notoriety in the Golden Age of aviation, but those who did remain well-known today.

One of these women was Louise Thaden (born Louise McPhetridge), who learned to fly after joining the Travel Air Manufacturing Company as a sales representative in Wichita, Kansas. Her salary included free flying lessons, and she earned a private pilot certificate in 1928. That year she also became the first pilot to hold the women's altitude, endurance, and speed records in light airplanes. She was the fourth woman in the United States to obtain an airline transport pilot certificate.

The general public was enamored with pilots, but not too keen on the idea of flying. Thaden admitted that her later job at Beech Aircraft Corporation was to convince prospective buyers that if a woman could fly airplanes, anyone could. And she was good at that job—from 1929 to 1931 she sold 25 aircraft, a high number for anyone considering the depressed economy.

By now the nation had begun following the exploits of male pilots in local and national air races, but women were not allowed to participate in those events. That changed in 1929 with the first women's transcontinental Air Derby, flown from Santa Monica, California, to Cleveland, Ohio. Thaden competed against Amelia Earhart, Pancho Barnes, Ruth Elder, Phoebe Omlie, Blanche Noyes, and 14 others in a multi-day event that saw one fatality, several engine failures, and a few suspected instances of aircraft sabotage. Ironically, humorist Will Rogers dubbed the event a "Powder Puff Derby" after he spotted some racers freshening their makeup before meeting news photographers at the stopover points.

But the race was no beauty pageant for the contestants. Thaden barely made it to the starting point. While ferrying her Beech Travel Air to California, Thaden, seated low behind the Wright J5 engine, inhaled carbon monoxide fumes that nearly put her out of the running altogether. She landed at Fort Worth, Texas, where her boss, Walter Beech, ran a four-inch pipe from the leading edge of the cowling into the cockpit to provide a source of fresh air.

Thaden went on to win the heavy class, while Phoebe Omlie won the light class. By the finish line, the racers had become friends, trading maintenance tips and joking about the chicken dinners they consumed during the stopovers.

Not wanting to let go of that camaraderie, the racers talked about forming a club for women pilots. Thaden, Earhart, and others established The Ninety-Nines in November 1929. Of the 117 licensed women pilots of the day, 99 became charter members of the organization and took the name from their number. The Ninety-Nines International Organization of Women Pilots, headquartered in Oklahoma City, continues today with more than 5,000 members.

Women were prohibited from competing against men in air races in 1934, after Florence Klingerman crashed and died while flying a Gee Bee in a race in Chicago. The ban was lifted in time for Thaden, flying with Blanche Noyes, to take home the first-place cup in the Bendix Transcontinental Speed Race at the National Air Races in Los Angeles in 1936. They were the first women to win the Bendix Trophy. They flew from New York to Los Angeles in 14 hours and 55 minutes in a Beechcraft C–17R Staggerwing.

You can see Thaden's trophy, her pilot's license signed by Orville Wright, and other artifacts in the Louise Thaden Library at the Beechcraft Heritage Museum in Tullahoma, Tennessee.

Air racing continues to draw crowds. Some 35,000 to 40,000 people each year head to Reno, Nevada, to watch high-performance aircraft careen around pylons at the National Championship Air Races. The Red Bull Air Race has millions of viewers, thanks to the fact that the races are televised and streamed online. And women from around the United States still gather annually to compete in the VFR cross-country Air Race Classic, a direct descendant of the Women's Transcontinental Air Race.

Jacqueline Cochran

A hairdresser at Saks

'The best female pilot in the U.S.'

Humble beginnings are two words used often for people whose hard work and ingenuity make them legends. Such is the case of Bessie Pittman, er, Jacqueline Cochran, also known as the Speed Queen, director of the Women Airforce Service Pilots (WASP), colonel of the U.S. Air Force Reserves, first woman pilot to "go supersonic," and recipient of the Distinguished Flying Cross.

Cochran was one of five children in the Pittman family in the Florida panhandle. By some accounts she married at just age 14 to Robert Cochran, kept his last name after their divorce in 1927, and gave herself a new first name—Jacqueline, setting a course to get out of Florida and into an eventual job at Saks Fifth Avenue in New York City. She learned to fly at Roosevelt Field on Long Island and had her license within three weeks. She won the Bendix Trophy in 1938.

Among other firsts in her lifetime of flying were: the first woman to take off and land on an aircraft carrier, the first woman to fly a bomber across the North Atlantic, the first woman to pilot a jet across the Atlantic Ocean, the first woman to break the sound barrier, and the first woman president of the Fédération Aéronautique Internationale. And that's the short list. She was a magazine reporter, a cosmetics company mogul, and a consultant for the Northrop Corporation. Cochran was instrumental in the formation of the WASP, having written a letter to Eleanor Roosevelt proposing a women's flying division of the U.S. Army Air Corps.

Cochran married Floyd Bostwick Odlum, in 1933 one of the wealthiest men in the United States. The couple gave to charitable causes, and Cochran-Odlum ran for Congress in 1956. Thermal Airport in Indio, California, was renamed Jacqueline Cochran Regional Airport after the Indio resident's death in 1980.

Jacqueline Cochran is congratulated by Vincent Bendix after her 1938 Bendix race victory (below right).

New York's La Guardia Airport was the height of architectural efficiency at the time of its construction. It is currently undergoing a multi-billion-dollar makeover to include glass-enclosed air bridges that will allow passengers to look down on taxiing jets as they walk to connecting concourses.

A NEW DEAL FOR AVIATION

'Our greatest primary task is to put people to work'

FDR's approach to the Great Depression was summarized in a well-known quote: "It is common sense to take a method and try it. If it fails, admit it frankly and try another. But above all, try something." Among the most radical things the new administration tried was the experiment of hiring large numbers of the unemployed to make public improvements, either directly under federal contracts or through grants to state and local governments.

Keeping track of the "alphabet soup" of relief agencies that resulted was difficult then and hasn't gotten easier since. Among the best known today are the Civilian Conservation Corps (CCC), which put young, unmarried men to work improving public lands; the Public Works Administration (PWA), which undertook massive endeavors such as the Grand Coulee Dam and the Overseas Highway to Key West; and the Works Progress Administration (WPA, later the Work Projects Administration), which paid the cost of labor on smaller projects where state or municipal governments furnished the materials. A separate branch of the WPA, known as Federal Project Number One, commissioned work in the visual arts as well as literature, music, and theater. Two and sometimes all three came together in the construction and improvement of airports.

New Deal airport projects spanned the continent, and then some. Maine's affiliate of the WPA's predecessor, the Federal Emergency Relief Administration (FERA), built the airports in Bangor and Augusta. An expansive CCC portfolio in California's Death Valley included the original runway at Furnace Creek. The airfield on Howland Island, where Amelia Earhart hoped to refuel while crossing the Pacific, was constructed with federal funds by graduates of Hawaii's Kamehameha School. New Deal programs bolstered the development of airports in Portland, Oregon, and Portland, Maine; Nashua, New Hampshire, and Nashville, Tennessee; Chicago, Illinois, and Chico, California.

Notable artistic and architectural triumphs were achieved along the way. At the Garfield County Airport near Bryce Canyon, Utah, WPA workers built a corporate-sized hangar from local ponderosa pine harvested to curtail a beetle infestation; the bores left by the beetles are still visible in the sawn logs. The hangar built in 1937 in Chilton County, Alabama, was listed among

LA GUARDIA AIRPORT
ALL FLIGHT
OPERATIONS
OFFICIAL
GRUEN
AIRPORT TIME
TELEPHONE
TELEPHONE
SHELTER

"OUR GREATEST PRIMARY TASK IS TO PUT PEOPLE TO WORK. THIS IS NO UNSOLVABLE PROBLEM IF WE FACE IT WISELY AND COURAGEOUSLY." —FRANKLIN DELANO ROOSEVELT

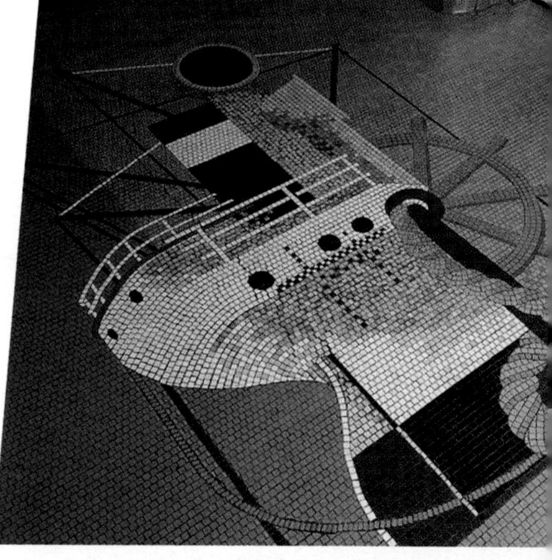

that state's most endangered historic sites before it was salvaged by a community pilot group and reopened in 2010. Enrique Alferez's "Fountain of the Four Winds" still graces New Orleans Lakefront Airport. Murals on the floor of the 1941 terminal building at Long Beach, California, were rediscovered after carpet was removed in 1990 and promptly declared a cultural landmark; the airport is now considered one of the best surviving examples of New Deal airport design. And the interior of the Marine Terminal at New York's La Guardia boasts "Flight," the largest of all WPA murals. The exterior is graced by a flying-fish motif in tribute to the huge flying boats that provided the earliest transatlantic service.

La Guardia was, at the time, the largest New Deal airport, but it's scarcely the only current air-carrier field to trace its roots to that era. A small strip on what was then called Hog Island was built into Philadelphia International Airport. Major airports built or dramatically improved during the 1930s also include Los Angeles, San Francisco, Honolulu International, Boston's Logan, Cleveland-Hopkins, Memphis International, and Atlanta's Hartsfield-Jackson. Slightly smaller destinations include Charleston International/Joint Base in South Carolina and Yeager Field in Charleston, West Virginia; Chicago's Midway International; Atlantic City; Albuquerque, New Mexico; and the McGhee-Tyson Airport in Knoxville, Tennessee.

Some of this artistry has escaped the march of so-called progress. Outstanding examples of terminal architecture have been turned into museums at what were once Wichita Municipal and Houston Hobby airports. The dramatic former terminal of the Manchester airport now houses the Aviation Museum of New Hampshire. Other beautiful historic buildings have found other uses. The former Albuquerque Municipal Airport terminal, a two-story adobe structure graced by fountains outside and fireplaces within, houses the Transportation Security Administration (TSA) offices for Albuquerque's Sunport. The exterior and lobby are still open to visitors, although the best available parking is said to be at the post office across the street. And Chandler Field in Fresno, California, is cited as one of the most pristine WPA-funded airports remaining. To boost employment as widely as possible, four separate contracts were let for the design and construction of the terminal, administrative annex, electrical control building, and bathroom complex—a decision entirely in keeping with the Roosevelt administration's approach to public works.

Reflecting the overall aesthetics of New Deal public works, prominent artists such as Arshile Gorky, shown at Newark Airport (top), collaborated to create airports that weren't just functional, but beautiful as well. Long Beach Airport's WPA mosaics (above) were rediscovered decades later under carpet. At New Orleans Lakefront Airport (formerly Shushan Airport), art deco murals by New Deal artist Xavier Gonzalez were hidden behind panels until 2005, when floodwater from Hurricane Katrina damaged the terminal and restorers seized the opportunity to revitalize the historic art. It's unknown whether this airport mural was funded by New Deal programs (right).

NC81243

Aside from the addition of a fourth seat, this rugged, versatile, well-mannered taildragger remained nearly unchanged through its 13-year production run. Seventy years after the last "new" example was assembled from spare parts, Fairchild 24s are still prized as antique airplanes that are both useful and affordable—at least relatively speaking.

FAIRCHILD 24

A step up in comfort and style

Unlike modern aircraft offerings, where your choices sit in the narrow categories of relatively low-cost Light Sport aircraft, mid-range trainer, or high-end speedster, the Golden Age had a range of price points and styles to appeal to a broad base of pilots.

The Fairchild 24 sat squarely in the middle of the range. Considerably more capable and expensive than a Piper Cub, but much more reasonable than a Beech Staggerwing, the Fairchild offered the range, capability, and style of a true middle-class flier. It was also meant as an early bush plane—with stout oleo landing gear and a high propeller clearance, the 24 can operate out of unimproved runways.

Fairchild made more than 2,000 of the 24s, some of which went to the military to help the war effort in World War II.

One unusual feature of the 24 is that it came with a choice of either a straight six Ranger engine from Fairchild, or a Warner radial. The Ranger also supplied the power to the PT-19, a primary trainer of World War II pilots. Because so many were built, parts remain available to this day.

TECHNOLOGY IN THE GOLDEN AGE

Fast airplanes, daredevil feats, and leaps forward

The 1920s and 1930s, the historical period known as aviation's Golden Age, was a time of unprecedented public fascination, capital investment, and technological advancement in flying. There was a flood of aviation speed, distance, and altitude records; supercharged and turbocharged engines of ever-increasing power; all-metal airplanes; better construction methods; and navigation and instrumentation that allowed "blind flying" in clouds and low-visibility conditions.

Air races were among the most popular public displays and rivaled professional sports, and pilots such as Roscoe Turner and Jimmy Doolittle were national heroes. Large U.S. manufacturing firms such as Ford Motor Company created pioneering airliners including the Trimotor and individual flying machines like the Flivver, and the company anticipated duplicating its success in mass-assembling cars with airplanes.

The beginning of corporate aviation also began to take shape in the Golden Age as fast, relatively reliable, and increasingly luxurious aircraft such as the Beech 17 Staggerwing, Howard DGA-15, and Stinson V-77 Reliant became both travelers and aerial status symbols with art-deco flair.

Long-distance flights such as Charles A. Lindbergh's 1927 Orteig Prize-winning solo flight from New York to Paris showed aviation's growing sophistication, promise, and risk-taking ethos.

All of these advancements were powered by leaps forward in engine technology. At the end of World War I, the most powerful U.S. aircraft engine was the 12-cylinder, liquid-cooled Liberty L-12, an up-to-450-horsepower powerplant that also came to be used in cars, trucks, and tanks. By the end of the Golden Age, however, radial engines with innovations such as superchargers, turbochargers, and water injection were putting out close to 3,000 horsepower and flying at high altitudes that dramatically increased true airspeed and range.

Technological advancements during the Golden Age of aviation set the stage for the rise of American air power in World War II, when U.S. manufacturers, such as Douglas Aircraft Company, produced aircraft for the war effort.

Howard Hughes

What you didn't know about Howard Hughes

From screaming speed to 'Hell's Angels'

Already a pilot at age 19 when he inherited Hughes Tool Company from his father in 1925, Howard Robard Hughes Jr. became a successful American businessman, investor, philanthropist, and aviation magnate. Among many other accomplishments he founded the Hughes Aircraft Company in 1932, and went on to modify and design aircraft, set a number of world airspeed records, and eventually purchase Trans World Airlines.

Two aircraft stand out. The streamlined Hughes H-1 Racer featured flush rivets for completely smooth skins, retractable main gear, a hydraulically actuated tail skid, and a Pratt & Whitney R-1535 radial engine producing more than 1,000 horsepower. In 1935 it set a world speed record of 352.39 mph; in 1937, flying with longer wings, Hughes averaged 322 mph in a Los Angeles-to-Newark nonstop.

The H-4 Hercules flying boat was conceived during World War II for transatlantic troop transport, when German U-boats were sinking many cargo ships. Dubbed the *Spruce Goose*, the behemoth was made primarily out of wood—albeit birch—because aluminum was not available. Both the world's largest flying boat and largest aircraft made from wood, the H-4 had a wingspan of 319 feet, 11 inches. The 24,000 horsepower from its eight Pratt & Whitney R-4360 Wasp Majors carried it aloft only once, on November 2, 1947, when Hughes flew it about one mile at a maximum altitude of 70 feet.

While most pilots are aware of those aircraft, few know many details of Hughes's Hollywood years—especially the 1930 film *Hell's Angels*, which he produced and directed. Sound motion-picture technology was introduced during filming, and Hughes decided to incorporate it into the in-production silent film, replacing some of the cast in the process.

High-altitude physiology, weather, and radio navigation also became better understood during this period. Pioneering aviator Wiley Post, wearing a primitive pressure suit, flew a Lockheed Vega to 50,000 feet where he was the first to take note of the powerful, high-altitude winds that would later be known as the jet stream.

To harness the additional power of these new engines, inventors created a series of variable-pitch, then constant-speed propellers, which allowed propeller blades to twist so that they could maintain optimum angles for climb and cruise. The first practical pilot-control-

lable propeller was introduced in 1932. In the United States, propeller manufacturer Hamilton Standard won the prestigious Collier Trophy in 1933 for its hydraulically actuated constant-speed propeller. Top-of-the-line civil aircraft from airliners to racers quickly adopted these more efficient propulsion systems.

Some civil aircraft outperformed military models during the Golden Age. But that changed with the outset of World War II as aviation firms were drafted into the war effort and tasked with producing trainers, fighters, and bombers on an unprecedented scale.

The theoretical underpinning of jet engines also was spelled out during the Golden Age, but the high-temperature, high-strength materials and precision manufacturing required to make them weren't commercially available.

Aviation technology surged during the war years, which also brought industrialization and the advent of jet aircraft. But the era of the barnstormer, aviation pioneer, and individual entrepreneur that typified the Golden Age was over.

By January 1, 1939, there were 9,635 certificated U.S. civil aircraft of more than 400 horsepower.

Wiley Post's (in suit) experiments with high-altitude flying and the development of pressure suits led to the discovery of the jet stream.

MONOCOUPE 90

Bye-bye, biplanes—the Monocoupe ushered in a new era

In an era dominated by big, slow biplanes, aircraft designer Don Luscombe shook up the flying scene with his speedy, efficient Monocoupe.

The single "mono" wing and side-by-side "coupe" seating went on to become mainstays of future aircraft design, but they were rare in 1930 when the Monocoupe 90 was introduced.

Monocoupe Aircraft produced several models with a variety of small radial engines in the 1930s and 1940s. More than 300 were built, and the vast majority went to a growing number of private owners in the United States who were attracted to their speed, efficiency, and sporty appearance. The Monocoupe was a pioneer of "personal aviation," in which small, light airplanes with fully enclosed cockpits were used for both flight training and cross-country travel.

Biplanes outnumbered monoplanes until 1931, when 308 monoplanes were produced compared to 237 biplanes, according to statistics from the Civil Aeronautics Administration.

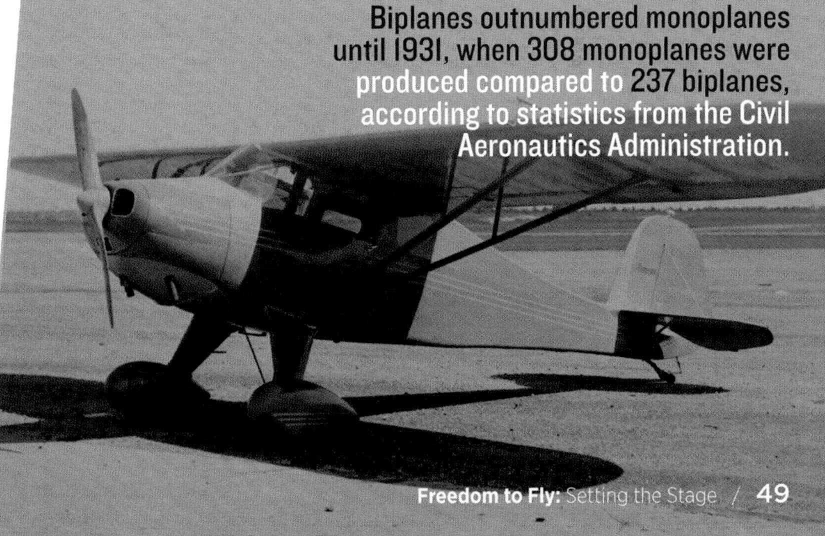

2. AN IDEA TAKES FLIGHT

Being present at AOPA's creation

The Aircraft Owners and Pilots Association was born in the environs of Philadelphia. In the 1920s and 1930s, this area had all the ingredients necessary for fostering a healthy level of personal flying. Philadelphia supplied the area with men of means—professionals who earned their livings in commerce, industry, and private practice. The vast suburbs provided land well-suited for airports. Flying clubs sprouted up left and right, and pilots and aircraft owners eagerly joined them in order to both pursue their sport and enjoy the social atmosphere. The friendships and acquaintances made through one such flying club would be pivotal to the birth of AOPA.

This was the Pylon Club. It was based at Patco Field, near Norristown, Pennsylvania. Every weekend there was good flying weather, members would flock to Patco, fitted out in leather jackets, helmets, and flying goggles. Typically, each weekend's flying would involve a group flying event. One weekend it might be an airborne treasure hunt, in which pilots were to land at various locations in order to pick up clues as to the "treasure's" location. Another weekend might require that pilots fly a specified course in a test of navigation skill or the pilot's ability to conserve fuel. Some weekends, though, were spent just flying for its own sake.

One fly-out was to a private island in the Saint Lawrence River, owned by brothers Philip T. and Laurence P. Sharples, industrialists specializing in the manufacture of centrifuges. For unknown reasons, the Sharples brothers got lost en route. By the time they neared the island it was becoming dark, so they landed at a friend's airport and spent the night. That friend was Edwin Link, the inventor of the Link trainer. Link's houseguest was Edward J. Noble, who later became the chairman of the Civil Aeronautics Authority (CAA), the forerunner of the Federal Aviation Administration. It was autumn 1937.

Founding members (clockwise from above) are C. Townsend Ludington, Philip T. Sharples, Joseph B. "Doc" Hartranft Jr., John Story Smith, and Laurence P. Sharples. Alfred L. Wolf (facing page) spearheaded the association's organizational meetings, became a founding trustee, and served as its first secretary.

By the time the Sharples brothers met Noble again, they had been busy exploring the idea of forming a pilot association with like-minded Pylon Club members. One of them, Philadelphia lawyer Alfred L. Wolf, had written a letter to Carl Friedlander, president of the Aeronautical Corporation of America (Aeronca). Friedlander had written an article for *The American Aviation Daily* in which he argued for an association to represent the interests of private airplane manufacturers, the Private Pilots Association, the United Pilots and Mechanics Association, and the Association for the Advancement of Aeronautics. Without a more focused, businesslike lobbying organization, Wolf and his compatriots feared that "miscellaneous aviation"—as general aviation was called then—would come out second best in political battles.

Those compatriots—all from the Philadelphia area—included Wolf, C. Townsend

"THE WORLD OF THE AIRLINE PLANE, AND THE WORLD OF THE MILITARY PLANE, WAS A DIFFERENT WORLD THAN THE ONE IN WHICH CARL WAS MAKING HIS AERONCAS." —ALFRED L. WOLF

and Wolf agreed. "The world of the airline plane, and the world of the military plane, was a different world than the one in which Carl was making his Aeroncas," Wolf said.

There were parallels in the pilot world—for example, the Private Fliers Association (PFA) and the Sportsman Pilots Association (SPA)—but Wolf felt that the SPA was just for fun, and that the PFA "wanted to be all things to all men in aviation," according to one letter. Other groups proved equally ineffective, and made for a confusing scene that divided interests. There was the American Pilots League,

Ludington (owner of The Ludington Line, an air shuttle service that flew between Newark and Washington), the Sharples brothers, and John Story Smith (secretary-treasurer of the Jacobs Aircraft Engine Company).

Meanwhile, a student at the University of Pennsylvania was busy networking. Joseph B. "Doc" Hartranft Jr. had made a name for himself at a very young age—he was founder and president of the Cloudcombers, the university's flying club. The Cloudcombers were an especially active

group, with some 100 members. Under Hartranft's leadership, with the participation of William Strohmeier, president of Amherst College's flying club (later to become a marketing executive with Piper Aircraft Corporation), and the help of other college flying clubs, the National Intercollegiate Flying Club (NIFC—later to become today's National Intercollegiate Flying Association) was formed. The idea behind the NIFC was to bring students from many colleges together in activities such as regional and national air meets, plus two annual symposiums.

Hartranft invited Wolf to speak at the NIFC's spring 1938 symposium, held at Washington, D.C.'s Willard Hotel. Wolf agreed. At the symposium, Hartranft talked about the need for a national association to represent the interests of general aviation. During a break in the lecture schedule, Hartranft happened to meet up with Wolf, who complimented Hartranft on his presentation, then mentioned that a group of serious-minded pilots in Philadelphia had been thinking along the same lines. Would Hartranft meet with this group to further discuss the matter? Of course he would. It was the first time the nervous, 22-year-old Hartranft would meet all the principals in this influential group, and the meeting would align all their convictions.

The Philadelphians

The group awaiting Hartranft was impressive. It included some of Phila-

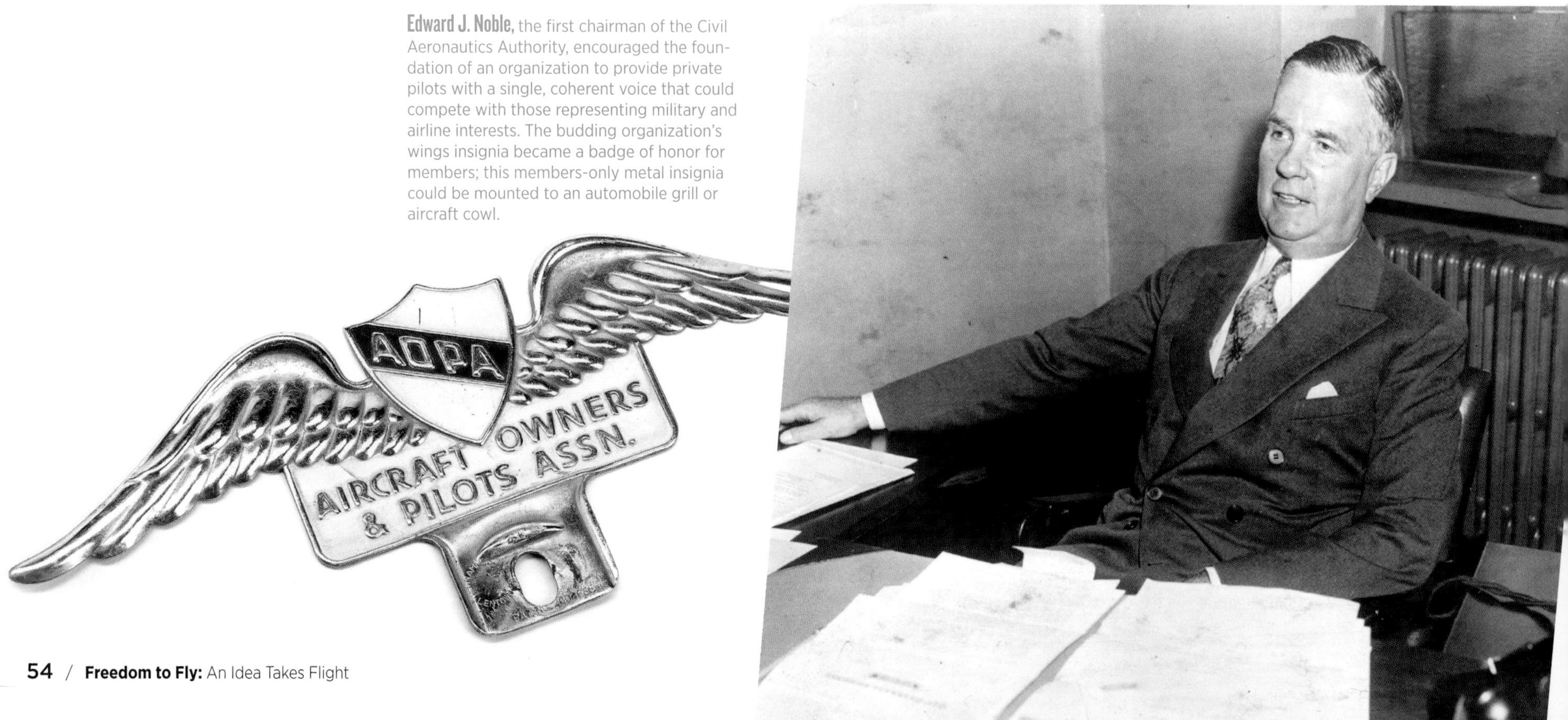

Edward J. Noble, the first chairman of the Civil Aeronautics Authority, encouraged the foundation of an organization to provide private pilots with a single, coherent voice that could compete with those representing military and airline interests. The budding organization's wings insignia became a badge of honor for members; this members-only metal insignia could be mounted to an automobile grill or aircraft cowl.

THE FLEDGLING ASSOCIATION'S AIM WAS "TO MAKE FLYING MORE USEFUL, LESS EXPENSIVE, SAFER, AND MORE FUN."

delphia's most successful and influential businessmen and lawyers—all of them pilots, and all of them members of the Philadelphia Aviation Country Club, the one situated near Philadelphia's Wings Field. It was at this club that many early organizational meetings took place. Today, a bronze plaque in PACC's lounge serves as a reminder of AOPA's birthplace.

Ludington, president of Ludington Airlines, inventor, and in charge of the Franklin Institute's aviation affairs, was perhaps the figure best known to the public. But the legal and business community also knew the Sharples brothers and Wolf. Philip T. "P.T." Sharples was an officer of the Sharples Corporation, served on the board of directors of the Lehigh Valley Railroad Company, and played a major part in many civic associations and charitable endeavors. Laurence P. "L.P." Sharples was a vice president of the Sharples Corporation and winner of many air races and aviation trophies. Both Sharples brothers owned airplanes: P. T., a Waco F-2 and F-3 and a Cabin Waco; and L.P., a J-6 Travel Air and a Monocoupe.

Smith was now the secretary-treasurer of the Jacobs Aircraft Engine Company, founder of Wings Field, president of PACC, and a member of the board of governors of the Aeronautical Chamber of Commerce of America, the forerunner of today's Aerospace Industries Association.

Of course, Wolf was also in attendance. Wolf was the spark plug of the group and, for all practical purposes, the initiator of all of the early organizational meetings. He owned a Fairchild 24, equipped as a floatplane.

Hartranft's first meeting with the five Philadelphians addressed general aviation in a very broad fashion. As was the case in previous meetings, all agreed that general

MEMORANDUM TO

Mr. Hartranft

Mr. L. P. Sharples

Talked to Hon. Edward P. Warner, who is now a member of the Civil Aeronautics Authority, about our new venture Wednesday, and he was indeed friendly and very much impressed. Regarding the commercial hook-up, he saw that as a possible method of certain objections that we had not contemplated, e.g. the fact that we are a local or Philadelphia group in the eyes of the Industry to date. He stressed certain things.

Firstly, though private fliers think private flying is very important, no one else is convinced of that and whenever anyone comes for governmental cooperation or assistance they are faced by a lack of proof that there is anything beyond a luxury involved.

Secondly, someone must set out to prove the relationship between private flying or the type of flying we are going to represent and the National Economy, the National Defense, etc.

I told him that we were not considering members of the Authority as sponsors at this time, which I hope was in line with all of our thoughts. I thought it would have been abrupt to do so during the interview.

A.L.W. 4/21/39

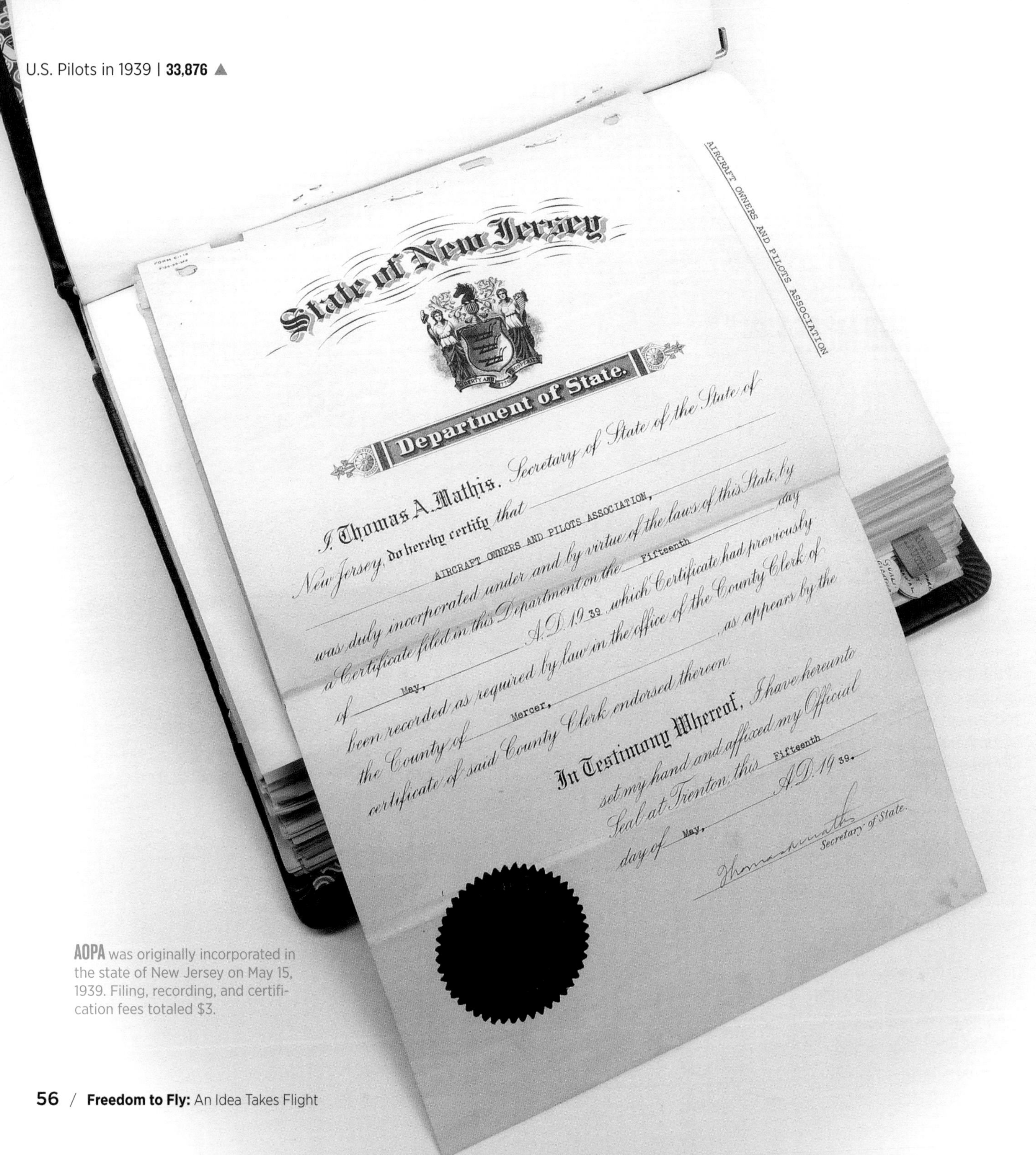

AIRCRAFT OWNERS AND PILOTS ASSOCIATION

State of New Jersey

Department of State.

I, Thomas A. Mathis, Secretary of State of the State of New Jersey, do hereby certify that AIRCRAFT OWNERS AND PILOTS ASSOCIATION, was duly incorporated under and by virtue of the laws of this State, by a Certificate filed in this Department on the Fifteenth day of May, A.D. 1939, which Certificate had previously been recorded as required by law in the office of the County Clerk of the County of Mercer, as appears by the certificate of said County Clerk endorsed thereon.

In Testimony Whereof, I have hereunto set my hand and affixed my Official Seal at Trenton, this Fifteenth day of May, A.D. 1939.

[signature] Secretary of State.

AOPA was originally incorporated in the state of New Jersey on May 15, 1939. Filing, recording, and certification fees totaled $3.

aviation had no unified voice at the federal, state, or local levels and suffered from a poor public image. For a general aviation association to be successful, the group reasoned, it must work as a businesslike operation and not like the many other splinter groups vying for the general aviation pilot's allegiance. The group parted, resolving to meet again. Hartranft, having graduated from the University of Pennsylvania the previous year, returned to Washington, D.C., to fulfill his obligation to serve as a naval officer.

The Philadelphia group was to receive some additional encouragement later in 1938 as a result of a fly-out to southern Georgia. The Sharples brothers took Noble, by now the chairman of the Civil Aeronautics Authority, on a turkey hunting expedition. While sitting in a turkey blind waiting for their quarry, Noble proceeded to tell the brothers how aviation groups representing the airlines and the military presented their arguments in a professional, convincing manner—and usually got their way. Private pilots soliciting a hearing from the CAA, on the other hand, presented their cases individually. Many times, Noble related, these pilots' demands and opinions were of an oddball nature, which furthered the image of general aviation as a sort of lunatic fringe. Without a coherent, single voice, he averred, the interests of general aviation would always be in jeopardy. Wolf heard the same thing from a member of the CAA, Edward P. Warner, as he related to Hartranft in a letter dated April 21, 1939: "Though private fliers think private flying is very important, no one else is convinced of that, and whenever anyone comes for governmental cooperation or assistance, they are faced with a lack of proof that there is anything beyond a luxury involved.... Someone must set out to prove the relationship between...the type of flying we are going to represent and the national economy, the national defense, etc."

"I'M TIRED, AND GOING TO BED. I PROPOSE WE CALL IT WHAT IT IS—THE AIRCRAFT OWNERS AND PILOTS ASSOCIATION."
—C. TOWNSEND LUDINGTON

When word of Noble's and Warner's opinions reached the Philadelphia group, they decided to act. After all, here was the government—the organization that had caused general aviation all of its troubles—giving advice on how it best could be influenced. Without a more focused, businesslike organization, Wolf and his compatriots feared that private fliers would come out second best in political battles unless they had a better lobbying organization.

As with many other dates in AOPA's early history, it is impossible to pin the exact date of the first serious organizational meeting between Hartranft and the men who would later become AOPA's first trustees. We can surmise, however, that it took place in April 1939 at the Barclay Hotel in Philadelphia's Rittenhouse Square.

All agreed on the goals of the organization to be promoting the economy, safety, and enjoyability of personal flying, as well as promoting, protecting, and representing the interests of members. The wording of the organization's mission statement—to make flying less expensive, safer, more useful, and more fun—was incorporated into official documents and continues to live as today's goals. The founders also agreed that the organization's trustees should serve without pay, as a confirmation of their purity of purpose.

But first there was the matter of deciding this new organization's name. P.T. Sharples favored "Pilots, Incorporated," arguing that this conveyed a more professional approach. L.P. Sharples, Ludington, Smith, and Wolf

The numbers of the first 93,505 AOPA members were recorded by hand in a series of five hardbound ledgers.

Charting the course

AOPA's board drives the mission

Providing leadership for the newly formed association were members of the board of trustees: C. Townsend Ludington, Lawrence P. Sharples, Philip T. Sharples, J. Story Smith, and Alfred L. Wolf. Over AOPA's eighty-year history, thirty-three pilots and aircraft owners have served on the board, committing their service to preserve pilots' freedom to fly and ensure that AOPA maintains its leadership role on behalf of our members and GA—all serving without compensation.

G.C. Whalen	1946 – 1948
C. Townsend Ludington	1939 – 1960
J. Story Smith	1939 – 1972
George C. Sparks	1970 – 1973
Philip T. Sharples	1939 – 1975
Lawrence P. Sharples	1939 – 1977
Alfred L. Wolf	1939 – 1985
D. Charles Merriwether	1974 – 1985
Joseph B. Hartranft Jr.	1961 – 1990
Lawton S. Lamb	1988 – 1994
Elaine Harrison	1977 – 1997
Tristram C. Colket	1989 – 1997
John L. Baker	1987 – 1998
Fitzgerald S. Hudson	1972 – 1999
John J. Serrell	1967 – 1999
William B.L. Hudson	2000 – 2004
John S. Yodice	1973 – 2007
Philip B. Boyer	1995 – 2009
Anne Blake Garrymore	1998 – 2011
Craig C. Fuller	2009 – 2013
R. Anderson Pew	1970 – 2014
Paul C. Heintz	1975 – 2015
William C. Trimble III	1993 – Present
Burgess H. Hamlett III	1998 – Present
H. Neel Hipp	2000 – Present
Darrell W. Crate	2004 – Present
Lawrence D. Buhl	2004 – Present
James G. Tuthill Jr.	2009 – Present
Matthew J. Desch	2011 – Present
Amanda J. Farnsworth	2012 – Present
James N. Hauslein	2012 – Present
Mark R. Baker	2013 – Present
Luke R. Wippler	2016 - Present

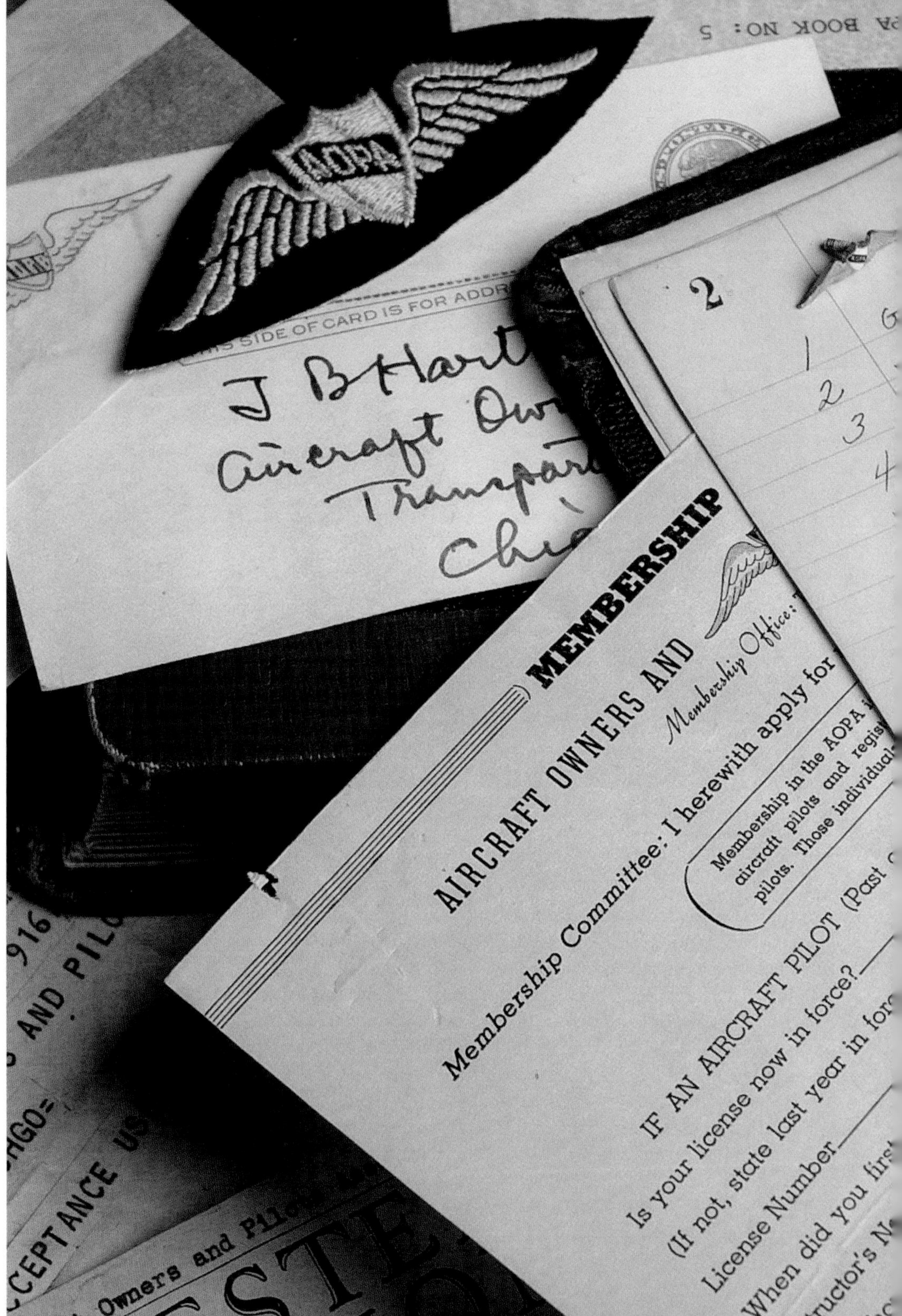

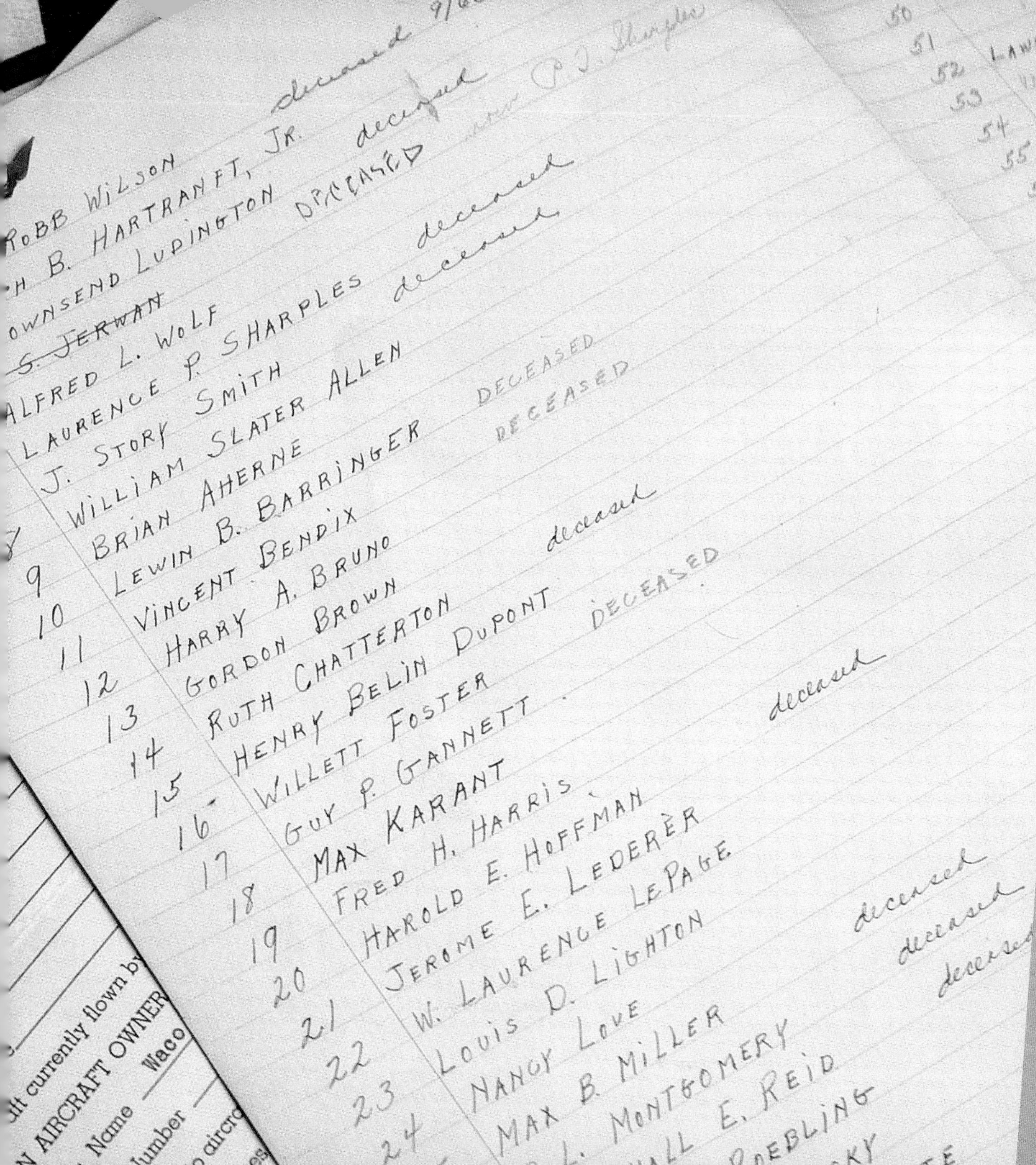

❮ THE WAY WE WERE

The first members couldn't simply join AOPA. They had to apply for membership, with approval subject to verification of their credentials as pilots and/or aircraft owners.

In addition to the founders, early members included film and stage actors Brian Aherne and Ruth Chatterton, industrialists Vincent Bendix and Henry Berlin DuPont, publisher Guy Gannett, and future *AOPA Pilot* editor Max Karant.

The wings have been a constant element of AOPA's logos since the beginning, appearing on items such as letterheads and mastheads, pins and patches, license plate holders, decals, and stickers.

U.S. Pilots in 1940 | **69,967** ▲

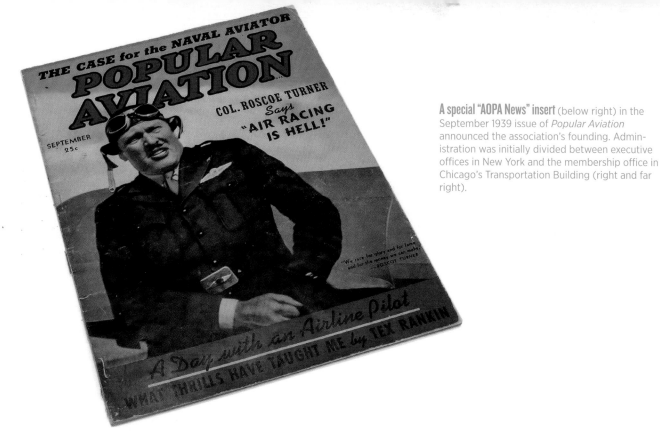

A special "AOPA News" insert (below right) in the September 1939 issue of *Popular Aviation* announced the association's founding. Administration was initially divided between executive offices in New York and the membership office in Chicago's Transportation Building (right and far right).

each had their own ideas. As the meeting droned on at the hotel, the clock reached 2:30 a.m., and Ludington had had enough. "I'm tired, and I'm going to bed," he said. "I propose we name it just what it is—the Aircraft Owners and Pilots Association."

The deal was done. On May 15, 1939, AOPA's charter was signed. The Sharples brothers, Ludington, Wolf, and Smith became the founding trustees of the infant AOPA. Ludington was elected as AOPA's first president, and Hartranft was hired as the first employee, with the title of executive secretary.

The Ziff-Davis deal

The founders knew that for an organization to thrive, it needed a means of communicating its message to members, potential members, and the rest of the flying community. Without a highly visible publication, this would be impossible. Anticipating all this came the agreement of March 4, 1939, between the Ziff-Davis Publishing Company and the as-yet nameless organization, represented by Ludington, the Sharpleses, Smith, and Wolf. Under the terms of this agreement, Ziff-Davis (publishers of *Popular Aviation*, to become *Flying and Popular Aviation* in August 1940, and *Flying* magazine in January 1943) agreed to provide the fledgling organization (called simply "fliers" in the contract) with $500, then $1,000, monthly cash payments for the purpose of establishing the membership base. It also agreed to give the "fliers" 30 column inches of free editorial space in each monthly issue of *Popular Aviation*, one page per issue of free advertising for a period of one year, and editorial assistance and desk space at the Ziff-Davis Chicago headquarters.

For their part, the fliers agreed to make *Popular Aviation* their official publication and repay Ziff-Davis's up-front money in monthly installments.

But Ziff-Davis drove a hard bargain. Written into the contract was a clause that required the association to obtain 70 pilots and/or aircraft owners as sponsors. These sponsors' names "should be of some advertising value," according to the terms. Furthermore, the agreement could be canceled if the association failed to obtain 2,500 members within one year. The pressure was on, but the Philadelphians now had their publication, their seed money, and some office space.

Hartranft worked out of AOPA's new office in Chicago, located next door to the Ziff-Davis offices at 608 South Dearborn Street, known as the Transportation Building. This marked a great improvement over AOPA's first office, which was located in the same building used by Ludington's firm of Markham, Chalmers, and Ludington, at 1425 Walnut Street in Philadelphia. There, Hartranft was installed in an office on the fourth floor, surrounded by film cans and boxes of potatoes. (Ludington produced a popular film called *Crime Does Not Pay*, and also perfected a means of vacu-

New Capital Airport

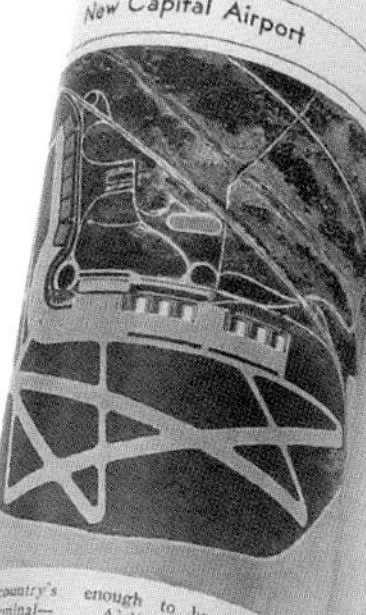

An Italian Pursuit

AIRCRAFT OWNERS AND PILOTS ASSOCIATION

53

AOPA NEWS

By GILL ROBB WILSON

THE Aircraft Owners & Pilots Association—long overdue—has just been born. You ought to see the kid! Healthy, happy, kicking the slats out of the cradle and already asking where babies come from. We call him AOPA for short. Got a connecting rod to teeth on and some of the neighbors' goats to play with. With 60,000 pilots as his godfather just watch him grow!

What's It All About

Well, to be brutally frank, everybody on the runway has a bandwagon but we of the great unwashed fraternity of common everyday variety of pilots. The airline pilots have their Air Line Pilots' Association and the manufacturers have their organization. The airlines have their Air Transport Association and the public has its NAA. Those organizations really serve their clientele. Who serves us? We've been eating off the kitchen table with the rest of the beggars—too long, far too long.

G. R. Wilson

But that's all over now and we're all set to go. Well financed, backed by some of the leading lights in aviation, the AOPA already has begun to win laurels for the pilots it represents.

Among Our Sponsors

There's a man named Bendix, for example, whose name is on most of the equipment to be found on practically every airplane. Then there's a man named Sikorsky, whose flying boats are known over the seven seas—though a bit beyond the purses of most of us plain folks. Then there's a fellow named Gannett who owns more newspapers than you or I can read, and Henry DuPont who has owned more airplanes than some of us ever saw. Hollywood, too, contributed its share with Ruth Chatterton and Brian Aherne. As a matter of fact, if you want to know anything about any of our 40-odd sponsors, just buy a who's who in America and look up the deep water citizens. And every last one of them is an aviator at heart. . . .

Among Our Officers

There's our president, Townsend Ludington. He was running a great airline without a mail contract before Mr. Black ever left Alabama. He and Bob Hewitt were racing old Sport Farman's when Jennie still was a respectable gal. He had to have some help in getting AOPA lined up so Philip and Larry Sharples, who run banks and factories and such like, were drafted as vice-president and treasurer respectively. Alfred Wolf, of flying breakfast fame, runs the minutes. He's secretary. J. B. "Doc" Hartranft, Jr., former president of the Intercollegiate Flying Clubs, is executive secretary. Gill Robb Wilson, who flies because he's getting too old to walk, is executive consultant. They all own ships and they all fly and have for years.

Doc Hartranft is in charge of the organization office in the Transportation Building, Chicago. The good-looking secretaries are all married so no use dropping around, none of you pilots, unless you just want to see how hard Doc has to work—or if you have something on your mind. The Philadelphia office, where Mr. Ludington presides, is at 1424 Walnut Street. Now there's the place for hospitality; you'll feel better just for having met him. And Presidents don't have to work so hard either. And when in Philadelphia look up the Sharples boys. They are liable to ask you out for dinner and make you take a plunge in the pool that trickles out of the side of the mountain where they live. At least, that's what they say. But don't fall for that boloney; that water comes right out from underneath the North Pole! And, if you feel like crossing the Delaware River, come up to Trenton where Gill Wilson hangs out—when he isn't in Washington trying to get something done for the AOPA.

But We've Just Circled the Field . . .

Figured you'd want to look around a little before you landed. Mighty good idea. Gives a pilot a kind of homey feeling when he knows what he's sitting down on. The AOPA is a friendly sort of landing place. No brass hats, no big smoke stacks, no steam rollers on the runways. If you have soloed an airplane you can get in. That's what you might call being baptized into aviation, that solo requirement. So they made that the mark of eligibility. Of course, if you own or ever did own an airplane that lets you in also. AOPA figures a fellow's heart is likely to be where his dough is so that makes an aviator out of an owner. You see, the whole thing isn't just to have another organization in aviation, but to have an agency to gather up all the intelligence and faith and spirit that has been floating around loose and weld it into a great force for constructive progress in non-commercial aviation.

There's a whale of a lot of work to be done. Private aviation can't put that responsibility off on some one else. It's easy to sit around and bellyache. It's always been a favorite hangar sport to moan about something. The AOPA is the actuation force to mobilize miscellaneous pilots both to protect and promote their interests in an organized and aggressive fashion.

Work Already Has Started

For example, the civil pilot training program got stuck under pressure of work in the Senate Committee. Senator Bennett "Champ" Clark was chairman. His father used to visit Gill Wilson's dad, off and on. Old Champ was one of the real empire builders. His boy just has to be prime timber. You can always talk to a man like that, so Gill wandered in and asked respectfullike if he wouldn't do all us boys a favor by bringing up that bill for consideration. Didn't tell him a darn thing but that we thought it was sound and badly needed. Didn't try to do any lobbying. Didn't ask for any commitments. Didn't get any either, but a wire came several days later saying he had called the bill up for hearing—and you know how swell were the results. Don't claim AOPA moved that bill at all. Merely telling you we were there and Senator Clark was perfectly swell about it. These Missourians can kick as hard for you as against you.

C. T. Ludington

Two other members of the Senate Committee were especially helpful: Senators Warren Barbour of New Jersey and Claude Pepper of Florida. Barbour once was amateur heavyweight boxing champion, so he's just naturally a good sportsman. And is that guy big! He wanted to know if the AOPA could get him a *Cub* with a *Cyclone* or *Wasp* in it for commuting to Washington. We told him we could fix that up all right, but it might be a better plan to get a DC-5 with a Continental "40" and then he could take all his friends along.

Things To Be Careful About

The Army carried the mail for a spell and washed out some pilots. That raised a lot of trouble. It happened because there wasn't time to get set for the job. We could wash out our training program the same way. There will be a lot of hitherto unconsidered factors to deal with. For example, the economic factor will be different. With someone else paying for the time, the student will want to pile up his flying hours and get through. He doesn't know that time is a maturing factor in flight training. He never has studied habit evaluation or, as the psychologists call it, maturation. We old timers learned about it by watching results.

Economic pressure will likewise be on the operator. He will be pushed to get all the hours handled. So what? So the student flies too much in too short a time without having time to mentally and nervously digest what he is learning. That leads to accidents or makes bad pilots. The Army and N

Wings Field

A visit to AOPA's birthplace

One summer day in 1929, two pilots of the Pylon Club, Lewin Barringer and Alfred L. Wolf, were flying north of Philadelphia, over Montgomery County, Pennsylvania. They spotted a large meadow on a farm near the small village of Blue Bell and decided to land there.

A discussion with the farmer ensued. Wolf and Barringer learned the 134-acre dairy farm—Twin Springs Farm—together with its farmhouse (built in 1776) and a barn was for sale. This bit of news was passed on to Pylon Club members Jack Bartow (president of the Bartow Beacon Company, maker of airport lighting systems and airway beacons) and John Story Smith (vice president of the Pottstown Stove Company, a machine firm that made the Brownback Tiger Kitten engine that powered early Taylor Cubs; and later, president of the Jacobs Engine Company).

Smith bought Twin Springs. Because the Patco Field used by the Pylon Club was getting crowded, he built a new airport on the farm. He called it Wings Port, and created an adjacent social center he called the Philadelphia Aviation Country Club (PACC). In 1931 two hangars were built—of stone, a rare building material for a hangar, then as now. As for Wolf, he bought an adjoining lot, where he built a house and his own airstrip.

Many of AOPA's early business, organizational, and social events took place at the PACC at Wings Port—now called Wings Field. Today, a bronze plaque in the PACC lounge serves as a reminder of what many call AOPA's birthplace.

The house that became the headquarters of the Philadelphia Aviation Country Club (shown here in 1948) still stands just across the access road from this active GA airport in the Philadelphia suburbs. Airspace restrictions shut down flying activities at Wings Field during World War II, but the airport bounced back after the war, when it was often host to air regattas and social events.

Aircraft Owners &
NATL SERVICE HDQTS Chicago

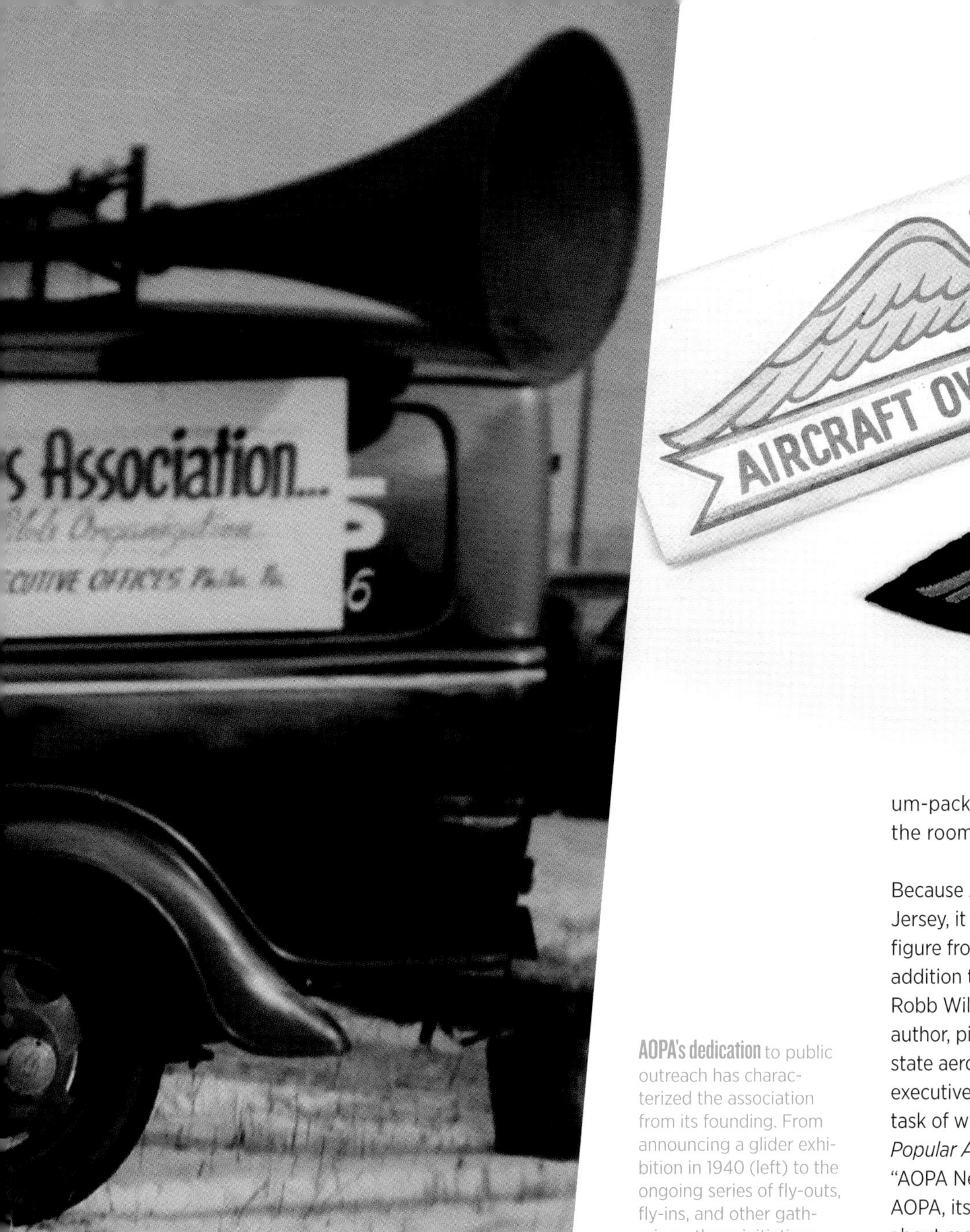

AOPA's dedication to public outreach has characterized the association from its founding. From announcing a glider exhibition in 1940 (left) to the ongoing series of fly-outs, fly-ins, and other gatherings, these initiatives have shown thousands of attendees the benefits of membership.

um-packing French-fried potatoes; he used the room for storage.)

Because AOPA was incorporated in New Jersey, it was felt that a prominent aviation figure from that state would be a proper addition to the staff. For this reason, Gill Robb Wilson, a former Presbyterian minister, author, pilot, and director of New Jersey's state aeronautics commission, was hired as executive consultant. He was assigned the task of writing AOPA's editorial section in *Popular Aviation*. This department, titled "AOPA News," contained information about AOPA, its goals and initiatives, and news about member activities. It was bound into magazines destined for subscribers who were members of AOPA—it did not appear in newsstand or general circulation copies.

"AOPA News" first appeared in the September 1939 issue and was four columns in length. In November 1939, an additional AOPA article, running four pages and titled simply "AOPA Section," became a regular feature written by Hartranft and Wilson. By March 1940, "AOPA Section" had swelled to nine pages, and each opened with a full-page photograph by famed aviation photographer Hans Groenhoff.

First initiatives

AOPA's first order of business was enrolling members, so advertisements for *Popular Aviation* were designed and published, along with posters and other promotional material. To encourage pilot proficiency, entertainment, and a sense of community, AOPA organized "breakfast flights"—fly-in events that also served as a grassroots method of raising awareness of the new association. The first of these flights was held at Glenn Curtiss Field in Glenview, Illinois.

AOPA's first political activity was to urge the passage of a Senate bill that would establish the Civilian Pilot Training Program (CPTP). Apparently, Wilson's contacts with Senators Bennett Champ Clark (D-Mo.), Warren Barbour (R-N.J.), and Claude Pepper (D-Fla.) were instrumental in gaining a consensus and enacting the bill into law. This very important piece of legislation allowed thousands of people to earn their pilot certificates under a government subsidy. It also stimulated general aviation activity and aircraft sales, and provided solid aviation education for those who would later serve in the air forces in World War II.

AOPA also secured a reduction in the medical examination fee (from $10 to $6), urged the CAA to construct more airports to handle the increase in flying activity, and conducted the first study of the various state aviation fuel taxation policies. Discussions with the National Advisory Council for Aeronautics (NACA—the National Aeronautics and Space Administration's predecessor organization) centered on design parameters for an easily affordable single-engine airplane. A program that recognized a pilot's long history of accident-free flying was also established. This drive to recognize general aviation safety was part of a greater effort to secure favorable insurance rates for AOPA members, an effort that came to fruition several years later.

Wilson, speaking at a conference of aviation manufacturers on October 12, 1939, urged that the government assist manufacturers in the development of safer aircraft and engine designs, a hot topic at the time, when stall/spin and engine-failure-related accidents were the most common. He also expressed AOPA's strong belief that all aircraft manufacturers should standardize the design of their cockpit instruments and other equipment, and provide all aircraft with stall warning indicators, as well as maintenance and inspection manuals. These items, taken for granted today, were provided only after AOPA began to apply pressure in 1939.

The year ended on an upbeat note: 2,000 members had signed up, thanks to the diligence and commitment of the founders and original handful of employees. But greater challenges lay ahead. What began with Imperial Japan's invasion of China in 1937 and Nazi Germany's occupation of Czechoslovakia's Sudetenland region in 1938 had expanded into a worldwide conflict with the German invasion of Poland in September 1939. World War II had begun.

"THE AIRCRAFT OWNERS AND PILOTS ASSOCIATION—LONG OVERDUE—HAS JUST BEEN BORN. YOU OUGHT TO SEE THE KID!" —GILL ROBB WILSON, "AOPA NEWS"

Breakfast flights and simulated emergency drills—such as this hurricane relief drill conducted in Greenport, Long Island, in July 1940—brought pilots together while demonstrating GA's value to the general public.

AOPA number one

Gill Robb Wilson bestowed gravitas on the fledgling organization

Who is Gill Robb Wilson, and why is he the first AOPA member? When AOPA was in its gestation, the association was looking for the day's big names in general aviation. The candidates had to have name recognition, no small degree of fame, and a certain gravitas to enhance AOPA's sense of purpose. No flamboyant publicity-seekers or barnstormers need have applied.

Wilson fit the bill. Born in Allegheny County, Pennsylvania, and the son of a Presbyterian minister, Wilson and his brother traveled to France during World War I. After driving ambulances, he served with the French Escadrille 66 (not the Lafayette Escadrille) and the 163rd American Squadron. He earned the Croix de Guerre and learned to fly at an aviation school in Tours, France.

After the war, Wilson became a Presbyterian minister; served as a pastor in Trenton, New Jersey; and became the national chaplain of the American Legion. In 1927, it's reported that Wilson lost his voice after his first wife and child died of influenza. Recovery meant that he couldn't use his voice so he left the ministry and, drawing on his aviation background, became New Jersey's director of aeronautics in 1930. Also in the 1930s, he was an airport consultant to the Works Progress Administration, an advisor to the U.S. Bureau of Air Commerce, and was a president and vice president of the National Association of State Aviation Officials. He participated in the investigation of the Lakehurst, New Jersey, crash of the zeppelin *Hindenburg*, and traveled to Germany in 1938. The trip convinced him that Germany was preparing for war.

Sometime in April 1939, Joseph B. "Doc" Hartranft Jr. named Wilson an executive consultant in the runup to AOPA's formation. The following month, Wilson became AOPA's first member. Wilson had a flair for writing, so once AOPA launched its "AOPA News" section in *Flying and Popular Aviation* magazine (now *Flying* magazine), he was named the section's first editor. Based on his impressions of a militant Germany, Wilson was instrumental in promoting the idea of a civilian group focused on coastal patrol and general preparedness should war break out. This conviction was instrumental in AOPA's forming its Air Guard in 1940.

In December 1941 the Civil Air Patrol was established, AOPA's Air Guard was incorporated into it, and Wilson was made the CAP's first executive officer. During World War II, he was a correspondent for the *New York Herald Tribune*. After World War II, Wilson returned to writing full-time, writing poetry and a book (*The Airman's World*, 1957), and serving as editor of *Flying* magazine from 1952 to 1962. He was also president of the U.S. Air Force Association. He died in Los Angeles in 1966.

Today's Mid-Ohio Valley Regional Airport (PKB) in Parkersburg, West Virginia, was originally named Gill Robb Wilson Field. And the CAP's highest award is named after him.

May 3 1939

Mr. Bradley A. Rogers, Jr.,
Jacob Reed's Sons,
1424 Chestnut St.,
Philadelphia, Pa.

Dear Brad:

Regarding your inquiry as to the qualifications of Gill Robb Wilson, State Director of Aviation of New Jersey for speaker, I may advise as follows:

According to an announcement of a radio address over KYW from the Poor Richard Luncheon March 28, the following qualifications were listed:

Mr. Wilson was with French Escadrille 66 American Squadron 163, decorated with the Crox de Guerre; N. J. Distinguished Service Medal, with the French Ambulance Corps; the Aviation School at Tours, graduated from W & J, 1915; Western Theological Seminary, 1920, National Chaplain of the American Legion, 1927.

At the present time Mr. Wilson is a reserve Military Aviator; Aerial Machine Gunner, Governor of the NAA, Past Vice-Pres. & President of the Ntl. Assn. State Aviation Officials, Technical Adviser to U. S. Bureau of Air Commerce, a member of "Quiet Birdmen," Airport Consultant, W. P. A., an ordained Presbyterian minister, completing eight years service on Adjutant-General's Staff, N. G. N. J.
Executive Consultant of Aircraft Owners & Pilots Association

If and when I may be of further service, ple

Sincerely,

J. B. Hartranft, Jr.

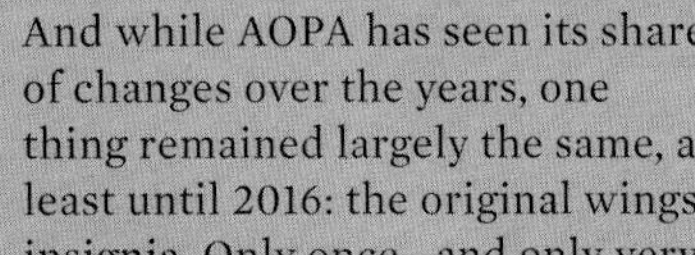

About those wings

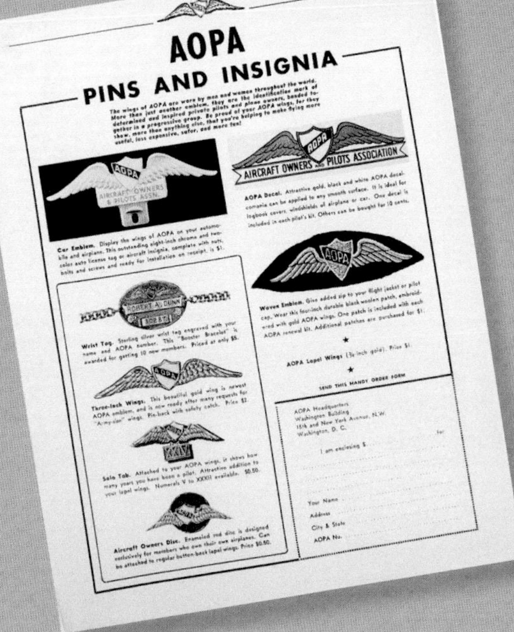

AOPA

PINS AND INSIGNIA

The wings of AOPA are worn by men and women throughout the world. More than just another emblem, they are the identification mark of determined and inspired private pilots and plane owners, banded together in a progressive group. Be proud of your AOPA wings, for they show, more than anything else, that you're helping to make flying more useful, less expensive, safer, and more fun!

Car Emblem. Display the wings of AOPA on your automobile and airplane. This outstanding eight-inch chrome and two-color auto license tag or aircraft insignia, complete with nuts, bolts and screws and ready for installation on receipt, is $1.

AOPA Decal. Attractive gold, black and white AOPA decalcomania can be applied to any smooth surface. It is ideal for logbook covers, windshields of airplane or car. One decal is included in each pilot's kit. Others can be bought for 10 cents.

Wrist Tag. Sterling silver wrist tag engraved with your name and AOPA number. This "Booster Bracelet" is awarded for getting 10 new members. Priced at only $5.

Woven Emblem. Give added zip to your flight jacket or pilot cap. Wear this four-inch durable black woolen patch, embroidered with gold AOPA wings. One patch is included with each AOPA renewal kit. Additional patches are purchased for $1.

★

AOPA Lapel Wings (¾-inch gold). Price $1.

★

Three-inch Wings. This beautiful gold wing is newest AOPA emblem, and is now ready after many requests for "Army-size" wings. Pin-back with safety catch. Price $2.

Solo Tab. Attached to your AOPA wings, it shows how many years you have been a pilot. Attractive addition to your lapel wings. Numerals V to XXXII available. $0.50.

Aircraft Owners Disc. Enameled red disc is designed exclusively for members who own their own airplanes. Can be attached to regular button-back lapel wings. Price $0.50.

SEND THIS HANDY ORDER FORM

AOPA Headquarters
Washington Building
15th and New York Avenue, N.W.
Washington, D. C.

I am enclosing $ .... for

Your Name
Address
City & State
AOPA No.

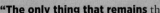

AOPA wings have graced the association's products and publications since the design was finalized in 1939—and rightly so. How can you fly without wings?

"The only thing that remains the same is change," goes an old saying. And while AOPA has seen its share of changes over the years, one thing remained largely the same, at least until 2016: the original wings insignia. Only once—and only very, very briefly—did the legacy wings undergo a significant design change. For a period of one week in late 1939, members were issued Gothic-looking wings, an attempt to establish a more "modern" look. Those wings were a flop; members called and wrote, stating in very clear terms that they didn't like the new wings and that they wanted the old ones instead. After that brouhaha, no one could bring themselves to alter the design that was chosen in the spring of 1939. A strong feeling of tradition has always surrounded AOPA's wings, which have decorated millions of automobiles, hats, jackets, lapels, banners, and who knows what else over the years.

The original wings were conceived by Joseph B. "Doc" Hartranft, who favored the drooped design used by Great Britain's Royal Air Force. It made for a good compromise in those times. The trick was to avoid any confusion that could be caused by having wings that resembled the military wings issued to U.S. flying officers and yet still convey a sense of national pride. By adapting the RAF design to suit their tastes, AOPA settled on a design that was both uniquely their own and still carried a sense of nationalism. After all, Great Britain has been America's staunchest ally and, in early 1939, all could sense that another world war would soon break out.

Nevertheless, the selection process was tedious. Before Hartranft decided on the design—and the trustees approved it—many alternatives were discussed. These consisted not only of Hartranft's own sketches, but those advanced by several jewelers eager for the business of representing the fledgling association. Bailey, Banks, and Biddle of Philadelphia came up with rigid-looking designs that seemed to mimic the wings of the Axis powers.

Spies Brothers Inc., of Chicago, was finally chosen as the designer of the first lapel pins. Their wings resembled Hartranft's design, but the shield was different.

At the last moment, just before Hartranft was about to settle the deal with Spies Brothers, a young jeweler from Salt Lake City visited Hartranft. Obert C. Tanner had just founded his own jewelry company and had learned of AOPA's formation. He asked to see a sample of the Spies Brothers' wings, and Hartranft showed him.

"I don't think this is the kind of message you want to convey about your membership," said Tanner. Hartranft was puzzled and asked for an explanation.

"The letters 'AOPA' appear in a bar sinister—running from the top right of the shield to the lower left. You want it to run in a bar dexter—from top left to lower right," said Tanner with an air of authority.

It seems that a "bar sinister" conveys a subtle, yet clear, message in the arcane language of heraldry. Tanner proceeded to enlighten Hartranft: A bar sinister means that the bearer is of illegitimate birth.

His lesson finished, Tanner left the office with a contract to produce AOPA's wings, including those for AOPA's wartime Air Guard. It was a relationship that was to last. The O.C. Tanner Co. still makes AOPA staff desk displays, issued to those with five, 10, 15, 20, 25, 30, 35, and 40 years of employment with the association. Members receive pins to recognize milestone years of membership. Member pins are now manufactured by the Pin Center of Las Vegas.

In 2016, AOPA updated its wings with a sleeker, more modern look (top left) after an extensive design and review process. The goal was to preserve the essential style elements of the original wings, so the shield mimics the legacy look—and yes, the wings still have that signature droop, although muted, and with less prominent feathers.

APOA
AOPA
THE BAIL
RESERVES THE
IDDLE COMPANY
STIMATE ON THIS DESIGN

3.

A WORLD IN TURMOIL

The "AOPA News" page in *Popular Aviation* magazine grew to an eight-page insert called "AOPA Section" (lower right) with the May 1940 issue of the magazine.

World War II transformed civilian flying in the United States

The 1940s dawned on a world in turmoil. But the United States had yet to enter the global conflict consuming Europe and Asia. The growth of private flying accelerated—and with it, AOPA membership grew.

For AOPA, the decade began with the expansion of existing programs and the addition of others. By March 1940, membership had risen to 4,000 pilots, so meeting the terms of the Ziff-Davis contract was no longer an issue. And membership continued to rise. One of the programs that helped stimulate AOPA's growth in this decade was the formation of AOPA Units—local pilot groups organized by AOPA members in the field. The first AOPA Unit was formed in January 1940 in Washington, D.C., by Herbert Berl. The second unit was formed shortly thereafter in Stockton, California, by John J. Cole. By May 1940, the "AOPA Section" reported the formation of 136 AOPA Units, which served as focal points for both social and instructional events. This growth in membership and activities meant that Hartranft had to hire an assistant—Lawrence Lawver—to travel the United States, keep records, and help with administrative work.

Rooftops, roads, and compass roses

Before radio navigation was common, pilots often used airmarks to guide them. Airmarking picked up steam with the public, mostly thanks to Amelia Earhart and Phoebe Omlie. It is said that Earhart sold the government on the program by arguing that general aviation must be made safe—like driving—before the public would buy in.

In 1935, the Bureau of Air Commerce appointed Blanche Noyes to run the program. More than 30,000 airmarks were said to have been completed before December 1941. Airmarks were painted on roofs of theaters, hotels, and railroad stations; on water towers and roads; and made out of rocks and shrubs on hillsides. But the program was halted after the attack on Pearl Harbor; the war department ordered all airmarks within 150 miles of the coasts to be blacked out for safety. After the war, the program started up again, but with new standards for letter size and color, and the addition of coordinates and north-pointing arrows at each mark.

The original airmarks were paid for by the Works Progress Administration; they were later funded by state commissions and local chambers of commerce. The program ran through the 1970s, and today The Ninety-Nines still paint airmarks and compass roses at airports around the country.

OAKLAND 9

EMERYVILLE

BURY THE WIRES...
NOT THE PILOT!
AIRCRAFT OWNERS AND PILOTS ASSOCIATION
SAFETY CAMPAIGN

Fly-ins and social activities were the main draws of belonging to one of the growing number of local AOPA Units in the association's early days. Members of the Camden, New Jersey, unit attend a dinner in 1940 (opposite page). An AOPA safety campaign urged cities to remove obstructions near airports (left) and to include future airports in their planning.

In its representation of member interests, AOPA focused much attention in 1940 and 1941 on the problem of airport access and landing fees. Like so many other issues, the problems of the early days bear an uncanny resemblance to those that general aviation continues to face today. Of particular concern was the imposition of a $5 fee on pilots landing general aviation aircraft at New York City's brand-new La Guardia Field. AOPA also lobbied the Civil Aeronautics Administration to allow general aviation pilots the use of CAA designated emergency landing fields as conventional airports.

AOPA offered technical guidance to pilots wanting to establish "AOPA Airhavens"—low-cost airports with prefabricated hangars. Other accomplishments included a reduction in the reexamination period for airmen written exams from 90 to 30 days; airmarking of many prominent buildings, an initiative that coincided with the AOPA pressure to begin the construction of emergency runways near certain highways; and the association's successful efforts to convince local authorities to bury power lines near many airports—"Bury the Wires, Not the Pilots" said one slogan. The year 1940 also saw the first use of airport questionnaires to provide members with firsthand information on services and facilities (this was to later become the seed of *AOPA's Airports USA* and *AOPA's Aviation USA* airport directories) and the first member benefit discounts—agreements to provide discounts to members using the Hertz Driv-Ur-Self System (now Hertz Rent-A-Car) and Transcontinental and Western Air (which became Trans World Airlines).

In early 1940, AOPA established the Emergency Pilot Registry, a cooperative venture between AOPA and the American Red Cross. Pilots who joined were given training in first aid and disaster relief mis-

CRESCENT
BEVERAGES

Cubs, Coupes, and Cruisers

The prewar general aviation fleet

Leading up to U.S. involvement in World War II, the Piper Cub was America's airplane; more than 3,000 J-3 Cubs, J-4 Cub Coupes, and three-seat J-5 Cub Cruisers rolled off Piper's Lock Haven, Pennsylvania, assembly line in 1940 and almost 2,900 more in 1941. They joined a plethora of other light, high-wing monoplanes designed for the sportsman-pilot, such as the Aeronca Super Chief; Fairchild 24; the Funk models B and L; the Interstate Cadet; Luscombe's Model 8 Silvaire; the Monocoupe Model 90 series; the Porterfield 90, CP, and LP; the Rearwin Speedster, Sportster, Cloudster, and Skyranger; the Stinson 105; the Taylorcraft; the Welch OW; and the Wendt W-2.

Among low-wing monoplanes, the Bellanca Crusair, Culver Cadet (designed by Al Mooney), Ercoupe (designed by Fred Weick and distinguished by its innovative new tricycle landing gear), Ryan S-C, and Swallow LT-65 were popular choices.

The businessman-pilot had his choice of roomier, more powerful models, such as the Beech 17 "Staggerwing" series and the Waco models E, N, and S (all cabin biplanes); Cessna Airmaster; Howard DGA-15; Monocoupe Zephyr and Zenith; Spartan Executive; and Stinson Reliant.

Multiengine corporate models were gaining in popularity. Companies could choose a Beech 18, Bennett Monoplane, Cessna T-50, or Lockheed 12.

For those pilots engaged in amphibious operations, the single-engine Fleetwings Sea Bird or twin-engine Grumman Widgeon (at right) were available. And for those intrigued by rotary-wing flight, a Kellett or Pitcairn autogiro could be had (and more exciting developments were on the horizon—the world got its first view of Igor Sikorsky's revolutionary VS-300 helicopter in 1941).

V203

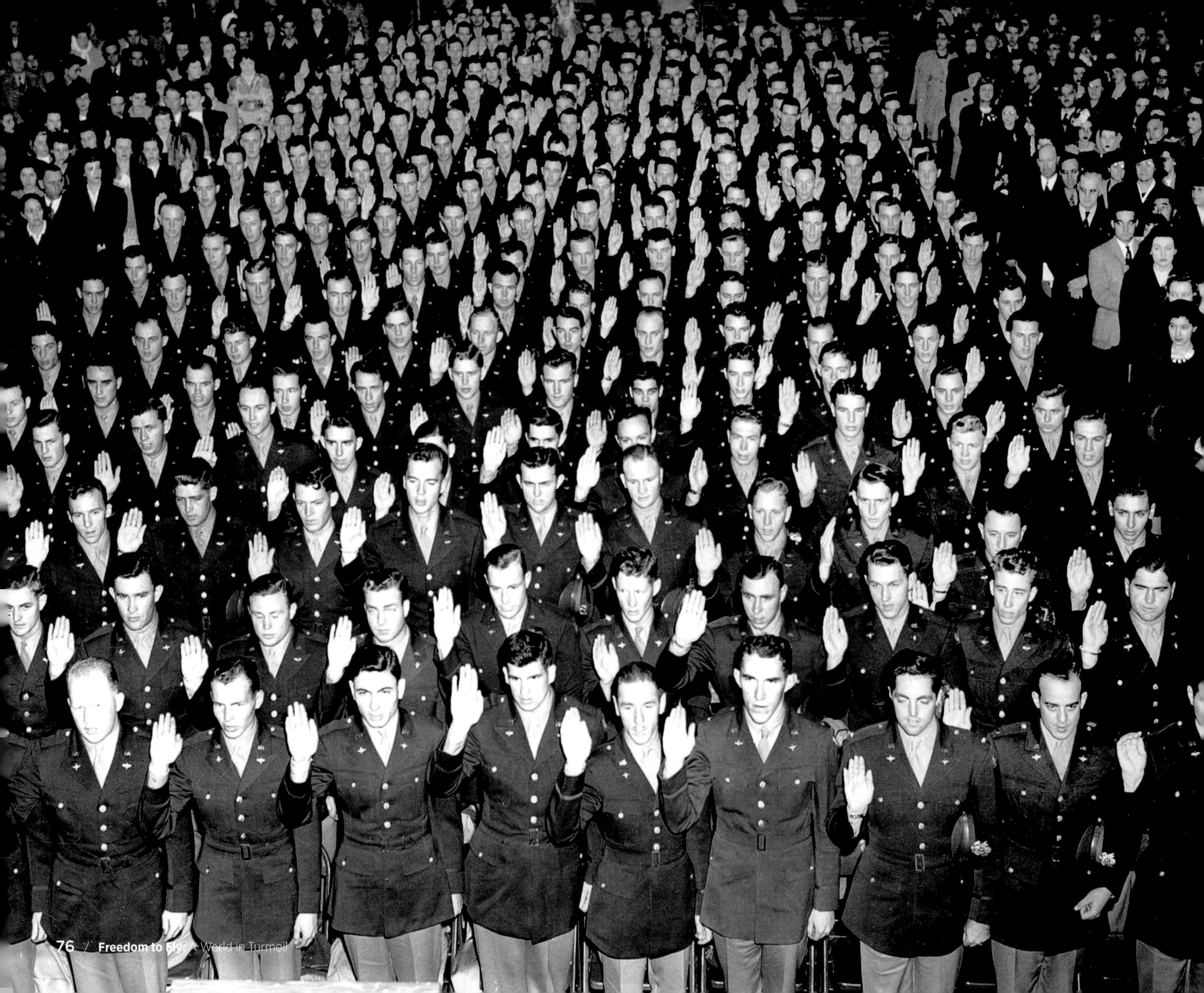

Civilian Pilot Training Program graduates were sworn into the U.S. Army Air Forces (left) as newly minted officers. AOPA Air Guard applicants had to pass written tests, such as the "One Star" examination at right.

sions and called into service when floods, major fires, and other disasters required air operations. Some 3,000 AOPA members joined the registry.

By the summer of 1940, France had fallen to the Germans, and the Battle of Britain was underway. American attitudes toward intervention were shifting. The U.S. Civilian Pilot Training Program, in effect since February 1939, began to turn out pilots in earnest. Within a year, some 52,000 pilots graduated, and the U.S. pilot population jumped from 31,000 to more than 100,000 in 18 months, in large part because of the CPTP.

Anticipating the need for qualified pilots to help in service of national defense, AOPA in August 1940 announced the formation of the AOPA Air Guard. This was a program designed to introduce civilian pilots to military rules and procedures

In the Guard

Sample questions from an Air Guard application

Air Guard applicants were tested on their knowledge of military customs and discipline, Army administration, first aid, engines, navigation, and more.

True or false? **You are permitted to fly within 100 feet of the water provided it is open water and no ships are within one-half mile.** (False)

True or false? **In a four-stroke-per-cycle, seven-cylinder radial engine, turning at 1,400 rpm, #7 cylinder should fire 700 times in one minute.** (True)

Does the Army **supply food, clothing, shelter, and entertainment for the enlisted men?** (Yes)

True or false? **Any person subject to military law who behaves himself with disrespect toward his superior officer is punishable under the Articles of War.** (True)

ONE STAR AIR GUARD EXAMINATION

(Lawyer giving this examination will kindly sign here after the examination has been completed.) To the best of my knowledge the examination has been fairly taken.

David B Evans
(Lawyer's Signature)

Student will kindly fill in the following, clearly written:

Date Oct 24, 1940

Your Name Willis Scott

Mail Address #4
Webster City, Iowa

I hereby promise that I will not use any outside help of any nature whatsoever in answering the questions in this examination and will use nothing but my memory and intelligence.

Student sign here: Willis Scott

You are to complete this examination within two hours and hand it back personally to the person who opened it for you.

Each question is to be answered by noting after it either "y or "no," or "true" or "false" as the wording obviously indicates.

The scoring will be as follows: For each correct answer yo receive a score of + 1, for each question unanswered, a score of and for each question answered wrongly, a score of - 1. Thus, don't know the answer, it is better not to answer than to guess

There are no "trick" questions, in which, for instance, t wording would be used to obscure the meaning. There are, of plenty of frankly false statements concerning which you have enough to label them as false.

Army Administration

(Answer each question either "yes" or "no.")

1. Does the Army supply food, clothing, shelter, and ente tainment for the enlisted men?

2. When a private in the Army wants to see a doctor, do he have to pay the doctor?

3. Is the normal method of transporting troops overla to send them in standard railroad cars rather than Army-owned railroad cars and busses?

official inter-Army mail repl below the original forwarding it, sheet as i

AOPA members joining the Emergency Pilot Registry wore a badge (left) and were trained in first aid and disaster relief operations. Advertisements in a 1940 issue of *Flying and Popular Aviation* (right) drove up enrollments in the Air Guard and boosted AOPA membership.

and to provide a manpower base from which the air forces could draw additional pilots. This program was conducted independently of the CPTP; those who had soloed an airplane were eligible. Some 5,000 pilots participated in the Air Guard.

Three courses of instruction were offered. The one-star course required students to understand the basics of aerial photography, map reading, flight theory, military discipline, ranks, and codes of conduct. Prospective air guardsmen mailed their requests for test materials to AOPA's service headquarters—which had moved to 415 Lexington Avenue, New York City (member registration headquarters was still at the Chicago address)—and the association would mail back a textbook, plus question and answer forms. After a period of study, the student was required to take the test to a local lawyer, who was to serve as proctor. The proctor sealed the completed test sheets, then mailed them back to AOPA for grading. If a student passed, he was eligible to wear an AOPA-designed uniform.

The two-star course worked in much the same fashion but involved a more difficult test and flight training, as both a pilot and observer. The three-star pilot received advanced flight, observation, and photography instruc-

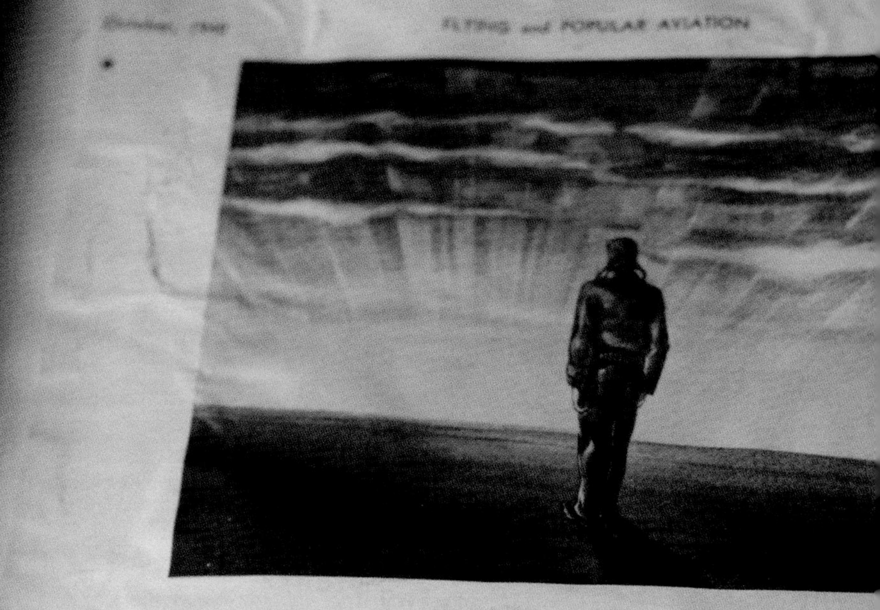

FACING A NEW HORIZON...

Today the AOPA stands on the threshold of a new horizon. Today, more than ever, air strength is needed to cope with any national emergency. To meet this challenge the AOPA has formed, as a component part of its organization, the AIR GUARD . . . a civilian air reserve open to every American who has soloed a plane.

Through the newly formed AIR GUARD the Aircraft Owners And Pilots Association offers a volunteer civilian military course of instruction consisting of the following three parts.

★ ONE-STAR COURSE—A study course covering important phases of military procedure . . . compiled from actual training given Army pilots. ★ ★ TWO-STAR COURSE—Primary flight training . . . a 20-hour military familiarization flight training course. ★ ★ ★ THREE-STAR COURSE—Advanced flight training including instrument familiarization . . . highest rating in the AIR GUARD.

What does the formation of the AIR GUARD signify? To civilian pilots it brings an opportunity to join a great patriotic volunteer movement to give America "Maximum Emergency Strength in the Air." To the AOPA it brings new opportunities for service and helpfulness.

Write today for complete information on the AIR GUARD. A post card will do.

AIR GUARD

AIRCRAFT OWNERS AND PILOTS ASSOCIATION

415 Lexington Avenue, New York City

I'M PROUD TO BE AN AOPA PILOT!

Today over 6,000 civilian pilots . . . men and women from seventeen to seventy in all parts of the United States . . . take great pride in being affiliated with the Aircraft Owners and Pilots Association. As registered members of AOPA—the largest and most progressive non-scheduled flying organization of its kind—they cherish their new and more important status as private pilots.

appreciate the many special services and valuable

are automatically accorded AOPA regis-

civilian pilot who has soloed, you

is making non-scheduled

and more fun

AIRCRAFT OWNERS AND PI

ASSOCIATIO

Office of President: 1424 Walnut Street,

National Service Office: Transportation

tion. Once a three-star candidate's test was passed, he was eligible to fly on certain military observation missions using fuel provided free of charge by the armed forces.

The units' breakfast flights and other fly-in activities continued—until December 7, 1941, when the Japanese attacked Pearl Harbor, Hawaii. America's entry into World War II had finally come, and it brought a drastic change to civilian flying.

Nation at war

Hours after the attack on Pearl Harbor, the Civil Aeronautics Administration grounded all civilian flying in the United States—17,000 private airplanes and more than 80,000 pilots, according to an AOPA Section report. Titled "AOPA in Action!" the article describes pilots around the country reasoning, "It has come; the total eclipse of private flying fought so hard and so long by 'Doc' Hartranft and the AOPA. It will be a blow to him. It will shut down AOPA for the duration; all of its struggles will be forgotten.

"Excellent reasoning, but poor information," it continued. "At that moment 'Doc' never felt better. Then, at the crisis of the nation's shock, 'Doc' was ready. No haymaker, the government's sudden order merely put the AOPA on its back on the floor. Thanks to more than a year of preparation and conditioning, 'Doc' and his AOPA organization got up off the floor and began to slug." AOPA was instrumental in establishing an emergency pilot registry and identification program that convinced the CAA and the military to allow registered pilots to fly in all airspace, save the newly instituted West Coast, East Coast, and Canadian

AOPA member Zack "Smilin' Jack" Mosley (below) penned an air-minded, syndicated cartoon. On December 9, 1941, urgent telegrams were sent by AOPA to all AOPA Units, urging them to comply with FBI fingerprinting after the attack on Pearl Harbor in Hawaii (bottom). Civil Air Patrol sub chasers from Atlantic City, New Jersey, don "zoot suits" in case of ditching (right).

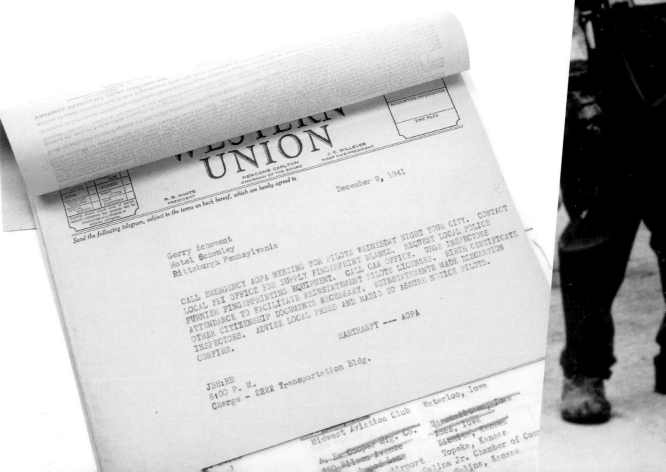

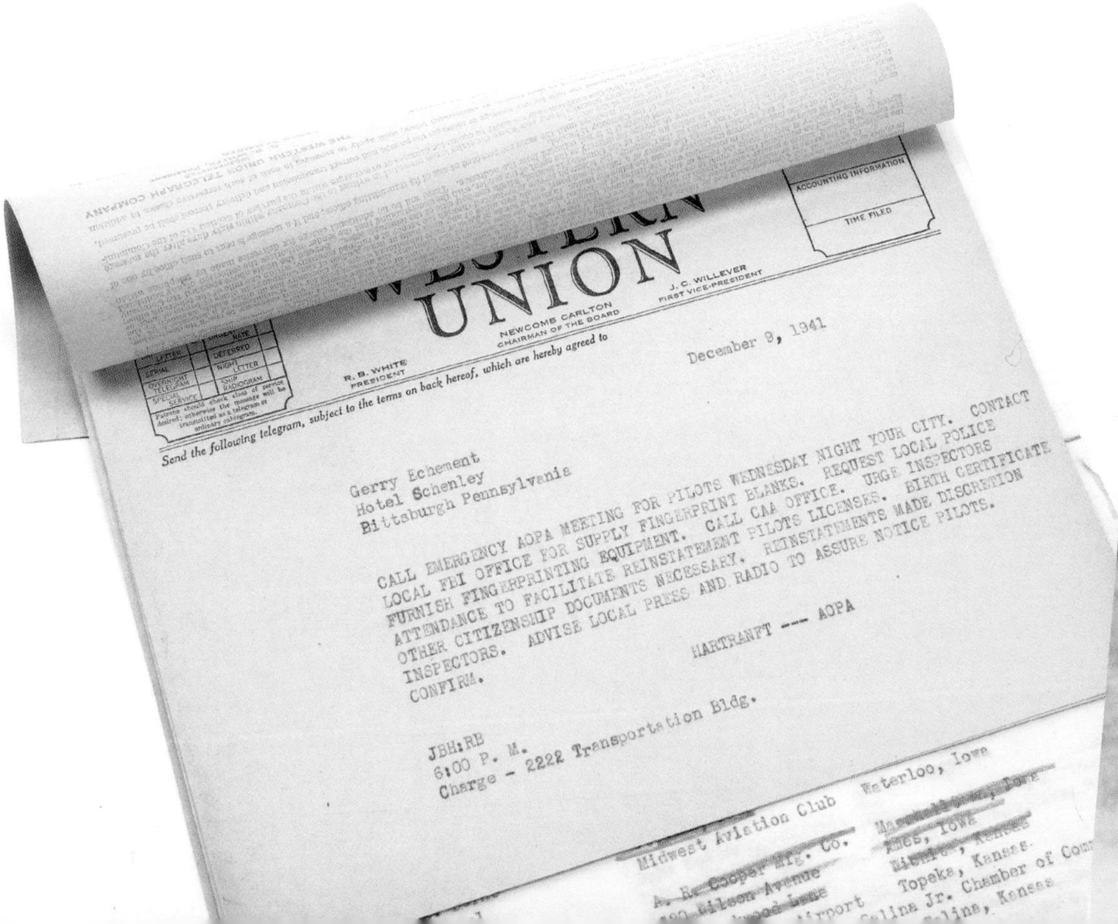

UNION

R. B. WHITE, PRESIDENT — NEWCOMB CARLTON, CHAIRMAN OF THE BOARD — J. C. WILLEVER, FIRST VICE-PRESIDENT

Send the following telegram, subject to the terms on back hereof, which are hereby agreed to

December 9, 1941

Gerry Echement
Hotel Schenley
Pittsburgh Pennsylvania

CALL EMERGENCY AOPA MEETING FOR PILOTS WEDNESDAY NIGHT YOUR CITY. CONTACT LOCAL FBI OFFICE FOR SUPPLY FINGERPRINT BLANKS. REQUEST LOCAL POLICE FURNISH FINGERPRINTING EQUIPMENT. CALL CAA OFFICE. URGE INSPECTORS ATTENDANCE TO FACILITATE REINSTATEMENT PILOTS LICENSES. BIRTH CERTIFICATE OTHER CITIZENSHIP DOCUMENTS NECESSARY. REINSTATEMENTS MADE DISCRETION INSPECTORS. ADVISE LOCAL PRESS AND RADIO TO ASSURE NOTICE PILOTS. CONFIRM.

HARTRANFT --- AOPA

JBH:RB
6:00 P. M.
Charge - 2222 Transportation Bldg.

Midwest Aviation Club — Waterloo, Iowa

R. EARLE
D07
CAPT.
NEWCOMB

New warriors

Diversity in the second world war

With the nation engaged in a conflict of unprecedented scale, the demands of World War II brought significant social changes to the United States, with women and minorities filling roles previously thought the domain of white men.

Tuskegee Airmen

The first black U.S. military aviators were the Tuskegee Airmen—started as a pursuit squadron and bombardment group; they were training B-25 crews by war's end—trained in Tuskegee, Alabama. In addition to the pilots, the navigators, bombardiers, maintenance and support staff, instructors, and others were known collectively as Tuskegee Airmen.

The military chose the Tuskegee Institute—today Tuskegee University—to train pilots for the formerly all-white U.S. Army Air Corps. The segregated unit was created in response to pressure from black newspapers and a lawsuit by civil rights organizations, which had sought full integration of the armed forces.

The Tuskegee Airmen flew combat operations and heavy bomber escort missions, initially with Curtiss P-40 Warhawks and eventually with P-51 Mustangs—the airplane for which they are best known. The pilots of the 332nd Fighter Group painted the noses and rudders of their P-51s red, and the group became known as the Red Tails.

The Tuskegee Airmen flew 1,578 combat missions and 179 bomber escort missions, and destroyed 112 enemy aircraft. Because they

stayed close to the bombers they escorted and did not pursue fleeing enemy fighters, the 332nd did not rack up as many kills as other fighter groups. Enemy aircraft shot down 27 of the bombers they escorted—but the average number of bombers lost by other escort groups of the Fifteenth Air Force was 46, nearly double the number.

At the war's conclusion, many of the Tuskegee Airmen went on to careers in the military. In 1950, George S. Roberts, deputy commander of the 332nd Fighter Group, became the first black man to command a racially integrated unit in the new U.S. Air Force. He retired a colonel.

"If they did not demonstrate that they were far superior to the members of the six non-black fighter escort groups of the Fifteenth Air Force with which they served, they certainly demonstrated that they were not inferior to them, either," said Daniel L. Haulman, chief of the Organizational Histories Branch of the Air Force Historical Research Agency.

The WASP

As World War II gained momentum and the need for factory personnel intensified, women went to work on assembly lines, producing aircraft and other goods for the war effort. Women were not allowed in military combat roles.

Male pilots were shipped overseas as fast as they could be trained, which left no one to ferry new training airplanes to military flight schools. Nancy Harkness Love, a test pilot and air racer, and Jacqueline Cochran, an air racer and speed record holder, founded two programs aimed at training civilian women pilots to ferry the aircraft. The two programs—Women's Auxiliary Ferrying Squadron and Women's Flying Training Detachment—became the Women Airforce Service Pilots. Graduates were stationed at 122 air bases around the United States.

From 1942 to 1944, 1,074 women ferried every aircraft the U.S. Army had, including the P–51D Mustang, the P–47 Thunderbolt, and the B–26 Marauder. They also towed gunnery targets, transported equipment and nonflying personnel, and flight-tested aircraft that had been repaired. Thirty-eight WASP died while serving—11 during training, and 27 while on active duty missions. Their nonmilitary status meant that their families had to pay for their funeral expenses.

In 1944, the WASP were disbanded. In spite of their wartime service, the women were not given U.S. military veteran status until 1977.

Military airfields—like this one in El Paso, Texas—popped up all over the nation as the United States prepared for war. Many would go on to serve the public for decades.

Thanks, Uncle Sam

Hundreds of airfields built by the armed forces now serve the flying public

Seen from the air, many have a characteristic shape: a more-or-less equilateral triangle formed by three intersecting runways. Others look like a cross or plus sign with a third, diagonal runway joining two of the tips. Those built as outlying or auxiliary landing fields more often consist of a single strip.

Around the country, hundreds of airfields built or vastly expanded as part of the war effort remain in active use as civilian airports, spanning the range from the 1,800-foot gravel runway of Cordova Municipal Airport in Alaska, to a combined 41,476 feet of asphalt at Miami International.

The triangular configuration was a particularly appealing layout for training facilities, guaranteeing that trainees would never have to face more than a 30-degree crosswind. This was also helpful to the Civil Air Patrol pilots flying Cubs and Taylorcrafts on submarine patrols from the freshly built air stations along the coasts. Not all have retained that admirable characteristic.

Military projects—for purposes such as training, manufacturing, and support—brought aviation to remote communities such as Eagle Pass, Texas, whose former Army Air Field is now Maverick County Memorial. Some formerly isolated auxiliary fields, however, have been enveloped by seven decades of development. The Army's Lomita Flight Strip was renamed for local hero Louis Zamperini (Olympic runner, B-24 bombardier, and prisoner of war) after being first handed over to and then swallowed up by the city of Torrance, California—and, of course, Santa Monica, America's most threatened airport, rolled out thousands of C-47 and C-54 transports to help win the war. B-17 pilots learned to trundle their unwieldy charges down the runways of what's now Cincinnati/Northern Kentucky International. B-17 crews were also trained at Geiger Field in Washington, later renamed Spokane International. Future Wildcat, Hellcat, Avenger, and Corsair pilots honed their craft on the 3,000-foot runways of Naval Auxiliary Air Station Manteo on North Carolina's Outer Banks while PBY crews practiced offshore. These days it's known as Dare County Regional. Newark Army Airfield was a logistics hub, while the airport in nearby Linden, New Jersey, tested and delivered fighters and dive bombers built at the former General Motors auto plant across the street. In Michigan, Ford's production of the B-24 Liberator at the Willow Run Airport in Ypsilanti reached one every 63 minutes—faster than the Army could accept them. By the war's end, Ford built nearly 7,000 aircraft and manufactured parts for another 1,893 to be assembled elsewhere, accounting for nearly half the total production run of about 18,500.

Airline passengers alighting in Austin, Texas; Cleveland, Ohio; Milwaukee, Wisconsin; Richmond, Virginia; and Great Falls, Montana—among many others—enjoy the lasting benefits of the World War II construction boom. So do GA pilots touching down for a vacation at Fernandina Beach, Florida; a hunting trip outside Bethel, Alaska; or legislative business at the St. Paul Downtown Airport just across the river from the Minnesota State Capitol. It doesn't compare with national survival, but a rich aviation infrastructure is yet another gift to modern America from the Greatest Generation.

Warplane production skyrocketed overnight (below) after Pearl Harbor, with factories putting on extra shifts to produce airplanes such as the North American B-25 Mitchell medium bomber.

border Vital Air Defense Areas. The only other civilian pilots allowed similar freedoms were those in the Civil Air Patrol, which was formed December 1, 1941, and publicly announced the day following the Pearl Harbor attack. (The Civil Air Patrol was the brainchild of Gill Robb Wilson, AOPA member number 1.)

To be properly registered, pilots had to carry a card bearing their pilot certificate number, photograph, and thumbprint. Cards were made at designated sites and times by AOPA Units and at AOPA's registration headquarters in the Transportation Building in Chicago. This program did not only apply to AOPA members; the federal government empowered AOPA to register any and all American pilots who presented themselves for registration. AOPA ran photos of the registrations in an ad in *Flying and Popular Aviation* boasting that within 72 hours of the attack, 124 units were performing relicensing.

In high gear

The transformation that took place in aviation manufacturing during World War II was unique in industrial history. U.S. aircraft manufacturers in the late 1930s relied on skilled craftsmen who produced small numbers of airplanes, mostly by hand. It was a highly specialized cottage industry that ranked forty-first in revenue terms among industry in the United States.

Within five tumultuous years, aircraft manufacturing was transformed to the top U.S. industry, and more than 2.1 million people came to work in huge factories—some of them among the largest structures in the world—where they mass produced bombers, transports, trainers, and fighters at unprecedented, and formerly unimaginable, rates.

The numbers tell part of the story. In 1939, all U.S. factories produced about 3,000 new airplanes annually. Five years later, in 1944, that number spiked to nearly 100,000—a more than 30-fold increase. At some factories, such as the Douglas facility in Long Beach, California, more than 80 percent of the workers were women.

When the United States entered World War II, the relatively small number of general aviation aircraft were grounded or commandeered for military use. The top corporate aircraft of their day—Beech D-17 Staggerwings and Howard DGA-15s—became military liaisons. Trainers such as Piper J-3s and Waco and Stearman biplanes were drafted to train military pilots. And airliners such as the Douglas DC-3 began serving as military transports.

U.S. auto manufacturers Ford and General Motors became aircraft builders during the war, and Ford's plant at Willow Run, Michigan, produced B-24 Liberator bombers at the astonishing rate of one every 63 minutes, 24 hours per day, in 1944. From July 1940 through August 1945, the United States churned out almost 296,000 warplanes.

BOUNDARY OF AIR DEFENSE
BOUNDARY OF VITAL DEFENSE AREA
AIR DEFENSE ZONE BOUNDARY OF VITAL
VITAL DEFENSE
DANGER AREA
PROHIBITED AREA
WASHINGTON
BALTIMORE
HAGERSTOWN
Gettysburg
Hanover
Westminster
Frederick
Annapolis
Manassas
Waynesboro
Martinsburg
Taneytown
Rockville
Bowie
La Plata
Cambridge
Easton
St Michaels
Havre de Grace
Aberdeen
Chestertown
Centerville
Warrenton
Culpeper
PA
MD
W VA
VA
C & O CANAL
POTOMAC R
CONGRESSIONAL
BLUE RIDGE
TOWER 278 KC 126.18 Mc
WASHINGTON RADIO
BALTIMORE RADIO
Under Contact flight rules, when passing the Indian Head danger area,

This sectional chart from 1944 shows an especially sensitive area of the United States during World War II—the nation's capital and the coastal areas with their many military facilities. Civilian pilots had to steer clear of Vital Defense Areas such as the ones portrayed here.

U.S. Pilots in 1945 | **299,333** ▲

Civil Air Patrol subchasers, such as this Fairchild 24, patrolled America's coastlines (at right). CAP pilots operated up to 200 miles offshore.

Called up for duty

More than 16 million served in the U.S. military during World War II. Hartranft and Wolf were called up for duty in the Army Air Corps. Wolf, one of AOPA's founders and original trustees, served in the South Pacific, ferrying aircraft to combat theaters of operation. He was to earn the rank of brigadier general. Hartranft's job sent him to Washington, D.C., where he served in several capacities. One was on the Interagency Air Traffic Control Board (IATCB), a panel of representatives of the Army (and Army Air Corps), Navy, and CAA who ruled on operational disputes between civilian and military operations.

Hartranft's job was to fill the role of a participant with a neutral background, and to take any unresolved disputes to President Roosevelt for a final disposition. In this capacity, he was effective in assuring that general aviation was not unnecessarily excluded from the growing amount of airspace allotted for military training. "Keep 'Em All Flying!"—a play on a U.S. Army recruiting slogan, "Keep 'Em Flying"—was the motto proclaimed on bumper stickers distributed by AOPA.

Another of Hartranft's goals was to create a home defense role for the Air Guard. Certain three-star graduates were given the task of assisting the Navy in searching for enemy submarines along coastal sections of the United States. Many searches were successful in identifying and locating submarines that were later sunk.

Hartranft's third job was as general manager at AOPA's new Washington, D.C., offices, located first in the Carpenters Building at 1003 K Street NW (from September 1942 to November 1945), then at the International Building at 1319 F Street NW (from November 1945 to September 1947), followed by the Washington Building at 15th and New York Avenue NW (from September 1947 to June 1951).

During the war years, most of the day-to-day responsibilities of running AOPA's service office rested with Ann Shryock, Hartranft's assistant, who headed up a staff of six in the Washington office; registration work was still done in Chicago.

Prior to U.S. involvement in the war, AOPA membership had risen to approximately 10,000; at the war's height, about 3,000 members temporarily dropped out to serve in the armed forces. But the number of American pilots skyrocketed: The Army Air Forces graduated 233,198 from its primary pilot course between Pearl Harbor and the end of the war, according to the Aerospace Industries Association. When the war ended, millions of service members returned home to resume their civilian lives in a changed nation.

The staggering number of new aircraft, a surge in pilots and mechanics, and the construction of airports and manufacturing centers around the country would shape general aviation for decades to come.

"KEEP 'EM ALL FLYING!"—A PLAY ON A U.S. ARMY RECRUITING SLOGAN, "KEEP 'EM FLYING"—WAS THE MOTTO PROCLAIMED ON BUMPER STICKERS DISTRIBUTED BY AOPA.

April, 1942
FLYING
KEEP'EM ALL FLY
NOT every good pilot is in the armed service. There are posts in civilian and "semi-military" life that the private flyer can fill to perfection. Here are just a few: Guarding Airports, Serving as Air Couriers, Searching for Lost Aircraft, Towing Aerial Gunnery Targets, Ferrying Planes Cross-Country, Observing Back-Country Regions, Helping Train Air-Raid Watchers, Transporting Defense Council Leaders, Aiding Military Ships at Civil Airports, Helping Evacuees by Highway Traffic Patrol.
In any of these capacities, civilian flyers may possibly aid the Civil Air Patrol in its staunch efforts to "Keep 'Em ALL Flying" and to keep the air safe for Democracy's airmen. The Aircraft Owners
& Pilots Associat
AOPA pilots, he
Sam's civilian and
their best individ
Now, more thar
important role in
more than ever be
plane owner look to
their flying problems
ful . . . Join the mass
flying's defense . .
about the strongest,
of aircraft owners and
coupon below, today or
FOR DEFENSE
BUY UNITED STATES SAVINGS BONDS AND STAMPS
AIRCRAFT OWNERS AND PILOTS ASSOCIATION
Registrar's Office—Dept. F42
Michigan Square Building
Chicago, Illinois
Please rush illustrated brochure telling how I can become a registered AOP
with complete information on how I can do my part in America's civilian air de
NAME
ADDRESS
PILOT LICENSE NUMBER
CITY & STATE
AFT OWNERS AND PILOTS ASSOCIA

All U.S. civilian pilots were grounded after Pearl Harbor, but those registered with an AOPA Unit or on AOPA's Emergency Pilot Registry were exempt and could fly in all but the most secure airspace.

GA dons khaki

Production priority goes to war trainers

When the United States was swept into the war in December 1941, civil aircraft production lines were immediately turned over to war production, which often did not involve building airplanes—although 27 aircraft manufacturers were immediately ordered to assign priority to the production of aircraft to assure an adequate supply of trainers for CPTP students. Many of the light aircraft manufacturers produced their prewar models in military configurations.

From 1942 through 1945, Piper Aircraft alone delivered almost 8,000 airplanes to the armed forces. Similarly, Aeronca built the L-3, training gliders for the U.S. Army Air Forces and U.S. Navy, an ambulance version of its Super Chief for the Civil Air Patrol, and a trainer version of the Super Chief. The Beech 17 was drafted by the U.S. Army Air Forces and U.S. Navy as the Traveler and the Model 18 as the Expeditor. Cessna's T-50 Bobcat was used as a multiengine trainer. The Fairchild 24 became the Forwarder for the U.S. Army Air Forces, U.S. Navy, and Royal Air Force, and the same services used the Grumman Widgeon (with the RAF calling it the Gosling).

The Howard DGA-15 became the Nightingale and was used as a transport, ambulance, and instrument trainer. Interstate provided the L-6. The Spartan Executive became the UC-71. The Stinson Sentinel served the U.S. Army Air Forces and U.S. Navy; the Reliant, the U.S. Army Air Forces and Fleet Air Arm. Taylorcraft provided its L-2 to the USAAF and a training glider to the U.S. Army Air Forces and U.S. Navy. Waco built some of the largest gliders ever made, some of which were used during the Normandy invasion as well as elsewhere in the European theater; in addition, powered Wacos served the U.S. Army Air Forces and other armed forces.

One of the most significant effects of the war was the priority that came to be attached to research into rotary-wing flight. By the end of the war, helicopters had been developed by Sikorsky, Platt-LePage, Bell, Higgins, Hiller, Landgraf, and Piasecki—and by the end of the decade, these companies would be joined by Firestone, Bendix, Brantley, Hoppi-Copter, Jov, Kaman, Kellett, McDonnell, Dornan, Helicopters Incorporated, Jensen, and Marquardt. Few of these companies ever entered full-scale production, but some of them established the basis of today's civil and military helicopter industry.

Piper Aircraft's line of Cubs became training and liaison aircraft (inset) during World War II. Cessna's T-50 Bobcat (right) first flew in 1939, and was used for training during the war for pilots stepping up to C-47s, B-25s, B-17s, and other larger aircraft.

12

4. BOOM TIMES

FBO fuel-price gouging is nothing new. This cartoon from a 1947 "AOPA Pilot" insert in *Flying* magazine reflected a growing awareness of general aviation's unfair treatment at the pumps—and a simmering conflict with airline interests.

High hopes in a postwar world

The United States wasted no time picking up the economic beat in the late 1940s. The war was over, and the Great Depression a distant, all-but-forgotten episode as the military returned to a peacetime footing and soldiers, sailors, airmen, and Marines returned home, started families, and embarked on their careers.

Many returning servicemen had been pilots in the war, and in the general aviation community there was every expectation that they'd want to resume flying as civilians. A jump in the U.S. civilian pilot population of more than 100,000 in a year—to 400,000 in 1946—was driven in part by military pilots converting their certificates. AOPA membership resumed its prewar rise: By the end of 1946, membership stood at approximately 20,000. General aviation flying activity took a proportionate increase, as returning pilots bought aircraft in unprecedented numbers, at least for a while. Many of these aircraft were surplus military aircraft, auctioned off at the end of the war. The CAA wanted to prohibit civil certification of these aircraft. In one of its first postwar legislative efforts, AOPA was successful in turning this around.

America returned to work, and one of the greatest economic expansions, after World War II. That included a burst of general aviation manufacturing. The Globe Swift assembly line is full of activity (facing page).

The massive number of surplus aircraft after the war had profound implications for general aviation. Thousands of war-surplus Stearman and Waco biplanes were available for bargain-basement prices. They became cropdusters, civilian pilot trainers, and airshow performers. B-17 Flying Fortresses, B-25 Mitchells, Lockheed Lodestars, A-26 Invaders, and C-45 Expeditors were refitted as corporate aircraft. PBY Catalina flying boats and TBM Avengers became aerial firefighters. C-46 Commandos and C-47 Dakotas were put into civilian hands as airliners and cargo haulers.

Meanwhile, excess aircraft manufacturing capacity was redirected to serve an anticipated boom in general aviation demand. Cessna, Piper, Aeronca, and others flooded the market with inexpensive trainers, while Beech, North American, and others produced higher-performing models for business and private use. But the then-widely accepted notion that the hundreds of thousands of

Postwar manufacturing

An upswing, slump, and modest recovery

When World War II ended, some firms never returned to the civil aviation market. Others entered it for the first time: Republic, with its amphibious Seabee; North American, with its Navion. Consolidated Vultee and Boeing tested the waters with two-seat designs, and Lockheed with a single-seater. And the Globe Swift's vestpocket-fighter profile revealed its designers' backgrounds.

Companies that had been building light aircraft all along reentered the civilian market with gusto. Piper built almost 7,800 J-3s and PA-12s in 1946 alone, convinced that the returning crop of military pilots would embrace general aviation. But Piper and the other companies that banked on massive civil production in the early days after the war were wrong. After a brief burst of sales, deliveries of general aviation airplanes declined precipitously.

Nevertheless, several exciting designs debuted between 1946 and 1950. Bell's Model 47 (left) would become the most popular helicopter in the world and would help revolutionize aeromedical evacuation techniques during the Korean War. Cessna launched its 120, 140, and 170 models, establishing a family of aircraft that would remain in production for almost 40 years. The Mooney M18 Mite, the forebear of another popular aviation family, was introduced. The Aero Commander L.3805 launched another. Piper continued to enhance its lightplane line. A quirky passion for flying cars emerged at this time as well—Consolidated Vultee experimented with its Flying Automobile and Fulton with its Airphibian.

And then there was Beechcraft. For several years, Beech had been working on an innovative design for a 20-passenger airliner. The Model 34 Twin-Quad, as the airliner was dubbed, went nowhere, but it shared one novel characteristic with an airplane that most assuredly did go somewhere: a V-tail. Beech's Model 35 Bonanza was introduced in 1947 and was an immediate success. Its direct descendant, with a conventional tail—the model G36—is still in production today.

S-23
S-24
FIRE HOSE

military pilots trained during the war would keep flying when they returned to civilian life was overstated.

Pilot advocate

With wartime concerns behind it, AOPA adjusted to a new peacetime role as a consumer and safety advocate.

To meet the demands of the postwar increase in flying activity, the CAA proposed greater equipment requirements, including the mandatory use of communication radios. AOPA initially opposed this proposal because the radios of the day, laden with tubes, weighed a great deal and compromised a light airplane's useful load. Ultimately, a satisfactory compromise was reached, which required communication radios in only the busiest airspace. New designs helped, too, as manufacturers such as Lear, Bendix, and Narco began to build more compact, efficient, and lighter equipment.

Navigation aids were another issue in the postwar years. The CAA sought to introduce very high frequency omnidirectional range (VOR) stations for en route navigation, and what was to become today's instrument landing system as the standard instrument approach facility—phasing out the old radio range stations. As with the communication radio question, AOPA objected because of weight penalties, claiming that ground-controlled approach procedures could be used. This question was also resolved once manufacturers built lighter sets. By late 1948, AOPA was assisting in the drive to educate pilots about VHF navigation. AOPA-published manuals describing VOR navigation were distributed to members, and AOPA participated in airborne testing of VOR and ILS equipment and helped manufacturers and government officials prepare specifications for the new receivers.

AOPA also devoted much effort to addressing the many unfair expenses levied on general aviation pilots. These

Still flying after all these years

The long life of war-surplus airplanes

Low prices for military surplus airplanes in the immediate postwar years gave those aircraft new life as cropdusters, civilian pilot trainers, and airshow performers. And later, war surplus airplanes morphed again. Waco (far right) and Stearman biplanes, some of them discarded or neglected, enjoyed a renaissance in the 1990s and 2000s as some were immaculately restored into collector's items. Former fighters such as P-51 Mustangs (right) that sold for a few thousand dollars immediately after the war became multimillion-dollar objects of affection and gleaming status symbols for their current owners. A few transports such as DC-3s have become flying museums that tell the story of the transformative time when they were produced, and the world they helped to shape. Some of these irreplaceable pieces of aviation history are sure to continue flying long after the "greatest generation" that produced them, and went to war in them, are gone—and that's quite a legacy.

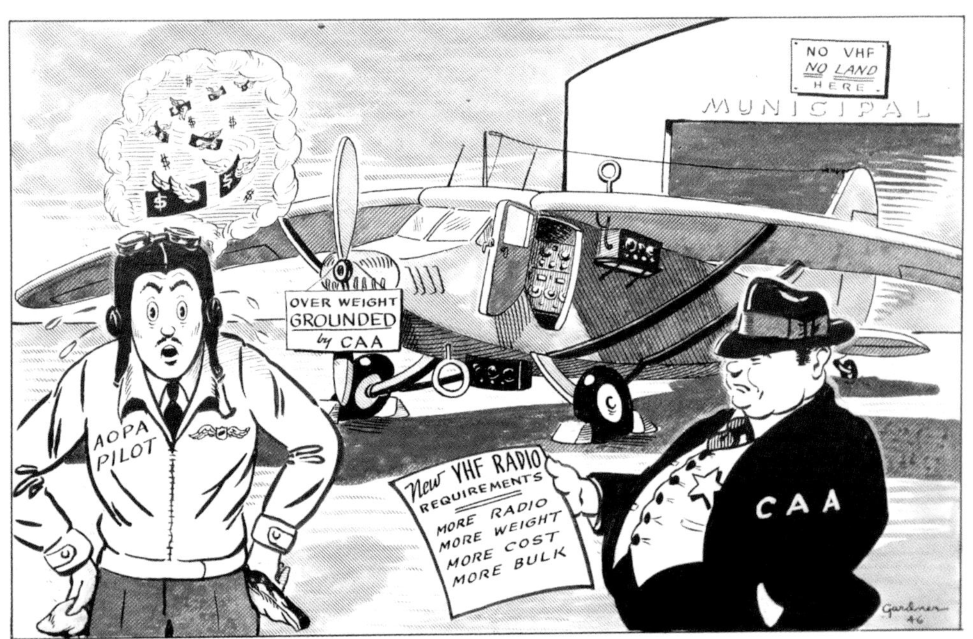

Federal mandates for communications radios in 1947 at first brought pushback from AOPA as shown by an "AOPA Pilot" cartoon (left).

Mooney Mite

This small but mighty single-seater was the forerunner of speedy aircraft

Mooney Aircraft has a history as long and winding as the road John Lennon and Paul McCartney immortalized. The company has blossomed and gone bankrupt; pulled itself out of financial straits with new owners only to collapse again; and then come back with new investors. Through it all, Mooney has maintained a legion of fanatical owners and a reputation for manufacturing speedy single-engine aircraft.

But the whole thing started with a single-seat wooden and fabric design called a Mite.

The Mooney M18 Mite was meant to be an affordable, mass-produced airplane for the business traveler, and affordable it was—the aircraft sold for just less than $2,000, and promotional pamphlets said it burned 1.3 cents per mile in fuel, compared to 3.6 cents per mile for the average car. The first four prototypes were built with 25-horsepower Crosley automotive engines, but production aircraft flew with 65-horsepower Continental or Lycoming engines. The Mite held just 11 gallons of fuel and had a useful load of up to 330 pounds, including a baggage capacity of 75 pounds. Its range was 380 miles, and you could do a cool 125 miles per hour in cruise.

The Mite featured the distinctive forward-swept tail that most pilots recognize as belonging to a Mooney, and surprisingly, it had retractable gear. Because the airplane had no electrical system, the gear had to be hand-cranked up and down.

The Mite was produced from 1949 to 1955, with about 290 airplanes coming out of the factory. Growing interest in metal, two- and four-place aircraft caused Mooney to move forward with its own variant on those designs, and the Mite halted production. An attempt was made in the 1970s to resurrect the Mite in kit form, but apparently only one such kit was ever sold, according to an article by Don Downie, which appeared in the January 1984 issue of *Private Pilot*.

AOPA asked for examples of poor treatment at airports and FBOs starting in the late 1940s. The association mailed postcards to members so that offenders—as well as standouts—could be graded and publicized (below). Newly issued AOPA logo decals boosted pride in membership, and served as not-so-subtle reminders to service providers.

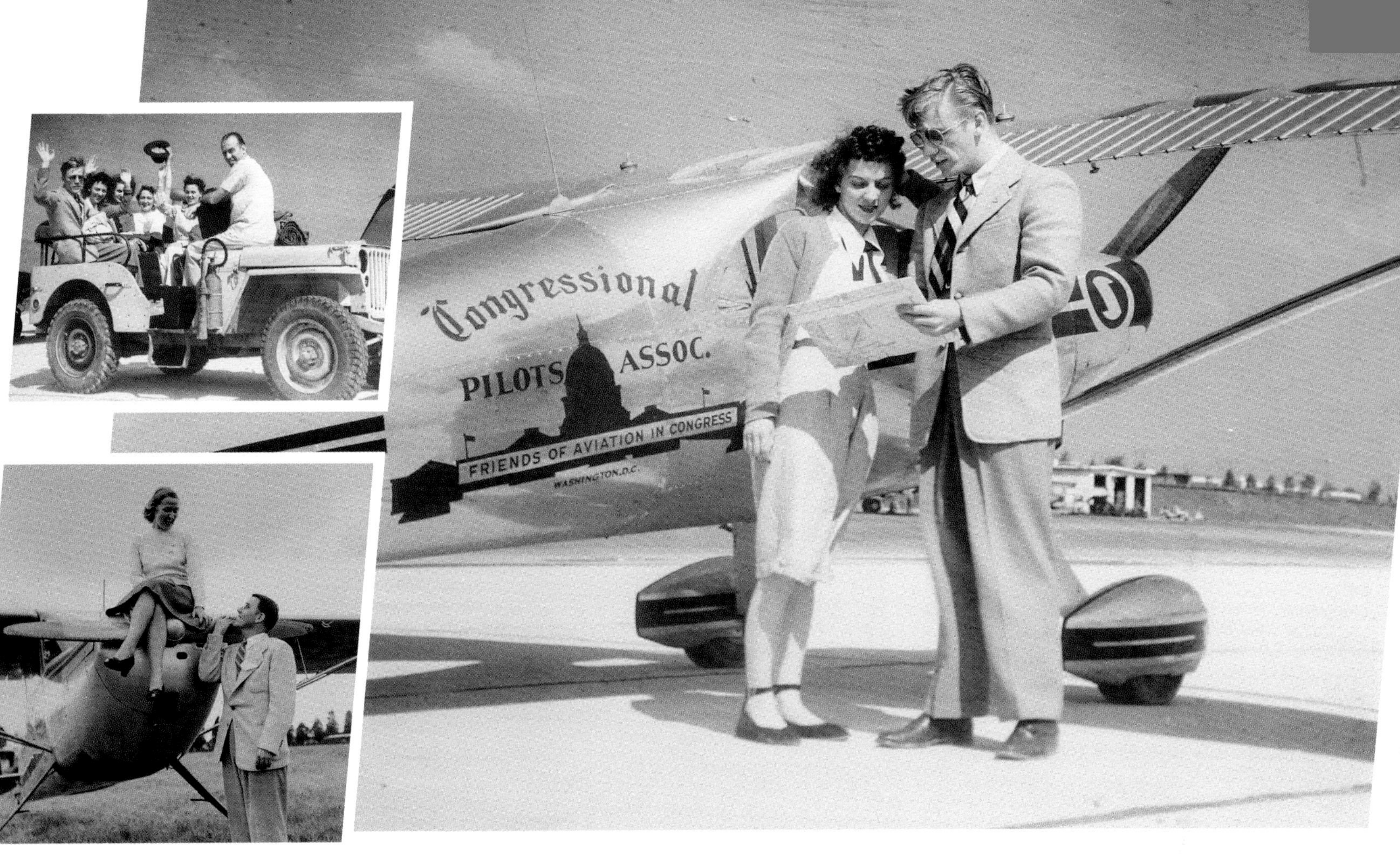

Congressional staffers and club members gather at the Congressional Flying Club, based at the Montgomery County Airpark in Gaithersburg, Maryland. That's Joseph B. "Doc" Hartranft Jr. sitting backwards in the Jeep.

overcharges, collectively called "the bite" in "AOPA Pilot" editorials (in 1943, the "AOPA Section" was eliminated, replaced by the first "AOPA Pilot" inserts), included excessive repair charges and escalating landing fees, hangar rents, tiedown fees, and local taxes. The "AOPA Pilot" inserts publicized those who charged too much, advising members to stay away from the offenders. Once again, AOPA's consumerist initiatives foreshadowed those in place today.

Several pilots even volunteered to test mechanics to see if they'd entice customers into paying for unnecessary repairs. The pilots would land at an airport, complain about a nonexistent problem, and report any cases of fraudulent and/or overpriced proposed work estimates. Reporter Don Downie later documented the quality of honesty of repair work across the country for what by then was *The AOPA Pilot*, an independent magazine. Downie visited 70 repair shops around the nation. At each stop he complained of engine or other mechanical problems. The author would loosen a spark plug, or disconnect a wire, to see if mechanics would make a fair assessment of the situation. By and large, he reported in the April 1961 issue of *The AOPA Pilot*, the treatment was fair.

The late 1940s were also when AOPA began its influential role as a major lobbying organization. To facilitate this, Hartranft helped form the Congressional Flying Club, an organization that still exists today at the Montgomery County Airpark in Gaithersburg, Maryland. With the help of manufacturers (who donated aircraft) and a cadre of volunteer instructors (who held ground school and provided flight instruction), many legislators and their aides learned to fly. By the end of 1947, the club had a Luscombe Silvaire, a Piper Cub, and 30 or so members—among them California Representative Carl Hinshaw, vice chairman of the Joint Congressional Aviation Policy Board. It was a brilliant and innovative way of both educating and influencing senators and representatives.

The Korean War brought its own set of pressures to bear on the U.S. airspace system in the 1950s. New Air Defense Identification Zones (ADIZs), similar to the Vital Defense Zones of World War II, were established along the East and West coasts, Hawaii and Alaska, along the Canadian border, and over New Mexico and Tennessee—areas where nuclear testing and research were taking place. Pilot identification cards were issued. Flight plans were mandatory in ADIZs. As in the previous war, AOPA cooperated in these national security measures. This time, AOPA was made a member of a civil aviation advisory committee to the U.S. Air Force's Air Defense Command.

Safe skies

As more pilots took to the skies in the postwar years, "AOPA Pilot" went on a safety campaign, demonstrating concern over the

R.A. "Bob" Hoover

The 'pilot's pilot'

Bob Hoover was larger than life

When R.A. "Bob" Hoover told the stories of his life, one was apt to wonder *Is this for real?* The legendary test and airshow pilot's stories were larger than life—just like the man. Every pilot has a favorite Hoover story: performing a barrel roll while pouring a glass of iced tea; his tanks filled with jet fuel instead of avgas and the design of the Hoover Nozzle; his medical certificate revocation—and reinstatement; rolling and looping a Shrike Aero Commander; his famous radio call: "Gentlemen, you have a race" at Reno; teaching pilots in the Korean War how to dive bomb; and his escapades in World War II.

The young Hoover was at first so airsick, he feared his dreams of flying were over before they even started. "I loved the idea of flying since I was 6 or 7 years old. I thought, *wouldn't it be wonderful to fly*. I dreamed about it," he said. "I soloed at 16 after eight hours; 15 minutes each weekend. I was so worried about getting sick. But I just had to overcome it."

Later, enlisting for World War II at the age of 18, his dream to fly in combat was also nearly dashed. "When I enlisted the physician said, 'I hate to tell you this, but you need to read the bottom of the eye chart. I'm going to leave the room for 20 minutes. When I come back, let's see if you can read the chart.' I memorized that chart," Hoover said. "Later he told me he'd made the best decision passing me. He was proud of my accomplishments."

Those accomplishments included a daring escape from a prisoner of war camp in Germany after he was shot down in a malfunctioning Spitfire in 1944. "I made several attempts at escape and spent time in solitary confinement," he said. "After 16 months, at the end of the war I escaped and flew to the Netherlands in a Fw 190."

After the war, Hoover became a test pilot for North American Aviation and tested and flew its most famous aircraft, including the F-86 Sabre and the P-51 Mustang. He's best known for his Mustang—N51RH—known as *Ole Yeller*. Hoover was awarded military honors including the Distinguished Flying Cross, Soldier's Medal, the Purple Heart, and France's Croix de Guerre. He was an honorary member of the Blue Angels and the Thunderbirds, and was awarded the Smithsonian Institution's National Air and Space Trophy in 2007, and an honorary doctorate by the U.S. Air Force Test Pilot School in 2010. He met Orville Wright, and General James H. Doolittle once called him "the greatest stick-and-rudder pilot who ever lived."

Of his flying life, Hoover said: "I had some mishaps that I don't mind admitting were terrifying, but I got back into the cockpit and pressed on. I did what had to be done."

Bob Hoover's many lives (opposite page), clockwise from lower left: he flew the North American P-51 in airshows beginning in the 1960s; as an airshow pilot flying a Rockwell Shrike Commander; and as an F-100 pilot after the Korean War.

EVERGREEN
EVERGREEN
"Bob" Hoover
F100D
EJECTION SEAT
DANGER
DANGER
KICK

One of AOPA's many safety campaigns after World War II focused on the dangers of low flying and "buzz jobs," as shown in this early "AOPA Pilot" cartoon.

growing number of fatal accidents involving low-altitude flying and low-altitude stalls and spins. In many editions, pages of pictures of crashed airplanes were published in an effort to drive home the seriousness of the problem. And AOPA was the first civilian organization to urge the installation and mandatory use of shoulder harnesses in light airplanes.

Another piece of safety equipment—stall warning indicators—continued to receive emphasis by AOPA. The organization wanted universal installation of this equipment in all light airplanes, even though the CAA tried—unsuccessfully, thanks to AOPA's efforts—to ban stall warning devices from being used in practical flight tests for a certificate or rating. In fact, AOPA was so strongly committed that it marketed Safe Flight Instrument Corporation's stall warning indicator for many years, selling it to members at a bargain-basement price of $37.50. It was a message that AOPA was to broadcast for years to come, until adoption of these devices as standard equipment was finally accepted by general aviation manufacturers. AOPA also endorsed the new castering "crosswind" landing gear developed by Goodyear Tire and Rubber Company and used in the Cessna 195 series of airplanes.

Concern with aviation safety took other forms. Today's system of Malfunction and Defect Reports was established with AOPA support. AOPA also mailed technical

The wild success of the 'Beaverton Outlaws'

Oregon tinkerers create a new aviation category

The tiny group of flying enthusiasts called themselves the "Beaverton Outlaws." These Oregon fliers were amateur aircraft builders, tinkerers, and iconoclasts who—in the spirit of the Wright brothers—wanted to design and fly their own aircraft without excessive government regulations.

Their home state gave them a legal loophole through its state aircraft licensing program. But after World War II, the Civil Aeronautics Administration claimed the sole right to regulate aviation matters on a national level—and the Beaverton Outlaws feared they would be permanently barred from flying their homebuilt aircraft.

George Bogardus (right) responded by flying his single-seat, homebuilt airplane to Washington, D.C., to personally convince the CAA that individual Americans should be allowed to continue designing and building their own aircraft, just as the Wright brothers had done in 1903. Bogardus wasn't immediately successful on his first trip in 1947, so he repeated the exercise in 1949 and 1951.

In 1952, the CAA created an exception to aircraft licensing requirements that, for the first time, carved out the relatively permissive rules that would govern the new Experimental amateur-built aircraft category. The creation of what would come to be known as the Experimental amateur-built category led Paul Poberezny (far right), then a Wisconsin Air National Guard pilot and amateur aircraft designer and builder, to create the Experimental Aircraft Association (EAA), which he and wife, Audrey, initially ran from their home.

The first EAA fly-in took place in Milwaukee in 1953 and fewer than 150 people attended. The group expanded, however, and moved its fly-in to Rockford, Illinois, in 1959 where it put on an airshow that drew antiques, warbirds, and aerobatic performers.

A decade later, former air racer and original EAA member Steve Wittman brought the EAA fly-in to Oshkosh, Wisconsin, where it has grown into one of the aviation world's premier events. EAA itself has expanded with more than 170,000 members, and the Experimental category has achieved a size, sophistication, and level of aircraft performance far beyond anything that the Beaverton Outlaws could have anticipated.

In the 1970s, designer Burt Rutan created a series of highly efficient, canard, pusher aircraft kits that popularized the movement. Other designers and entrepreneurs such as Frank Christensen, Lance Neibauer, and Tom Hamilton launched their own companies creating kits for the Christen Eagle aerobatic biplane, Lancair series of low-wing composite aircraft, and Glasair two- and four-seat aircraft, respectively.

Now, the Experimental category includes helicopters, turboprops, and jets, and it spawned an entirely new group of noncertified avionics that offer innovative and relatively inexpensive glass

“I’VE LEARNED MORE ABOUT PEOPLE THROUGH MY ASSOCIATION WITH AVIATION **THAN I EVER DID ABOUT AIRPLANES.”**

—PAUL POBEREZNY, FOUNDER OF THE EXPERIMENTAL AIRCRAFT ASSOCIATION

and service bulletins to members, informing them of mechanical problems with various aircraft. Together with the Cornell University medical school, a crash injury research project was conducted.

The 1950s began with an air of crisis for aviation, the result of several midair collisions in 1949 between scheduled air carriers and general aviation airplanes. You could argue that this was inevitable, given the continued growth in both airline and general aviation travel; the piston airliners of the day increasingly shared airspace with smaller aircraft. Often, investigators ruled that the probable causes were the airliners' failure to see and avoid traffic; AOPA found itself in a vigorous debate over an Air Line Pilots Association (ALPA) proposal that would have banned

panels and autopilots with safety features that show traffic, terrain, and adverse weather.

EAA also helped create the Light Sport aircraft category that consists of mechanically simple lightweight one- and two-seat aircraft that can be flown under sport pilot rules. AOPA and EAA have worked closely together on a variety of aviation issues, including third class medical reform, finding a replacement for leaded avgas, and opposition to aviation user fees.

About 15 percent of the single-engine piston airplanes on the FAA aircraft registry today are licensed in the Experimental category. Homebuilders are adding more than 900 new single-engine piston aircraft annually—about the same number as all FAA-approved manufacturers combined.

The biggest kit manufacturer of all is Van's Aircraft of Aurora, Oregon, not far from the former meeting place of the Beaverton Outlaws. More than 10,000 of the Van's series of RV aircraft have been built and flown—and Van's founder Richard VanGrunsven helped restore Bogardus's pioneering airplane in 2006.

The pioneering pilot who made those long trips to promote experimental aviation succeeded far beyond anything he or his fellow Oregon builders could have imagined.

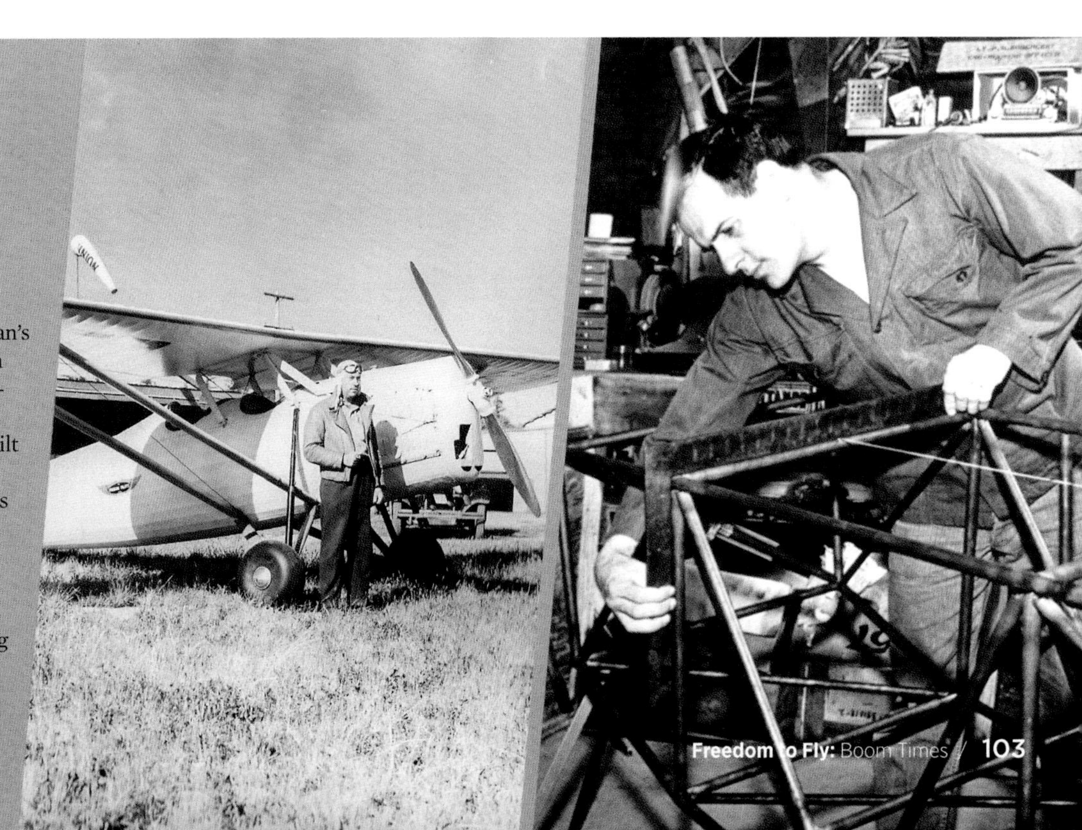

general aviation from airports used by air carriers. AOPA prevailed and joined with the CAA in opposing the use of straight-in approaches by airliners landing at nontowered airports.

In a related move, AOPA brought about the designation of a common VHF communications "party line" frequency, so that pilots could share weather and other information, and inform each other of their locations and intentions. Government and industry concurred that this was a good idea, and thus was born the unicom (a term coined by Joseph B. "Doc" Hartranft Jr. and Max Karant that stood for "universal communications") frequency.

In another demonstration of its commitment to safety, AOPA in 1950 formed the AOPA Foundation, a nonprofit organization dedicated to general aviation pilot safety and education. This organization would later come to be known as the AOPA Air Safety Foundation (ASF). Today, it's known as the AOPA Air Safety Institute (ASI); a reconstituted AOPA Foundation serves as a charitable fundraising organization.

In 1950, the total general aviation accident rate was 46.68 accidents per 100,000 flight hours; the fatal accident rate was 5.17 per 100,000 flight hours. Newspapers and accident reports were replete with stories of fatal buzzing accidents, forays by VFR-only pilots into instrument weather, and stall-spin accidents. Today, the accident and fatal accident rates have plunged to an estimated 5.32 and 0.84 per 100,000 hours, respectively. Many factors have contributed to the drop, but one of the big ones is the work of AOPA's safety organization.

In the early 1950s, the AOPA Foundation's efforts were focused primarily on making grants. The first grant went to the Cornell Aeronautical Laboratory Inc., of Buffalo, New York, in October 1953 for the design of an airborne emergency ground lighting system. The idea was to develop an airborne light for use in night emergency landings—one that would replace the flares used in general aviation airplanes of the day. The light had to be powerful enough to illuminate a large landing area, yet draw little current and weigh less than 25 pounds. Cornell came up with what it called the Strobalume system. This used a battery-powered, slow-flashing strobe lamp that, from 1,050 feet above

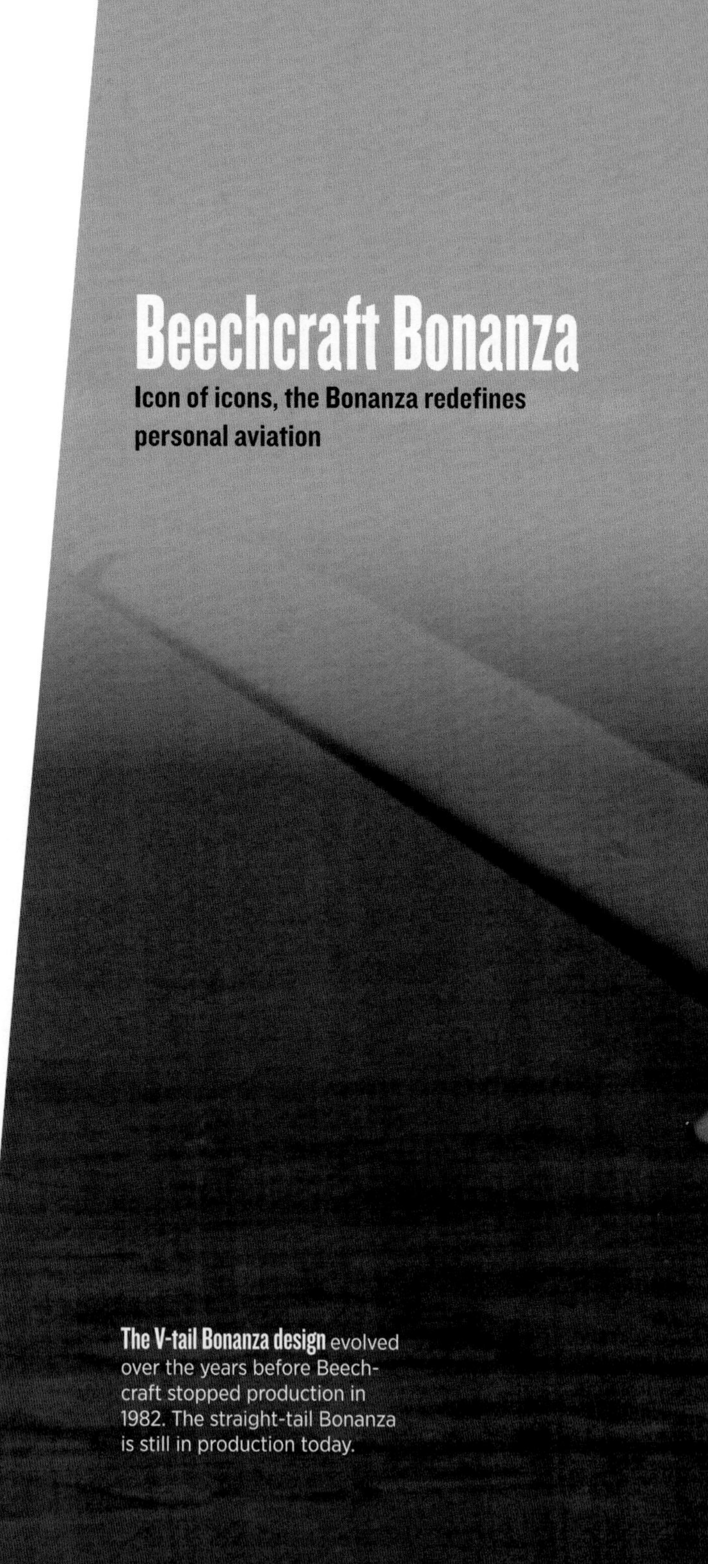

Beechcraft Bonanza

Icon of icons, the Bonanza redefines personal aviation

The V-tail Bonanza design evolved over the years before Beechcraft stopped production in 1982. The straight-tail Bonanza is still in production today.

The debut of the Beechcraft Bonanza in 1947 was almost like a tear in the space-time continuum of general aviation. Compared to other immediate post-war models, the Bonanza was all new and radical—as if it came from another dimension. All-metal fuselage, low wings, horizontally opposed engine, retractable tricycle landing gear, and those unusual magnesium ruddervators. The speedy Bonanza took off and has never looked back, continuing in production ever since—the longest continuously produced airplane in history.

More than 17,000 have flown out of the Wichita factory. Dozens of models have been produced and are in use throughout the world in personal aviation, training, charter, and military service. The models fit primarily into three categories: the V-tail versions, which continued in production until 1982; the straight-tail Model 33, which started out as a Debonair but was later rebranded Bonanza, started in 1959 and continued until 1995; and the Model 36, a stretched version, which began production in 1968 and continues today as the glass-cockpit G36.

Excellent handling, good performance, quality construction, and strong resale value have all contributed to the line's success. As a result of the famed handling, performance, and reliability, more Bonanzas have made round the world flights than any other single-engine airplane. Even seven decades after its introduction, the Bonanza is seen by many as the most desirable piston airplane of all time—at least in this dimension.

Fred Weick

Safer, easier to fly, more efficient

Legendary designer served GA well

Fred Weick's contributions to aviation extend far beyond the Erco Ercoupe and the Piper Cherokee, the two designs for which he is most recognized. Few today even know that an aircraft once bore the name of this storied engineer who dedicated his aeronautical career to making airplanes safer, easier to fly, and more aerodynamically efficient. Although his work emphasized light aircraft, the advances he forged made their way to larger airplanes as well.

As a new University of Illinois graduate in 1922 with a degree in mechanical engineering, Weick went to work for the U.S. Air Mail Service, where—among other things—he helped to modify surplus military de Havilland DH-4s to carry mail. After learning to fly and a job in the U.S. Navy's Bureau of Aeronautics, he joined the National Advisory Committee for Aeronautics (NACA)—NASA's predecessor. There, Weick designed and built a 20-foot-diameter wind tunnel, four times larger than NACA's largest existing such facility, for testing full-scale propellers. He also led the development of low-drag cowlings for air-cooled radial engines that still provided sufficient cooling, resulting in the "NACA cowl."

Later, Weick—with help from his wife, Dorothy, and NACA coworkers—built the Weick W-1 in his garage. The prototype made its first flight in 1934. Many of his safety-enhancing ideas—tricycle gear, limited elevator travel to prevent stalls, and interconnected ailerons and rudder to prevent spins—were soon incorporated in the Engineering and Research Corporation (Erco) Ercoupe, which first flew October 1, 1937.

After World War II, he joined the engineering faculty at what's now Texas A&M University, where he designed the Texas A&M College AG-1. The single-seat, single-engine prototype—it was the only one built—may have been the first aircraft specifically designed for aerial application. The AG-1 design eventually evolved to become the Piper PA-25 Pawnee.

Along with Fred Thorpe, Weick co-designed for Piper the all-metal, low-wing, four-place PA-28 Cherokee. It was conceived as a less expensive alternative to the high-performance Piper PA-24 Comanche, and descendants of the Cherokee remain in production today. Weick once said that the Cherokee design used half as many parts as the Comanche, and required only half as many rivets.

He also was involved with the PA-32 Cherokee Six, among other projects. The Cherokee's signature, constant-chord "Hershey bar" wing design also was employed in the PA-32R Lance; later PA-32R airframes with a newer, tapered wing design were named Saratogas.

Weick retired from Piper in 1969, when he was 70. However, he continued flying until age 84, and remained very involved in the Experimental aircraft community—he was a regular at EAA AirVenture in Oshkosh, Wisconsin—until his death at age 93 on July 8, 1993.

Fred Weick's W-1 (opposite page, above) was one of the first aircraft to employ tricycle landing gear. Despite its unconventional look, many of its features were carried over into the extremely successful Ercoupe, which debuted in 1939. Weick posed with an Ercoupe (opposite, below) at the Erco factory in Riverdale, Maryland.

ground level, could light up an area the size of a football field to the level provided by full moonlight. The strobe light was to both conserve energy and yield maximum light, but there was a flaw. Cornell researchers discovered something we're now all warned about: that flashing strobe lights can cause disorientation and vertigo, especially if they're used in clouds or fog at night. For this reason the project was shelved, but in the years to come, when strobe lights became common, the lessons learned from the Cornell project were applied in the form of FAA-mandated placards warning about the use of strobe lights in conditions of limited visibility.

Other grants awarded to the Aviation Crash Injury Research facility of Cornell University's medical college in 1954 and 1955 funded the first research into the feasibility of installing shoulder harnesses, which extended to innovations that would later produce the inertia reel harness, and included catapult testing of dummies. The first type-specific accident research was begun under terms of another grant to the Washington, D.C.-based aviation research firm of Ray and Ray. Other research projects focused on a stall-warning system and a basic wing-leveler.

Another grant, which funded a University of Illinois study on loss of control in instrument conditions, gave rise to one of the AOPA Foundation's most popular courses. By the end of the 1950s, thousands of pilots had taken advantage of the AOPA Foundation's renowned "180-degree rating" course, an educational program designed to provide non-instrument-rated pilots with the skills needed to extricate themselves from an inadvertent encounter with instrument meteorological conditions. The foundation was—and ASI still is— funded by voluntary contributions from AOPA members, fundraising efforts, and endowments. The fund-raising philanthropic arm of the association overall is now called the AOPA Foundation.

Expanded services

AOPA began offering chart subscriptions to members in July 1949, and the same year saw the awarding of certificates of merit to 708 of the nation's 6,200 civil airports judged to have superior facilities and services, based on results of a member poll. AOPA also was able to secure lower-cost insurance for members' airplanes through an arrangement with Lloyd's of London.

"WHAT IS CHIEFLY NEEDED IS SKILL RATHER THAN MACHINERY." —WILBUR WRIGHT

Until May 1951, general aviation pilots had been paying discriminatory life insurance premiums. In that month, thanks to AOPA's help, Minnesota Mutual Life Insurance Company began offering AOPA members group life insurance at reasonable rates. Providing fairly priced insurance for pilots had always been one of the major objectives of AOPA's founding trustees, and the Minnesota Mutual agreement was a substantial first step. More were to follow. Later in the decade, in January 1957, AOPA endorsed the hull and liability insurance programs offered by the American Mercury Insurance Company (Americo). These policies offered the most preferential rates yet available to the pilot population.

Navigating new airspace

As the brand-new network of VOR stations was being installed, AOPA provided general aviation's points of view regarding this modernization effort. In May 1951, the CAA announced its plan to shut down 53 low-frequency radio range stations, all at once.

N3369P
Piper

Rise of the personal twin

The evolution of owner-flown aircraft takes the next step

Cheap gas probably didn't hurt. Neither did a growing national sense of prosperity, or the increasing appetite for power and speed it fostered. Quite possibly, manufacturers wanted to appeal to the large share of returning military pilots who'd flown multiengine bombers, transports, or attack airplanes. Or maybe it had more to do with the emergence of the horizontally opposed engine as a cost-effective alternative to more complicated radials.

Whatever the reasons, the early 1950s saw the sudden development of a robust market for twin-engine airplanes designed for individual owners. Prewar twins such as the Beech 18, Lockheed Model 10 (Electra), and Douglas DC-3 were large airplanes intended for commercial use. It wasn't until 1939 that Cessna began to experiment with a lightweight model more suitable for private use.

The prototype of the five-seat T-50 Bobcat made its first flight on March 26 of that year. An order placed by the U.S. Army the following year drew almost the entire run of 5,400 into military use, where they served as primary multiengine trainers and light liaison aircraft. Anticipating that surplus airplanes would flood the civilian market after the war, Cessna ended production after fulfilling its military contracts. By that time, a fabric-covered airplane with wooden spars and ribs had also come to seem obsolete, even by civilian standards.

The first new postwar design came from a brand-new competitor. While the war still raged, Douglas designer Ted Smith formed the Commander Aircraft Company. The prototype of what became known as the Twin Commander, an unusual high-wing design whose landing gear retracted into the engine nacelles, made its first flight in April 1948. CAA certification was achieved in June 1950. To demonstrate its "exceptional single-engine performance," the company flew a fully loaded example from Oklahoma City to Washington, D.C., with the left propeller stowed in the baggage hatch (conveniently reducing drag). Commercial production began in August 1951. The U.S. Air Force selected the Commander 520 for President Eisenhower's personal transportation, citing its "exceptional performance characteristics."

Walter Beech and his design team were not far behind. Aware of Smith's initiative, and eyeing an Army bid for a light twin-engine airplane, Beech scrambled his design team and got the prototype Twin Bonanza (Model 50 T-Bone) into the air in November 1949, just seven months after the initial engineering drawings. Its most important feature was invisible to the pilot: the massive wing spar from the much larger Model 18. Its stout construction earned Beech that Army contract: Everyone on board walked away unhurt after a factory pilot attempting a short-field landing stalled from 50 feet in a fully loaded T-Bone during field trials. Impressed by the airplane's toughness, the U.S. Army placed its first order. Production began shortly after the type certificate was awarded in 1951.

Piper's entry began with a paper design acquired as part of its 1950 purchase of Stinson. The original "Twin Stinson" was a true oddity, a twin-tailed tube-and-fabric airplane with engines of just 125 horsepower each. The 1952 prototype's flight characteristics proved lamentable, so it was redesigned with a conventional single tail, aluminum skin, 150-horsepower engines, and a bulbous fuselage often compared to a sweet potato. Production began in 1954. It also gained a new name—the Apache (at left). Its lower acquisition and operating costs made it a favorite in the training market, where it gave new multiengine pilots unforgettable proof of the hazards of single-engine operation.

Cessna may have reached the party late after sending the invitations, but when it got there, it arrived in style. The spindly landing gear, retractable step, sleek fuselage, and distinctive tip tanks make successive generations of the Model 310 instantly recognizable. It became the fastest competitor in the field, although by a narrow margin, over the Twin Commander—and on 240 horsepower per side versus 260 in the Commander (and 295 in the Beech Twin Bonanza), with corresponding savings on fuel. The first prototype flew in January 1953, with commercial deliveries beginning late the following year.

So in the course of three and a half years—from June 1951 to December 1954—the choices available to buyers who wanted personal airplanes with the speed and perceived security of a second engine grew from zero to four. Depending on needs and budget, prospective owners could opt for small and slow (the Piper Apache), large and slow (the Twin Bonanza), large and fast (the Twin Commander), or medium-sized and even faster (the Cessna 310) at prices ranging from $30,000 to more than double that. Twins would remain a desired step-up and a mainstay of courier work and light package delivery for another 50 years before ever-increasing operating costs and a new generation of fast, reliable singles began to shrivel their sector of the market.

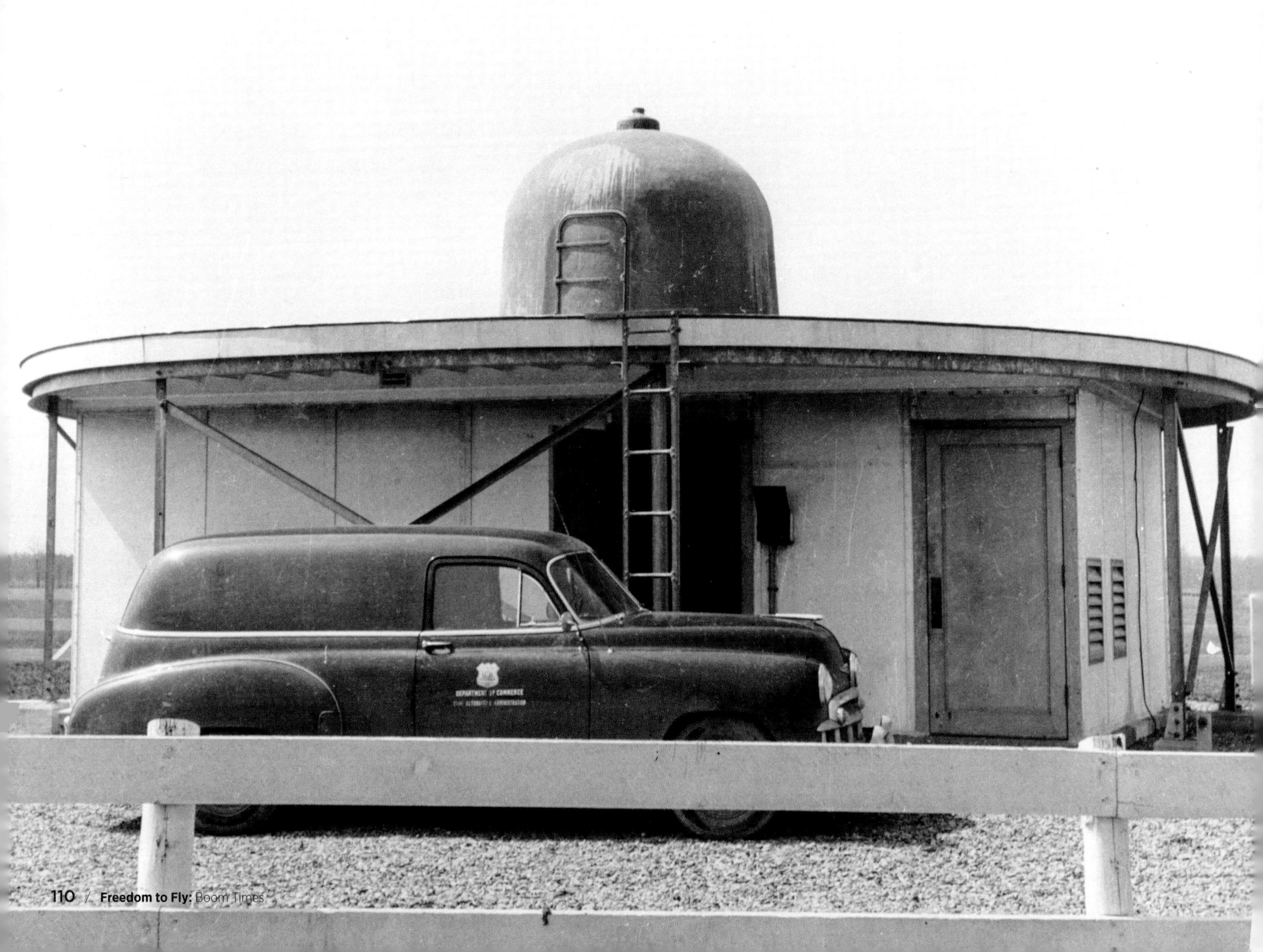
DEPARTMENT OF COMMERCE

A new system of navigation was introduced, using a nationwide network of VHF omnidirectional range (VOR) stations (opposite page). Among the first of the new VHF transceivers was one built by William P. Lear's Lear Developments (left). Lear also invented the eight-track music player system—and the Learjet.

These ranges continued to serve many pilots and aircraft still equipped with low-frequency receivers; AOPA argued that to remove them all at once would create a safety hazard. General aviation pilots needed time to buy the new VOR receivers and wanted reassurance that the new VOR stations would broadcast weather information the way the radio ranges did. Once again, the message came through and the result was a gradual decommissioning of the radio ranges.

Of course, adoption of the VOR system had a ripple effect through other government products. And where the CAA allowed important details to fall through the cracks, AOPA was quick to point them out. For example, new sectional charts were being published without depicting the locations or frequencies of the new VOR stations. At AOPA's insistence, the CAA added the necessary symbology, along with compass roses aligned with magnetic north—another AOPA initiative. AOPA was also responsible for keeping highways on sectional charts and for adding depictions of drive-in theaters, the latest rage in the prosperous, car-crazy, highly mobile lifestyle of the 1950s.

Max Conrad

The 'Flying Grandfather'

Every era has its hero, and Max Conrad was the aviation darling in the 1950s and early 1960s. President John F. Kennedy said in 1961 of Conrad's distance and endurance records: "Your numerous long-range flight records in small aircraft are a tribute to your courage and professional ability. You have helped much to prepare young people for the complex and serious responsibilities of the aerospace age. In addition, your work and example have brought goodwill to many parts of the world."

Conrad's career started tragically when the young flight instructor tried to stop a woman from walking into a spinning propeller. The woman died, and the prop struck Conrad in the head, rendering him incapable of speech and with some brain damage that took him years to overcome. He persevered through many careers, including owning a flight school and working for Northwest Airlines and Honeywell, and he became famous for setting nine lightplane records for distance, speed, and endurance.

A Minnesotan, like Charles A. Lindbergh, Conrad was also the second man after Lindbergh to fly solo from New York to Paris. Conrad crossed the Atlantic and the Pacific more than 200 times in his lifetime. He set records that stood well into the 2000s, such as a flight of 7,668 miles in a Piper Comanche from Casablanca to Los Angeles in 1959; a round-the-world flight in 1962 with average speeds of 123.2 mph; and a distance flight from Cape Town, South Africa, to St. Petersburg, Florida. Conrad was awarded the Louis Blériot medal in 1952 and the Harmon Trophy in 1964. He amassed more than 50,000 flight hours before his death at 76 in 1979.

Conrad was known as the "Flying Grandfather" because he fathered 10 children and had 37 grandchildren.

N9AP

PIPER APACHE AND AZTEC

A tale of three twins

The Piper PA-23 began as a paper airplane—the unrealized "Twin Stinson" drawings acquired when Piper bought Stinson from Consolidated Vultee in 1950. The prototype chiefly served to demonstrate that peculiarity doesn't necessarily provide performance. That design—a tube-and-fabric airframe with a double tail, powered by a pair of 125-horsepower Lycoming O-290-Ds—proved enough of a handful to push Piper's engineers in a more conventional direction. The PA-23 Apache debuted in 1954 with a single tail, aluminum skin, and a pair of 36-gallon bladder tanks feeding 150-horsepower Lycoming O-320-As. It also sported the famously bulbous fuselage that makes it instantly recognizable even today.

That configuration held for four years. The 1958 model was fitted with O-320-B engines that boosted horsepower to 160 per side, but in 1960 Piper signed the Apache's death warrant by introducing the PA-23-250 Aztec (at left), whose 250-horsepower Lycoming O-540-A1Ds boosted cruise speed by 20 knots and maximum gross weight by 1,000 pounds—nearly half of which went into doubling standard fuel capacity to 144 gallons with a corresponding increase in range. The 1962 introduction of the Apache 235 (also powered by O-540s) failed to save the smaller twin, which ended production in 1965 having ceded the lower-cost segment of Piper's multiengine market to the faster and more efficient Twin Comanche, introduced in 1963.

The Aztec gained a longer nose with baggage compartment in 1962, the same year turbocharging was first offered. Fuel injection became standard in 1964 (along with dual alternators and hydraulic pumps). Maximum gross increased from 4,800 to 5,200 pounds, and production continued through 1981. Nearly 7,000 PA-23s were assembled: more than 2,000 Apaches and almost 5,000 Aztecs. The "Az-Truck" continues to enjoy acclaim for its high payload and short-field capabilities—and tolerance for the high fuel burn and modest cruise speed accompanying those virtues.

The implementation and standardization of the VOR network provided AOPA with its biggest challenge. The problems didn't just center on the decommissioning of low-frequency range stations. All through the early 1950s, the CAA championed VOR and VOR/DME as the next-generation navaid. Pilots and the rest of the aviation community made their plans accordingly. But in June 1955, it was learned that the military had persuaded the CAA—in secret negotiations—to alter its plans. The armed forces wanted TACAN (the tactical air navigation system) as the standard navaid system. This abrupt turnaround had the effect of galvanizing support behind AOPA, which argued that such a decision, made without the benefit of consulting general aviation, amounted to a cynical, scandalous waste of money and effort. For many months, it appeared that the general aviation community would have to scrap its preparations for VHF-based navigation in favor of the UHF-based TACAN. All the receiver systems, airspace rules, and procedures would have to be thrown out the window if TACAN were to be the system of the future. At one point, a timetable called for a phase-out of existing VORs by 1965.

Thanks largely to AOPA's persistence, a compromise was worked out. Instead of VOR/DME or TACAN, the solution called for vortacs, colocated VOR and TACAN stations. Civilian use of electronic distance information was retained, the military obtained its TACAN, and the rest of the

Ted Smith

Ted Smith's first Aero Commander design (right) was sleek for its day.

Master of Commanders

Smith's designs speak for themselves

Ted Smith's aircraft designs included military and general aviation airplanes—and they all emphasized speed, parts commonality, and two powerful engines.

Smith was a California native who grew up in the golden state's vibrant aircraft industry and later founded his own production firm there.

After high school in Oakland, he graduated from the Boeing School of Aeronautics in 1929. He began his career at the Douglas Aircraft Company in Southern California as a tool designer on the company's B-18 and B-23 bombers. He rose quickly within the firm at a time of explosive growth fueled by World War II, and Smith became the company's lead engineer on the A-20 Havoc, a highly maneuverable, twin-engine attack airplane that was produced in large numbers (more than 7,000) and flown extensively by U.S. and allied forces.

Under the tutelage of legendary designer Ed Heinemann, Smith played a central role in developing the Havoc's successor, the Douglas A-26 Invader.

In the 1950s, Smith focused on general aviation aircraft at Rockwell, where he designed the Aero Commander family of twin-engine, high-wing business airplanes. The Aero Commander line was popularized by airshow star R.A. "Bob" Hoover, who performed a stunning demonstration that included engine-out aerobatics and dead-stick, spot landings. The Aero Commander line later included stretched, turboprop, and jet versions.

The pinnacle of Smith's general aviation designs, however, was the Aerostar—a record-setting, no-compromises piston twin with astonishing speed, performance, and sporty handling qualities. Aerostar production began in 1967 and grew to include pressurized and turbocharged models.

Smith and a small group of investors believed so much in the Aerostar that they bought the company in 1972—and their long-term plans included building an entire family of aircraft based on the Aerostar to include turboprop and jet versions.

The oil embargo and recession of the early 1970s disrupted those plans, however, and then Smith died suddenly in 1976 at age 70. Piper Aircraft bought the rights to the Aerostar in 1978, then moved production from California to its main plant in Vero Beach, Florida. Piper halted Aerostar production in 1984 after a total of about 1,000 of the speedy twins had been produced.

For all the flamboyance of Smith's aircraft designs, the man himself was quiet, reserved, and not at all boastful. Instead of making extravagant claims, he said he preferred to let the performance of his aircraft speak for itself.

airspace users would continue to use VORs. It was the best resolution possible, and it was satisfactory to all, even if nerves were strained in the process.

But as with so many other issues, the casebook never completely closed on the navaid standardization question. In 1958 and 1959, AOPA and other general aviation user groups found themselves once again fighting to keep what they had won. Through the International Civil Aviation Organization (ICAO), several foreign nations attempted to make the Decca navigation system the universal standard. Decca, developed in England during World War II, used master and slave stations for navigation, so it operated much like loran. But at an ICAO conference, AOPA and its allies defeated the proposal. The VOR system was saved again.

Other changes—and portents of the future—in airspace rules were proposed in the 1950s. In August 1955, the CAA announced a proposal for an "experimental" High Density Air Traffic Zone (HDTZ) located around Washington, D.C's then-National Airport, today Ronald Reagan Washington National Airport. It was the forerunner of today's Class B airspace. This HDTZ, which went into effect in April 1957, extended from the surface to 3,000 feet agl, had a maximum radius of some 15 nautical miles, required one mile of visibility for VFR operations, and imposed a 180-mph (156-knot) speed limit within its confines. It was with AOPA's advice that the speed limits were set. The speed limit remained in force until it was replaced in 1998 with a blanket, 200-knot speed limit when flying in Class C and D airspace, or below Class B airspace.

Then—as now—AOPA lodged its protest against the proliferation of this type of "experimental" system. And experimental it remained—for the time being. It was to be many years later that the concept would be revitalized, in the form of the Terminal Control Area, and now Class B airspace. But

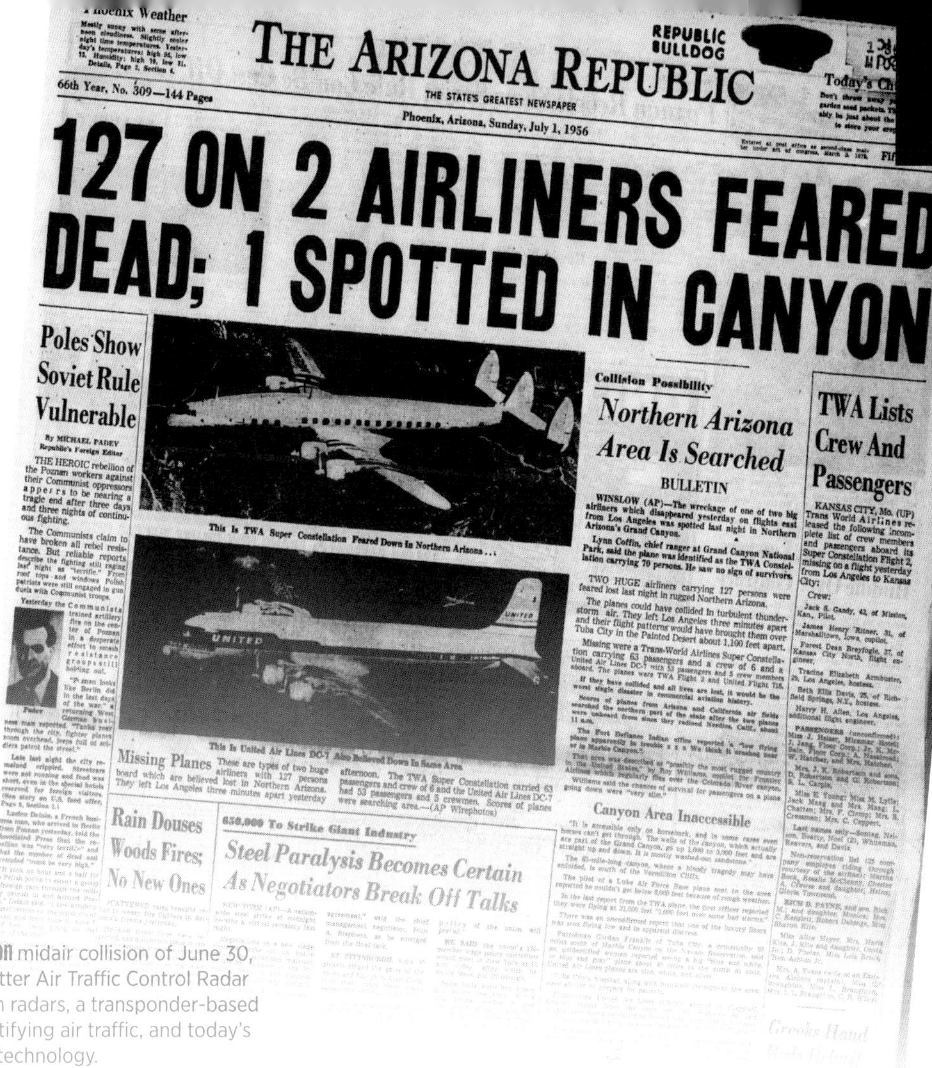

THE ARIZONA REPUBLIC

THE STATE'S GREATEST NEWSPAPER

66th Year, No. 309—144 Pages

Phoenix, Arizona, Sunday, July 1, 1956

REPUBLIC BULLDOG

127 ON 2 AIRLINERS FEARED DEAD; 1 SPOTTED IN CANYON

Poles Show Soviet Rule Vulnerable

By MICHAEL PADEV
Republic's Foreign Editor

THE HEROIC rebellion of the Poznan workers against their Communist oppressors appears to be nearing a tragic end after three days and three nights of continuous fighting.

The Communists claim to have broken all rebel resistance. But reliable reports describe the fighting still raging last night as "terrific." From roof tops and windows Polish patriots were still engaged in gun duels with Communist troops.

Yesterday the Communists trained artillery fire on the center of Poznan in a desperate effort to smash resistance groups still holding out.

Padev

"Poznan looks like Berlin did in the last days of the war," a returning West German business man reported. "Tanks roar through the city, fighter planes zoom overhead, jeeps full of soldiers patrol the street."

Late last night the city remained crippled. Streetcars were not running and food was short, even in the special hotels reserved for foreign visitors. (See story on U.S. food offer, Page 5, Section 1.)

Ludes Delain, a French business man, who arrived in Berlin from Poznan yesterday, told the Associated Press that the rebellion was "very terrible" and that the number of dead and wounded "must be very high."

[illegible]

This Is TWA Super Constellation Feared Down In Northern Arizona . . .

This Is United Air Lines DC-7 Also Believed Down In Same Area

Missing Planes These are types of two huge airliners with 127 persons aboard which are believed lost in Northern Arizona. They left Los Angeles three minutes apart yesterday afternoon. The TWA Super Constellation carried 63 passengers and crew of 6 and the United Air Lines DC-7 had 53 passengers and 5 crewmen. Scores of planes were searching area.—(AP Wirephotos)

Collision Possibility

Northern Arizona Area Is Searched

BULLETIN

WINSLOW (AP)—The wreckage of one of two big airliners which disappeared yesterday on flights east from Los Angeles was spotted last night in Northern Arizona's Grand Canyon.

Lynn Coffin, chief ranger at Grand Canyon National Park, said the plane was identified as the TWA Constellation carrying 70 persons. He saw no sign of survivors.

TWO HUGE airliners carrying 127 persons were feared lost last night in rugged Northern Arizona.

The planes could have collided in turbulent thunderstorm air. They left Los Angeles three minutes apart and their flight patterns would have brought them over Tuba City in the Painted Desert about 1,100 feet apart.

Missing were a Trans-World Airlines Super Constellation carrying 63 passengers and a crew of 6 and a United Air Lines DC-7 with 53 passengers and 5 crew members aboard. The planes were TWA Flight 2 and United Flight 718.

If they have collided and all lives are lost, it would be the worst single disaster in commercial aviation history.

Scores of planes from Arizona and California air fields searched the northern part of the state after the two planes were unheard from since they radioed Needles, Calif., about 11 a.m.

The Fort Defiance Indian office reported a "low flying plane apparently in trouble x x x We think it crashed near or in Marble Canyon."

That area was described as "possibly the most rugged country in the United States," by Roy Williams, copilot for Frontier Airlines which regularly flies over the Colorado River canyon.

Williams said the chances of survival for passengers on a plane going down were "very slim."

Canyon Area Inaccessible

"It is accessible only on horseback, and in some cases even horses can't get through. The walls of the canyon, which actually are part of the Grand Canyon, go up 1,000 to 3,000 feet and are straight up and down. It is mostly washed-out sandstone."

The 60-mile-long canyon, where a bloody tragedy may have unfolded, is south of the Vermilion Cliffs.

The pilot of a Luke Air Force Base plane sent in the area reported he couldn't get below 8,000 feet because of rough weather.

In the last report from the TWA plane, the first officer reported they were flying at 21,000 feet, "1,000 feet over some bad storms."

There was an unconfirmed report that one of the luxury liners was seen flying low and in apparent distress.

[illegible]

TWA Lists Crew And Passengers

KANSAS CITY, Mo. (UP) Trans World Airlines released the following incomplete list of crew members and passengers aboard its Super Constellation Flight 2, missing on a flight yesterday from Los Angeles to Kansas City:

Crew:

Jack S. Gandy, 42, of Mission, Kan., Pilot.

James Henry Ritner, 31, of Marshalltown, Iowa, copilot.

Forest Dean Breyfogle, 37, of Kansas City North, flight engineer.

Tracine Elizabeth Armbruster, 29, Los Angeles, hostess.

Beth Ellis Davis, 25, of Richfield Springs, N.Y., hostess.

Harry H. Allen, Los Angeles, additional flight engineer.

[illegible]

Rain Douses Woods Fires; No New Ones

[illegible]

650,000 To Strike Giant Industry

Steel Paralysis Becomes Certain As Negotiators Break Off Talks

[illegible]

The Grand Canyon midair collision of June 30, 1956, led to better Air Traffic Control Radar Beacon System radars, a transponder-based system of identifying air traffic, and today's ADS-B-driven technology.

the association was successful in keeping Washington, D.C.'s airspace open and accessible to general aviation.

Landmark midair

June 30, 1956, must certainly go down as a dark and pivotal day for U.S. civil aviation. This was the day that a United Air Lines DC–7 and a Trans World Airlines Lockheed Super Constellation collided in the skies over the Grand Canyon. Both aircraft were on IFR flight plans, but the collision occurred in airspace where traffic control services were not provided. All 128 on board the two airplanes died in the crash. This catastrophe provided the impetus for the further refinement of air traffic control's primary radars, paved the way for the development of transponder-based traffic identification, and fueled political pressure for the creation of an independent federal agency for aviation. AOPA supported the need to explore new and more effective ways of separating air traffic. Today's system of using airborne transponders and GPS-based ADS-B Out technology as the means for aircraft sequencing and separation can be directly traced to the Grand Canyon midair collision.

In November 1956, AOPA hired Victor J. Kayne as a consultant on ATC affairs so that the organization could share his expertise in an area that promised to be more and more challenging in the future. Kayne had previously served as an assistant chief of the CAA's Division of Airways Operations, a CAA representative to ICAO, and a tower chief at Washington National Airport. He also held the first air traffic controller certificate, issued to him in 1938.

In another augury of the future, AOPA supported a 1956 Senate bill that would establish the CAA's independence from the Department of Commerce. In November 1958, the aviation community got its wish, and the Federal Aviation Agency was born. However, the first FAA administrator,

Twin Commander 690A

‹ FASTER, FARTHER...AND FIRST

In 1944, with the war just turning the corner toward victory, no sensible observer would have bet on who might succeed in any postwar general aviation market, and odds are that no one would have put money on a company that hadn't existed on New Year's Day—except, perhaps, the Aero Design and Engineering Company's eventual founders, officers, and investors.

Foremost among them was Ted Smith, whose insight into fast, unconventional designs ran from the Douglas A-26 Invader through the later Aerostar models (built as Piper, Smith, or Aerostar). By the end of 1944, he'd formed the company and attracted the financial backing to make its drawings reality. The Aero Commander's initial design was finished in 1946; the prototype flew less than three years after V-E Day. Certification followed on June 30, 1950.

If the machine looked odd—a snub-nosed, high-wing configuration whose main landing gear retracted into the nacelles housing geared 260-horsepower Lycoming GO-435-C engines—it flew well, with a 175-knot cruise speed, 1,600-pound useful load, and 700-nautical-mile range. Its 1954 selection as President Eisenhower's civilian transport didn't hurt sales, but new owner Rockwell International's hiring of fighter ace Bob Hoover to fly the pointed-nose Shrike version in his trademark airshows really got the public's attention. Aerobatics on two engines, then one, then none flown with Hoover's inimitably precise energy management established the credentials of an airplane that, despite its performance, had been considered stodgy.

The first to enter the light-twin market, the Aero Commander line was also the last to leave. After more than 3,100 deliveries and numerous changes of ownership, production ended in 1984. The Aero Commander piston twins were built until 1980. In 1972, a series of Twin Commander twin turboprops evolved, beginning with the Model 690. The last of the Twin Commanders, the Model 1000, was delivered in 1985.

AOPA often clashed with FAA Administrator Elwood Quesada (at left) in the late 1950s.

Elwood R. (Pete) Quesada, appeared to carry a bias against general aviation. Troubles began almost as soon as Quesada's appointment was announced. According to law, the administrator of the FAA must be a civilian. But Quesada was a lieutenant general in the U.S. Air Force at the time of his nomination. To circumvent the letter—if not the intent—of the law, Quesada resigned his commission to accept the FAA post. (Later, when he left office, his commission was reinstated by Congress.) However, Quesada carried many of his military convictions into the office of FAA administrator.

Quesada allowed the expansion of restricted and military operations areas, much to AOPA's forceful dissent. Higher VFR ceiling and visibility minimums also were proposed, and defeated, in large part due to AOPA's influence. Quesada hoped to expand the experimental High Density Air Traffic Zones, but AOPA responded by proposing a new concept designated the airport traffic area—less restrictive airspace with a radius of five miles and a ceiling of 3,000 feet. The proposal went through, proving that many types of busy, controlled airspace do not require expensive, burdensome solutions in order to have safe, orderly flows of traffic.

The Twin Bonanza, big and stately, took the prize for ramp presence in a piston twin from its start in 1951.

BEECHCRAFT TWIN BONANZA

What's in a name?

With essentially no parts in common, why did Walter Beech borrow the name of his company's flagship single for its first light twin? One theory holds that this was to reassure buyers concerned that the Bonanza had "only one engine." Or he might just have wanted to piggyback on the V-tail's success. In any case, he was a man in a hurry. Development of the Model 50 was spurred by his desire to make up ground on the fledgling Aero Commander company—particularly in pursuit of an Army contract, the lifeblood for small-airplane manufacturers in the uncertain postwar market. Ralph Harmon's design team responded in seven months with an airframe as nearly unbreakable as the commercial market had yet seen: test articles had no difficulty passing load tests at an unheard-of 8 Gs.

Everything about the original 1951 model was big: a front bench seat that comfortably sat three across, nacelles that accommodated major maintenance without removing the geared Lycoming GO-435s, two-bladed propellers nearly eight feet in diameter, and fuel burns exceeding 15 gph per side. Blame those big nacelles for some of that, and also for leisurely cruise speeds (around 160 knots): Intended for larger supercharged Franklin engines, they were never redesigned after Franklin abruptly left the aviation market. They went on to house progressively more-powerful mills in the GO-480 family: 275 horsepower in 1954, 295 horsepower with three-bladed propellers in 1956, and a supercharged 340-horsepower version in 1957.

Production numbers were never high. Just less than 1,000 were built before the last rolled off the line in 1963, 20 percent were bought by the military. By 1960 they were being outsold by Beech's next twin. The smaller, lighter, and much more economical Travel Air was derived from the Bonanza—and subsequently evolved into the Baron.

CESSNA 310

Fast company

After completing its military T-50 contracts, Cessna spent a few years catching its corporate breath, focusing on its strut-braced tailwheel singles. The 310 marked a complete departure: Cessna's first tricycle-gear model was a low-wing retractable-gear twin whose 240-horsepower Continental O-470-Bs lived in unusually snug nacelles thanks to in-line mounted pressure carburetors. Most distinctive, of course, were the 50-gallon tip tanks. Unlike the Aero Commander and Twin Bonanza, its dimensions were governed by the imperative of fitting the airplane into a standard T-hangar. Cessna also slotted it to come in below the Commander in cost and weight while rivaling or exceeding it in speed and payload.

The engineers hit their marks. Factory aerodynamicist Harry Clements recalled that the second prototype was faster than the first and the initial production units were a little faster than that. The tip tanks—which became a hallmark of all Cessna piston twins—allowed the wings to be unusually thin, contributing to exceptional aerodynamic efficiency. Over its 27-year production run engine output was only increased by 45 horsepower per side (compared to 200 in Beech's Travel Air/Baron series).

Fuel injection became standard in 1959 and the clumsy-looking "tuna tanks" were streamlined and angled into "Stabila-Tips" in 1963, increasing dihedral and reducing the inertia-driven overbanking tendency that made transition training exciting. That year's cabin stretch added a sixth seat. Turbocharging was offered via a nominally different model, the 320 Skyknight, in 1961; this was redesignated the Turbo 310 in 1969.

In all, more than 6,000 (including almost 600 Skyknights) were built before Cessna ceased production in 1981.

Max Karant (below, left) joined AOPA to work on "AOPA Pilot" in 1948, then rose to top leadership positions in the association during his 30-plus-year career.

Leadership changes

In May 1948, Hartranft hired Max Karant, formerly the managing editor of *Flying* magazine, to serve as assistant general manager of AOPA and editorial director for "AOPA Pilot," replacing Gill Robb Wilson—who went to *Flying*, where he assumed the editor's post. The team of Hartranft and Karant was to set the leadership style for the next three decades of AOPA history, during which AOPA membership would quadruple from 50,000 to more than 200,000 members. The organization that began with one staff member sharing a room with French-fried potatoes had come a long way.

Other association developments in the early 1950s included the move of AOPA's offices from Washington, D.C., to suburban Bethesda, Maryland. In June 1951, AOPA moved into the Keiser Building at 4644 East-West Highway in Bethesda. In October 1952, Hartranft, who had been running the day-to-day operations of AOPA, was named president and general manager. C. Townsend Ludington, AOPA's first president, was made honorary president.

AOPA Pilot made its debut as an independent magazine with the publication of its first issue in March 1958. This marked the end of the business

C. Townsend Ludington, AOPA president 1939-1952

Champion of 'freedom of the air'

AOPA's first president was a wide-ranging aviation businessman

Charles Townsend Ludington is most well known for the airline that bore his name, but he left an indelible mark on general aviation through his role as the first president of AOPA.

Ludington started Ludington Air Lines with his brother Nicholas in 1930. The airline provided the first scheduled service between New York, Philadelphia, and Washington, D.C.—"flights every hour on the hour." Service expanded to Norfolk, Virginia, and Nashville and Knoxville, Tennessee—and in 1933, Ludington Lines merged with the Eastern Transport Company, the predecessor of Eastern Airlines. Ludington also served as president of a manufacturer of aviation and hospital lighting; operated transcontinental contract airmail routes; was a director of Keystone Aircraft Company; co-founded and held leadership roles in the Jacobs Aircraft Engine Company, Kellett Aircraft Company, and other aviation businesses; and wrote about aeronautical subjects. His book *Smoke Streams: Visualized Air Flow* was used as a textbook on aerodynamics.

Ludington helped found AOPA in 1939 and served as president until 1952. "In Mr. Ludington's wise philosophy can be found the roots of most of AOPA basic policies and programs of today. The concept that public airports belong to the people and should not be dominated by the proprietary demands of the airlines; the concept of first come, first served; the policy that our air navigation system should accommodate all classes and users (and not that users should accommodate themselves to the system); the see-and-be-seen concept—these and many more of the principles of "freedom of the air" were the aviation credo of Mr. Ludington and the other AOPA founders," wrote then-AOPA President Joseph B. Hartranft Jr. in a tribute in *The AOPA Pilot* on the occasion of Ludington's death in 1968.

U.S. Pilots in 1955 | **643,201** ▲

connection with the Ziff-Davis Publishing Company and the beginning of one of the world's greatest aviation magazines. Karant served as the independent magazine's first editor.

Time for fun

The 1950s weren't all work for AOPA. As AOPA Unit activities were gradually phased out in favor of a stronger, centralized voice, AOPA began to sponsor a large annual fly-in. From 1947 to 1956, this was held at the Rehoboth Beach, Delaware, airport. With each successive year, more and more members and their guests attended the event. In an effort to locate a national convention at a more central spot, AOPA held its first Plantation Party at the Edgewater Gulf Hotel in Edgewater, Mississippi, in October 1956. Attended by a boisterous and enthusiastic crowd of members and their families, this was the first of AOPA's annual conventions, which came to be known as AOPA Expos.

There was plenty to celebrate. AOPA had close to 80,000 members, many unfavorable regulatory restrictions had been reversed or satisfactorily modified, and general aviation activity was on a new upswing. But the seeds of future challenges had already been planted. There were strong hints of increasing regulation with the VOR controversy and the High Density Air Traffic Zone proposal. The beginnings of radio frequency congestion and a reduction of general aviation weather services gave indications of future trends. Compared to the problems awaiting the association in the years to come, the 1950s in retrospect would seem trouble-free.

AOPA Units held many fly-ins and breakfast flights in the 1940s and 1950s, such as this one at the Rehoboth Beach, Delaware, airport in 1952.

Aircrafters
MASTER REBUILDERS OF Aircraft and Engines
AOPA HEADQUARTERS
N-Z
AVIATION

U.S. Pilots in 1956 | **669,079** ▲

AOPA SWEEPSTAKES ›

AOPA has a tradition of giving away airplanes in member contests and sweepstakes. The first such prizes were in 1956, when a Champion Sky-Trac (right) was awarded to Donald G. Rhodes of Midvale, Utah, and a Piper Tri-Pacer was awarded to William J. Meehan of Elon College, North Carolina. The lucky winners received the keys from "Doc" Hartranft (opposite page, on right) while on the air. WTOP-TV (today's WUSA), Washington, D.C.'s local CBS affiliate, staged the ceremony in a hangar at Washington National Airport for the Arthur Godfrey Show; Godfrey, an AOPA charter member, acted as master of ceremonies from New York through a split-screen process. Edward M. Moore won a Champion Tri-Traveler in a 1957 contest (inset) for submitting the best letter giving his reasons for joining AOPA. In recent history, a new tradition—refurbishing legacy classics for a sweepstakes—began in 1993, with the transformation of a well-used 1974 Cessna Skyhawk into a state-of-the-art example of modern avionics. Similar rags-to-riches overhauls have been made in subsequent years, with airplanes chosen for their enduring popularity or historical significance. The step-by-step upgrade model, whereby each airplane was flown from shop to shop for each step of the restoration process, has changed over the years to include some turnkey projects conducted by such companies as Aviat and Yingling Aviation.

AOPA SWEEPS

1956	Piper Tri-Pacer Champion Sky-Trac
1957	Champion Tri-Traveler (Second prize was a Spartan Sprite boat)
1958	2 Forney Aircoupes (promotion for Hertz)
1989	Piper Archer
1993	Good as New Cessna 172
1994	Better than New Cessna 172
1995	First New Cessna 172
1996	First New Cessna 182 Skylane
1997	Ultimate Piper Arrow
1998	Timeless Tri-Pacer
1999	Aero SUV Cessna 206
2000	Millennium Mooney 201
2001	Bonanza V35
2003	Centennial of Flight Waco UPF-7
2004	Win A Twin Piper Twin Comanche
2005	Commander Countdown Rockwell Commander 112
2006	Win A Six in '06 Piper Cherokee Six
2007	Catch A Cardinal Cessna 177B
2008	Get Your Glass Piper Archer
2009	Let's Go Flying Cirrus SR22
2010	Fun to Fly Remos GX
2011	Crossover Classic Cessna 182
2012	Tougher than a Tornado Aviat Husky
2014	Beechcraft Debonair
2015	Reimagined Cessna 152
2017	Cessna 172
2019	Piper Super Cub

THE VOICE OF GENERAL AVIATION

'AOPA Pilot,' over the years

By the end of World War II, AOPA's success was evident. In 1946 membership was 20,000 and climbing—twice the pre-war level. Ziff-Davis' fortunes were also looking good, as its page count climbed on the popularity of stories featuring military aircraft. In August 1940, *Popular Aviation* had been changed to *Flying and Popular Aviation*; in January 1943 its name was changed to *Flying*, the name it retains to this day.

AOPA's editorial representation in *Flying* grew as well. In April 1943, the last "AOPA Section" was run and was replaced in May with "The AOPA Pilot." By 1948, it was clear that AOPA was on a roll. Membership hit the 50,000 mark and kept rising, which meant that more and more issues of *Flying* had to carry "The AOPA Pilot," that each of those issues had to bear the special AOPA cover stamp, and that those issues had to be mailed to a separate list consisting only of AOPA members. And all the while, the size of "The AOPA Pilot" in *Flying* kept increasing. To Ziff-Davis, this additional overhead must have been burdensome.

Meanwhile, to keep up with the extra editorial duties, Hartranft hired the colorful and outspoken Karant, who had been *Flying's* managing editor, to be both editorial director of "The AOPA Pilot" and AOPA's assistant general manager. In a musical chairs move, Wilson then left AOPA to become *Flying's* new editor in chief. By all these developments, it's easy to see how *Flying*, AOPA, and "The AOPA Pilot" were intertwined in both business and interpersonal relationships.

According to what little remains of AOPA's historical records, these relationships were to become tense. An encapsulated summary of the issues leading to AOPA's decision to self-publish "The AOPA Pilot" appears in an August 28, 1956, memorandum of a meeting between Ziff-Davis' Benjamin G. Davis and AOPA's Charles P. Miller (who would soon serve as "The AOPA Pilot's" managing editor). The 10-year publishing contract between Ziff-Davis and "The AOPA Pilot" was up for renewal in October 1957. Both parties said they wanted to continue the business arrangement, but the memo makes it clear that their interests were diverging.

Miller recounts Davis as saying that *Flying* was facing a postal rate increase, and that increases in the cost of producing the magazine meant that any increase in the size of "The AOPA Pilot" was "definitely out unless we [AOPA] would bear the cost."

NO TC, NO PROBLEM
AOPA PILOT
The Voice of General Aviation
www.aopa.org | September 2012
Time for ADS-B?
GARMIN'S GDL 39 RECEIVER p.95
French Lessons
FLYING CLUBS GET IT RIGHT p.58
MARCH 1971
APRIL 1983
AOPA PILOT
OPS IN CHOP
DIVIDING THE SKY
CESSNA 206
Dare
Pilot with Rhythm
The Voice of General Aviation
de Havilland DHC-1
Freedom to Fly:

N34270
SKYHAWK
CESSNA

CESSNA 172 SKYHAWK

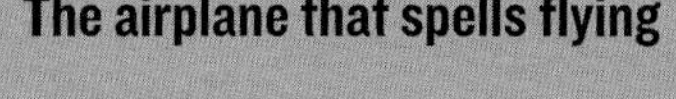

The airplane that spells flying

When Clyde Cessna formed his eponymous company in 1927, could he have foreseen that a tricycle-gear trainer bearing his name would one day become the world's most-produced aircraft?

The 172 was originally envisioned as a tricycle-gear version of Cessna's 170C; the 172 offered the same reliability but easier flying characteristics. The first year of production turned out more than 1,400 aircraft. They were powered by 145-horsepower Continental O-300 engines.

Rising costs from product liability lawsuits caused Cessna to terminate production of single-engine aircraft in the 1980s. With the passage of the 1994 General Aviation Revitalization Act, the company kicked back into gear and resumed 172 production with the R model, which was introduced in 1996.

Cessna, purchased by Textron in 1992, continually updates the 172 in response to customers' desires. Tweaks range from more modern avionics—all new Cessna 172s are sold with glass avionics instead of the traditional analog gauges—to a larger fuel capacity and a maximum gross weight increase. Engine horsepower increased from 145, to 160, to 180 horsepower. There are more than 21 distinctive models of the 172. These include the Cutlass RG—a retractable-gear 172 with a 180-horsepower engine—and the 172Q, which was a Cutlass with fixed gear.

Almost everyone who's flown an airplane in the past 60 years has had some contact with a Cessna Skyhawk—whether learning to fly in one or transitioning to one on the way to bigger and higher-performance aircraft. The Cessna 172 does so many things well that it is considered a great airplane for flying clubs, flight schools, and first-time owners.

Cessna's venerable four-seater wasn't always a Skyhawk. Introduced in 1956, the airplane was originally just a 172. The Skyhawk name came from an optional package, starting with the 172B in 1961, the same model year as the airplane shown here.

Active U.S. Pilots in 1958 | **354,365** ▼
FAA active pilot numbers, including student pilots

'The AOPA Pilot' editor Max Karant started the magazine and served as its head for 18 years. He previously worked for *Flying.*

Moreover, Davis said that AOPA was "at the end of the period where they could expect a 'bargain' rate for their magazine." Rather, Davis argued, AOPA should pay more for Ziff-Davis to publish "The AOPA Pilot." To keep up with costs, Davis said that AOPA should increase the cost of membership; establish new, nonpilot classes of membership; and end AOPA's free services to members.

For its part, AOPA wanted to sell its own advertising, something that Ziff-Davis definitely didn't favor. In the memo, Miller recalls Davis saying, "The only commercial value to the Ziff-Davis organization, which our relationship held, was that of advertising." Then Miller quotes Davis as making a comment suggesting that the idea of AOPA's breaking away had already come up in earlier conversations. "If advertisers who run ads in *Flying* magazine were able to reach the AOPA membership in any other manner except through *Flying*, i.e., through publications of our [AOPA's] own, it would completely nullify the advertising advantage that Ziff-Davis has," Davis reportedly said. "And there would be absolutely no value in continuation of the AOPA-Ziff-Davis affiliation." Davis went on to say that he wouldn't have "any great trouble in maintaining subscriptions among pilots by going directly to AOPA members and getting the full subscription rate."

Davis also reportedly said that, "AOPA would never attempt to publish their own magazine if they were in their right mind."

GA on the silver screen

Aviation in the movies, 1950-1969

In 1946, The penetration of TV sets in American households was 9 percent; by 1955 it was 65 percent.

In a period dominated by war movies, general aviation took a back seat in media in the years following World War II. The most famous movies featuring pilots and aircraft told stories about World War I, World War II, and the Korean War. Most notable among them is *The Bridges at Toko-Ri* (1954), about accomplishing a mission of destroying bridges, even though it means that pilots become collateral damage.

Several movies in the postwar years also deal with war veterans or make airliners the subject of their tale. For example, *The Tarnished Angels* (1957, based on a novel by William Faulkner) deals with a World War I flying ace's inability to adapt to civilian life as a barnstormer. *The High and Mighty* (1954) recounts an airliner's in-flight emergency and fixates on conflicting views of the veteran captain and his second in command.

However, general aviation had its own standouts. In 1957, *The Spirit of St. Louis* premiered, starring James Stewart—himself a pilot—as Charles A. Lindbergh, recounting the latter's historic flight from Roosevelt Field, Long Island, to Le Bourget, Paris. Three replicas of the *Spirit of St. Louis* were made for air-to-air and in-studio shots.

In 1965, *Those Magnificent Men in their Flying Machines* hit the box office. Set in 1913, it is a comedy about an international aircraft race set to win glory for Great Britain, directed by Royal Air Force veteran Ken Annakin. The aircraft shown in the film are life-size models, as well as replicas. Out of a total of 20 triplanes, monoplanes, and biplanes, six actually flew, albeit only in favorable weather conditions—they were as finicky as the originals. In the film, competing aviators battle the same perils as pilots today: low visibility, weather, spatial disorientation.

But leave it to TV to accomplish what aircraft manufacturers hoped to achieve—turning service members returning from the war into civilian pilots and kindling an interest in general aviation. So "Out of the clear blue of the western sky comes... *Sky King*," a television series about an Arizona rancher-pilot, his niece Penny, and their aircraft *Songbird*. Where the local sheriff had to admit defeat, Schuyler "Sky" King came to the rescue, supported by Penny, also a pilot. The aircraft used in the movie was originally a Cessna T-50 Bobcat, and in later episodes a twin-engine Cessna 310B. Cessna, realizing the potential of the show, provided the airplane, as well as Bill Fergusson, the pilot. Kirby Grant, the actor who played Sky King, was also an accomplished pilot.

The impact of this show was phenomenal. It's what kids talked about at school after they watched, reliving the scenes. Gloria Winters, who played Penny, in an interview remembered receiving letters from pilots, telling her they were inspired by the show to pick a career in aviation. Once, as passenger on an airliner, she was heralded over the intercom by the pilot as having been responsible for him becoming a pilot.

Not as famous, a real-life general aviation experience was depicted by Stanley Kubrick,

"THE EDITORIAL POLICY OF 'THE AOPA PILOT' WILL BE TO EDUCATE, ENTERTAIN, AND INFORM, AND TO DO SO OBJECTIVELY, FORCEFULLY, AND FEARLESSLY." —MAX KARANT, EDITOR IN CHIEF, 'THE AOPA PILOT'

Kirby Grant and Gloria Winters as Schuyler "Sky" King and Penny.

who in 1951 made a documentary, *Flying Padre,* about a Catholic priest in New Mexico, Father Fred Stadtmueller. As his parish was large, he used a Piper Cub named *Spirit of St. Joseph* to travel between settlements.

In this era, general aviation was male-dominated. In the movies, women were usually flight attendants, as in *Air Hostess* (1944), *Come Fly With Me* (1963), or *The Stewardesses* (1969). Most were chasing men, often pilots. But not all of them: *The Lady Takes a Flyer* is a drama about a pilot couple running a business shipping goods. The female lead, played by Lana Turner, one day decides to leave the baby with her husband in order to fly a shipment. The husband (Jeff Chandler) in turn takes the baby on a trip to London.

And then there are oddities such as the 1957 *Go Fly a Kit,* an animated movie about a cat raised by an eagle that learns to fly and teaches consecutive generations the skill, as well as *Thunderbirds,* a British science fiction television series that relies on electronic marionette puppetry, about an international rescue team using all kinds of flying vehicles. And Jimmy Stewart plays the pilot of a Fairchild C-82 that makes an emergency landing in the Sahara in *The Flight of the Phoenix* (1965), where a model-airplane aficionado saves the day.

AOPA has a long history of research-based program initiatives. In the early 1950s, a study at the University of Illinois and funded by the AOPA Foundation showed how VFR-into-IMC accidents occurred.

180 degrees to safety

The birth of a legacy

In 1953, federal accident statistics showed that 50 percent of all fatal general aviation accidents were attributable to VFR-only pilots inadvertently flying into instrument weather. In those days, relatively few pilots were instrument-rated, and a 1954 University of Illinois study proved just how a VFR-into-IMC crash was most likely to occur.

THE 180-DEGREE RATING COURSE KICKED OFF WHAT WAS TO BE A DECADES-LONG TRADITION OF NATIONWIDE COURSE OFFERINGS.

The university received an AOPA Foundation grant to study pilot loss of control in instrument meteorological conditions. When noninstrument-rated pilots were suddenly placed in instrument conditions, for 19 out of 20 a bank ensued, the nose of the airplane dropped, airspeed increased, the pilot would see his altimeter showing a rapid descent, and he would exert back-pressure on the control column to stop the descent. This tightened the turn, which consequently caused an even greater descent rate. The dynamics of what had been called the graveyard spiral had been quantified, and the germ of one of the foundation's most popular programs was born—the 180-Degree Rating Course.

The University of Illinois researchers were given another grant to come up with a course curriculum designed to teach noninstrument-rated pilots how to extricate themselves from instrument conditions. In 1956, the university's Institute of Aviation accordingly developed a six-hour course, and the AOPA Foundation ponied up some more money to allocate as scholarships aimed at instructors who would teach the course.

University student Ralph F. Nelson, a standout in the fledgling instructor corps, caught the attention of Hartranft, then the president of both AOPA and the foundation. Hartranft offered Nelson a job at the foundation, heading up the 180-Degree Rating Course and the rest of the foundation's educational efforts. Two years before he was to graduate, Nelson landed the title of project director of the AOPA Foundation, then located in Bethesda, Maryland. In June 1958, he graduated, moved to Bethesda, and immediately began plans to teach 50 instructors (one from each state) how to present the techniques. The course made its public debut in October 1958 at AOPA's Plantation Party in St. Petersburg, Florida.

This course kicked off what was to be a decades-long tradition of nationwide course offerings, many of them involving several hours' worth of in-flight and classroom instruction. At the time, there were no other courses like the 180-Degree Rating Course. As with so many other foundation and Air Safety Institute initiatives, it was the only course available that effectively addressed a genuine safety problem.

That tradition continues today, as pilots interact with the organization's cutting-edge safety programs, including engaging safety videos, podcasts, online resources, and in-person seminars. The organization now goes by the name AOPA Air Safety Institute, but retains its faithfulness to its original charter, written down in A. Felix DuPont Jr.'s Wilmington, Delaware, law offices in 1950: "To promote safety in every manner in all phases of aviation, and to engage in research and investigation upon, and the dissemination of, the science and scientific aspects of aviation and kindred subjects."

Let there be no doubt: We're all better, safer, more educated pilots thanks to the AOPA Air Safety Institute's work.

The 180-degree turn experiment, by the numbers

178 seconds Average time for subjects to reach an incipient dangerous flight condition.
19 of 20 Number of subjects who placed the airplane in a graveyard spiral on the first attempt to fly by instruments.
1 The other subject put the airplane in a whip-stall attitude.
59 of 60 Number of times those same subjects successfully exited the simulated emergency scenario after completing the University of Illinois course.

Safety Timeline

1950 AOPA Foundation is created.

1958 180-Degree Rating Course rolls out nationwide.

1961 360-Degree Rating Course debuts.

1963 Pinch-Hitter course is unveiled.

1964 *Come Fly With Me Darlene* kicks off the AOPA Foundation's involvement in educational films.

1967 AOPA Foundation becomes AOPA Air Safety Foundation to reflect its work.

1972 *Aviation Weather* debuts on PBS stations.

1977 ASF begins offering flight instructor refresher courses (FIRCs).

1988 ASF establishes the Emil Buehler Center for Aviation Safety and develops the general aviation accident database.

1991 The first *Joseph T. Nall* report is published.

2000s ASF offers its first online courses.

2010 ASF becomes the AOPA Air Safety Institute, a division of the newly formed AOPA Foundation, AOPA's fundraising arm.

2017 ASI is removed from the AOPA Foundation to become a part of AOPA.

"KEEP THY AIRSPEED UP, LEST THE EARTH COME FROM BELOW AND SMITE THEE." —WILLIAM KERSHNER

After this meeting, AOPA leaders made up their minds. There would be no more arrangement with Ziff-Davis. The 17-year relationship that helped found and fund AOPA, solicit its first members, and give voice to the association, was over. AOPA would produce its own publication of *The AOPA Pilot*, and do it with production values, a format, and an editorial style that would put it in direct competition with its former business partner—which stood to suddenly lose 63,000 AOPA member-subscribers.

Now the ball was in AOPA's court, and decisions had to be made quickly. Hartranft (by then AOPA's second president), Karant, and Miller planned to put out the first issue of *The AOPA Pilot* (the magazine used the title *The AOPA Pilot* until 1979) in November 1957. A printer had to be selected, staff hired, story lineups decided, advertising representatives commissioned, advertising rates set, and production values determined.

Initially, the idea was to put out a 48-page, standard size, glossy magazine with black-and-white contents (with some spot color here and there), and color front and back covers. A September 28, 1956, internal memo argued against going with a pocket-sized format, which some favored. This smaller format was envisioned as having 96 pages. But Miller thought a small-format magazine would seem too much like an imitation of *Air Facts*, a popular monthly general aviation magazine published by Leighton Collins. Moreover, Miller

'AOPA Pilot' highlights

An editorial in the March 1958 issue of *The AOPA Pilot* outlined the publication's mission to serve AOPA members exclusively, with a range of content including "new developments in civil aircraft and their accessories, safety devices and practices, flight techniques, rules and regulations; interesting people, interesting flights, airports and their operators." Here's a sampling from the past six decades:

In the August 1966 issue of *The AOPA Pilot*, Alcor Aviation's Al Hundere introduced readers to a radical new way of monitoring engine performance: Alcor's exhaust gas temperature gauge. The EGT brought engine analysis to pilots for as low as $189, when previous engine analyzers had cost as much as a small airplane.

"With the introduction of the exhaust gas temperature method of mixture control, pilots discovered that an EGT indicator is also a trouble detector."

In the May 1977 issue of *The AOPA Pilot*, readers were treated to two articles written by Charles A. Lindbergh. Both involved Lindbergh bailing out of his mail plane at night, over an undercast of fog.

Beech Aircraft Corporation ceased production of its V-tail Bonanza in 1982 after a spate of inflight breakups. "Bonanza Besieged," a February 1981 feature by longtime contributor Barry Schiff, debunked the notion that V-tailed airplanes were inherently unsafe.

"It is intriguing to reflect upon how such a storm of controversy can be created about a design that has been regarded as a standard of excellence for more than a third of a century. And yet, upon close examination, the storm is little more than a tempest in a teapot or, as Shakespeare said, 'much ado about nothing.'"

"Satellites Instead," a July 1982 article by Dr. Gerard K. O'Neill, advanced a GPS-based method of collision avoidance and navigation. It was a prescient article that envisioned today's GPS.

The terrorist attacks of September 11, 2001, and their implications for GA, were the subjects of November 2001's "America Under Siege" collection of articles. This somber section also included *AOPA Pilot* staffers' experiences on the day of the attacks. Some were in the air at the time, and had to land immediately.

February 2015 marked *AOPA Pilot*'s first Destinations theme issue in what became an annual tradition of highlighting the many places general aviation pilots can access by air—from tropical island getaways to Arctic tours of polar bear country.

said that after members had been receiving a full-size *Flying* for so many years, they might feel cheated if they received a smaller magazine in its place. Eventually, the full-size magazine argument won.

The advertising rates of the day seem laughable now. You could buy a full-page, one-time advertisement in the first issue of *The AOPA Pilot* for $425, or buy the back cover for $850. But then again, everything cost less 60 years ago. For example, AOPA membership was $10 per year, and the first staff writer for *The AOPA Pilot* earned $6,000 a year.

The editorial staff had offices at AOPA headquarters, then at 4644 East-West Highway in Bethesda, Maryland. But freelance writers—or AOPA members—wrote most of the 1958 magazine content. Some of the stories needed a lot of editorial help before publication. The rewriting and other tasks took the staff by surprise. Unaccustomed to the heavy demands of starting a brand-new magazine, it took several months for the team to get its act together. Karant and Miller did most of the editorial work, and they were swamped. That first issue's publication date kept being pushed back. That's why *The AOPA Pilot* debuted with a cover date of March 1958—four months later than its target date. It mailed one month later than that.

The first cover of 'The AOPA Pilot' (opposite) featured an air-to-air photograph of the Cessna 182 Skylane. AOPA photographers have refined the art of air-to-air photography, capturing the energy and magnetism of aircraft in dynamic angles and stunning environments. This contemporary Cessna 180 entices readers to fly the Copper River Basin in Alaska (below).

"Additional editorial help is a must if we wish to continue publishing the sort of magazine we're trying to put out," said a March 27, 1958, memo from Miller to Karant. "We cannot operate as we have during the past three months. It has been a hand-to-mouth proposition during the past two months. This method of operation has resulted in expensive alterations, missed deadlines, and a book that doesn't quite meet our desires or capabilities. Of course, I am not including an important personal item—an exhausted staff. We have a total of two people to do the work being done by six persons, plus clerical assistance, on *Flying* magazine. I have had a total of five free days since January I."

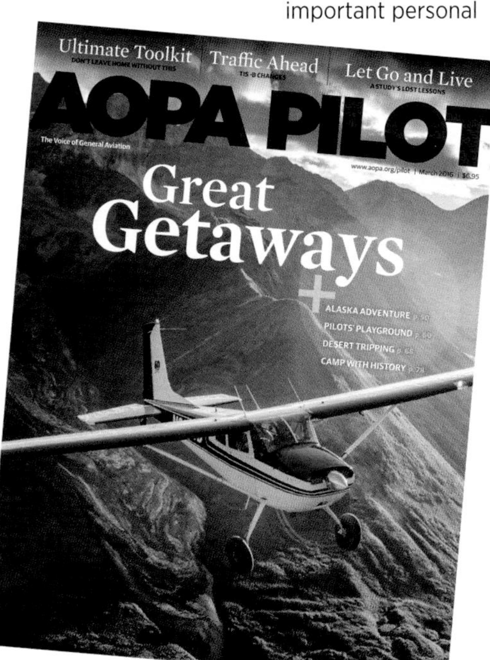

Hartranft balked at hiring another editor, but finally relented just days before the magazine went to press. Sue Timberlake was hired as the magazine's first associate editor, and soon began generating articles for upcoming issues. Once the staff got its sea legs, editorial content improved steadily and, as expected, the magazine's advertising revenue grew with each issue. *The AOPA Pilot* also served as a great vehicle for recruiting new members. By the end of 1958, AOPA rose to 80,000 members—a 17,000-member increase over the previous two years. AOPA and *The AOPA Pilot* were off and running, and there was no turning back.

Was the decision to start our own magazine a good one? *AOPA Pilot* is, by far, the world's largest-circulation general aviation magazine, staffed by award-winning writers, contributors, graphic artists, and photographers, consistently bearing the best design and photography in the business—and earning the awards to prove it. It may have gotten off to a shaky start in 1956, but those days are long gone.

Old friends

AOPA's longtime writers

What's the first page of *AOPA Pilot* that you read? For some it's "Never Again," the monthly oops column of fellow pilots. For many others it has been the columns of Barry Schiff (above, left) and John S. Yodice (above, with trophy), the longest-running writers in the magazine's history.

John Yodice began writing for AOPA as a young attorney in 1965, just six years after the formation of his private practice outside Washington, D.C. Over the years Yodice came to be known for his direct style and piercing rebuke of government overreach as it related to pilot certification. His career has been dedicated to helping pilots out of tough situations with the FAA. While writing for AOPA he helped to educate hundreds of thousands of pilots on their rights and responsibilities. Yodice's "Pilot Counsel" column stopped in 2018, 53 years after he first started writing it for *AOPA Pilot*.

Although most readers know Barry Schiff through his "Proficient Pilot" column, the former airline captain has only been writing in that spot since the early 1990s. His tenure as a writer for AOPA goes back much further. In June 1963 AOPA ran Schiff's first published article. The subject was one we still discuss today—how to navigate properly. Over the years Schiff's stories have caused countless pilots to dream, think, and discuss almost every facet of aviation. From peace flights in the Middle East to soaring high in the U-2, Schiff is the type of aviator many long to be.

5.

GROWTH AND CHALLENGE

More pilots, more aircraft—and more conflict

The 1960s and 1970s were a pivotal time for the country, for the aviation world, and for general aviation. Expansion, modernization, and increasing complexity characterized the aviation world of the 1960s. A decade that began with radial-engine transports ended with the Concorde and a man on the moon. By the dawn of the 1970s, Boeing 747 jumbo jets were taking more passengers farther, faster.

Comparatively few airlines of the early 1960s later swelled into a network that threatened to dominate the airspace infrastructure. A fairly primitive means of identifying and separating air traffic gave way to a much more sophisticated, transponder-based method. And it was in the 1960s that we would begin to experience the expansion of the federal government's involvement in aviation affairs to an unprecedented degree. The tumult and uncertainty prevalent in much of the country was found in all areas of aviation, as well. Incredible engineering achievements were tempered by high-profile accidents that split the aviation world and created significant challenges for general aviation.

The Cessna 150—slow, small, but sturdy—became the most popular trainer in the general aviation fleet. Production began in 1959, followed in 1978 by the Cessna 152. The 150 and 152 were the backbone of the hugely successful Cessna Pilot Center network. For thousands of new pilots in the 1960s and 1970s, these were the airplanes that taught them to fly.

The trainer era

Two decades that defined entry-level aviation

With the massive growth in the pilot community that occurred during the 1960s and 1970s, it follows that there would have been a large and diverse fleet of training airplanes to make it happen. Tens of thousands of trainers came from Cessna, Piper, and Beechcraft. Many are still in use today. While the decades prior featured the Piper Cub and the Curtiss Jenny, this era marks the definition of what we still consider to be a great training aircraft.

Far and away the most popular training aircraft of the time were the Cessna 150 and 152. With more than 30,000 coming off the line in Wichita, Kansas, the little Cessna that could had the perfect combination of power, gross weight, and handling characteristics that continue to make them sought after some 50 years later.

Sometimes assumed to be the precursor to the larger 172, the 150 was actually a smaller, simpler version of the 172 that came about approximately four years later. The two-seat, all-metal 150 was introduced in 1959, coming off the production line with a 100-horsepower Continental O-200 engine. Priced at a reasonable $7,000 for the base model (about $61,500 in today's dollars), Cessna sold 600 units on the day it was announced.

Although some of the PA-28-series Pipers were used for training, it took Piper nearly 10 years to answer Cessna's dominance of the two-seat training market. Despite being late to market and of an inferior design, the Tomahawk sold respectably. Introduced in 1978, production ran for only four years, and stopped at almost 2,500 airplanes. The "traumahawk" nickname comes from a pronounced tail wag during spins, and the model had some fatal accidents.

Beech was never in the training market in a big way, but did see opportunity in the huge need of the late 1970s. The company produced the Skipper for only a few years. With its bubble canopy, low wings, and T-tail, it looks surprisingly like the Tomahawk. Only about 300 were built.

Meanwhile, more pilots were using more airplanes than ever before. The annual increase in gross domestic product averaged about 4.5 percent in the 1960s and 3.2 percent in the 1970s. And with the Vietnam War's GI Bill and baby boomers coming of age, general aviation manufacturers were having a heyday, introducing new models left and right and producing an average of more than 9,000 airplanes per year. This is the era of the "Spam can" designs that pilots continue to fly today. The U.S. pilot population more than doubled in two decades, from 360,000 in 1959 to 814,000 in 1979. It was a busy time for aviation in America—and for AOPA, still more challenges lay ahead.

Growing pains

In times when all aspects of an industry—aviation—are expected to grow, conflict among the parties is a given.

According to assurances given when the Federal Aviation Act of 1958 was enacted, AOPA was to have been granted the opportunity to participate in rulemaking activities, providing input to FAA rulemaking, and allowed to appeal penalties against airmen to the Civil Aeronautics Board (CAB). In this, AOPA had the support of, among others, Senator Clair Engle (D-Calif.), an influential member of the Senate appropriations subcommittee dealing with aviation affairs.

But it was not to be. In 1960, general aviation had to face Elwood R. Quesada, the FAA administrator whose controversial approach to regulations and aviation safety often put him at odds with AOPA. Quesada, a retired three-star general in the U.S. Air Force, acted as judge and jury for airmen charged with violations of the regulations—there was no means of appeal.

In spite of Quesada, there were successes during what was to be his last year in office. The FAA's 1960 budget of just less than $511 million included $195 million earmarked for expansion of navaids. An attempt to cut $10 million from the weather bureau's $60 million budget was defeated, an act that helped retain and expand many programs designed to improve general aviation pilot briefings. Continuous broadcasts of aviation weather were instituted at 87 low-frequency navaids. Money was appropriated for a newer primary radar system, one capable of more easily detecting radar returns from airplanes in flight. A "flash advisory service" was begun at flight advisory weather service centers (the precursor of today's flight service stations); this informed pilots of severe weather conditions in much the same way as today's convective sigmets. And in September 1960, flight following services—now called VFR advisories—were made available to VFR pilots flying cross-country. With more flying activity came the need for more communications frequencies, and 75 additional VHF frequencies were allotted in 1960.

A voice for private fliers

Changes were in store in the early 1960s, starting with leadership in the White House. The October 1960 issue of *The AOPA Pilot* carried a statement by presidential candidate John F. Kennedy, who strongly sympathized with AOPA's attitudes. Kennedy said: "I, personally, see a threefold problem at this time. One concerns the balance needed between the rules and regulations required by safety and the guarantee of civil rights of private pilots. The second is the question raised by AOPA about former military men filling the top civil positions in aviation. The third is the lack of public awareness of the percentage of air time recorded by civil aviation as related to commercial aviation and the resultant apathy toward civil aviation."

After Kennedy's election, AOPA and general aviation experienced a turnaround. President Kennedy appointed Najeeb E. Halaby as FAA administrator. Halaby, formerly the deputy assistant secretary of defense for international security affairs from 1946 to 1954, brought a more analytical, reasoned tone to the FAA. After two years of Quesada, and despite also being a former military man, Halaby was like a breath of fresh air. For America's 349,000 pilots flying a total of 76,000 general aviation airplanes, he came just in time.

Halaby began his fresh slate with a visit to AOPA headquarters, where he received an in-depth briefing on the association's work and goals. Before the first four months of his term had passed, Halaby instituted what he called "Air Share" meetings—opportunities at the grassroots level for general aviation pilots to question him and share their views on the issues at hand. Before the end of 1961, Halaby had attended more than 100 such meetings at locations all across the United States. These did much to alleviate the mutual suspicions that for too long had characterized the FAA-general aviation relationship.

A cherished line of single-engine aircraft

The J-3 Cub is such an icon that it's the airplane most people associate with Piper Aircraft. But the long-lasting, durable Cherokee line is a runner-up in the nostalgia department.

All Piper PA-28s and -32s are direct descendants of the original Cherokee, introduced in 1961. The Cherokee's low-wing, all-metal design was said to be the result of a challenge from William T. Piper to designer Fred Weick, who had told Piper he could design an airplane more economical than the tube-and-fabric aircraft for which the company was known.

The first Cherokee was a four-place, 160-horsepower aircraft with distinctive wings given the nickname "Hershey bar." In 1974, Piper changed the wing to a tapered shape to improve performance and safety.

Shortly after the first Cherokee arrived on the scene, Piper began producing variations, including 150- and 180-horsepower models and a two-place version. Future variants would include the retractable-gear Arrow and the six-seat Cherokee Six, thus providing step-up aircraft for loyal customers. As these evolved, names such as Warrior, Challenger, Archer, Pathfinder, Dakota, and Saratoga replaced the Cherokee moniker.

Piper continues to produce single-engine PA-28 aircraft at its factory in Vero Beach, Florida.

Active U.S. Pilots in 1962 | **365,971** ▲

The new administrator also commissioned a study—Project Horizon—to investigate the nation's aviation problems. Project Horizon came up with 24 goals for the national aviation system. Among them was the need to "accelerate the growth of general aviation, recognizing it as an essential and expanding element of the national air transportation system." Another goal of the program was to "plan and implement a long-range, nationwide system of airport and terminal development capable of keeping pace with the projected growth of air traffic." This was music to general aviation's ears. Out of Project Horizon came the necessary support for the passage of Engle's bill—S.447—that provided safeguards and appeals to the CAB in cases against certificate holders.

Another of Halaby's initiatives—Project Tightrope—was highly critical of former administrator Quesada's methods of enforcing federal aviation regulations. Tightrope recommended a skilled staff of investigators to check out reports of violations and explore trial-type hearings for final rulings. When he announced this study, Halaby said, "We shall adopt no more regulations than are strictly necessary and shall appeal to the pilot's common sense so that those we do adopt will be respected."

Yet another study—Project Beacon—advocated for the increased use of transponders in the air traffic system of the future. AOPA

'The AOPA Pilot' magazine wasn't AOPA's only publication. *AOPA's Airports USA* listed virtually all airports in the United States, with entries including a wide range of information. The *AOPA Handbook for Pilots* was a small-format compilation of aviation rules, safe practices, telephone numbers to contact for weather, and distillations from the then-*Airman's Information Manual* (AIM).

Pilot resources

AOPA worked hard to offer useful benefits

The 1960s marked an expansion in AOPA's offerings of products geared toward making flying easier and less expensive. The year 1961 saw the publication of the first *AOPA Airport Directory,* later renamed *AOPA's Airports USA*. In March 1965, *The AOPA Pilot* carried the first aircraft and engine directory, another reflection of the healthy state of the expanding general aviation industry. In another development, AOPA terminated its group insurance agreement with the American Mercury Insurance Company and endorsed the insurance provided by the Aviation Employees Insurance Company (Avemco) in December 1962.

As the 1960s progressed, members were offered a growing variety of services and benefits. AOPA's flight planning department—which provided AAA-style trip planning—grew by leaps and bounds, as did the departments providing other pilot information and services. The AOPA Air Safety Foundation, under Executive Vice President Ralph F. Nelson, added more courses to its flight training curriculum. Automatic flying-only life insurance, group life insurance, and preferential auto rental and travel programs continued to expand.

"WHEN I FIRST BECAME ADMINISTRATOR OF FAA, IT WAS OFTEN CHARGED THAT THE AGENCY ONLY LISTENED TO SPOKESMEN FOR THE AIRLINES AND SPECIAL INTERESTS AND THAT WE WERE REALLY NOT INTERESTED IN THE 'MAN-ON-THE-STREET' OF AVIATION—THE WEEKEND PILOT, THE PERSON WHO FLEW FOR PART BUSINESS AND PART RECREATION." —NAJEEB E. HALABY, IN A MEMO TO PRESIDENT JOHN F. KENNEDY

President John F. Kennedy (right) with Najeeb E. Halaby, Federal Aviation Agency administrator, at the November 1962 dedication of Dulles International Airport outside Washington, D.C.

disagreed with the transponder provisions at the time, arguing that the equipment was not yet capable of being fully implemented. But in other areas, most notably the recommendations to use climb and descent corridors in congested airspace, AOPA concurred with Project Beacon's final report. One AOPA comment the FAA acted on was the association's insistence that all high-performance aircraft should be segregated from other aircraft in the terminal area.

Halaby presided over a continued expansion of the airspace infrastructure, a theme that ran through the 1960s and 1970s. More direction-finding equipment was installed at tower and flight service facilities, more flight service stations (the "flight advisory weather service center" name was dropped) were established, new towers were commissioned, and new vortacs and ground-based weather radars were put in service across the United States. But all of this was very expensive and drew considerable public attention. The FAA's 1962 budget amounted to $695 million; 1963's was $756 million; by 1964, the agency was asking for $810 million. The construction of Virginia's modern Dulles International Airport outside Washington, D.C., would cost $175 million alone.

In a misguided attempt to save money, the FAA, for the first time in what would prove to be a series of occasions, proposed eliminating 42 flight service stations. AOPA took the lead among aviation user groups in protesting this move. In spite of this, however, 21 flight service stations were consolidated out of existence by 1965. Ever since that time, AOPA has been adamant in its efforts to preserve and upgrade the quality and quantity of aviation weather information, a goal made much easier in today's world of digitally transmitted data over the internet and through smartphone apps.

Conflict in the skies

Halaby resigned as FAA administrator in July 1965 and was replaced by an appointee with dubious credentials. The Johnson administration named William F. McKee for the job. As with Quesada, McKee was a career (albeit retired) military officer. This, and the fact that McKee had no flying experience, raised all the old questions about military influence on a civilian agency. AOPA emphatically pointed out that the position required a civilian, but McKee (known as "Bozo" to acquaintances) was confirmed anyway. President Lyndon B. Johnson obtained special legislation that allowed McKee to keep his retired military status throughout his tenure at the FAA.

President Johnson had other, more far-reaching plans for the aviation community. In his 1966 State of the Union message, Johnson called for a new

Early corporate airplanes included Lockheed's JetStar (left), with four engines and sumptuous interior. Beechcraft's Model 90 King Airs (above) were the first of a line practical and comfortable turboprop twins. The Learjet 23 (top right) was a speed demon appealing to magnates and rock stars alike. Gulfstream's GI (right) was a stately turboprop twin that hinted at the Gulfstreams to come.

Corporate aviation's first airplanes

After World War II, aviation-minded companies had few choices if they wanted to start their own flight departments. Some converted surplus transport airplanes, but their radial engines and other dated technology meant high upkeep. Others opted for the Lockheed JetStar or North American Sabreliner. But the JetStar, with its four Garrett turbojet engines, gulped fuel and its heavy (44,500-pound) maximum takeoff weight meant long takeoff runs—and long runways to accommodate them. Still, it was the VIP airplane of choice for the government and military, and JetStars did look sexy. Sabreliners, transport trainers for the military, were also turbojet-powered and weighed half what the JetStar did, but carried fewer passengers. Both created ear-splitting noise levels.

The first true, purpose-built corporate airplane was the Grumman G159 Gulfstream I, better known as the GI. It was powered by twin Rolls-Royce Dart engines of 2,210 shaft horsepower each, could seat eight to 12 passengers in comfort, cruised at 300 knots, had a maximum range of 2,200 nautical miles, and needed just 4,300 feet of runway for a balanced field length, despite its 35,100-pound maximum takeoff weight. It looked elegant and had some advanced features: an auxiliary power unit, water-methanol fuel injection for better hot-and-high takeoff performance, and a crew advisory system that used an annunciator panel to warn of faults. Between 1957 and 1978, 200 GIs were built. They sold for around $2.5 million; today they can go for as little as $300,000—if you can find one.

Renowned inventor William P. Lear laid the groundwork for the business jet industry to come when he built the Learjet 23 in 1963. The Lear 23—with its wings and other design elements borrowed from a prototype Swiss attack jet called the P-16—looked aggressive on the ramp and had the performance to match, with its maximum 13,000-pound weight driven by two 2,950-pounds-static-thrust General Electric CJ610 turbojet engines and providing Mach 0.82 cruise speeds and a ceiling of 40,000 feet. Together with its performance and sleek, head-turning ramp presence, the eight-seat Lear 23 became a cultural icon. Movie stars, rock stars, and celebrities flocked to the Lear 23—the ultimate personal jet then—and "jet-setters" were born. Between 1962 and 1966, slightly more than 100 Learjet 23s were sold. Today, only a handful are left. The early Learjets were demanding to fly, and many crashed. Their loud turbojet engines can't meet current noise rules, so GE-powered Lears are banned from most airports. Today they mainly live in museums. But the Learjet 23 and its immediate successors,

the Learjets 24 and 25, were followed by a long line of ever more sophisticated and capable models that are very much in evidence—the Learjets 28, 31A, 35/36, 40, 45, 55, 60, 70, and 75.

Beechcraft's King Air 90 series made its debut in 1964 and was an instant hit. These 550-shaft-horsepower Pratt & Whitney PT6A-20/21-powered twin turboprops quickly dominated a growing niche among those who didn't need a jet, but wanted hard-working, multi-role transport airplanes with interiors that passengers loved. And with maximum takeoff weights well below 12,500 pounds, the 90-series King Airs could be flown single-pilot, making them the airplane of choice for small business owners and others with the need to fly six to eight passengers. With cruise speeds and ranges of 220 knots and 1,000 nautical miles, the "baby" King Airs were the perfect launch platform for those who found themselves needing to step up to the King Air product line. Because the design was scalable, ever-larger, more powerful, and capable King Airs followed: the E90, F90, 100, 200/B200, 250, 300, and 350-series King Airs. In all, more than 6,500 King Airs of all models have been sold, making them the most popular turboprops of all time. But it all started with the 90 series, which alone accounted for more than 2,000 sales. C90GTx models are still on the assembly line today and sell in the range of $3.8 million. It's obvious that Beechcraft got the King Air design right, from the very beginning.

AOPA's Plantation Parties served as fly-ins and social events of the year starting in 1956. They followed on the heels of a tradition of pilot get-togethers established at the local level by the AOPA Units of the 1940s and early 1950s. Between Plantation Parties, AOPA Conventions, and Expos, AOPA has returned to Las Vegas eight times.

cabinet-level department—the Department of Transportation (DOT). Some 34 agencies dealing with various aspects of transportation would be reorganized and placed under the proposed DOT, and the Federal Aviation Agency would be one of them. So would the Civil Aeronautics Board's Bureau of Safety. Under the proposal, the Federal Aviation Agency would be renamed the Federal Aviation Administration (FAA), and the Bureau of Safety would be renamed the National Transportation Safety Board (NTSB). Both would report to the secretary of the DOT.

AOPA and Senators A.S. (Mike) Monroney (D-Okla.), the principal author of the Federal Aviation Act of 1958; Warren Magnusen (D-Wash.); and Abraham Ribicoff (D-Conn.) disagreed with the DOT idea. AOPA had always believed in an independent FAA and felt that subordinating aviation affairs to a politically appointed DOT secretary could have an adverse effect on the safety, efficiency, and fair treatment of all segments of the aviation community. Nevertheless, the bills creating DOT were passed into law on October 15, 1966, over the reasoned objections of many aviation experts and congressional allies. The debate over McKee's qualifications as administrator faded away with the nomination of Alan S. Boyd (an aviation lawyer, and formerly a chairman of the CAB) as DOT's first secretary, and the nominations of the first five members of the newly created NTSB.

The FAA under DOT took a more serious look at transponders and began installing more newly designed secondary ATC radars—radars specifically designed to read and record transponder returns. At first only a few terminal areas had secondary radar, and the codes were few: 0600 for VFR flights, 1100 for IFR en route, and 0400 for IFR aircraft on approach. Slowly, more transponders were installed in general aviation airplanes, and more terminal areas received secondary radars. And by 1966, more avionics manufacturers introduced several affordable Mode A (non-altitude-reporting), 4,096-code transponders. (Mode C, altitude-reporting, models would not see widespread use until the 1970s.)

LEADERS AMONG US >

AOPA policy was guided by a growing board of trustees, including (left to right), R. Anderson Pew, Paul Heintz, and John S. Yodice. Pew's background included stints as the vice chairman of Bryn Mawr College and the directorship of the charitable asset management firm Glenmede Trust Company. Heintz was a lawyer specializing in estate planning, fiduciary and tax law, and Orphans Court litigation. He served on the Board of Governors of the Philadelphia Bar Association, and as a high school student, he visited AOPA's first offices in Bethesda, Maryland. Today Pew and Heintz serve as trustees emeriti of AOPA's Board of Trustees. Yodice has practiced aviation law since graduating from the George Washington University School of Law in 1959. He helped to establish AOPA's Legal Services Plan and argued successfully in a number of pivotal lawsuits, among them actions against landing fees at Boston's Logan Airport and R.A. "Bob" Hoover's fight to regain his medical certificate.

Two midair collisions in 1967—one between a TWA DC-9 and a corporate Beech Baron B55 over Urbana, Ohio, on March 9, the other between a Piedmont Airlines Boeing 727 and a corporate Cessna 310 over Hendersonville, North Carolina, on July 19—helped edge public opinion about transponders away from voluntary use toward favoring mandatory use of these new instruments.

AOPA's response was to cite the NTSB findings. In both cases, the airliner was found to be at fault for not seeing and avoiding the conflicting traffic. AOPA also reiterated its support of dedicated climb and descent corridors for high-performance airplanes and putting a high priority on the development of a proximity warning indicator that could alert pilots to the presence of nearby aircraft.

The recent midair collisions contributed to a revival of the high density traffic airport—again—in April 1968. American general aviation had faced the concept under another name in 1964, when the FAA called it "airport terminal service" or "terminal area radar service." Like the 1957 concept, the 1964 plan called for an experimental period of operation, beginning in the Atlanta area. The idea was to provide radar sequencing and separation to participating pilots using ATC's primary radar and two-way communications. In the Atlanta program, different levels of service to VFR aircraft were provided and called Stage I (traffic information and limited vectoring), Stage II (advisory and sequencing), and Stage III (sequencing and separation).

But there were difficulties. Primary radar relied on detection of echoes from an aircraft's aluminum skin (an unreliable "skin paint"). More accurate transponders and secondary radar had yet to be perfected or introduced, and poor resolution and interference from precipitation echoes frequently made aircraft identification impossible when using primary radar. Because the volume of traffic exceeded the experimental system's capacity, traffic

"I SAID, 'BILL, I'VE GOT TO BE HONEST WITH YOU. RENO IS WIDE OPEN AND IT'S WONDERFUL, BUT IT'S NOT ENOUGH POPULATION TO SUPPORT THE COST OF AIR RACING.'"

—BOB HOOVER, RECOUNTING A CONVERSATION WITH BILL STEAD

delays were common. In the end, plans to expand this service to 25 additional airports were scrapped.

In 1968, the FAA proposed seven high density traffic airports by year-end, with airspace restrictions that would limit many general aviation pilots' access to airports such as New York's La Guardia and Washington, D.C.'s National Airport. The original proposal called for an upper level of airspace 60 statute miles in diameter and extending from 5,000 to 10,000 feet above the primary airport's elevation. Only IFR flights were to be allowed in this layer. The next layer would have extended from 2,200 to 5,000 feet agl and have a diameter from 30 to 40 statute miles. IFR and "controlled VFR" flying would be allowed in this airspace. The layer nearest the surface also would be open only to IFR or CVFR flights.

Two more midair collisions in 1968 helped create additional pressure for HDTA rules. On March 27, an Ozark Airlines DC-9 collided with a Cessna 150 just past the departure end of Runway 17 at St. Louis, Missouri's Lambert Field. On August 4, a North Central Airlines Convair 580 hit a Cessna 150 at 2,200 feet, 11 miles southwest of the Milwaukee airport. In both cases, the airline crew was faulted for not seeing and avoiding the Cessnas.

AOPA maintained its opposition to the HDTA concept, arguing that the proposed measures were unnecessary, would effectively exclude many general aviation aircraft from flying to the affected airports, and overreached by determining which portion of the public could use public facilities. During the verbal battles that dragged on through the rest of 1968, several other developments challenged the energies of the AOPA staff. On July 31, McKee resigned as FAA administrator and was replaced by David D. Thomas, who served temporarily until John H. Shaffer was appointed in March 1969.

The same day McKee resigned, AOPA filed a lawsuit against the Port of New York Authority (PNYA), arguing that PNYA's

Gentlemen, you have a race

Air racing comes back in a big way

For millions of Americans, their only exposure to aviation before the wars was stunts and the thrilling world of air racing. Beyond the spectacle, prewar air racing significantly advanced aviation technology, usually in pursuit of big purses.

After the wars, the show was back, but the motivations were different. Now it was about fun, competition, and the chance to own and fly a piece of history. Although races had always been held sporadically, the era of postwar racing was on when Bill Stead offered up his ranch outside Reno, Nevada, in 1964 and the Reno National Championship Air Races were born. Surplus T-6s and SNJ-5s could be purchased for $4,000, and mightier warbirds weren't that much farther out of reach.

Today Reno is the only place you can find closed-course close racing, but soon after the event began in 1964, races popped up everywhere from Cleveland to Phoenix, and Miami to Mojave, California. In its inaugural year, Reno featured the Formula One, Biplane, and Unlimited classes. The T-6 class started in 1968, and immediately solidified its status as the closest of all race classes. Winner Hendrik Otzen beat Richard Sykes by two-tenths of a second. Those kings of speed, the Unlimited racers, started at a high bar that keeps being raised. Bob Love's P-51D *Bardahl Special* qualified at 395 miles per hour in 1964. In 2011, Steve Hinton set the record for the fastest Unlimited qualifying ever at Reno, flying the P-51 *Strega* at 499 miles per hour.

Courses galore

Growth of the AOPA Air Safety Foundation

One of the AOPA Foundation's early hits was the Pinch-Hitter course, aimed at nonflying pilot wives. Scores of women signed up for the course (above left), then received dual instruction (facing page, top right) in how to communicate and land in case of inflight emergencies. Ralph F. Nelson (center, at left, with AOPA Government Liaison Robert G. Armstrong) led the AOPA Air Safety Foundation for more than 30 years.

The AOPA Foundation's influence grew considerably during the 1960s and 1970s. Its 180-Degree Rating Course became obsolete when the FAA came up with a new ruling. Impressed by the voluntary course's success and publicity, the FAA went a step further in March 1960 by requiring private pilot applicants to demonstrate their proficiency in reversing course by reference to instruments only. The 180-Degree Rating Course had relied on the aircraft's inherent stability, calling for pilots to remove their hands from the wheel and focus on trim and rudder use. However, the FAA wanted pilots to have their hands on the controls, and execute their turns by reference to the attitude indicator—a method dubbed "positive manual control."

What could have been a blow to the organization became an opportunity to collaborate with the FAA and advance the safety mission of both organizations. The foundation's Ralph F. Nelson set about developing a new course that accommodated the new rules. Called the "360-Degree Rating Course," this curriculum called for four hours of ground school and four hours of flight instruction. Pilots flocked to the course by the thousands, at sites all across the United States. Those who took the course were exempt from taking an FAA checkride to demonstrate their competence and, under an arrangement with the FAA, an FAA Blue Seal was affixed to their pilot certificates. The first courses were held at the 1961 AOPA Plantation Party, and the flight training manuals used for the course were published in the November 1961 issue of *The AOPA Pilot* magazine.

Buoyed by the 360-Degree Rating Course's success, the foundation started embracing more advanced training. Instrument nav/com, instrument en route, and instrument approach courses followed. Then came the vanguard of a blizzard of even more specialized courses to follow—the Flight Training Clinics. These two-day weekend courses were set up at airports across the nation, with the cooperation and endorsement of the National Association of State Aviation Officials.

With that initiative came flight training and knowledge-test preparation courses called weekend ground schools, on topics such as instrument procedures, mountain flying, written exam preparation, and practical weather. By the mid-1980s, more than 100,000 pilots had taken one or more of these courses. Nelson would need even more instructors for a wildly successful course—the Pinch-Hitter—that made its entrée at the 1963 AOPA Plantation Party in Palm Springs, California. The Pinch-Hitter course came about as a result of two accidents involving pilot incapacitation.

The idea was to offer training that would enable a nonpilot to navigate to an airport, talk with air traffic control, and land an airplane safely without any assistance. There would be four hours of classroom instruction and four hours of flight instruction. The Ohio State University School of Aviation developed the curriculum, but Ohio State's research indicated that nonpilots believed it took a Superman to fly an airplane; some predicted that students would be afraid of failing the course. Nelson was warned that if his new course didn't draw at least five people it would be immediately canceled. At Palm Springs, 143 women and one teenage boy took the course.

Pilots would fly their spouses and other family members to designated venues, in their own airplanes; while one spouse

took a weekend ground school course the other would take the Pinch-Hitter. By 1966, half of the 4,000 Pinch-Hitter graduates had gone on for more flight training; one third earned their private pilot certificates. "We didn't really mean it to be a tool for recruiting new pilots, but that's what happened," Nelson recalled.

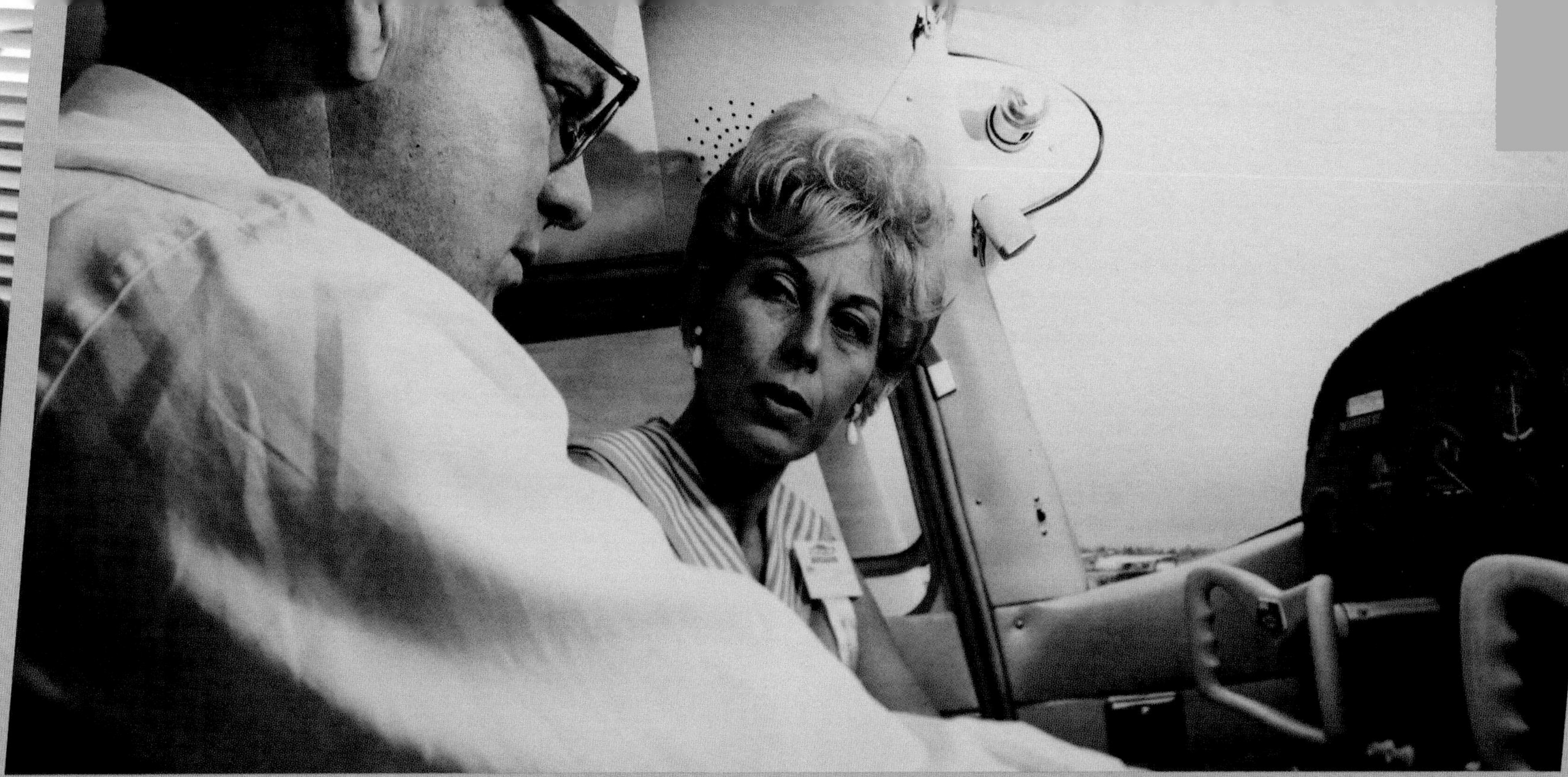

The key to the program's success was its nonthreatening approach to flying. There were no heavy discussions about aerodynamics and no complex procedural advice—just the bare essentials necessary to fly an airplane to a safe landing. Instructors were chosen for their affability (the course supervisor was Hal Shevers, then working as an instructor, but who soon would launch Sporty's Pilot Shop), and the main ground rule was that no one would flunk the course. The pressure to succeed was removed, so real, unfettered learning could begin.

The foundation's first involvement in educational films began in 1964, with *Come Fly With Me, Darlene,* a short feature aimed at the Pinch-Hitter crowd. Other films would soon follow, covering topics such as stalls and spins, weather, and airspace.

The group was renamed the AOPA Air Safety Foundation in 1967 to better reflect the nature of its work. *Aviation Weather,* the first and only public television program that provided aviation weather information, began airing over Public Broadcasting Service stations in 1972, thanks to an ASF grant. Annual grants continued as the program, renamed *AM Weather* in 1986, expanded to some 360 stations by the early 1990s. PBS canceled the program in 1993 in favor of *Bloomberg Business News*.

ASF also began an ongoing program that continues today as flight instructor refresher courses (FIRCs). In 1965 the FAA initiated a Flight Instructor Refresher Program to provide standardization in updating flight instructors. A rule was enacted requiring biennial recertification of flight instructors, and the FAA began to hold recertification courses around the country. It soon became evident that the FAA didn't have the manpower or resources to deal with a project of this magnitude. Based on the AOPA Air Safety Foundation's demonstrated competence in aviation education, the FAA empowered ASF to conduct the recertification courses in 1977. Thousands of CFIs renew their certificates every year under this extremely popular course.

In 1977, William R. Stanberry succeeded Nelson as ASF executive director. Under his tenure ASF's courses continued to grow in popularity.

Hal Shevers may be best known as the founder of Sporty's Pilot Shop, but in the 1960s he was an instructor (right) at ASF Flight Instructor Refresher Courses.

Starting in 1962, the International Council of Aircraft Owner and Pilot Associations (IAOPA) began representing general aviation's interests around the world. At right, an IAOPA delegate holds forth at a meeting of the International Civil Aviation Organization (ICAO) in Montreal.

sudden imposition of a $25 landing fee at La Guardia Airport was arbitrary and discriminatory. AOPA argued that the proposed 400-percent increase in the minimum landing fee for private aircraft at PNYA airports during peak hours violated federal grant assurances requiring airports to be "available for public use on fair and reasonable terms and without unjust discrimination."

Then events suddenly piled up. In September 1968, the Professional Air Traffic Controllers Organization (PATCO) staged a slowdown in its handling of air traffic. In what would become a familiar strategy, PATCO brought aircraft movements to a crawl by suspending procedural shortcuts and strictly following the rules and procedures in the ATC controller manual. This slowdown particularly affected the New York, Washington, and Chicago metro areas.

In October, the FAA published a notice of proposed rulemaking that would establish a reservations system for arrivals into and departures from the Chicago, New York, and Washington, D.C., terminal areas. Reservations would be required to enter the affected airspace, and IFR airplanes would be required to use a transponder and have two-person crews. The worst aspect of the proposal, though, was its hourly allotments of general aviation arrivals and departures. At Kennedy International, general aviation had five slots per hour; at La Guardia, six; at Newark, 10; and at Washington National, 12 per hour. AOPA urged representatives from all segments of general aviation to attend the public hearings on this controversial proposal. Instead of the anticipated three, some 95 witnesses testified against the proposal.

GA interests, at home and abroad

AOPA goes international

On February 2, 1962, Doc Hartranft and Victor Kayne began the creation of the International Council of Aircraft Owner and Pilot Associations (ICAOPA, now IAOPA). This organization's goal was the representation of general aviation interests at deliberative meetings of the International Civil Aviation Organization (ICAO), which had been established by the United Nations. ICAO had become a group of delegates selected from aviation organizations and governments around the world, leaning heavily toward airline interests when it came to such subjects as standardization of navaids, procedures, and allotment of airport capacity. Too often, general aviation interests were ignored, causing difficulties in international travel by general aviation airplanes and, more significant, causing decisions insensitive to general aviation to become standardized at the international level.

IAOPA's first member organizations were AOPA-U.S., the Canadian Owners and Pilots Association (COPA), AOPA-Australia, AOPA-Union of South Africa, and the Philippines Airmen's Organization. The group obtained entry to ICAO (in itself a feat of creative politics) and attended its first ICAO deliberations and conferences on March 19, 1963, in Mexico City.

Today IAOPA has 73 member affiliates, representing nearly 500,000 pilots worldwide.

"THE ICAOPA SPOKESMAN MADE IT A POINT ON EACH OCCASION TO POINT OUT THAT THE NAME SHOULD BE PRONOUNCED 'IK-KAY-OH-PAH.' ONE COMMITTEE CHAIRMAN HOPED IT WASN'T SUPPOSED TO BE PRONOUNCED 'IK-KAY-OH-PAH,' BECAUSE IT MIGHT IMPLY THAT THE NEW ORGANIZATION WAS THE FATHER OF ICAO."
—"ICAOPA WINS WORLD RECOGNITION," MAY 1963 'THE AOPA PILOT'

Instead of lasting half a day, the hearings dragged on for three days. All to no avail, save the dropping of the two-person crew provision and earning a verbal commitment from Secretary Boyd to set aside $30 billion for the construction of new general aviation reliever airports.

Soon after, Boyd resigned. Richard M. Nixon was elected president, and his Republican administration promised changes from the way business had been done during the Johnson years. John A. Volpe, a former Massachusetts governor, was named DOT secretary in January 1969. John H. Shaffer was appointed administrator of the FAA in March.

AOPA called on members to contribute to a "war chest" in a campaign called SAGA (Save America's General Aviation). Within days, $8,000 had been raised, some of it coming from the National Aeronautical Corporation (Narco) and the American Bonanza Society.

However, HDTAs—reservations, transponders, and all—went into effect in June 1969 and lasted for six months. The HDTA policy would be renewed in one form or another over the next three years. And as with the 1964 Atlanta HDTA experiment, the June effort proved once again that the FAA was incapable of meeting the demands of the rapidly growing numbers of aircraft using the airspace system. A centralized Airport Reservations Office was established in Washington, D.C., to coordinate aircraft movements, but delays and congestion occurred anyway.

AOPA filed a lawsuit against Volpe and Shaffer, stating that HDTAs were a violation of the traditional first-come, first-served policy of airport access, and that the new rules would have the effect of granting exclusive rights to the airlines and air taxi operators. The lawsuit was rejected, as was another lawsuit against PNYA concerning the landing fees at La Guardia. It was another set of bitter defeats for AOPA.

And another FAA proposal was still to come in October 1969. Once again, a midair collision—on September 9, between an Allegheny Airlines DC-9 and a Piper Cherokee near the India-

"WHY FLY? SIMPLE. I'M NOT HAPPY UNLESS THERE'S SOME ROOM BETWEEN ME AND THE GROUND." —RICHARD BACH, PILOT AND WRITER

napolis airport—provided the impetus. As a result, a new type of airspace, the terminal control area (TCA), was proposed. The FAA suggested that it be put into effect at a total of 22 airports. The TCA airspace as proposed closely resembled that of its successor—today's Class B airspace. This proposal marked the maturation of the transponder as the day's most modern tool for air traffic management. Now that the FAA had more secondary radars in the busier terminals, it was only natural that transponder requirements should evolve as the price of admission to the airspace structure.

By January 1970, the moves to introduce TCAs had begun. The FAA began to hold informal hearings on the TCA concept all across the United States. In what was to become a pattern for future "participation" of general aviation pilots in rulemaking processes, these hearings were conducted with little or no advance notice to the pilot community—a practice that AOPA condemned then and continues to oppose to this day.

By March 1970, the FAA announced plans for two types of TCAs. Group I TCAs would surround the busiest terminal

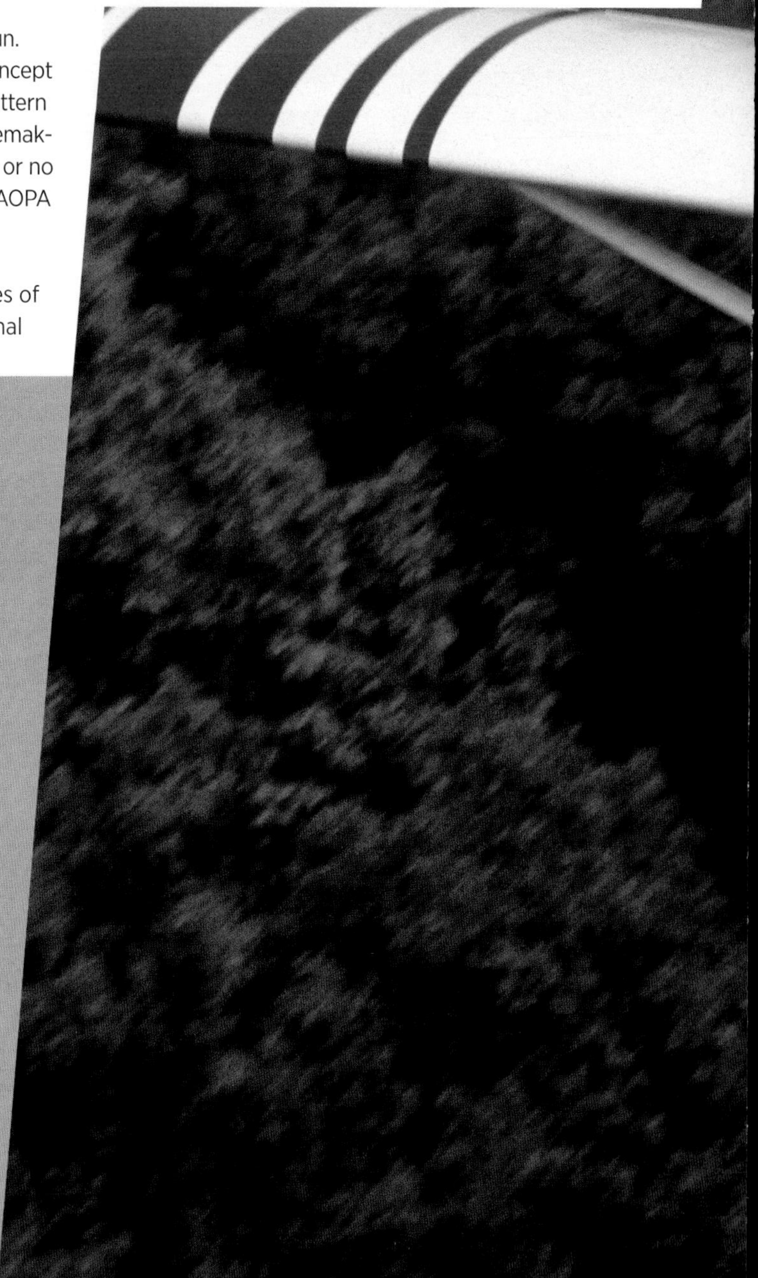

CITABRIA

Just for fun

The playfully named Citabria ("airbatic" spelled backward) was meant to be fun, inexpensive, and versatile.

A bigger, stronger version of the tube-and-fabric Champ trainer, the Citabria was introduced in 1964 and soon went on a growth spurt of its own. Its engine size grew from 100 to 115, 150, 160, and now 180 horsepower.

Gross weight increased, as did the durability of components. Wood wing spars were replaced with aluminum, and oleo struts were replaced with spring steel landing gear, then aluminum.

As subsequent models became more capable, Citabrias grew in popularity and versatility. More than 5,000 have been produced, and they're used for primary and aerobatic training as well as backcountry and personal flying. They're all stressed for aerobatic flight, and the most noticeable difference is flaps. (Only the 7GCBC model has them.)

The Citabria also gave birth to more specialized models with the larger "8-series." The Decathlon (8KCAB) is optimized for aerobatics with a symmetrical airfoil, constant-speed propeller, and inverted fuel and oil systems. The Scout (8GCBC) is made for the backcountry with flaps, big tires, and larger fuel tanks.

And the Citabria itself has become more refined with Adventure and Explorer versions made for aerobatics and backcountry flying, respectively.

The Citabria has been produced by several companies over the years: Champion Aircraft, Bellanca Aircraft Company, Champion Aircraft Company (different than the original), and American Champion Aircraft Corporation.

Through it all, the mechanically simple, rugged, and forgiving aircraft has maintained its honest flying characteristics and frisky nature.

Active U.S. Pilots in 1971 | **741,009** ▲

Boston's Logan International Airport (right) was the focal point of a legal battle in the 1970s, after jumbo jets began operations there. General aviation aircraft were assessed high landing and other fees in an attempt to exclude them. The effort failed.

areas; would require mandatory participation, two-way communications with ATC, VOR navigation capability, and altitude-reporting transponders; and would provide separation for all participating aircraft. Group II TCAs, which were envisaged as covering less crowded terminal airspace, would still require altitude-reporting transponders, but ATC services would only separate large turbine aircraft from other aircraft in terminal airspace. On May 19, FAA Administrator Shaffer approved the new rules. They were to take effect on June 25, beginning with a Group I TCA at Atlanta. Thanks to AOPA, the Atlanta TCA would have a central corridor to allow VFR-only traffic to transit this airspace.

AOPA was concerned for three good reasons. One was the absence of climb and descent corridors. The second was the absence of VFR terminal area charts; these were not to be published and disseminated until several days after the Atlanta TCA was in use. The third reason was that AOPA believed the ATC system could not safely handle the high level of traffic under the new radar environment. This last concern was made manifest in August 1970, when the FAA attempted to impose Group I TCA rules in the Washington, D.C., area.

The first day of the Washington TCA was a dismal flop. Controllers had to resort to three-hour delays in order to safely coordinate arrivals and departures. After just one day, the Washington TCA was put on hold while the FAA's airspace experts figured better methods of sequencing and separation. This TCA was to have been implemented on October 1, but additional problems ultimately delayed the implementation to February 4, 1971—the same day that the Los Angeles TCA went into effect.

The FAA had been studying the problem of airspace congestion since 1968, when DOT's Air Traffic Control Advisory Committee was formed to examine future alternatives for the nation's airports and airways. In early 1970, the committee issued a report that confirmed what AOPA and other

Training network

Cessna's imaginative pilot centers

Fifty years ago, the pilot population was more than 700,000. With that strong a number it may seem odd that a major aircraft manufacturer would want to start a program to grow the pilot population. But Cessna has always been synonymous with grassroots aviation, and by starting the Cessna Pilot Centers, the company cemented itself as the pilot training leader.

The CPC program began in 1970, and the goals of that original effort remain largely the same today. Cessna wanted to bolster the pilot population by providing a high level of training, and also have a network by which to sell training airplanes.

When the company restarted single engine piston manufacturing in the mid-1990s, each CPC was required to have a Cessna no more than two years old available for training or rent. Today that requirement has relaxed to be only a G1000-equipped Cessna. The deal has been good for the school partners and the manufacturer. Schools get Cessna's marketing muscle and a great training curriculum, and Cessna gets a nationwide network of branded partners and a single-engine piston sales outlet. Today there are about 125 CPCs, and together they sell about 8,000 training kits a year.

user groups had been saying for years: that "the air traffic control radar beacon system will saturate under traffic load characteristic of the denser hubs in the 1980s" and "the committee's studies indicate that data link will be necessary to meet the ATC communications load at major hubs."

Developments in the airspace system also showed a lack of responsiveness to the demands being placed on it. Using its traditional method of restricting access to airspace in order to bring about manageable traffic levels, the FAA lowered the floor of positive control airspace east of the Mississippi River from 24,000 to 18,000 feet mean sea level in August 1971. But these and other measures were judged inadequate. A series of FAA Alert Bulletins issued in March 1971 revealed 48 "control incidents" involving a loss of standard control separation because of ATC system faults. The FAA said that it would delay the implementation of additional TCAs (with the exception of the New York TCA) until after the AOPA/ALPA climb and descent corridors had been tested in the Boston airspace. In the Boston simulation, controllers were inadequately prepared for the simulation and had difficulty adjusting to the new flow patterns with such short notice. The FAA went ahead with its TCA implementations, much to AOPA's and ALPA's chagrin.

The NTSB report noted that an air carrier was made aware of a similar confusion at Dulles just six weeks earlier. The carrier issued a notice to flight crews after being notified through an anonymous safety awareness program.

This brought about a bill initiated by Senator Frank Moss (D-Utah) to introduce requirements for all airplanes in positive control airspace to have collision-avoidance systems. Development of collision-avoidance system technology had been coming along slowly, the result of private research. As early as 1970, Secretary Volpe had awarded a $279,032 contract to Control Data Corporation for the purpose of developing an airborne collision avoidance system.

A turning point for all segments of aviation came on December 1, 1974, when TWA Flight 514 crashed into a mountain on approach to Dulles International Airport. The crash was caused by the crew's descent below a published minimum altitude, but the accident raised important questions. Was the approach chart ambiguous in its portrayal of the proper altitude? Did approach controllers issue a confusing clearance? Was there fundamental, understandable confusion between crew and controllers?

Out of this accident came several important safety initiatives. AOPA's contribution was to ask for publication of a *Pilot/Controller Glossary*, which was granted. This document spells out in detail the definitions of words in the ATC and pilot lexicon. The glossary lives to this day and contributes a great deal to reducing the misunderstandings that can occur in pilot/controller communications. Another safety improvement was the beginning of minimum safe altitude warning advisories, which required controllers to advise pilots when dangerously low altitudes were reached.

But perhaps the biggest challenges of the decade followed the September 25, 1978, midair collision of a Pacific Southwest Airlines Boeing 727 and a Cessna 172 in San Diego, California. Relatively new FAA Administrator Langhorne Bond used the banner of safety as a rationalization to attempt to force through many ill-conceived regulatory proposals. One was a plan to increase the number of TCAs to 65 and impose an additional 149 TRSAs around less busy terminal areas. Another was a proposal to deny immunity to those who submitted reports to ASRS.

AOPA was quick to point out that the accident took place within a TCA and demonstrated the fallacy of depending on controlled terminal airspace as a cure-all for midair collisions. Furthermore, analysis of the accident showed a familiar pattern: The airliner was at fault for striking the Cessna while descending from behind it. AOPA, as it had done for decades, pointed out the insufficient visibility from airliner cockpits and emphasized that the pilots in the Cessna were participating in ATC services as required by the regulations and were both commercial pilots, not inexperienced neophytes.

In various public pronouncements, AOPA President John L. Baker used the occasion to criticize advocates of growth of controlled airspace. "The blunt truth is that the ATC system cannot accept growth," he reiterated.

Safety reporting comes with a price

The accident that started ASRS

In December 1974, a TWA Boeing 727 that had been cleared for an approach to Dulles International Airport hit a ridge west of the airport, killing all 85 passengers and seven crewmembers. United Airlines had reported an incident that foreshadowed the TWA crash to the FAA, but the FAA said it didn't know what to do with the information. So in 1975 the FAA created an Aviation Safety Reporting System (ASRS), which it soon handed over to NASA. NASA's new ASRS provided valuable examples of situations in which misunderstandings and lapses of attention (on the part of both pilots and controllers) created the potential for dangerous safety issues. By granting anonymity and freedom from prosecution for inadvertent violations, ASRS and its monthly publication, *Callback*, served as an essential educational tool. In March 1979, AOPA fought a proposal to eliminate the immunity provisions of ASRS—and won.

Active U.S. Pilots in 1973 | **714,607** ▼

Former fighter pilot, Senate legislative aide and corporate executive John L. Baker was named assistant administrator of the FAA's Office of General Aviation Affairs in the early 1970s—an office that no longer exists. In 1977 he was named AOPA president.

A hint of things to come

Baker brought a GA voice to FAA

In September 1970, FAA Administrator John Shaffer appointed John L. Baker to the post of assistant administrator in the FAA's Office of General Aviation Affairs. It was a bright moment, because Baker promised stronger general aviation input in decision-making processes. *The AOPA Pilot* carried an interview with Baker in its November and December 1970 issues. In them, Baker said, "I have some pretty firm ideas about this business of general aviation being treated as 'second-class citizens.' It has just got to come to a screeching halt."

About his new job, Baker said, "It isn't my intention to be the chaplain for general aviation. I intend, in effect, to be the advocate of general aviation.... I have the feeling the time has come when flying safety is going to get increased emphasis, and with that comes, of course, the threat of overreaction.... I hope we can retain our perspective on flying safety and work for positive solutions, rather than any repressive manner of achieving safety."

These were welcome words to AOPA and the rest of the general aviation community. With his background as a lawyer, congressional aide, corporate executive with Grumman Aerospace, and deputy director of DOT's Office of Congressional Relations, Baker's FAA appointment was a wise one. Few imagined that Baker would become AOPA's president within seven short years.

Although initially designed for a military contract, the Lockheed JetStar is considered the first dedicated business jet. The military contract was canceled before the JetStar was finished, and Lockheed decided to go ahead with the development for the business market. The JetStar entered service in 1961, and more than 200 were sold before production ceased in the 1970s.

But this did not prevent the FAA from proposing a rule that would have lowered positive control airspace to 10,000 feet msl and required "controlled VFR" (altitude-reporting transponders, VOR equipment, and two-way communications with ATC) for all VFR flights above 10,000 feet msl. Thanks to the diligence of a highly motivated staff and support from an increasingly informed and articulate membership (more than 43,000 negative comments were submitted to the FAA), this proposed rule was withdrawn in October 1979. It was a victory against the irrational hysteria that follows any major midair collision and another example of AOPA's growing power.

Money trail

In order to provide the funds for expansion of airports and air traffic services, Congress on July 1 passed the Airport and Airway Development Act of 1970. The plan would be carried out over a 10-year period. Spending levels of no less than $250 million per year for improvements to airways were established. A total of $2.5 billion would be spent for the construction and improvement of airports. The act required that a trust fund be established to pool the revenues, and that this fund be invested in interest-bearing accounts.

Airport and Airway Trust Fund revenues came from four principal sources. One was an annual tax on aircraft ($25 per year for aircraft with an empty weight less than 2,500 pounds and powered by reciprocating engines; an additional fee of two cents per pound for reciprocat-

CESSNA'S FIRST JET ›

"Cessna is selling a business jet? No way!" That was the prevailing opinion in 1968, when Cessna unveiled a mockup of its Fanjet 500. Cessna's hold on the piston single and twin market had been unassailed. Now, the Fanjet 500, powered by two Pratt & Whitney JT15D-1 engines, was built to mine the niche between $600,000 turboprop twins and $800,000 business jets. Most business jets typically fly routes of 600 nautical miles and carry fewer than three passengers. Why not offer a quiet, 330-knot jet capable of flying four passengers as far as 900 nautical miles? Plus, Cessna had experience making some 1,100 T-37 jet trainers for the military. On the first flight of the Fanjet 500 in September 1969, the airplane reached a maximum indicated airspeed of 225 knots—which gave rise to jabs that the airplane was susceptible to bird strikes from the rear. There was a perceived problem with the name, too. Fanjet engines were commonly used, and the "500" could be confused with the Aero Commander 500 and Lockheed L-500. Cessna settled on the Citation name based on the racehorse Citation that won the triple crown in 1948. By early 1970, Cessna had identified 100,000 or so potential customers. Part of the appeal was a marketing strategy emphasizing a network of Cessna-owned and -operated service centers. The first airplanes, now known as Citation Is, went for $695,000 and came with pilot training and a three-year airframe warranty. Today some 7,000 Citations of various types are flying, with one of them—the now-discontinued Citation X—capable of Mach 0.935. The Hemisphere, a 0.90-Mach, 4,500-nm, fly-by-wire large-cabin twinjet, is in development. You don't hear so many "Slow-tation" jokes any more.

500FJ

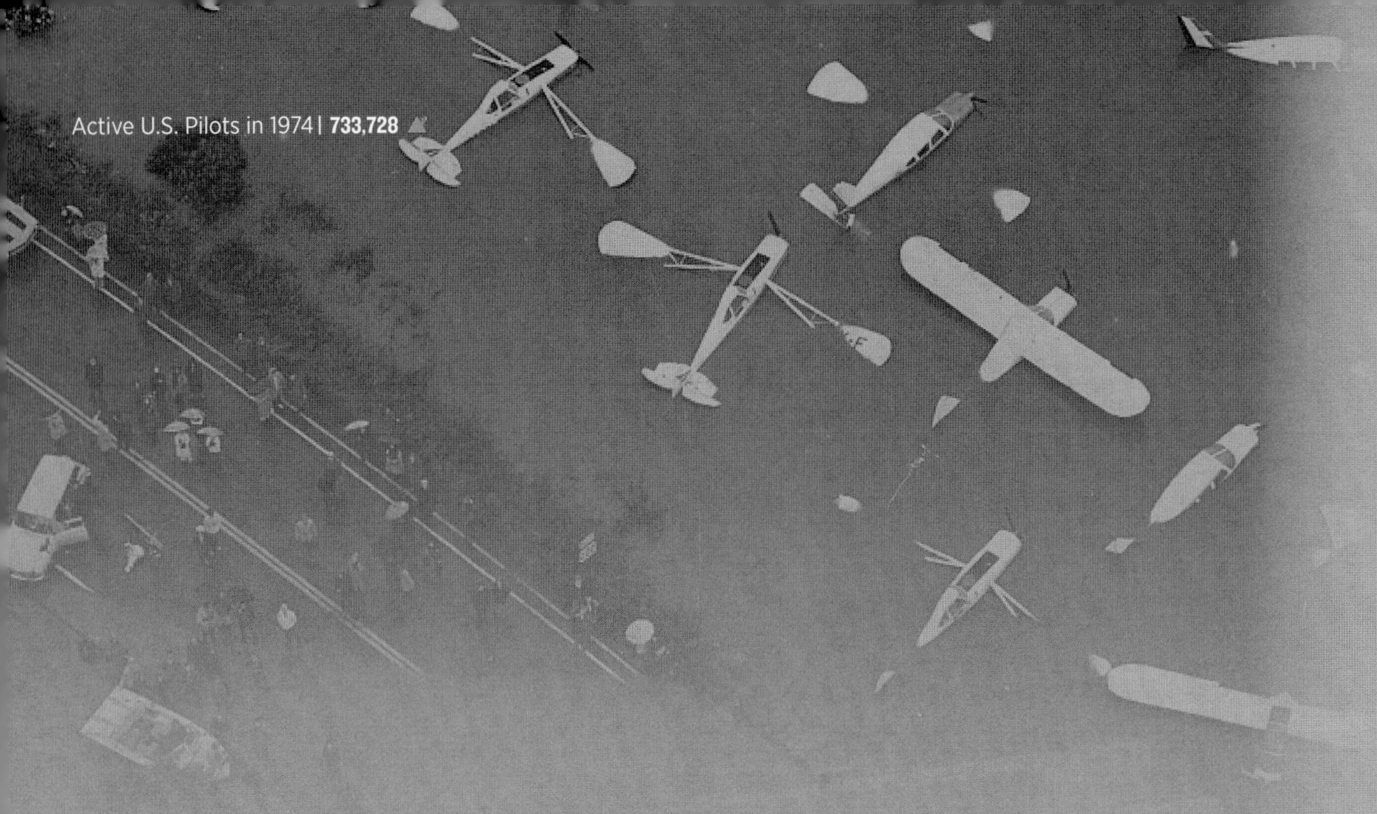

Washed up

Piper closes up shop in Pennsylvania after an epic flood

In hindsight, it may not have been the best decision to locate a major aircraft manufacturing plant near a river known to flood. Although, to be fair, a hurricane was such a remote possibility it was likely never considered a risk.

Hurricane Agnes in June 1972 is still lore in much of the mid-Atlantic and western New England, and the 100-year storm crippled Piper's manufacturing facility in Lock Haven, Pennsylvania.

Nestled on the banks of the western branch of the Susquehanna River, Piper's manufacturing facility saw 16 feet of water, enough for the company to call it quits in central Pennsylvania and consolidate manufacturing at its Vero Beach, Florida, plant. Although some suggest that Piper's Vero Beach plant had opened as a result of Agnes, the company had been building airplanes there since 1957.

Closing Lock Haven was a blow for the Comanche line of aircraft. Already on a downward trend, the Comanche tooling was so severely damaged in the flood that Piper decided to simply halt production. In fact, according to a story in *The New York Times,* the FAA required Piper to destroy most of its tooling at the plant. Trenches were dug near the Lock Haven headquarters, and millions of dollars worth of airplanes and equipment were bulldozed in. NASA purchased 32 aircraft that had sustained less damage. In all, the hurricane did about $24 million in damage, or more than $150 million in today's dollars.

It also spelled the end of an era for the historic company, which had ironically chosen Lock Haven as its base of manufacturing and operations after a fire had forced it from its Bradford, Pennsylvania, home some 39 years earlier.

GA and the oil embargo

With fuel allotments, pilots felt the pinch

The 1973 oil embargo decision by the Organization of Petroleum Exporting Countries (OPEC) raised oil prices and brought what AOPA thought were irrational responses from the U.S. government. While automobile drivers faced gas shortages and long waiting lines, general aviation was presented with much more severe threats. It took considerable persuasive power to convince many in government and private industry that general aviation airplanes should not be lumped in the same category with recreational boats and snowmobiles, and face disastrously low allotments of avgas. In congressional testimony, Hartranft pointed out that "while general aviation has 98 percent of all aircraft, it uses only 8.6 percent of civil aviation fuels [while] 91.4 percent is used by the airlines."

The final 1973 aviation fuel allotments—based on percentages of 1972's consumption levels—worked out to 100 percent for the airlines, 100 percent for agricultural operators, 90 percent for "business" use, and a disappointing 75 percent for the category named "personal and instructional."

It was at this time that 80-octane avgas production was severely curtailed. Refineries claimed that the demand did not justify the continued production of this fuel, even though AOPA made strong arguments to the contrary. In the end, the association was able to persuade Exxon Oil Company to continue making 80-octane fuel available at FBOs in much of the United States.

ing-engine airplanes weighing more than 2,500 pounds; and for turbojet aircraft, a fee of $25 plus 3.5 cents per pound). A 7-cents-per-gallon charge was levied on all purchases of general aviation fuel. An 8-percent tax was levied on all airline tickets. Finally, a $3 ticket tax was charged on all tickets with international destinations.

It didn't take long for those in power to attempt to pilfer the trust fund. In January 1971, it was reported the FAA (on orders from the Office of Management and Budget) had asked approval for a budget plan that would divert taxes in the trust fund. Instead of being used for long-range capital improvements, the FAA wanted to use trust fund money to pay for the agency's day-to-day operating expenses. AOPA objected immediately and went to work lobbying Congress to ensure that this and any future misuse of the fund could not occur.

Thanks largely to AOPA and its allies, a bill was introduced on May 11 that would prevent the Nixon administration from using any aviation user taxes for purposes other than those intended by law. The bill passed on November 16, 1971. For the time being, it appeared that the trust fund was safe from administrative "raids." By October 1972, when Nixon was campaigning for his second term as president, the administration was able to claim that the aviation trust fund had spent $456 million in support of 896 airport construction projects. Nixon compared this with the relatively measly $75 million of annual airport expenditures before the enactment of the Airport and Airways Development Act. In addition, he noted that a planning grant program had been established under his first administration that helped fund 224 state and local airport planning projects. While true enough, there were other factors working against the full utilization of trust fund monies. One was that local governments, acting on input from concerned citizens, opposed the construction of new airports or runways because of perceived noise and safety problems. The other was that the Office of Management and Budget preferred that the trust fund be used as a means of offsetting deficits elsewhere in the federal budget.

Administration initiatives to use trust fund money to pay for the FAA's daily operating and maintenance expenses didn't abate, either. Eventually, in 1976, Congress relented. In an important and disturbing precedent, the FAA was allowed to use trust fund money to pay for the operation and maintenance of those installations and equipment

Burt Rutan

Confidence in nonsense

In the record books, but not the production line

Elbert Leander "Burt" Rutan's aircraft are unconventional, and they do the unthinkable. Two circled the globe nonstop without refueling (*Voyager* in 1986 and *GlobalFlyer* in 2005); SpaceShipOne was the first civilian rocket plane to make two successive suborbital space flights (and won the Ansari X-Prize in 2004); and the VariEze and Quickie were economical, efficient kit aircraft made from surfboard foam and fiberglass.

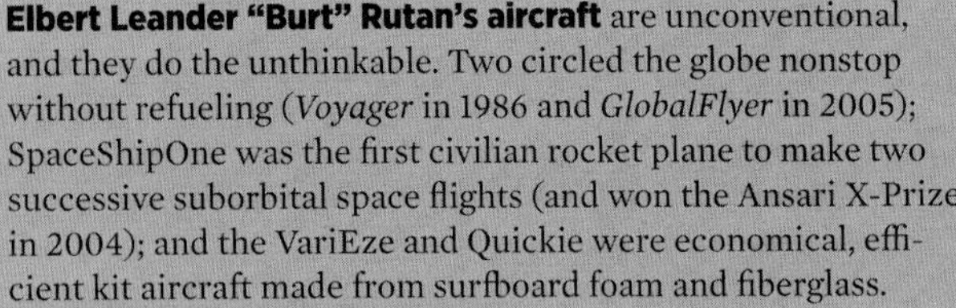

All five pioneering aircraft reside in the National Air & Space Museum, a testament to their—and their designer's—uniqueness. Rutan's designs are distinctive, yet the characteristics almost all of them have in common are flight efficiency, lightweight materials, and unusual lifting surfaces—in most cases, a movable canard in front. Few of Rutan's designs were ever FAA-certified, and none of those outside the kit industry were commercial successes.

Rutan was born in Oregon in 1943, studied aerospace engineering at California Polytechnic State University, learned to fly as a teen, and honed his experimentation skills as a civilian flight test engineer at Edwards Air Force Base in the California desert from 1965 until 1972.

He left to join Bede Aircraft and worked on the diminutive BD-5 single-seat kit airplane until 1974. Then he returned to California and started Rutan Aircraft Factory, a start-up firm that designed and marketed kit aircraft such as the VariViggen canard pusher and more refined VariEze and then Long-EZ, which became popular among homebuilders.

Rutan founded Scaled Composites in Mojave in 1982, and the company became world renowned for rapid prototyping. He also contracted with Beech in the 1980s to design the Beechcraft Starship, a twin-turboprop canard pusher that won a cult following but, for a variety of reasons, was a marketplace flop.

Rutan's fame spread when the long-winged *Voyager*, piloted by his brother Dick Rutan and Jeana Yeager, flew nonstop around the world in a nine-day marathon. The team won the Collier Trophy for that effort as well as a Presidential Citizens Medal from President Ronald Reagan.

Other notable aircraft from the prolific designer include the Solitaire glider; Defiant twin; ARES low-cost ground-attack jet; Grizzly STOL airplane; Boomerang asymmetrical twin; White Knight and Proteus high-altitude, heavy lift jets; and V-Vantage and V-Jet II, a very light jet that was a precursor of that aircraft category.

Rutan joined forces with Microsoft co-founder Paul Allen in the early 2000s to create SpaceShipOne, which also won the Collier Trophy. Virgin Galactic and businessman Richard Branson funded the development of SpaceShipTwo, a six-seat aircraft set to become a pioneer in the nascent space tourism industry.

Rutan retired from Scaled Composites in 2011, and now lives with wife Tonya in Coeur d'Alene, Idaho. But he hasn't completely left experimental aviation.

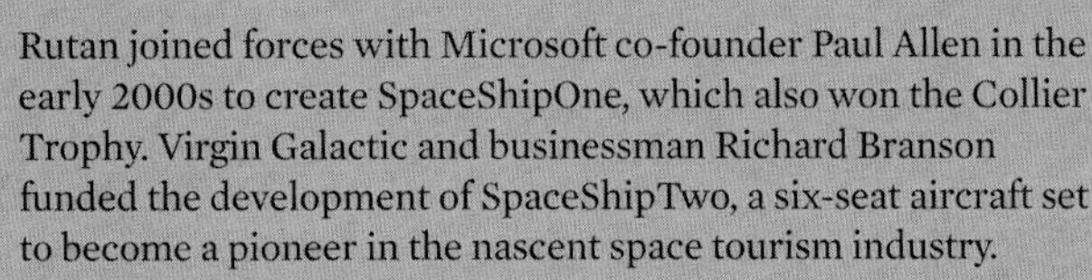

In 2015, he built and tested an amphibious, ultra-long-range aircraft called the SkiGull. He's given some public talks about the two-seat airplane, including a well-attended presentation at EAA AirVenture that year but—like so many of his designs—he said the research is being done out of his own curiosity and there are no plans to make the SkiGull a commercial product.

Rutan is a highly sought-after speaker, and one of his favorite topics is the nature of innovation. "To have breakthroughs, you must have confidence in nonsense," he said. "That's why only weird guys tend to have the breakthroughs. A sensible person won't have a breakthrough because he writes it off real quickly as nonsense and, therefore, he doesn't ever do something that's nonsense."

"USUALLY THE WACKY PEOPLE HAVE THE BREAKTHROUGHS. THE 'SMART' PEOPLE DON'T." —BURT RUTAN

Burt Rutan's unconventional designs such as the VariEze (left) and Long-EZ (back right) earned him a name in the homebuilt aircraft community. Composite construction enabled scaled flight demonstrators such as this smaller version of the Fairchild T-46 "next generation trainer," which as a subcontractor Rutan Aircraft Factory designed and flight tested.

Active U.S. Pilots in 1976 | **744,246** ▲

Pilot Bryan Allen pedaled his way across the English Channel. He later worked for ultralight manufacturer American Aerolights, then AeroVironment.

Pedal faster!

Human flight takes a new form

The environmental movement of the 1970s may not have had a big impact on general aviation as a whole, but it did spur some interesting engineering projects, including Paul MacCready's Gossamer Albatross. MacCready had previously won a purse with his Gossamer Condor, which called for a human-powered flight over a closed course. The next contest called for a human-powered flight across the English Channel, mimicking Louis Blériot's route in 1909.

For this flight MacCready's AeroVironment created what was basically wings, a canard, and a seat, all covered in plastic. The wingspan was nearly 98 feet long, yet the entire craft weighed only about 70 pounds without the pilot.

For the channel crossing on June 12, 1979, pilot and cyclist Bryan Allen pedaled for two hours and 49 minutes, covering 22.5 miles at an average altitude of about five feet.

Today AeroVironment is the U.S. military's largest supplier of small drones.

initially purchased with trust fund revenues. This was to be the first of many more trust fund raids to come.

FAA adrift

Nixon's second administration had brought new officials to DOT and the FAA. John A. Volpe resigned as DOT secretary and was replaced by Claude S. Brinegar, formerly an executive of Union Oil Company of California. Shaffer was replaced by Alexander P. Butterfield, the former deputy assistant to the president, as FAA administrator.

Butterfield faced difficulties from the start. In early 1973, the annual report required by the Airport and Airways Development Act criticized the FAA for a lack of long-range planning in the implementation of new projects. Once in office, Butterfield began advocating the levying of administrative fees for pilot certificates and written examinations. This raised considerable adverse comment from AOPA as well as other aviation user groups. (At one point, proposals called for a $17 charge for all written exams and as much as $157 for the issuance of a commercial, airline transport pilot, or certificated flight instructor certificate.)

Butterfield had not endeared himself to general aviation interests when he also began to speak of abolishing the Office of General Aviation Affairs. All of this, plus Butterfield's comment about general aviation airplanes in terminal airspace ("If you ride a bicycle, don't drive on the Beltway") started the new administrator off on the wrong foot.

Butterfield wasn't on very good terms with the executive branch, either. The Watergate scandal was in high gear by 1973. Butterfield had tried to spare Nixon any embarrassment by shelving a request to retain his military benefits (Butterfield was a U.S. Air Force colonel and pilot, with experience in the Vietnam War).

But on July 13, 1973, Butterfield dropped a bombshell during an investigative hearing of the congressional

Watergate committee. He recalled that while he was a White House aide for the Nixon administration, he knew of a taping system that recorded all presidential conversations. This was big news, and the controversy over the taping system and its recordings—or, more precisely, its erasures—went a long way toward Nixon's eventual resignation as president.

Under the burden of constant administration scrutiny, Butterfield resigned as FAA administrator in March 1975. In the same month, William T. Coleman succeeded Brinegar as secretary of DOT. Coleman helped establish guidelines to ensure that programs funded by the trust fund followed a logical path of implementation.

The House aviation subcommittee of the Public Works and Transportation Committee agreed, noting in an October 1975 hearing that it wanted an authorization for the next five years of $3.125 billion for airport development; 15 percent of this amount was to be earmarked for general aviation airports. These figures represented an increase of 140 percent over the airport expenditures of the past five years. But while construction projects were taking place with the help of the trust fund, not all the money was being used; by 1977 the trust fund had an uncommitted balance of more than $3 billion.

On the agenda

In 1977, John L. Baker was first named senior vice president, then president of AOPA. Baker had advocated for general aviation in his role as assistant administrator of the FAA's Office of General Aviation Affairs, but resigned when he realized the FAA under Butterfield was becoming more and more adrift.

The growing concern over airport noise provided Baker with his first challenges. The balance in the trust fund was steadily growing past the $4 billion mark and faced

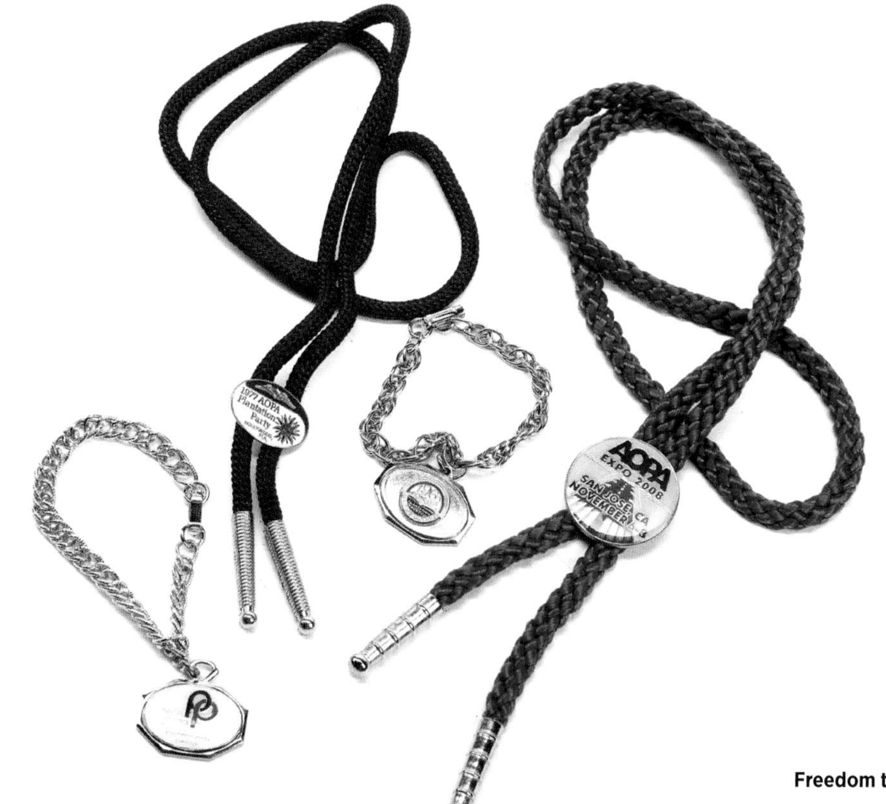

Bolo ties and bracelets, customized for each annual convention, became popular mementos.

Active U.S. Pilots in 1977 | **783,932** ▲

VAN'S AIRCRAFT RV-3

The design that launched 10,000 builds

The sleek, diminutive RV-3 was the first clean-sheet design that designer Richard VanGrunsven brought to market—but it wouldn't be the last.

The all-metal, low-wing, tailwheel aircraft became a sensation, and it spawned a series of two- and four-seat designs that have made Van's Aircraft far and away the most popular kit manufacturer in the world. More than 10,000 Van's Aircraft kits have been completed and flown—and although the RV-3 is the least numerous among them, it's the most influential.

The RV-3 incorporated VanGrunsven's "total performance" concept of doing many things well. The RV-3 can take off in less than 500 feet, cruise at almost 200 miles an hour, and cover 600 miles on just 30 gallons of fuel. It's light and nimble in the air, and it can operate off paved, grass, or gravel runways.

In 1974, the RV-3 competed in a real-world efficiency contest that measured both high- and low-speed performance and won by a large margin. Nothing else was even close.

Over the years, the RV-3 has developed an almost cult following among Van's Aircraft purists who see it as a no-compromise expression of VanGrunsven's design intent.

The first one built by the famously droll and understated designer is housed in the Experimental Aircraft Association's museum in Oshkosh, Wisconsin. The 800-pound airplane has a thinner airfoil than subsequent designs, no counterweights on control surfaces, a mechanical flap lever, and enough interior space to accommodate its 6-foot, 3-inch designer.

The original RV-3 had a 125-horsepower Lycoming engine, but most builders chose more powerful Lycoming O-320 models of 150 or 160 horsepower. The first RV-3s also came with a single fuel tank in the fuselage, but later versions had a pair of 15-gallon fuel tanks in the wings.

When kit buyers clamored for a second seat, VanGrunsven added a tandem seat with the RV-4. When kit buyers asked for side-by-side seating, he introduced the RV-6.

When they asked for a "real back seat" and more baggage and fuel capacity, he designed the tandem RV-8. And when they wanted a similarly proportioned, side-by-side airplane, he produced the RV-7. Requests for a four-seat airplane led to the RV-10, and customer demand for a Light Sport aircraft resulted in the RV-12.

Van's Aircraft naming conventions are confusing—but the RV-3's influence on future designs is obvious. The RV line consists of all-metal, stressed-skin, low-wing designs with fixed landing gear, bubble canopies, and horizontally opposed four- and six-cylinder engines. Flying characteristics across all models are remarkably similar with a light, well-balanced, responsive control feel.

VanGrunsven cracked the code for producing sporty, efficient, versatile aircraft—and the RV-3 formed the mold that his subsequent designs have followed.

increasing efforts to divert its monies into unauthorized projects. The latest challenge came from the airlines, which wanted a 25-percent reduction in their trust fund contribution so that they could use the money for retrofitting their airplanes to meet stricter noise standards. Baker immediately asked for a 25-percent reduction of general aviation's contribution. The airlines dropped their plan.

Baker also called on new FAA Administrator Langhorne Bond and DOT Secretary Brock Adams for "zero-based regulating." This was an initiative designed to review all FARs, evaluate them for cogency in light of current trends, and translate them into plain English so that they could be more easily understood.

AOPA spent the better part of 1977 and 1978 on a number of campaigns: to eliminate the aircraft use tax, to urge federal assistance be given to all public-use airports, to keep National Weather Service offices and FSSs from being closed down, to urge the consolidation of Parts II and III of the *Airman's Information Manual* into a single volume, and to lobby for an end to manual updates of the National Ocean Survey's two-ring instrument approach plate binders in favor of bound volumes that are thrown away with each revision cycle. To better represent members at the state and local levels, AOPA in 1978 established a network of regional representatives.

Because the Airport and Airway Development Act is up for renewal every five years, AOPA began to argue early for changes to the 1980 version of the law. AOPA

A helicopter for everyone

Frank Robinson transformed the rotorcraft world

Helicopters would never be considered an economical machine to operate. But before Frank Robinson and his innovative R22, R44, and R66 designs, they were out of reach for all but the wealthy and large corporate operators.

Robinson's designs focused on two key factors—cost and weight. Through his work at Hughes, Bell, Cessna, and Kaman, Robinson became transfixed with the idea of developing a light, affordable helicopter that could be used for training and smaller operators. He launched his company in 1973 out of his home, and only two years later had test flown the first R22 prototype at the Torrance Airport in California. Certification and deliveries came in 1979, and the era of the helicopter for everyone was born.

Although some deride the light weight and low-inertia main rotor, the R22 and R44 have some excellent design characteristics, including maneuverability and a highly responsive tail rotor. Moreover, the relatively low acquisition and operating costs mean more pilots can learn to fly helicopters, and even individuals can enjoy the challenge and joy of vertical flight.

Many had tried before, but the Robinson R22 was the first certificated helicopter that was relatively affordable to fly and own. By bringing down the cost and complexity, Frank Robinson opened up an entire segment of aviation to people who previously couldn't experience it. Even with new entrants on the market today, the R22 remains the world's most popular training helicopter, and has marked the beginning of thousands of careers.

ADVANCED
HELICOPTER
CONCEPTS
R22

Joseph B. "Doc" Hartranft Jr., AOPA president 1952-1977

'Our Doc'

AOPA's first employee led the association through its first four decades

He was AOPA member number 2, the association's first employee, AOPA president from 1952 to 1977, and chairman of the AOPA Board of Trustees from 1977 to 1985. Joseph B. "Doc" Hartranft Jr. led the association through wartime and peace, and through decades of challenges. His influence touched everything from the words pilots use to the markings on runways.

Hartranft learned to fly at Roosevelt Field, Long Island, New York, as a teenager. He eventually earned a commercial certificate with multiengine and instrument ratings, logging more than 17,000 hours of flying in more than 50 years.

Before AOPA's founding, Hartranft pioneered airborne newsgathering by flying newsreel cameramen over his hometown of Philadelphia to earn money for college during the Great Depression. In 1933, he founded the National Intercollegiate Flying Club (NIFC) while attending the University of Pennsylvania. Today it's the National Intercollegiate Flying Association (NIFA). He also founded the Cloudcombers, the University of Pennsylvania's flying club.

Hartranft helped found AOPA in 1939 as a young college graduate, and for several years he was the association's only full-time employee. As war loomed, he helped demonstrate the value of civil aviation; and after the attack on Pearl Harbor, he helped civilian pilots get back into the air.

Hartranft focused on airports early and often, starting with airport clean-up and painting projects. He proposed marking runways with magnetic headings, the system used today.

When pilots had difficulty obtaining affordable insurance, he worked with Lloyd's of London in 1946 to reduce pilot personal accident and liability insurance 20 to 40 percent.

Hartranft led AOPA's development of the basic VFR and IFR radio frequency plans for GA to alleviate congestion on VHF communications channels. He prepared the first pilot's manual on how to use the VOR electronic navigation system, and helped originate the word "unicom."

He formed the AOPA Foundation, which is today's AOPA Air Safety Institute, to promote safe flying. Hartranft also helped create public television's *A.M. Weather* program, which formerly aired every weekday morning on Public Broadcasting Service stations with a look at U.S. weather affecting aviation.

As AOPA had become the voice for general aviation in the United States, Hartranft realized that GA needed a voice at the international level as well. With GA representatives from Australia, Canada, the Philippines, and South Africa, he founded the International Council of Aircraft Owners and Pilots Associations (IAOPA) in 1962.

He retired from the board in 1990 and was named emeritus board member in 1998. He died in 2002 at age 86.

noted that the first Federal Airport Aid Act (enacted in 1946) set aside $1 billion for the construction of 6,000 airports. AOPA pointed out that since the trust fund was enacted in 1970 some $3.5 billion had been spent for airport improvements, but fewer than 3,000 airports had realized any benefit. AOPA called for extending the program for improvements but demanded that all designated airports (air carrier and general aviation) receive all earmarked trust fund money.

A series of midair collisions, a burst of technological innovations to meet this danger, a rapidly expanding number of pilots and airplanes in the airspace system, a profusion of bureaucratic overtures to give the impression of dealing with the strains of growth, and a propensity to spend and plan foolishly—or inadequately—marked the government's methods of dealing with civil aviation in the 1960s and 1970s. AOPA succeeded in representing general aviation interests at a time when big government began to listen only to big industry. The insensitivities, ignorance, and empire-building instincts that superimposed DOT over FAA affairs in the first place would remain alive and healthy in the 1970s and 1980s.

AOPA had demonstrated its expertise and political savvy in dozens of battles in the mid-twentieth century. And pilots took notice. At the end of 1969, AOPA membership stood at 141,000 and was still climbing. By the end of the 1970s AOPA was more than 245,000 members strong, and would need that power in the decade to come. While more than 18,000 new airplanes had been delivered in 1979, and AOPA could count on building on its tradition of representing member interests, the 1980s would bring challenges and opportunities of a kind unimaginable to observers in 1979. AOPA membership would continue its growth, and AOPA itself would continue to reorganize to better, and more quickly, represent member interests.

6.

THE FOREMOST ADVOCATE

Into the 1980s with a sense of purpose

AOPA faced the 1980s with a greater sense of purpose than ever before. At no other time in its history did the association propose more initiatives, provide more member services, or represent the interests of general aviation more effectively. This is the decade when AOPA and its employees would take their places among the most influential groups not only in Washington, D.C., but also in state and local political scenes.

To more effectively deal with political challenges in Congress, AOPA in 1980 formed its Political Action Committee (PAC). PACs became the principal means for lobbying organizations to contribute to political campaigns following the passage of the Federal Election Campaign Act of 1971. This legislation was designed to provide accountability for political contributions. As a result, PACs were formed by virtually all groups with interests in congressional initiatives. Today, AOPA's PAC ranks among the top 100 PACs in Washington, with funds substantial enough to contribute to many key members serving on aviation and transportation committees.

The first major political challenge of 1980 was to continue to manage the problems associated with the San Diego midair collision. The FAA's inclination was to impose wide-ranging airspace restrictions on general aviation pilots. AOPA countered with a specific plan for the San Diego area—a proposed redesign of the San Diego terminal control area (TCA) that would have provided climb and descent corridors for arriving and departing aircraft.

Considerable effort was invested by AOPA in designing a horseshoe-shaped TCA that was both easy to manage in terms of ATC workload, and easy for pilots to understand and comply with. Unfortunately, the FAA turned a deaf ear and instead established a confusing patchwork of airspace over San Diego.

Commentary on federal fiscal policy also occupied much of AOPA's time in 1980. Congress allowed the Airport and Airway Development Act to lapse in 1980, leaving the question of FAA funding to be handled by a supplementary authorization of money. This was a disappointment for AOPA, which had been lobbying hard for an additional provision to the 1980 act that would exempt large commercial airports (those able to fund their own improvements) from eligibility for trust fund money. But, largely because of AOPA's input, the supplementary authorization carried a sweetener: The user tax on noncommercial aircraft (the $25-plus annual tax, based on an aircraft's weight) was

Active U.S. Pilots in 1980 | **827,071** ▲

In 1983, AOPA executives appeared on more than 115 television and radio shows, and news from the association filled more than 100,000 column inches of space in America's newspapers. The association was becoming more visible to all segments of the population.

dropped from the books in exchange for an increase (from seven to 8.5 cents per gallon) in federal avgas taxes.

With the Airport and Airway Development Act in suspended animation, the trust fund drew the FAA's attention as a source for additional funding. The FAA requested $1.3 billion from the trust fund. It received $525 million.

It would need every penny, because serious problems were just around the corner. Ever since the summer of 1980, the Professional Air Traffic Controllers Organization (PATCO), the controllers' union, had threatened a strike. Just as ominous was a growing number of ATC radar computer outages. In 1979, some 873 failures occurred to the nation's aging system of IBM 9020 ATC computers. The airspace system was strained to capacity, mainly because of the growth of commuter and regional airlines, which came about as a direct result of the 1978 deregulation of the airlines.

The FAA had a plan for modernization—known as the National Airspace System Plan (NAS Plan or NASP)—but it also had delays in research and development, with politicians involving themselves in technical matters, and an administration concerned about a growing budget deficit. It all added up to a frustrating lack of progress.

The foot-dragging on modernization did the aviation community no favors when PATCO controllers finally did strike on August 3, 1981. On that day, close to 13,000 of the nation's 17,000 air traffic controllers refused to work, leading to the cancellation of 7,000 flights in the summer travel season. Two days later, President Ronald Reagan fired those who did not return to duty—more than 11,000 controllers. Reagan made sure fired controllers would never return, implementing a lifetime ban on rehiring the strikers. The controller workforce now comprised approximately 5,700 nonstriking controllers, 3,000 controller supervisors, and 800 military controllers called up for this special assignment.

Newly appointed FAA Administrator J. Lynn Helms (a former Piper executive who took over from Langhorne Bond on April 15, 1981) took measures to restrict the flow of air traffic. The General Aviation Reservation (GAR) program was put into effect on October 19, 1981, and was to remain in effect for the next two years. This program put quotas on the number of IFR general aviation flights in each ATC center's airspace. Initially, Helms decided on a daily six-hour ban on general aviation IFR flights. He called AOPA on October 6 to apprise the association, but by the end of the day Baker, with the support of the General Aviation Manufacturers Association and the National Business Aircraft Association, convinced Helms to switch to a flow-control method. This allowed for a certain amount of operations per hour, similar to what's used today during periods of intense traffic, such as EAA AirVenture at Oshkosh and the Super Bowl.

Baker did not leave it at that. On October 29, he appeared before the House Public Works and Transportation Committee, where he asked its chairman, Representative James J. Howard (D-N.Y.), for hearings to

The FAA's first IBM 9020 computer became operational at the Los Angeles ARTCC in 1970. A decade later, on the cusp of the personal computer revolution, the National Airspace System was still running on the same, now-antiquated computers (left). The strains of the nation's aging infrastructure and the growth of regional airlines after their 1978 deregulation came to a head when PATCO controllers staged a strike in 1981 (above).

Sean D. Tucker

Aviation zealot

Tucker's energy is palpable

A word often associated with aerobatic airshow pilot Sean D. Tucker is "intense." That's for a good reason—not only does Tucker maintain a rigorous physical fitness routine and do things such as climb Mount Kilimanjaro (twice) in his spare time, but he also practices his airshow routine three times a day during the season and his precious aircraft is disassembled, inspected, and rebuilt before each season. His solo routine was also intense—in his 13-minute "Sky Dance," Tucker performed maneuvers stressing to nine positive Gs and seven negative Gs; he flew at speeds up to 280 miles per hour; and a signature move was to fly straight down, tail first, at 100 mph. He retired from solo aerobatic performances at the end of the 2018 airshow season.

Tucker started flying at 17, even though he was afraid of crashing, and began a crop-dusting venture in his hometown of Salinas, California. Taking on aerobatics once he discovered "you could roll an airplane without falling out of the sky," Tucker has never looked back. But he gives back—he established the Bob Hoover Academy in Salinas to introduce at-risk teenagers to flight. He is an honorary Thunderbird and Blue Angel and has been enshrined in the National Aviation Hall of Fame. The second recipient of AOPA's R.A. "Bob" Hoover Trophy in 2017, Tucker also has served as chairman of EAA's Young Eagles Program.

Composite construction had made strides since the all-composite Windecker Eagle achieved FAA certification in 1969. The Rutan Voyager, constructed of lightweight graphite-honeycomb composites, set a new world closed-course distance record in July 1986 (right) before completing the first nonstop, nonrefueled flight around the world on December 23, 1986.

determine if equal access to the airspace system was being provided to all users. Of particular concern was the network of understaffed and underequipped flight service stations (FSS), upon which much of the burden of GAR fell.

A less expensive way to fly

The number of FAA-certificated pilots reached a peak of 827,071 in 1980. But student pilot numbers had already begun to slip, presaging a decline in the overall pilot population. AOPA sought ways to make it simpler and less expensive to fly. Concerned about the rising cost of flight training and the diminishing number of student pilots, the association in September 1981 proposed an amendment to FAR Part 61 that would allow a new type of pilot certificate: the recreational pilot certificate. Instead of a minimum of 40 hours of flight training to qualify (as with the private pilot certificate), recreational pilots would only need to have 30 hours. Under the terms of the proposal, recreational pilots would not be permitted to fly in TCAs, nor above 10,000 feet msl, nor at night, nor for hire. They would be limited to flying airplanes having no more than 180 horsepower and with fixed landing gear. Recreational pilots would be certified to fly airplanes having no more than four seats; however, recreational pilots would be allowed to carry only one passenger. The intent of the proposal was to make flying easier and more affordable. The FAA eventually published this proposal as a notice of proposed rulemaking on June 25, 1985. Although it was never widely utilized, the recreational pilot certificate set the stage for a later effort to create another more affordable entry point to flying: the sport pilot certificate.

AOPA also sought to reduce the cost of acquiring and maintaining a personal airplane. In September 1982, AOPA petitioned the FAA to amend FAR Part 23 to allow a new category of airplane—the Primary category, envisioned as encompassing airplanes with a single engine of no more than 200 horsepower and a seating capacity of no more than four. This proposal would allow relaxed certification standards so that manufacturers would be able to pass savings along to customers. It would also allow owners to perform more of their own maintenance and allow kit manufacturers to provide customers with more complete

N66430

Active U.S. Pilots in 1982 | **733,255** ▼

Washington, D.C.

Philadelphia, Pennsylvania

Bethesda, Maryland

OFFICES OVER THE YEARS

After many moves, AOPA sets up at its present-day home in 1983

AOPA's first "headquarters" were at 1424 Walnut Street in Philadelphia. It was really just a single room in a building housing the law offices of one of AOPA's founders, Alfred L. "Abby" Wolf. Joseph B. "Doc" Hartranft Jr., AOPA's first—and then, only—employee worked there.

In mid-1939, Hartranft moved to Chicago, where he could be near the offices of the Ziff-Davis Publishing Company, in the Transportation Building at 608 South Dearborn Street. At the time, Ziff-Davis published *Popular Aviation* (later to become *Flying* magazine), and AOPA published its first newsletter as an insert in the September 1939 issue of *Popular Aviation*.

AOPA's publishing activity continued in Chicago, but in 1940 AOPA set up its first administrative office in New York City, at 415 Lexington Avenue. AOPA's Air Guard had its offices there as well. From September 1942 to November 1945, AOPA's offices were in the Carpenter Building, at 1003 airplanes. (Kit manufacturers would not have to adhere to the traditional rules of the Experimental category that require builders to complete at least 51 percent of the work of assembly.) The Primary category proposal remained in limbo at the FAA before it was implemented a decade later.

Safety programs

The makeup of the pilot population had changed since the 1960s and 1970s. More pilots were instrument-rated, which meant less demand for the weekend flight training clinics the AOPA Air Safety Foundation had been providing. ASF responded by striving for overarching goals that would benefit the entire pilot population.

Archie Trammell, aviation educator and former editor of *Business and Commercial Aviation* magazine, became ASF's executive director in December 1980, replacing William R. Stanberry. Trammell began many ambitious nationwide programs, among them seminars on the use of weather radar, safety seminars on the most common problems during aircraft operations, and the mailing of VFR- and IFR-oriented safety pamphlets to virtually all certificated pilots in the United States. The publication *Flight Instructors' Safety Report* was expanded in size and distribution. Trammell also began ASF's Flight and Technology Laboratory, which investigated safety problems, such as the failure rates and modes of vacuum pumps—and a system-by-system evaluation of the Cessna 210, one of the most popular and capable single-engine airplanes. The film *Stall/Spin: Classic Facts and Myths* was produced in 1981.

To give an idea of the scope of ASF's work: By the end of 1981, ASF had held 82 weather radar seminars, 51 operational seminars, 184 weekend ground school sessions, and revalidated more than 9,000 flight instructors' certificates through scores of flight instructor refresher clinics.

Landmark research in human factors was begun in the mid-1980s and culminated, under the leadership of ASF Director of Operations Russell S. Lawton, in the publication of three aeronautical decision-making manuals in 1986.

Ralph Nelson was called back into service as executive vice president of ASF in late 1983, and he was succeeded in 1987 by retired Admiral Donald D. Engen, a former member of the National Transportation Safety Board, former Piper executive, and former FAA administrator. Engen's tenure, which ran until 1992, was distinguished by the establishment of the Emil Buehler Center for Aviation Safety and the development of its general aviation accident database. This database covers all general aviation accidents since 1982. Buehler, a New Jersey real estate executive, funded the center with several generous grants—the first amounting to $100,000. Using data from the accident database, ASF began a Human Factors Research department to provide information that made ASF's flight training programs even more relevant and safety-oriented. Vital grant-funded research on pilot judgment culminated in ASF courses and training manuals. This landmark work has since proven that pilot judgment can, indeed, be taught.

Engen also expanded the foundation's fundraising efforts. This helped bring about several publications, films, and videotapes directed at the issues surrounding single-pilot IFR operations. He also created the ASF's board of visitors—a group of general aviation notables who provide the foundation with ongoing technical guidance and financial support.

Airspace in review

The year 1982 was critical to the aviation community, not just because of the lingering effects of the controllers' strike, but because of the National Airspace Review (NAR)—a

K Street, NW, Washington, D.C. In November 1945 the association moved to D.C.'s International Building, at 1319 F Street, NW, followed by a September 1947 move to the Washington Building at 15th Street and New York Avenue, NW.

A growing staff, including personnel working on the "AOPA Section," the new title of AOPA's insert in *Flying*, prompted a move to the more spacious Keiser Building at 4644 East-West Highway in Bethesda, Maryland. In April 1972 headquarters moved two blocks away to the Air Rights Building at 7315 Wisconsin Avenue, where AOPA rented two floors in this high-rise structure. By the way, the Air Rights name had nothing to do with aviation or AOPA's advocacy. The building was constructed over a railway. The building's developers bought the "air rights" above the railway in order to build it.

In May 1983, AOPA moved to its current location at 421 Aviation Way, on the Frederick, Maryland, Municipal Airport. An adjacent building at 411 Aviation Way, built by Avemco Insurance, is also owned by AOPA, and now houses the AOPA Air Safety Institute and AOPA's You Can Fly Academy.

The number of FAA-certificated pilots peaked at 827,071 in 1980. But student pilot numbers had already begun to slip, presaging a decline in the overall pilot numbers.

THE POWER OF ONE

The birth of single-engine turboprops

Before the 1980s, the word "turboprop" usually had the adjective "twin" before it. After all, conventional wisdom went, how could you sell a turbine-powered airplane without the redundancy and safety of a second engine? Yet the idea of a certified single-engine turboprop persisted, with proponents touting the reliability of turboprops and the economy of a halved fuel burn and maintenance costs.

Beechcraft was the first to put its toe into the market. In 1982 it designed and flew its first BE-38P Lightning prototype. The five-seater used a Beech Baron B58P fuselage, Bonanza B36TC wings, and was powered first by a Garrett TPE-331-9 engine, then a 550-shaft-horsepower Pratt & Whitney PT6A-40. A 275-knot maximum cruise speed was advertised, along with a 1,200-nautical-mile range. Beechcraft sent out newsletters hyping the program and began taking deposits for the Lightning. But when the projected sales price reached the $1 million mark, the Lightning was canceled in 1984. Only two airplanes were built.

Cessna's Caravan also had its first flight in 1982, and a 2,100-plus production run began in 1984. The first model 208 Caravans had a 675-shaft-horsepower Pratt & Whitney PT6A-114A engine. Subsequent model 208B variants were stretched, made into cargo-hauling versions (FedEx bought 300 Cargomasters), given 10 to 14 seats, and amphibious floats were even offered. Aftermarket modifications of the Caravan offer 850-shaft-horsepower engines, and an Oasis option gave the normally utilitarian Caravan a luxurious leather interior. With a maximum cruise speed of 180 knots it was no speed demon, but this was the airplane for those needing to economically haul a big useful load (up to 3,300 pounds) over short distances. Or for a cult-like owner-flown community, to simply make a statement.

The Socata (later Daher) TBM series of six-seat single-engine turboprops, with more than 900 sales, has earned reputations as the Ferraris of single-engine turboprops. The first of the TBMs, the TBM 700, came out in 1990 and uses the 700-shaft-horsepower Pratt & Whitney PT6A-64 engine. Subsequent versions of the same basic design have undergone a number of weight and power increases (using the 850-shaft-horsepower Pratt & Whitney PT6A-66D), along with airframe, avionics, and interior improvements—including an aft flushing lavatory with hard doors. The latest versions—the TBM 910 and TBM 930—have maximum cruise speeds of 330 knots and maximum ranges of 1,730 nautical miles. For many, TBMs are the ultimate in personal transportation.

The Pilatus PC-12, introduced in 1994, was the last of the pioneering batch of turboprop singles. With a maximum cruise speed of 270 knots, it's slower than the TBMs, but makes up for it in cabin volume. Its interior can be configured for up to nine passengers in the executive configuration, which accounts for most of the PC-12's 1,600-plus deliveries. Later, PC-12NG models have the large-screen Honeywell Apex avionics suite. A "combi" interior allows for a combination of passengers and cargo; a high-density seating arrangement is available for charter use; and, if you remove the seats, the load can be all cargo. The PC-12's forward airstair door and large aft cabin door give it an airliner-like appeal. Its multirole capabilities make it a favorite for fractional operators, medical transport, military, and other uses.

Cessna Caravan

Socata TBM 700

Patty Wagstaff

'First Lady of Aerobatics'

Finding her place on the podium

Like the woman who set the records before her—Betty Skelton—Patty Wagstaff is the modern-day First Lady of Aerobatics. She won the award named in Skelton's honor six times from 1988 to 1994. Wagstaff was the first female on the U.S. National Aerobatic team (a six-time member) and the first woman to win the National Aerobatic Championship—and she did that three times.

Like Skelton, Wagstaff faced gender bias; aerobatics and the airshow circuit were a male-dominated field. The pressure drove Skelton to retire early (turning, ironically, to auto racing), but Wagstaff persevered.

She did not start flying until she was 30. Wagstaff was involved in a bush flying accident in Alaska when she realized she could learn to fly better than her hapless pilot. Her father had let his daughter take the controls of his DC–6 long ago when he flew as a captain for Japan Airlines, and she and her sister Toni had grown up around flying. Wagstaff took to the sport with zeal, earning her ratings quickly and competing in her first aerobatic competition just three years into her 30s.

She is famous for her signature maneuver, performing multiple vertical snap rolls. Her Goodrich Extra 260 is on display at the Smithsonian; she's been enshrined in the National Aviation Hall of Fame; and she won aerobatics' highest honor, the International Council of Air Shows Sword of Excellence. Today she teaches aerobatics at her school in St. Augustine, Florida. She's fought fires with Cal Fire and helped save wildlife in Kenya. Of her groundbreaking entry into the male-dominated world of flying she has said, "Do you think the airplane knows—or cares?"

program begun by Helms to reevaluate NASP with an eye to better traffic flow management and a redesign of the nation's airspace structure. It was NAR that made the first mention of "Model B" airspace—a concept that would come to life in 1984 as the airport radar service area, or ARSA. NAR also introduced the FAA's first plans to implement a microwave-based landing system (MLS) as the future replacement for the then-traditional ILS.

AOPA objected to the thrust of NAR for several reasons. For one, NAR's data were inconsistent with NASP's previous assumptions and projections. Moreover, the plans revealed a lack of coordination; relied on technologies and equipment that were not yet proven (e.g., MLS); and ignored the existing capabilities of satellite technology to provide navigation, communications, ATC, and search-and-rescue services. In addition to these shortcomings, the proposed NASP reconfiguration would require a disproportionately high tax package—some $50 billion over the next 10 years.

"ANYONE CAN DO THE JOB WHEN THINGS ARE GOING RIGHT. IN THIS BUSINESS WE PLAY FOR KEEPS." —ERNEST K. GANN

The lighter side

At the same time that AOPA's energies were devoted to the future of the airspace system, the association also had to recognize a new phenomenon that burst upon the scene in the early 1980s: ultralights. These lightweight, Dacron-and-aluminum aircraft began as crude, powered hang gliders but had evolved by 1981 to the point where a growing number of designs held a strong attraction for many who wanted a simple, economical means to fly recreationally. Some informed guesses put the number of ultralight aircraft at 10,000.

But for all the exuberance of ultralight designs and their enthusiasts, the activity was characterized by a lack of direction and leadership, and fraught with damaging rivalries among manufacturers. Recognizing that ultralight aviation was undeniably a part of general aviation, AOPA and ASF stepped up to the challenge of making ultralight flying safer and better represented in regulatory circles. In April 1982, AOPA formed an ultralight division and began to provide what would become a membership of more than 13,000 pilots with a bimonthly magazine, *Ultralight Pilot.*

ASF formed FAA-approved ultralight pilot competency programs, a program establishing training standards for ultralight pilot instructors, a program for registering ultralights, and an accident reporting program. These programs were administered by ASF's John Ballantyne, a well-known and accomplished hang glider and ultralight pilot. By the summer of 1983, ASF would earn from the FAA an exemption to FAR Part 103 (the rules governing ultralight flying) to allow two-place ultralight designs to be used for dual instruction. This went a long way toward improving the sport's rather dismal accident record.

Hampered by a lack of utility, negative media reports, and business failures, ultralight flying went into sharp decline by late 1984. Ultralight Division membership levels fell as drastically as the activity levels of the sport at large. In December, ASF transferred its ultralight programs to the U.S. Ultralight Foundation, an independent organization.

Pressure from the top

Elizabeth H. Dole became secretary of transportation in February 1983, succeeding Drew Lewis, who had served as Reagan's DOT secretary since 1981. (Neil Goldschmidt, 1979 to 1981, had succeeded Brock Adams and preceded Lewis.) Under Dole's leadership, the DOT sought a wider role in FAA affairs, to the dismay of both AOPA and FAA officials. One of her March 1983 initiatives was a plan to consolidate the nation's 311 flight service stations into 61 automated sites. AOPA was quick to point out that this amounted to circumventing the will of Congress, which had ordered that no consolidation was to begin until automated sites were fully in place, which they were not. AOPA went a step further and insisted that consolidation not take place until the automated stations were providing service equal to or better than that of the manned stations they replaced. For the time being, the FSS consolidation issue was on hold, awaiting further development and refinement of the software, computers, and other

PIPER MALIBU

A single landmark

Occasionally there's an airplane that fits a niche so perfectly, it endures. Although its beginning wouldn't have indicated such a long and successful history, subsequent updates and improvements have made the Piper Malibu a unique and capable airplane.

Like Apple's iPhone, which wasn't the first pocket computer with a phone but came to define the device, the Piper Malibu wasn't the first pressurized single-engine airplane, but its great design, pinpoint niche, and capable performance numbers have come to define this small segment for decades.

Mooney's M22 was first, coming to the market in the mid-1960s. By all measures the airplane was a failure, selling fewer than 10 a year over its five-year run. The Cessna P210 came as an evolution of the already popular 210 airframe. The P210 sold well and is still coveted by some pilots, but any time a design is adapted to fit a new role there are trade-offs.

The Malibu is different. It's a clean-sheet design that bested the P210 by 20 knots on the same fuel flow, and boasted an impressive 1,550-nautical-mile range. Although a true cabin-class airplane, the cabin is tight, but a rear clamshell door and club seating gave the airplane a certain comfort factor and panache the Cessna couldn't match.

Shortly after first deliveries in 1983, mechanical problems threatened to doom the design. Long before running an engine lean of its peak exhaust gas temperature was an accepted practice, Continental specified that the Malibu TSIO-520-BE be run well lean of peak. Whether the engine wasn't built properly to handle this environment, or whether owners ignored the advice is debated. Regardless, dozens of engine problems plagued the design early on. In fact, a failed cylinder on one airplane that resulted in a fatal accident brought a halt to manufacturing in 1998. An instructor was killed and his instrument student survived with serious injuries. The student sued and was awarded more than $32 million, at that time the largest settlement ever awarded in an aviation case to a single plaintiff.

Piper relaunched the airplane as the Malibu Mirage later that year with a Lycoming TIO-540-AE2A, among other changes. While the Mirage recorded much better reliability, the airplane also lost 500 miles of range, which has now rebounded to a range of more than 1,300 miles. With the introduction of the M600 turboprop, Piper now classifies the Mirage as the M350, featuring a Garmin G1000 panel and an array of modern safety features.

More than 35 years later, the Malibu/Mirage/M350 is the only certified pressurized piston single-engine airplane still in production—a niche it dominates.

hardware that would deliver FSS specialists from their antiquated teletype reports and blizzards of paper weather charts.

The remainder of 1983 saw AOPA successfully prevent yet another proposal to close FSSs (this time, 75 stations were threatened) and prevent a nighttime curfew on operations at Westchester County Airport in White Plains, New York. Less encouraging was the FAA's proposal that would establish test sites for the first airport radar service areas at Austin, Texas, and Columbus, Ohio. ARSA rules required that pilots establish communications with controllers prior to entering this airspace—but did not mandate the use of transponders. The FAA set a 30-day period aside for comments about this proposal, and AOPA argued—successfully—that in the interest of fairness, the period should be extended to the usual 90-day time frame. AOPA lent its tentative approval to the ARSA concept but expressed reservations that the increased workload on ATC could easily translate into delays and denials of entry into ARSA airspace. In the end, AOPA was proven correct. By 1986, 62 ARSAs were in place (and 26 more proposed), and complaints of restricted access, delays, and misunderstandings between pilots and controllers were widely reported by AOPA members.

FAA Administrator Helms resigned his position on January 31, 1984. Michael Fenello served as acting administrator until he was replaced on April 10, 1984, by Engen, the retired U.S. Navy vice admiral and former NTSB member. Shortly after Engen assumed his new duties, AOPA, other aviation user groups, and aircraft manufacturers responded to NTSB recommendations concerning the prevention of aircraft misfueling by endorsing the use of fuel filler restrictors on turbine aircraft and fuel filler placards.

Fight for access

If safety was at the forefront of concern at this time, the issues of airport capacity and access were, too. The pressures of deregulation were growing. More airplanes were seeking access to a fixed number of airports. Some felt that the answer to overcapacity was to deny general aviation access to certain major airports, even though federal funding carries with it the obligation to accept all classes of users. At John F. Kennedy International Airport, La Guardia Airport, Washington National (now Reagan National) Airport, and Chicago's O'Hare International Airport, auctions of landing slots were proposed, and People Express

Airlines even recommended that general aviation flights be prohibited at major urban airports during peak periods. Needless to say, AOPA argued strenuously against these sentiments, citing the federal funding obligations.

Baker, in testimony before the Senate transportation subcommittee in September 1984, stated the problem succinctly by saying, "The existing airport capacity problems are the direct result of unrestrained scheduling practices by the airlines." Baker went on to say that "airlines schedule up to 180 percent more flights at peak periods than airports can physically handle." In addition, Baker argued that general aviation traffic at major airports had actually declined, saying, "Since the August 1981 air traffic controller strike, general aviation traffic declined between 10 and 46 percent at five of the six busiest airports served by the airlines." This, Baker said, "along with the social decision made 15 years ago not to invest in the building of new airports and runways," was the real reason for the capacity problems.

AOPA urged the FAA to establish an office to monitor traffic in terminal areas, install more ILSs, provide more airport improvement program funds to outlying reliever and potential reliever airports, build more runways at existing airports, and designate more military airports as joint-use civil/military facilities. To date, these recommendations have been largely ignored, even though the FAA changed the emphasis of NASP and created the National Plan of Integrated Airport Systems, or NPIAS, to ostensibly put more effort into airport development.

A reassuring development took place in January 1985, when Engen announced that he did not envision consolidating all 311 FSSs into 61 automated sites. Instead, he advocated keeping 52 conventional stations in addition to the automated facilities, of which the first were commissioned in February 1986 at Cleveland and Dayton, Ohio, and Bridgeport, Connecticut.

Baker, in his 1985 annual report to members, acknowledged several of AOPA's more important contributions in the preceding year. Citing the growing importance of work by AOPA's regional representatives (organized later in the year under a dedicated headquarters staff in AOPA's Office of State Affairs), it was reported that the association successfully fought against the installation of tall towers near airports

John L. Baker, AOPA president 1977-1990

GA's fighter

Baker established a more aggressive political tone

It's safe to say that general aviation would not have thrived to the extent it has without the efforts of AOPA's John L. Baker. During his 13 years as AOPA president from 1977 through 1990, Baker faced down numerous threats to GA in his 13 years at the helm. His successes established a more aggressively activist tradition for AOPA—a tradition that benefited all GA pilots.

Baker, a U.S. Air Force fighter pilot, served in the Korean War in the 51st Fighter Group—a unit that suffered the deaths of all but two of its original members. He earned the Distinguished Flying Cross, the Air Medal with six oak leaf clusters, and sustained chronic back injuries as a result of ejecting from a crippled fighter. After the war, he served as a gunnery instructor at Nellis Air Force Base.

After the Air Force, Baker returned to Nebraska and earned a law degree at Creighton University, then started his long career in Washington, D.C. He started as a trial attorney for the Civil Division of the U.S. Department of Justice, and then served as a legislative aide on the staff of Senator Roman Hruska (R-Neb.). A stint as a lobbyist for Grumman Aircraft Engineering Corporation followed, and then Baker was named deputy director of the U.S. Department of Transportation. Subsequent jobs saw Baker working as assistant administrator of the FAA's Office of General Aviation Affairs, and as executive director of the Air Line Pilots Association.

By the time Baker joined AOPA—first as a senior vice president, followed by his selection as president in May 1977—his skill set as a Washington insider poised him to head up the association's advocacy efforts. One of his first initiatives involved establishing AOPA's legislative affairs department, with a staff located in offices near Capitol Hill. Baker also created AOPA's Political Action Committee and established AOPA's Communications Division, which centralized AOPA's media and public relations educational campaigns.

Long before the public became aware of the adverse effects of unrestrained, multimillion-dollar product liability judgments, Baker spoke out on the problem. Baker and AOPA's lobbying staff spent many days making members of Congress aware of product liability issues—setting the stage for eventual reform.

There were other landmark initiatives. One was the ongoing effort to make sure that the $4-billion-plus surplus in the Aviation Trust Fund was fairly distributed to more than 3,000 GA airports. Before Baker's presidency, it was common practice to divert trust fund money to projects unrelated to GA.

Baker identified the feasibility of creating a satellite-based navigation system—one that didn't rely on ground-based navaids. Long before GPS navigation was explored by the civil sector, Baker sought experts such as Princeton's Gerard O'Neill to advance the satellite cause.

In late 1989, AOPA's growing influence and widening member services caused membership ranks to swell to the 300,000 mark. Under Baker's leadership, AOPA's numbers nearly doubled from the time he took over as president.

John L. Baker is difficult to summarize in a single phrase. He flew fighters, but at heart saw himself as a Piper J-3 Cub driver, and he liked to build remote-control model aircraft. He was at home addressing opponents and speaking in public, but was secretly introverted, and had a sentimental streak. Those around AOPA's offices who knew him recall his many humorous asides, but he was never kidding when it came to GA's rights. As he said upon taking office at AOPA, "I have some pretty firm ideas about this business of general aviation being treated as a second-class citizen. It has got to come to a screeching halt."

Baker died in 2010 at the age of 81.

and airways in many states. The report also mentioned that AOPA successfully discouraged aviation fuel tax hikes in Arizona, Idaho, Nebraska, Oklahoma, Louisiana, and Maryland. Baker reported that AOPA's member count as of May 1985 had risen to a new high of 269,743 pilots and aircraft owners. Note was also made of the new AOPA Legal Services Plan, which made available to members a network of aviation lawyers across the country.

The Legal Services Plan, now offered as part of AOPA's Pilot Protection Services, was one of several pilot-focused products and services that debuted in the 1980s and continue in some form today. An AOPA forum on CompuServe served pilots with access to personal computers before the dawn of the world wide web; today, a robust website features news, videos, educational resources, flight planning tools, and more. An AOPA-sponsored credit card accepted for fuel at most fixed-base operations eliminated the need for members to carry gas cards in the 1980s; members now benefit from cash-back offers through an AOPA Mastercard. And the AOPA Air Power Loan presaged services provided by the present-day AOPA Aviation Finance Company.

It was also in the 1980s that AOPA stopped endorsing a single aviation insurer. In February 1986, AOPA announced its decision to terminate its agreement with Avemco Insurance Company, which had been closely aligned with AOPA for 24 years—some members had even assumed AOPA owned Avemco. AOPA later created its own insurance brokerage, incorporating the AOPA Insurance Agency in 1992.

An aging fleet

By the mid-1980s, the problems posed by growing costs of insuring newly manufactured aircraft against product liability claims threatened to choke off the nation's supply of new airplanes. The general aviation fleet at large was—and still is—rapidly aging. And where in 1979 manufacturers had been producing on the order of 18,000 new airplanes, that number had now dropped to approximately 1,700. Why? With $1-million-plus accident settlements now commonplace, each new airplane had to bear the product liability insurance premium burden for all other airplanes. Cessna Aircraft Company's chairman, Russell W. Meyer Jr., reported in 1985 that 20 to 30 percent of the cost of a new airplane reflected the cost of escalating product liability insurance.

Several senators and representatives set about rectifying this situation by proposing legislation to reform tort laws. Senator John C. Danforth (R-Mo.), Senator Nancy L. Kassebaum (R-Kan.), and Representative Dan Glickman (D-Kan.) all sponsored bills designed to curb the adverse legal climate for general aviation. Glickman's bill went so far as to ask for federal jurisdiction over general aviation product liability suits. Although these bills had been introduced into the legislative agenda, by late 1989 no action had been taken.

Other financial pressures were working against aircraft ownership at the same time. The Internal Revenue Service announced a proposal to do away with the 10-percent investment tax credit on December 31, 1985, denying prospective owners of business aircraft a considerable tax incentive. In a later congressional action (the Tax Reform Act of 1986), the investment tax credit was extended for one year, as long as aircraft purchased by the end of 1986 were put in service before July 1987.

Budget battles

In the spring of 1986, AOPA began to prepare testimony for the next reauthorization round of the Airport and Airway Improvement Act of 1982, which was due to expire in September 1987. While the association supported such programs as Doppler weather radar and the installation of more low-level wind shear alerting systems, it was more wary of the automated weather observation system (AWOS)—a system that then had shown a propensity to repeatedly malfunction. AOPA was also critical of NPIAS, stating that the exclusion of privately owned, public-use airports from funding eligibility was a major flaw: Pilots still paid into the trust fund, but many of the airports they flew from would receive no money.

Furthermore, the FAA planned for 85 percent of its $4.8-billion fiscal 1987 operations and maintenance budget to be paid from the trust fund.

The misuses of the trust fund, the lack of expertise and undue influence coming from the DOT, the over-budget and behind-schedule status of the FSS modernization effort, and the general mismanagement of other FAA modernization programs all indicated an aviation infrastructure that suffered from a lack of vision, and a lack of persistence and adherence to goals.

It all came to the fore when, in May 1986, Baker appeared before Representative William M. Lehman's (D-Fla.) House subcommittee on transportation, stating that the FAA should be removed from DOT. "Safety, technical, regulatory, and similar issues within the FAA can be better performed," Baker said, "'without an additional layer of bureaucracy to go through." It would be the first of many such appeals.

Electronic flight instrument systems such as the horizontal situation indicator in this Cessna Conquest made their way to general aviation cockpits in the 1980s. The heavy cathode ray tubes that characterized early EFISs have given way to lightweight LED displays today.

In support of another of AOPA's strong sentiments, Senator Kassebaum submitted in early 1986 a bill that would have removed the trust fund from the unified federal budget. This would have had the effect of taking the trust fund money off the federal government's general ledger, where it was used to offset the mounting federal budget deficit amassed under the Reagan Administration. The bill did not pass.

Landmark accident

As we have seen in past decades, each major aviation accident precipitates a chain of events that often results in rulemaking, and most certainly hones the aviation community's awareness of specific safety problems. For the decade of the 1980s, the midair collision between an Aeromexico DC–9 and a Piper Archer on August 31, 1986, would propel a pivotal sequence of events that would last well into the following year.

The accident took place eight nautical miles southeast of the Los Angeles International Airport in VFR weather at an altitude of 6,500 feet msl. The accident happened within the Los Angeles TCA, and the Archer pilot, whether confused by the depictions on his TCA chart or simply unfamiliar with the area, entered TCA airspace without a clearance. No traffic advisories were issued to either airplane because ATC did not observe the Piper's radar return, even though the airplane was equipped with a transponder and was squawking the appropriate code. The DC-9 collided with the Archer, killing all aboard each airplane and several on the ground.

FAA Administrator Engen responded by issuing several recommendations. AOPA endorsed many of them, including those calling for simplification and redesign of TCA airspace boundaries and dimensions, the standardization of TCA airspace, and the dissemination of specialized information and training for TCA operations. In this, ASF was especially helpful. The foundation began to hold courses on TCA procedures in cities around the nation; by the end of 1987, more than 25,000 pilots had attended these courses.

More challenges

AOPA faced another challenge in November 1987, when the FAA proposed suspending instrument approach procedures at airports relying on altimeter settings from remote sites, citing potential dangers from "nonhomogeneous weather conditions" and high terrain. This would have denied instrument approaches to more than 161 airports. By late 1987, AOPA and other user groups had convinced the FAA to drop this proposed rule, arguing that the rule was arbitrary and constrained the capacity of the airspace system to handle operations at reliever airports.

In June 1987, the Airport and Airway Improvement Act was reauthorized for an additional five years. The authorization called for annual expenditures of $1.7 billion and carried a provision authored by Representative Norman Mineta (D-Calif.) that would reduce the taxes paid into the trust fund whenever expenditures from the fund fell short of authorized amounts. At that time, the uncommitted balance in the trust fund stood at approximately $5 billion.

Another pivotal issue of 1987 concerned the proposed closure of the Linden, New Jersey, airport. A federal appropriations law contained language

GOING ON 50

The 1980s marked major milestones for AOPA

AOPA celebrated its golden anniversary in 1989 during its annual convention near Walt Disney World in Orlando, Florida. Some 60 charter members were present for the three-day event (most shown here), but absent were the men who founded the association in 1939. The 1980s had seen the deaths of founder and trustee Philip T. Sharples in 1980 and Alfred L. Wolf, the last surviving founder, one of AOPA's original trustees, and the first to propose the association's creation, in 1985.

The 1980s also were a time of transition for AOPA. In addition to a move to Frederick, Maryland, in 1983, the association saw several leadership changes. In 1985, R. Anderson Pew, who had formerly served as chairman and vice chairman of the board, was elected to chairman, replacing Hartranft. Paul C. Heintz was elected to the board's vice chairmanship. Hartranft would continue his duties as IAOPA's president until March 1989, when John Baker assumed these responsibilities.

that released the city of Linden from deed restrictions, freeing it to sell the airport property. The city wanted to sell the airport to make way for real estate development. AOPA argued—and Engen agreed—that the airport should be kept open because it received federal money and thus should continue to serve aviation users. As of this writing, Linden remains open. The eventual outcome of this issue has great significance because another 600 airports also are vulnerable to the same type of dismissal of local/federal agreements that apply to Linden.

Engen was made president of ASF in October, having resigned his post as FAA administrator on July 1, 1987. T. Allan McArtor, a former executive for Federal Express and an ex-Air Force fighter pilot, was appointed the new FAA administrator on July 22, 1987. He served until he was replaced by retired Admiral James B. Busey IV, who was sworn in February 1, 1989.

In a wide-ranging regulatory proposal, the FAA in February 1988 announced NPRM 88-2. This would have mandated the use of altitude-reporting transponders at or above 6,000 feet agl or 12,500 feet mean sea level (whichever is lower) and from the surface to 6,000 feet agl within a 40-nautical-mile radius of any airport served by terminal area radar. With AOPA's input, the final wording of the rule was softened. Instead of the originally proposed 6,000 feet, the floor was then raised to 10,000 feet msl or 2,500 feet agl, whichever is higher. Instead of the proposed use of Mode C altitude-reporting transponders within 40 nautical miles of any airport served by radar, the final rule is more specific. Mode C will be required in all TCA and ARSA airspace; from the surface to 10,000 feet msl within 30 nautical miles of a TCA primary airport; in the airspace above an ARSA to 10,000 feet msl; and within 10 nautical miles of additionally designated high density traffic airports. The new rules went into effect in stages, the first on July 1, 1989.

Active U.S. Pilots in 1988 | **694,016** ▼

Kolb Ultrastar

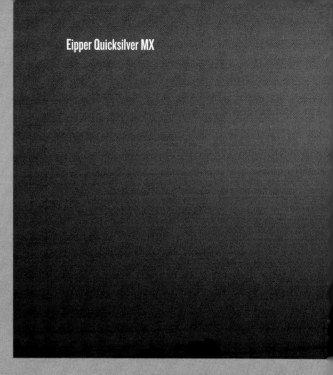

Eipper Quicksilver MX

THE ULTRALIGHT YEARS

Flying, with an independent streak

What happened when the first of the California baby boomers hit their 20s and wanted fun? If they were interested in flying, they were running and jumping off sand dunes and cliffs in hang gliders. But the flights were very short, and the trip back to the starting point was a physical and logistical challenge. By the early 1970s, they came up with the first power packs to extend their flights. A popular option was to bolt a McCullough chain saw engine to a propeller shaft. The pilot controlled pitch and bank by shifting his or her weight—like a hang glider—and the first engines were controlled by a blip switch, in the pilot's mouth. As long as the pilot had the switch clenched in his or her jaws, there was power; release the pressure and the engine quit. Controlling power meant opening and closing the switch to modulate power to achieve, say, a steady descent to a landing.

By the late 1970s and early 1980s, kit manufacturers were designing and selling a wide range of purpose-built, powered designs made primarily of aluminum tube airframes with flying surfaces of Dacron. Engines became more powerful, with some reaching 30 horsepower or more. Blip switches gave way to twist grips and conventional throttle levers. The number and style of designs and control configurations multiplied, and the ultralights phenomenon was born.

There were claims that 30,000 ultralight kits were sold. And the activity was completely unregulated. Some manufacturers and design-

Eipper Quicksilver GT500

ers lacked formal training or discipline, and responsibly, produced unsafe kit components and aircraft designs. Plus, no one knew exactly how many were out there. Ultralights were hyped as inexpensive (a typical kit might cost $3,000) and, above all, easy to fly, with the promise of the ultimate in wind-in-the-hair pleasure flying. But flight training programs were rudimentary and scarce. After all, no pilot or medical certificate is required to fly them. And an exemption allowing two-seat trainers didn't come along until 1982. Until then, an ultralight pilot's first flight was also his first solo flight. Unconventional control systems meant counterintuitive control inputs and steep learning curves, even for high-time pilots of certificated airplanes.

FAR Part 103, which finally gave the legal definition of an ultralight, came out in October 1981. It limited the aircraft to a single seat; a maximum empty weight of 254 pounds; a maximum power-off stall speed of 24 knots; a maximum cruise speed of 54 knots; and a maximum fuel capacity of five gallons. Flying was limited to day VFR conditions. Prior permission was needed before flight in controlled airspace.

Perhaps the most popular ultralight was the Quicksilver series. The first models had no ailerons and relied on elevator push rods for pitch- and yaw-induced rudder turns for directional control. Other designs were even sketchier. The Pterodactyl was a flying wing with weight shift for pitch and twist-grip controls to deflect wingtip rudders for turning. The Easy Riser was a biplane design with a similar control setup. But some had exemplary qualities, like the Lazair, with its Tedlar-covered wings; inverted V-tail; and twin, wing-mounted, 9-horsepower Rotax engines. At the peak of the ultralight phenomenon, 64 ultralight manufacturers were making 119 different models. The Powered Ultralight Manufacturers Association was formed to represent the new industry.

Ultralights were seen as a wave of the future that would bring hordes of young people into more conventional general aviation flying. In 1982, AOPA formed an Ultralight Division, complete with a registration program, training guidelines, and an accident reporting function. (Based on this effort, the National Transportation Safety Board investigated 167 ultralight accidents between 1983 and 1984. Inflight loss of control was ruled as a factor in 35 percent of fatal accidents; 26 percent were caused by inflight airframe or component failures.)

A bimonthly magazine, *Ultralight Pilot*, covered many aspects of ultralight flying; for its aircraft reports, the staff obtained 12 ultralight kits, built each of them, and then flew them. No flaw or quirk went unreported, and criticism flowed freely where needed. A rule of thumb emerged: Double the advertised time to build a kit.

At its height, the AOPA Ultralight Division had 13,000 members. EAA formed its own ultralight organization. AOPA held competitive events for ultralights at its annual conventions. EAA held a separate Oshkosh (now AirVenture) for ultralights a few days ahead of the main event.

In many ways ultralight flying's independent streak did it no favors. Whereas hang gliding became a model of self-regulation, with "Hang" ratings that standardized training and dictated which flights a pilot could undertake, ultralight pilots were slow to adopt self-regulation.

Ultralight Pilot ceased publication after its November 1984 issue, and the Ultralight Division was disbanded shortly thereafter. But for the ultralight movement, the beginning of the end came with the 1983 airing of ABC-TV's weekly *20/20* news magazine program. A segment titled "Ultralights: Flying or Dying?" showed a television news reporter on a training flight in a Pterodactyl. At approximately 1,000 feet, a wing failed, the airplane went out of control, and the reporter fell to his death. A subsequent investigation revealed that the reporter, a lapsed pilot of certified piston singles, intended to simulate an out-of-control condition for the camera by alternately pushing and pulling on the Pterodactyl's canard control surface. After the wing failed, the reporter, who reportedly was not wearing his seat restraint, was ejected. The *20/20* broadcast effectively stopped widespread ultralight flying in its tracks.

Ultralights are still flying today, are still governed by FAR Part 103, and the U.S. Ultralight Association (USUA) and American Ultralight Association (AUA) represent ultralight pilots and offer information on training, flying clubs, and safety programs.

FLYING FLOPS

Airplanes that didn't make the cut

The Beechcraft Starship looks great, was ahead of its time, and was an engineering marvel. But it was still a failure.

It may be unfair to call the twin turboprop a flop. After all, it had more modern avionics than its rival, decent performance, and a fantastic look. But cost overruns in development drove up the price well beyond the competition. The Starship cost more than some jets of the day, and was considerably slower.

Only 53 of the composite aircraft were built before production was finally halted, a terrible outcome for such a massive development program. Beechcraft was so fed up with the airplane the company purchased almost all of them back and sent them to the desert so there was no need to continue suffering through decades of support. A handful were not sold back and continue to fly.

The loser list

A small sampling from the long list of other designs that didn't make it:

Cessna 162 Skycatcher
With the 150/152 being such enduring designs, there was no reason to think Cessna wouldn't also make a hit in the Light Sport 162 Skycatcher. But a quirky design, cost overruns, and a soft market led the manufacturer to crush dozens of unsold aircraft as it scrapped the project.

Mooney M22 Mustang
The first pressurized piston single-engine aircraft made it through certification, so it's arguably successful. But as a marketable airplane, the Mooney M22 Mustang was a failure. Mooney sold fewer than 40 in the late 1960s. In light of Cessna and Piper's success with pressurized piston singles, Mooney's foray was a flop.

Windecker Eagle
Most pilots have never heard of the Windecker Eagle, and for good reason. Only two prototypes and six production aircraft were built, despite millions in development costs. The Eagle was the first certificated composite aircraft, but it never caught on commercially. Several attempts to revive the design have also failed.

The Beechcraft Starship is one of the most distinctive aircraft to ever be certified. Unfortunately development costs, performance shortcomings, and delays kept it from being a commercial success.

But if the outcome of NPRM 88-2 represented a compromise for AOPA, victory could be claimed in the case of the landing fee issue at Boston's Logan Airport. Under a plan known as the Program for Airport Capacity Efficiency (PACE), the Massachusetts Port Authority sought to exclude general aviation flights from Logan by imposing landing fees that could have ranged from $25 to $88 or more per airplane. AOPA asked DOT to rule on the legality of this move. AOPA argued that all airplanes should have equal access to the airport, inasmuch as all users pay into the federal funds that Logan uses. In November 1988, DOT's administrative law judge ruling on the case, Burton Kolko, agreed that PACE was discriminatory and ruled in favor of AOPA, setting an important precedent.

Another significant AOPA initiative potentially had the most far-reaching consequences for the future of the National Airspace System. In April 1988, Baker called on the nation's legislators and aviation experts to develop a unified, coordinated national aviation policy. The lack of such a policy had played havoc with the orderly development of the system's capacity to meet demand.

Congress had a receptive ear. On June 28, 1989, a resolution supporting the concept of a national aviation policy was entered in the House of Representatives by William F. Clinger Jr. (R-Pa.) and Dan Glickman (D-Kan.), along with 70 co-sponsors. One month later, a Senate resolution was entered by John McCain (R-Ariz.) and J. James Exon (D-Neb.). In addition, officials from the George H.W. Bush administration planned to meet with AOPA representatives. The goal: to achieve a consensus on plans for the future and to take steps toward enacting these plans into law.

Two other important victories also took place in 1989. A final rule enacting the recreational pilot certificate was made effective on August 31 of that year. And while AOPA disagreed with some portions of the new rule—principally those requiring an annual flight review for pilots having fewer than 400 hours total time—it represented an advance in the campaign to make flying more affordable for more pilots and prospective pilots.

The FAA also acted on AOPA's 1982 primary aircraft proposal, which would certify simpler, more affordable aircraft and allow owners to perform more of their own maintenance. An NPRM was issued in March 1989, outlining the scope of the Primary aircraft category. When enacted, the Primary aircraft category would complement the recreational pilot certificate in helping to make a new chapter in general aviation history.

As the 1980s drew to a close, AOPA membership continued its spectacular growth, even as total pilot numbers had plateaued. More than 280,000 active members were recorded at the beginning of 1989. As our history shows, the strength, commitment, and size of AOPA's membership remains at the core of its persuasive powers.

7.

COMING OUT SWINGING

Technology ascended, pilot numbers declined as the century closed

The transition to AOPA's sixth decade was made all the more symbolic by President John L. Baker's retirement at the end of 1990. Baker's 13-year tenure at AOPA's helm set a high bar for his successor, Phil Boyer. Any organization assumes the tone and personality of its senior leadership, and this came to the fore as Boyer took the reins. Where Baker had a background as a Korean War fighter pilot with experience in Congress, the FAA, and at the head of the Air Line Pilots Association, Boyer came to his term with a 32-year history in television broadcasting. But Boyer's world was also deeply intertwined with general aviation, having owned and flown everything from Cessna 150s to Cessna 340s in 48 of the 50 states. Early in his career he worked as an airborne traffic reporter for a Los Angeles television station. And by the time he got to AOPA, most general aviation pilots already knew him for his producing and hosting of a popular video series called ABC's *Wide World of Flying*. In short, he was a master communicator—one with an intense interest in technology in general, and avionics in particular.

He'd need every bit of that talent from day one. He put it to good use when issues with the FAA's National Airspace System Plan (NASP) came to the fore. The plan would take 10 years to modernize U.S. airspace, and more than $27 billion. That's a lot of money, but it was estimated as being only enough to cover 28 projects—and the list of projects had recently been expanded from 90 to 187. Thus began AOPA's strong advocacy for a shift to a satellite-based navigation system. It would save money, Boyer testified before congressional committees, and the global positioning satellite (GPS) system was already in place. "Review the NASP to eliminate programs inconsistent with GPS," Boyer reiterated in early 1991. "The way it is now, the FAA has just $10 million set aside for a satellite program office. That's not enough."

By the late 1980s, loran had become the latest, most modern evolution to civilian avionics. In spite of its limitations, it caught on and found its way into more and more instrument panels. Nice, but only the beginning of what was to come. Boyer kept pushing, and at AOPA's annual Expo in 1991, then-FAA Administrator James B. Busey IV told a rapt audience that "GPS would be fully operational and certified in 2010."

AOPA helped move the timeline along. The first tests aimed at GPS instrument approach capability came in late 1992 when a Nike missile system tracking radar was used to follow test approaches at

AOPA President Phil Boyer (right) and FAA Administrator David Hinson flew the United States' first operational stand-alone GPS instrument approach in Frederick, Maryland, in July 1994. At the time, fewer than half of the nation's 5,000 public-use airports were served by instrument approaches. Since then, the FAA has published close to 7,000 RNAV (GPS) approach charts, including about 3,900 providing ILS-style guidance and localizer performance with vertical guidance (LPV) minimums.

the FAA's Atlantic City, New Jersey, research facility. By then, the FAA had committed to 500 loran nonprecision approaches, up from its promise of 250 loran approaches a year before. Was "GPS In, Loran Out?" as *AOPA Pilot* Editor in Chief Mark R. Twombly wrote in an editorial at the time? Not yet, but he wasn't far off. A blizzard of ever-evolving handheld GPS units had already flooded the market by the early 1990s, and they were being snapped up by pilots in record time. It was a sign of increased appreciation of the functionality, accuracy, and situational awareness offered by GPS navigation.

What was the next hurdle? Certification of GPS for use under instrument flight rules (IFR). By 1993, the first panel-mount GPS units had hit the market, but they were not IFR-certified. Because certification testing for IFR use wasn't yet complete, pilots wanting to fly approaches and procedures under IFR had to use existing approach profiles and data—with the GPS navigation data serving in an overlay capacity.

Then came the big day. In July 1994, Boyer welcomed then-FAA Administrator David Hinson to AOPA headquarters at the Frederick, Maryland, Municipal Airport, and together they flew the first stand-alone GPS instrument approach to Frederick's Runway 5 in AOPA's Better-Than-New Cessna 172 sweepstakes airplane. The initial, intermediate, and final approach fixes were later named PHILB, DEFND, GEEAY. Get it?

IFR GPS navigation was on its way. Today, it's become the "new normal," replacing and augmenting more and more ground-based, VHF-sourced instrument approaches.

Taking stock

Of course, IFR GPS certification wasn't the only challenge facing AOPA. Far from it. It pales in comparison to a trend that was becoming ever more ominous, because all the GPS approaches in the world don't mean a thing if there's no one to fly them. Boyer cited gloomy statistics in the article "Taking Stock" in the April 1991 issue of *AOPA Pilot*: a pilot population that had declined by 125,000 in the past 10 years, and more than 1,000 public airports that had closed since the 1980s. If this steady loss of pilots wasn't reversed, general aviation would face an existential threat that would alter its fate for generations to come.

Under Boyer's leadership, AOPA Conventions became AOPA Expos, with exhibit halls, airport displays, and policy discussions from industry leaders.

POWER UP ›

Diamond Aircraft has always been an engineering-focused company. Stemming from Europe's active glider community, the Diamond designs feature high aspect ratio wings; relatively tight cockpits; and wide, expansive views. From the humble DA20 Katana (right), FAA-certified in 1994, to the fast and efficient DA62 twin, Diamond has developed more capable and enticing airplanes. Powerplant flexibility is so important to the company that when another diesel engine manufacturer folded, Diamond founded its own, Austro—something unheard of in modern times.

The modern avionics revolution began in the 1990s. Each advancement was more amazing than the last. Magellan Corporation launched the first portable consumer GPS device in 1989, the same year Garmin was founded. With a simple CDI display, the Garmin GPS 155 was the first GPS receiver to be certified for instrument approaches (below). Avidyne introduced general aviation's first certified multifunction display in 1997 (bottom). The Garmin G1000 followed a few years later in 2004 (right). For an industry used to incremental progress in avionics, these additional capabilities were astounding.

At AOPA's annual Expo in 1991, then-FAA Administrator James B. Busey IV told a rapt audience that "GPS would be fully operational and certified in 2010."

With this in mind, Boyer initiated a new AOPA program: Project Pilot. Launched in March 1994, Project Pilot was designed to boost student pilot starts—which had been decreasing for years, and had ended 1993 at 69,000, the lowest since the early 1960s. It was also aimed at getting lapsed pilots back in the air; the total number of active pilots had dropped from a high of 827,071 in 1980 to 665,069. To this end, AOPA developed Project Pilot newsletters and videos,

plus an 800-number hotline for those with questions about flight training. Project Pilot Mentor and Project Pilot Instructor programs were also developed.

The idea was for AOPA members to identify pilots as serious prospects, then volunteer one to two hours per week to encourage them to take up flight training or, in the case of lapsed pilots, to help renew their interest in returning to the cockpit. A special publication—*An Invitation to Fly*—was produced by AOPA's magazine staff for mass distribution.

The goal was to have 10,000 new student pilot signups by the end of 1994. And the Project Pilot programs came close to hitting the target, with 9,000 students and 8,000 Project Pilot mentors participating in the programs. However, the FAA's data still showed a discouraging picture, with 1994's new student pilot starts dropping by 13 percent over the previous year. AOPA responded by ramping up its efforts and beginning Project Pilot II. This brought the tally of signups in the program to 11,118 students, 10,287 mentors, and 1,200 instructors by the summer of 1995.

Other AOPA outreach programs—Fly-A-Leader, Fly-A-Reporter, Fly-A-Friend, and Fly-A-Controller, which had been in existence since 1991, augmented the Project Pilot cause by exposing influential cohorts not familiar with general aviation to first-hand experiences. And a GA Team 2000 program launched with broad industry support in 1996; the AOPA- and General Aviation Manufacturers Association (GAMA)-led program, which ultimately became Be A Pilot, sought to increase student starts to 100,000 a year by rekindling the public's interest in flying. Although many manufacturers signed on to the effort, support gradually waned as the expected boost was slow to materialize.

The Project Pilot programs continued, and by the end of 1999 approximately 30,000 pilots had been actively encouraged by 24,000 Project Pilot mentors. AOPA also joined with GAMA in the effort by donating $150,000 to Be A Pilot for its 1999 activities. Partnerships were formed with many of the other aviation alphabet groups. But student starts—and the pilot population as a whole—continued a steady drop. Clearly, something fundamental was at work at the cultural and sociological levels. Something that deflected popular interests away from flying. Countering that challenge would continue to attract a good deal of AOPA's attention over the coming years.

Project Pilot was one of many AOPA initiatives aimed at increasing the pilot population. The program formalized mentorship in the flight training process, building on the idea that having a seasoned pilot as a friend and mentor increased success. Other programs included the industrywide Be A Pilot and Fly-A-Controller.

The VLJ days

The very light jet (VLJ) phenomenon burst on the scene in the early 2000s. With single-pilot certification, maximum takeoff weights as low as 6,000 pounds, cruise speeds hovering around 300 knots, and ranges in the neighborhood of 700 to 1,000 nautical miles, they appealed to a crowd wanting to step up—way up—from piston singles and twins. In those days the hype flowed freely, with predictions that thousands of VLJs would soon create a vast aluminum overcast.

First on the scene was the Eclipse 500. Its initial sales price of less than $900,000 was wildly unrealistic and caused a buzz. But problems plagued the six-seater from the project's start in 1998. First, its original Williams engines were replaced by more powerful, 900-pound-static-thrust Pratt & Whitney PW610F engines. Eclipse Aviation, founded by ex-Microsoft executive Vern Raburn, then went into bankruptcy, obtained funding from Sikorsky and others, and in 2013 it certified the new Eclipse 550 (now at $2.5 million), which came with a high-tech panel that included autothrottles and synthetic vision. Even so, production stalled in 2015, with some 270 500s and 550s out the door. One Aviation was formed to purchase Eclipse and merge it with Kestrel Aircraft—the whole thing run by Cirrus Aircraft co-founder Alan Klapmeier. Although it has plans to certify the Eclipse 700, a slightly larger airplane, the company continues to struggle and in 2018 was placed into a managed bankruptcy.

Other manufacturers hopped on the VLJ bandwagon but met with generally discouraging results: Diamond Aircraft's D-Jet, Piper's Altaire, and VisionAire's Vantage never made it to market. But Cirrus' single-engine SF50 Vision Jet is making a strong showing among owners of Cirrus' Continental-powered SR22T models. Cessna's Mustang, a $4 million, 340-knot, 1,340-nautical-mile six-seat twinjet had its best years between 2008 and 2009, but kept a following until 2018, when production ceased.

By 2018, the market essentially turned away from VLJs. The term came to be shunned in response to the VLJs' notable performance, payload, and range compromises. In the end, customers turned to bigger, more powerful new designs with bigger payloads.

ECLIPSE 500

"LEARNING TO FLY IS ONE OF HUMANKIND'S MOST INSPIRING ACHIEVEMENTS. WHEN YOU LEARN TO FLY IT CHANGES WHO YOU ARE AND HOW YOU THINK OF YOURSELF FOREVER."

—JOHN KING, CO-FOUNDER OF KING SCHOOLS

Out of the flying business

A corollary of the declining pilot population was another major issue facing general aviation in the 1980s and 1990s—if pilots were walking away from general aviation, then so were the aircraft manufacturers.

The problem was huge, multimillion-dollar product liability settlements. Often, a general aviation crash was followed by a legal action against the aircraft's manufacturer. These lawsuits demanded compensation for design, manufacturing, or other flaws alleged to have contributed to an accident, no matter how trivial, and no matter how old the aircraft. Accidents can be tragic, and where compensation is justified it should be awarded. But the way things were by the late 1980s, there were no caps on awards, no limits on attorney's fees, and—most important—no "tail" (statute of limitations) on awards. A current manufacturer could be sued for an accident involving a 30- or 40-year-old airplane.

The situation was so bad that general aviation manufacturers claimed they could no longer afford to build airplanes. Where manufacturing peaked in the roaring 1970s, culminating with almost 18,000 airplane deliveries in 1979 alone, by the mid-1980s it had slowed to a trickle, with Cessna Aircraft Company, the biggest player in the market, ceasing production of its 152, 172, 182, 206, and 210 models altogether.

Since then, Senator Nancy Kassebaum (R-Kan.) had been submitting bills seeking to change general aviation product liability laws. She did so again in 1991, with S.B. 645—a bill that received endorsement from all of general aviation's interest groups, including AOPA. It was the sixth year in a row that bills to reform product liability legislation had been submitted in the U.S. House of Representatives and Senate. Each time, there was a failure to reach consensus. The Association of Trial Lawyers of America (ATLA) was especially effective in blocking any movement forward.

The situation dragged on until the summer of 1994. That's when Cessna Chairman and CEO Russ Meyer promised to build 2,000 airplanes in the first year after product liability reform legislation made it into law. AOPA kept up the pressure by sending out a National Pilot Alert to every one of its 330,000 members, asking them to urge their legislators to vote for product liability reform.

By twists and turns, it came to be. The key was to focus on a statute of repose, whereby no civil action for damages arising out of a general aviation accident could be brought against the aircraft manufacturer if the accident occurred more than 15 years after delivery of the aircraft to the first purchaser.

JET SET

'Turbine Pilot,' through the years

***AOPA Pilot* has always** tried to address the needs and interests of a wide range of general aviation pilots. That means seeking out stories with appeal to everyone from student pilots to high-time jet pilots. It also means covering everything from Light Sport aircraft and classic tube-and-fabric designs, to more recent piston singles and twins or Experimental-category aircraft and even warbirds and the most high-end airplanes. It can be a tough balancing act at times. But we know who our core audience is: those who fly piston singles built under FAR Part 23. By far, this segment receives most of our attention.

AOPA Pilot began devoting sections aimed at both ends of the pilot spectrum. For student pilots (and their instructors) we began "New Pilot" in August 1992. For those flying turbine-powered airplanes, "Turbine Pilot" was launched in May 1991; four times a year, additional pages were added to the magazines sent to selected members.

With the purchase of *Flight Training* magazine in 1998, AOPA instantly acquired a full-size monthly magazine targeting those learning to fly. It more completely addressed the pilot training environment, so the "New Pilot" section was retired from *AOPA Pilot* in 1999.

Later, "Turbine Pilot" articles were added to the full run of every *AOPA Pilot*, until 2010. In October 2007 and 2008, special standalone issues of *Turbine Pilot* were run for distribution around the National Business Aviation Association convention time frame.

In 2010, driven by the growth of the single-engine turboprop market, the appeal of the very light jet segment, and a new generation of advanced light jets, the section in *AOPA Pilot* became the monthly *AOPA Pilot* Turbine Edition. This version of the magazine is provided to members with type ratings in turbine aircraft; who own turbine or select high-performance piston aircraft; who hold a current Pro Pilot membership; or who have asked to receive the content. Currently, 55,000 AOPA members receive the *Turbine Pilot* edition, either in print or digitally.

A GOOD PILOT IS ALWAYS LEARNING

Resources for student pilots

Opening *AOPA Pilot* and reading about the latest airplane, an advanced instrument technique, or the ups and downs of aviation advocacy is an enriching experience. But for many student pilots the stories can be a confusing mix of technical jargon, abstract concepts, and coverage of airplanes far beyond their comfort level.

This is one reason *Flight Training* magazine was created. By targeting student pilots, *Flight Training* can explain concepts in simpler language than a student would find in a traditional aviation publication.

Started in 1988 by the Specialized Publications Company (SPC) of Parkville, Missouri, *Flight Training* was one of several training-related magazines the company published. Its owner, Gary Worden, was an avid pilot who saw an opportunity to reach students and serve flight schools.

Worden used a novel technique to distribute magazines. Although the FAA released names and addresses of student pilots, SPC went to the source. By sending copies directly to flight schools, *Flight Training* was able to gain recognition and credibility. The company also offered students a six-month free subscription, an enticing benefit to someone excited about learning to fly. The CFI also received copies when he or she recommended a student for a subscription, enabling both to use the magazine in the student's training process.

AOPA purchased *Flight Training* in late 1998, and began publishing the magazine with the April 1999 issue. The magazine provided an important avenue for AOPA to talk directly to students and it gave students access to AOPA's many resources, including a flight training hotline, flight planning, and weather.

The magazine celebrated its thirtieth birthday in 2018, a testament to its adherence to the core mission of helping students—and proof that a good pilot is always learning.

In due course, Representatives Dan Glickman (D-Kan.) and James V. Hansen (R-Utah) introduced H.R. 3087 in the House, and Kassebaum submitted her bill, S. 1458, in the Senate. This time, legislation moved with more resolve. The House bill bogged down, but longtime AOPA ally Senator James M. Inhofe (R-Okla.) filed a discharge petition, which meant that the bill would bypass the House Judiciary Committee and go straight to the House floor for a vote. It passed. On the Senate side, Kassebaum was successful in blocking all other bills and forcing a compromise among opponents of her product liability reform bill. In the end, a compromise was reached on an 18-year statute of repose and the newly minted General Aviation Revitalization Act (GARA) went to President Bill Clinton's desk, where it was signed into law on August 17, 1994.

The GARA was a mere three pages long, but Cessna and other manufacturers went back to building aircraft and hiring employees. Cessna's 172 and 182 went back on the assembly line in 1996, and the Cessna 206 in 1998. Piper Aircraft Corporation resumed building its PA-32 Cherokee Six/Saratoga, PA-44 Seminole, and PA-34 Seneca IV and Seneca V piston twins. Some credit the GARA with saving the then-financially troubled Piper Aircraft Company.

Paying in

It wasn't the first time the concept was mentioned, and it most certainly wouldn't be the last, but a proposal to privatize air traffic control services came up in 1993. Proponents of the idea argued that running air traffic control would be most efficient, and maximize economic return, if it were conducted by a private firm—not the federal government. But AOPA and other general aviation interest groups disagreed, saying that a privatized firm would have to earn a return on its investment, plus pay wages and benefits as well as federal, state, and local taxes. The current, government-operated system, set up to maximize public benefit and provide universal access to all, remained the best way to go.

This private-versus-public funding issue dragged on for years and became enmeshed with a debate on funding for the Airport and Airway Trust Fund, which is fed by airline ticket taxes, aviation fuel taxes, and air freight taxes. Forces behind privatization and user fees saw a European style of funding including landing, airway, communications, navigation, and other charges as the way to avoid what they argued could be chaos in the system. Because the trust fund's taxing authority was set to expire in January 1997, a sense of urgency pervaded their arguments.

President Bill Clinton signs the General Aviation Revitalization Act while Vice President Al Gore (red tie in back), AOPA President Phil Boyer (dark suit far right, at the corner of the desk), and other guests look on. GARA's impact on general aviation continues to be debated, but what's not in dispute is that the major manufacturers of the day restarted single-engine production as a direct result of its passage.

A privately run U.S. Air Traffic Services Corporation was advanced as a way forward. A new commission, the National Civil Aviation Review Commission, argued that unless user fees were levied there would be massive trust fund and FAA funding shortfalls, airline delays, and airport access issues. Boyer gave testimony before the commission, pointing out that under the terms of the Taxpayer Relief Act of 1997, the FAA's budget had been reduced each year of the Clinton administration, so there was no budget crisis. The trust fund kept growing at the same time the FAA's budget was curbed, and because of the spending caps, the federal budget itself was balanced for the first time since 1969.

If any additional funds were really needed, Boyer said, then more of the aviation fuel taxes could be appropriated. Aviation fuel taxes were 19.3 cents per gallon at the time, but 4.3 cents of that amount went to the general tax fund. AOPA has always argued that all of the aviation fuel tax should go to the Airport and Airway Trust Fund.

By 1999, cynicism ran high at times in the funding debate. Representative James L. Oberstar (D-Minn.) had suggested that the administration would first propose a budget with inadequate funding, then propose user fees to solve the self-created budget problems. Boyer said that "the real agenda is to evade the limits of the budget enforcement act, and spend aviation funds on nonaviation programs."

In the end, the measures proposing privatization and user fees went down in defeat. It was a success for AOPA and the rest of general aviation, but it wouldn't be the last time that these issues would surface. The federal budget comes up for renewal every year, and every year would become another opportunity for user-fee advocates to regroup and create another challenge. If

'AOPA Pilot' advertiser parties at the annual EAA AirVenture offered a chance to get in character and mingle with fellow pilots.

privatization or user fees were shot down again, the typical procedure would be to renew FAA funding once more—with minor adjustments for inflation—under a continuing resolution, then raise the issue again during the next budget cycle.

Keeping airports open

Troublesome as they were, budget issues certainly weren't the only problems facing general aviation in the 1990s. Airport issues regularly emerged. Among the first major challenges was the court settlement of a 1988 landing fee levied by the Massachusetts Port Authority (Massport) on general aviation airplanes arriving at Boston's General Edward Lawrence Logan International Airport. By 1991, the fees added up to $2.68 million. AOPA was the lead organization in securing a U.S. Department of Transportation ruling that the fees were unlawful. A program to refund the fees was put into effect; all pilots had to do was submit claims. Another discriminatory Massport initiative would have imposed landing fees at Logan based on peak-demand pricing. In times of slack traffic flows general aviation airplanes would have paid $25 per landing; during rush hours the fee would be $90. Fortunately, AOPA was central in making sure that this Program for Airport Capacity Efficiency never came to be.

Other airport-related issues drawing AOPA involvement included an Ohio airport-use tax that was reversed by Ohio legislators; the FAA's exemption of general aviation airplanes from the strictest-security areas at major airports, which allowed easier ramp access; the denial of a building permit for a proposed McDonald's restaurant site in a runway clear zone at the Oxnard, California, airport; and the reversal of yet another building permit for a movie theater complex that would have encroached on Republic Airport in Farmingdale, New York. Incredibly, a 197-foot-tall hotel—topped by a tower with an ornamental lighthouse—was proposed for a site near Boston's Logan. It would have been more than 100 feet taller than the FAA's own 95-foot height limit. These and other building proposals were reversed thanks to AOPA's newly established Department of Regional Affairs, fed by information from AOPA's new Airport Support Network—a nationwide program with volunteer observers at local airports.

Airport closure initiatives had become the other top-line concern by the mid-1990s. Local pressures to close such airports as Atlantic City, New Jersey's Bader Field/Atlantic City Municipal; Fall River, Massachusetts's Municipal Airport; and California's Reid-Hillview of Santa Clara County Airport arose; and

The first new production Cessna 172 after the passage of the General Aviation Revitalization Act rolled out of the Independence, Kansas, factory in November 1996 and was delivered to Sharon Hauser, winner of AOPA's 1995 sweepstakes prize.

Unknown to much of the general aviation market prior to the development of the PC-12, Swiss manufacturer Pilatus created a hit with the turboprop single in the early 1990s. With pressurization, competitive speed, and great useful load, the PC-12 offered many advantages over the other single-engine turboprops of the day. Pilatus stayed true to form and ensured the PC-12 could handle unimproved strips with ease.

The prolonged battle to preserve Reid-Hillview brought a young airport advocate to the attention of AOPA leadership in the early 1990s. Bill Dunn's bulldog tactics ultimately brought relief to the historic field and brought Dunn from California to AOPA headquarters in Maryland as vice president of airports where he continued to battle for airport protections across the nation. Although he has officially retired, he continues to support AOPA as a contractor, leading the charge to save the Santa Monica airport, and working with airports to assure fair and reasonable access for pilots.

Boyer made fighting these closures one of AOPA's biggest priorities. Conventional wisdom at the time held that general aviation airports were closing at a rate of 50 per year—almost one per week.

One particularly troublesome airport closure conflict involved Chicago's Merrill C. Meigs Field Airport. Even though Meigs supported 54,000 operations per year, created 1,500 jobs, and provided $57 million in annual economic contributions to Chicago, Chicago Mayor Richard Daley was set on closing Meigs. He wanted to build a park on its grounds, even though his administration had accepted four federal airport aid grants for Meigs since 1986. These grants were worth $1.2 million, and carried with them the provision that the money must be applied to maintaining and improving Meigs in the name of the public good.

AOPA's Department of Regional Affairs reacted by meeting with 50 elected representatives of communities neighboring Meigs, forming a support group—Friends of Meigs Field—and sending mailings to 11,000 AOPA members in Illinois encouraging action against the proposed closure. In spite of this, Daley briefly closed Meigs. But thanks to AOPA's pressure on the Illinois legislature it was reopened in February 1997. Moreover, the legislature's proviso required that Meigs remain open for five more years, and that it install an instrument approach, make runway repairs, and extend its tower's operations to midnight (it closed at 10 p.m. previously). For the time being, it looked like AOPA had saved Meigs.

As for Reid-Hillview, AOPA acted by working with state and local leaders, plus San Jose Mayor Susan Hammer and the FAA's San Francisco Airport District Office. The task: to reverse the Santa Clara County Board of Supervisor's 20-year stand to close Reid-Hillview. It worked, using tactics that once more pointed out that by accepting federal grant money, an airport must continue operating to the benefit of the taxpayers who help finance it.

Under pressure

Other moves also threatened general aviation interests. A 1990 amendment to the Clean Air Act could have prohibited leaded-avgas-burning engines later in the decade. This amendment could have had the practical effect of grounding some 195,000 piston engines in the general aviation fleet. AOPA argued against the move, inasmuch as avgas accounted for only 2.3 percent of all aviation fuel, and represented just 0.3 percent of all gasoline sales. Fortunately, the Environmental Protection Agency said in 1991 that aviation engines were not affected.

Members facing onerous and pricey airworthiness directives (ADs) benefited from still other AOPA actions. After unexplained crashes of Piper PA-46 Malibus, for example, the FAA grounded the airplane from flying in instrument meteorological conditions, turbulence, and icing while also prohibiting the use of its autopilot. AOPA successfully argued that more specialized training in the slippery, technologically

advanced high-performance airplane was the proper answer to the problem—not a 60-item special certification review.

Then there was an AD calling for initial and repetitive corrosion inspections of certain Lycoming O-320 and O-360 engine crankshafts, plus mandatory replacement of the crankshafts within five years. Over the years, this would mean some $10,000 in repair cost burdens to owners of those engines. With AOPA's influence, the AD was changed to much less expensive internal, visual inspections for inner-diameter corrosion pits, followed up by dye-penetrant inspections if any pits were found.

Of course, AOPA's influence in the rulemaking area also brought member benefits. To enhance drug interdiction enforcement, the FAA proposed that pilots pay for a new airman certificate with an embedded photo. In congressional testimony, AOPA President Boyer argued that a driver's license or passport photo could serve as acceptable photo substitute, and pilots could keep their existing certificates. Soon enough, the FAA signed off on the idea.

Another big opportunity to serve member interests came in 1997, with a rewrite of FAR Part 61—the rules covering pilot certification. Thanks to vigorous AOPA input, several rules were changed without sacrificing safety. One was the elimination of the requirement to log 125 hours before becoming eligible to earn the instrument rating; now, newly minted private pilots could pursue the instrument rating immediately after passing the private checkride. For student pilots, another rule change made 150 nautical miles the new minimum distance for a long cross-country; before, it was 300 nautical miles. For pilots with the new recreational pilot certificate, additional training would serve as the official go-ahead to fly cross-country; before, recreational pilots could fly only 50 nautical miles from their point of departure. Last but not least, the rules for those with instrument ratings to earn instrument proficiency were changed. The requirement to log six hours

Saving an airport is a long game. AOPA often fights for decades to ensure an airport stays open. With Merrill C. Meigs Field in downtown Chicago (left), the fight was especially brutal. AOPA worked with user groups, the city, the state legislature, the FAA, and Congress to try and preserve one of the few remaining downtown city airports. The association won a hard-fought victory in 1997, but more trouble was on the horizon.

of actual or simulated instrument time in the previous six months was eliminated. Now, the requirement is to perform six instrument approaches, holding patterns, and interception and tracking of navigation courses. Credit for performing these and other maneuvers in a flight training device or simulator was also granted.

Another rulemaking effort sprang from the nation's war on illicit drugs. Ever since the 1980s, more drugs were being flown into the United States via general aviation airplanes coming from, or through, Mexico and the Bahamas. In 1998, Representative Paul Coverdell (R-Ga.) added a rider to, of all things, an anti-tobacco smoking bill (H.R. 3858) that would allow the interception and forcedown of any suspected drug flights. Obviously, this carried the potential for misidentification, or worse, for many innocent pilots returning to the United States. This wasn't a new idea. In the 1980s a bill was introduced with provisions for the U.S. Coast Guard to shoot down any general aviation airplanes suspected of smuggling illicit drugs inbound from the Bahamas. It didn't make any headway, thanks to AOPA's influence. And the Coverdell rider didn't either. AOPA's Legislative Action office, together with Senator Inhofe, contacted Coverdell to talk things over. Later, in a conference committee meeting, the forcedown provision was eliminated.

One of the 1990s' last discriminatory moves was the FAA's "On the Spot" enforcement action proposal. It amounted to a traffic-ticket-style ramp check, whereby an FAA inspector could immediately write up, and begin the administrative steps, of an enforcement action. AOPA countered by saying that such an action could affect a pilot's insurability, employment, and future enforcement actions—all without due process. The situation was resolved when the

Thanks to AOPA's pressure on the Illinois legislature Meigs Field was reopened in February 1997. For the time being, it looked like AOPA had saved Meigs.

FAA agreed to skip the idea and agreed to giving pilots a 30-day time frame to respond to any charges.

Into the new millennium

Does history repeat itself? When it comes to recent general aviation history, the answer is a resounding "yes." The effort to enact user fees to finance the FAA's annual budget would present annual challenges. Under the Clinton and George W. Bush administrations there was a strong effort to curb budget deficits and control the cost of government—so much so that President Clinton put budget caps in place, and otherwise tried to curtail spending. Clinton's spending caps worked wonders at the macro scale; the budget was balanced for the first time in 28 years.

But the caps didn't work well for the FAA, because of the rising costs associated with the development of the future NextGen air transportation system, flight service station modernization, airport improvements, and the highly advertised demands created by rising levels of air traffic. With budget caps, the FAA said that there wouldn't be enough money to carry out these projects without finding funds elsewhere. That, in brief, is what drove the idea of levying user fees as a way to circumvent budget caps.

MEETING MEMBERS WHERE THEY ARE

AOPA evolves with the internet

AOPA has always sought to meet its members where they are, including on the digital frontier, before pilots knew much about it.

In the mid-1980s, the association hosted a forum on the CompuServe Information Service, but not enough members had personal computers at the time for it to take off. That had changed by January 1993, when AOPA Online was launched on CompuServe. CompuServe software offered a graphical user interface that foreshadowed today's web browsers. Jeppesen also briefly hosted an online service for AOPA.

As computers became ubiquitous and broadband internet slowly became available, AOPA Online transitioned to the web. The first iteration of its website, in 1995, was a single page with the association's address and phone number—common in those days. But the site quickly grew, and a comprehensive AOPA Online went live December 20, 1995. AOPA's CompuServe presence was rolled in during March 1996.

That original site faced a challenge, however. "There was actually a cybersquatter who had reserved aopa.org," said Seth Golbey, then AOPA's director of internet services and AOPA Online's first webmaster. Instead of paying a hefty ransom to gain control of its desired domain address, as many businesses were doing, AOPA became one of the first companies to challenge the squatter, and win.

The website grew, adding news and *AOPA Pilot* articles, then other resources. The organization was a pioneer in using integrated data online, and online commerce. "It was clear that automating some of the processes could save the association a lot of money," Golbey said. Early on there were essentially two websites, one for members and one presenting information to the public; members could seamlessly transition between them. A members-only section was introduced in 1997; more than 27,000 members registered in the first four months.

Golbey credited Phil Boyer for the association's technological leadership in this era. "We were an early adopter, and I think a lot of the credit in that regard goes to Phil. He was visionary and was willing to take some risks," Golbey said.

AOPA's digital philosophy also led to the creation of the weekly *AOPA ePilot* email newsletter, which published its first edition on Friday, October 29, 1999. It was joined by *AOPA ePilot Flight Training*—intended for student and new pilots—in December 2001. Nineteen years after *ePilot* debuted, the two newsletters had nearly 300,000 subscribers.

Soon after the terrorist attacks of September 11, 2001, airmen who had received proper briefings found themselves flying into temporary flight restrictions—some issued with very little notice. To increase awareness of these "pop-up" TFRs, AOPA began emailing airspace bulletins to members, advising them of temporary flight restrictions. AOPA used georeferenced address data to deliver these bulletins to members based on their distance from the TFR's location.

TODAY'S CHECKLIST

Preflight.
Dial 1-800-GO2-AOPA
Claim your free membership kit
Install AOPA customized software
Get a free month & 10 FREE Hours!

Take Off!
Click onto AOPA ONLINE's Icon
Retrieve Jeppesen WX Map
Generate/File Flight plans with EMI
Retrieve Fillup Flyer Fuel Finder reports
Enjoy 24-hour access to the AOPA Forum
Conference with G.A. Leaders
Talk with Pilot Magazine editors
Browse AOPA's extensive libraries
Get information on buying or selling a plane
Connect with the world from one source

Break the Information Barrier with AOPA ONLINE and Get 10 Free Hours — Plus a Free Month of CompuServe!

For instant access to the latest weather reports, N-Number registration database, AOPA's Aviation USA Airport Directory, calendars of aviation events, fellow pilots and members and more aviation information than you knew existed, climb aboard AOPA ONLINE. And there's no need for a separate on-line service for your non-aviation needs — AOPA has teamed up with CompuServe to bring you the whole wide world in one, easy-to-use service. Best of all, you can try it all now, absolutely free for a month. News, stock quotes, travel services, e-mail, movie reviews, and lots more. In fact, you get 10 free hours online to access over 3,000 products and services including AOPA ONLINE — FREE!

Then break the information barrier permanently for just $9.95 a month. Then you'll get 5 free hours online each month so you can access AOPA ONLINE! Whether you're a computer whiz or a complete beginner, join your fellow AOPA members right now and take off for the future. Just call 1-800-GO2-AOPA today!

CompuServe
AN H&R BLOCK COMPANY

AOPA ONLINE

Call 1-800-GO2-AOPA
and connect with the world from one source!

In the era of dial-up internet, AOPA Online offered 10 free hours plus a free month of CompuServe. Bruce Landsberg (right) led the production of AOPA Air Safety Foundation programs and publications such as DVD courseware and the *Joseph T. Nall Report*.

SAFETY TO GO

Safety programs evolved with the times

Bruce Landsberg came to the AOPA Air Safety Foundation as executive director in 1992. An aviation marketing and safety executive, flight instructor, and writer with experience at the Cessna Aircraft Company and FlightSafety International, Landsberg continued the foundation's tradition of providing a high volume of quality safety information and initiatives to every segment of the general aviation pilot population.

Under Landsberg, the Air Safety Foundation played an increasing role in general aviation safety education, and ASF management served on FAA, NASA, and other special committees to provide technical and educational expertise from a general aviation perspective. ASF took the lead in safety issues such as runway incursions, operations at nontowered airports, and the challenges associated with the transition to GPS navigation. Other research addressed such issues as personal computer-based training devices.

ASF decided to lay the groundwork to expand its offerings with a variety of online safety programs on topics including weather, airspace, runway safety, and radio communication. Thus, ASF began to develop interactive online courses, videos, webinars, quizzes, and publications, which made it possible for pilots to brush up on their aviation knowledge, no matter where they were.

Missing from this vast lineup were the programs that employed flight training as part of the curriculum. In 1992, ASF discontinued flight training as part of its traveling "road show" of courses. Costs were prohibitive, liability became an issue, and it was determined that ASF wasn't reaching as many pilots as it could or should. Some flight training programs were still conducted on a contract basis with such agencies as the FBI and other law-enforcement organizations.

AOPA took the lead in pointing out that money for these projects was already available in the Airport and Airway Trust Fund (AATF). The AATF, funded by aviation fuel taxes, airline ticket taxes, and cargo fees, was building a then-$8 billion (and growing) surplus. Trouble was, money in the trust fund—intended to be held in trust and used solely for aviation purposes when needed—was sometimes diverted and used for nonaviation efforts.

The answer, endorsed by Boyer in numerous appearances before Congress, was to "unlock" the trust fund, meaning that it should be brought out from under any spending caps and used to augment the FAA budget to meet the needs of modernization.

A bill sponsored by Representatives Oberstar and Bud Shuster (R-Pa.) of the House Transportation and Infrastructure Committee, sought to unlock the trust fund in their AIR-21 (Aviation Investment and Reform Act for the Twenty-First Century) bill and free it for spending. This would guarantee that all trust fund money would be spent on aviation, and that FAA budgetary needs would be met—at least in the short term. At first, the bill wasn't accepted by the Senate and faltered in 1999. A renewed push to move AIR-21 forward came in early 2000, and AOPA supported it.

In a victory for all of general aviation, Clinton signed AIR-21 into law on April 5, 2000. It was designed to provide the FAA with $40 billion over the next three years, with $3.2 billion for airport improvements in 2001 (a 64-percent increase over the previous year's amount) and $10.1 billion over the following three years. Until the following year's budget cycle began anew, user fees were out of the picture. Even so, by the end of 2000 there were more calls to privatize the air traffic control system. Running ATC as a business would be the only way to effectively deal with the rising amount of air carrier traffic and its attendant delays,

There are other airplanes with parachutes. There are other airplanes with glass panels and sophisticated autopilots. And there are other airplanes that fly just as fast with just as much payload. But combine those attributes in a package of composite skin and quality leather seats and you have the dominant Cirrus SR20 and SR22.

CIRRUS

The airplane with the parachute

"Where's the parachute?" Every pilot has heard this question. For some reason passengers love the idea of a parachute and always want to know where it is on the airplane. Many are disappointed to find one usually doesn't exist.

Cirrus owners and pilots don't have this problem. The Cirrus Airframe Parachute System (CAPS) is a whole-airplane parachute meant for saving all the occupants, a task it has excelled at since its introduction in 1998.

Being such a revolutionary invention, it's not surprising that the parachute system has defined Cirrus and its models over the years. The idea to make the parachute standard equipment on all Cirrus aircraft came after founder Alan Klapmeier was involved in a midair collision in 1985. Alan and his brother Dale Klapmeier began Cirrus in 1984 as a kit-manufacturing company with the VK-30, a composite-construction pusher design. They sold about 40 VK-30 kits, later transitioning to the Cirrus SR20.

The SR20 was certified in 1998, with the SR22 following soon after. Since then every airplane Cirrus has produced has come with CAPS standard.

Cirrus has continued to push design and safety improvements, looking more than any other manufacturer to the luxury car market for inspiration. As such, it is one of the few aircraft manufacturers to celebrate new model editions each year. The marketing strategy has been effective. In 2004 Cirrus became the biggest seller of single-engine airplanes, a position it holds most years.

The company's focus on safety also led to a robust factory-approved training program, developed in part with input from the owner community. The model's initial poor accident record saw a marked improvement as the training became more widespread. Part of that training calls for specific situations and methods for operating the parachute. This normalization of using the parachute resulted in more deployments, and thus fewer fatalities.

proponents argued. Boyer, in a letter to senators, argued that AIR-21, with its $8 billion commitment to ATC modernization over the next three years, would provide more than enough money to streamline air traffic procedures and improve runways and taxiways—the weak points that cause delays. Privatization proposals, he said, "...fail to recognize the inherent conflict between keeping safety paramount, and others' [the airlines'] interests in an economic bottom line. ATC is not a business, it's a vital safety service."

Pressure to privatize also came from the Reason Foundation, a conservative Los Angeles think tank. Its director, Robert Poole, an advisor to incoming President George W. Bush, also argued for annual fees for registering general aviation aircraft (such as $250 for a Cessna 172, and $950 for a Beech Baron) and user fees (among them, $10 for a weather briefing, $18.50 to file a flight plan).

Airport closures, user fees, ATC privatization, rules changes, the dwindling pilot population—all are issues that would follow AOPA's and general aviation's timeline to the present day. However, with the new millennium would come challenges more momentous and revolutionary than many could possibly imagine.

8.

HIGHER STAKES

Flying in the new millennium

At 8:46 a.m. on September 11, 2001, an American Airlines Boeing 767 hijacked by the terrorist group al-Qaida flew into the north tower of New York City's World Trade Center. At 9:03 a.m., a United Airlines 767, also hijacked and flown by an al-Qaida terrorist group, flew into the trade center's south tower. At 9:37 a.m. an American Airlines Boeing 757 flew into the Pentagon, and at 10:03 a.m. a United 757 crashed in the countryside near Shanksville, Pennsylvania—its flight into the U.S. Capitol building cut short by rebelling passengers. In all, the attack claimed the lives of 2,977 victims, and another 6,000 were injured.

It was one of the United States' defining moments, rivaling the Japanese attack on Pearl Harbor that began the United States' involvement in World War II. The number of dead in each attack was similar, and the 9/11 attacks also were responsible for drawing the United States into a war, this time in Afghanistan, against the Taliban and al-Qaida. Bombing of Taliban and al-Qaida camps in Afghanistan began the following month.

The United States' response to the 9/11 attacks was swift. Fighter jets were scrambled. NATO's Article 5, which deems an attack on one of its members an attack on all, was invoked for the first time. All civil aircraft flying over the United States were ordered immediately grounded at the nearest airport at 9:42 a.m. At 10:20 a.m. orders were issued to shoot down any commercial aircraft positively identified as being hijacked. Thousands of passengers—and general aviation pilots—were stranded at airports large and small across the country. That included 41,800 aircraft grounded at 282 airports within what was soon dubbed "enhanced Class B" airspace—which extended from the surface to infinity; horizontally to the extent of the Class B boundary; and would, by later in September, require ATC communications and clearances, monitoring of 121.5 MHz, and flight along defined routes.

Staff at AOPA headquarters watched the events play out the way the rest of the country did—on live television, starting with the second airplane hitting the south tower. After the shock subsided, people went into action. The prime directives were to keep all pilots—not just AOPA members—informed about changing restrictions. Some of this work was done via AOPA's Pilot Information Center 800 numbers, but AOPA's website was continually updated. In the first week after the attacks, there were more than 500,000 page hits on www.aopa.org. AOPA's then vice president of Air Traffic Services, Melissa Bailey Rudinger, was

Radar screens went dark in the hours after the attack as civilian air traffic was grounded. Some 4,500 airplanes were guided to landings in three hours, according to the National Air Traffic Controllers Association.

dispatched to FAA headquarters, where she was central in facilitating the resumption of general aviation operations.

An equally important goal was to provide a means whereby grounded general aviation pilots could return to their home airports. Some airline flights resumed on September 13, but Boyer asserted that limiting the resumption of flights to the airlines was unfair, citing the fact that airliners accounted for only eight percent of the civil aircraft fleet. As a result, limited Part 91 IFR operations were permitted the following day, provided that certain requirements were met. But national security officials reversed that decision only one hour after it was announced. This left some general aviation pilots—who thought they had taken off legally—subject to F-16 interceptions and FAA enforcement actions.

As issues cropped up, AOPA, through Boyer, Rudinger, and staff at the Frederick, Maryland, headquarters, dealt with them. For the unlucky pilots mentioned above, a "no enforcement" promise was secured from the FAA's Flight Standards Office. But no sooner than one problem was resolved, others took its place. One was the rule that created prohibited areas around each of the nation's 86 nuclear power plants. The rule was created via notice to airmen, which provided the latitude and longitude information for each plant. But the 10-nautical-mile radii around the plants were not charted visually. This set a trap whereby unwitting pilots could stray into the suddenly enacted prohibited airspace. AOPA took the initiative; its staff made the visual plots themselves, and put them on AOPA's website for all to see. Other, constant notam changes were updated in near real time and sent via email to those pilots within 250 nautical miles of an area affected by a notam or temporary flight restriction (TFR); they're still sent today as TFR airspace alert emails. In all, AOPA employees put in 8,000 hours of overtime during the first few weeks after 9/11.

It wasn't until mid-2003 that most security issues were resolved and operations, for the most part, returned to normal. But have no doubt: Things would never be "normal" again. For pilots and other Americans alike, there was life before 9/11, and a "new normal" life after. The 9/11 attacks gave us more and bigger TFRs; the Department of Homeland Security (DHS);

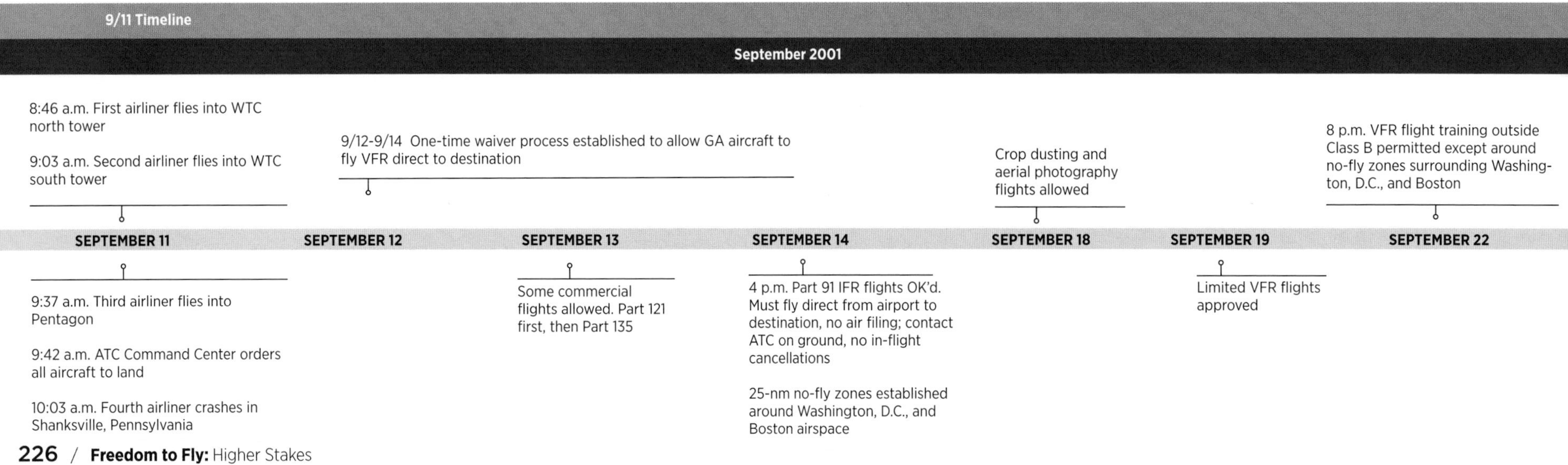
9/11 Timeline
September 2001
SEPTEMBER 11
8:46 a.m. First airliner flies into WTC north tower
9:03 a.m. Second airliner flies into WTC south tower
9:37 a.m. Third airliner flies into Pentagon
9:42 a.m. ATC Command Center orders all aircraft to land
10:03 a.m. Fourth airliner crashes in Shanksville, Pennsylvania
SEPTEMBER 12
9/12-9/14 One-time waiver process established to allow GA aircraft to fly VFR direct to destination
SEPTEMBER 13
Some commercial flights allowed. Part 121 first, then Part 135
SEPTEMBER 14
4 p.m. Part 91 IFR flights OK'd. Must fly direct from airport to destination, no air filing; contact ATC on ground, no in-flight cancellations
25-nm no-fly zones established around Washington, D.C., and Boston airspace
SEPTEMBER 18
Crop dusting and aerial photography flights allowed
SEPTEMBER 19
Limited VFR flights approved
SEPTEMBER 22
8 p.m. VFR flight training outside Class B permitted except around no-fly zones surrounding Washington, D.C., and Boston

the Transportation Security Administration (TSA); and, in the case of the airspace around the nation's capital, a special flight rules area (SFRA) with some procedures that still mimic those used in enhanced Class B airspace in the weeks after the attacks.

AOPA's job after the attacks was to do its part to help ensure that such an event could never happen again. To that end, AOPA created the Airport Watch program. This included an online video showing reenactments of suspicious behavior around airports and airplanes. This, together with an Airport Watch hotline (1-866-GA-SECURE)—established in December 2002—gave pilots guidelines for how to conduct themselves and report to authorities.

The 9/11 attacks heightened security concerns about flight training operations at general aviation airports, chiefly because some of the terrorists flying the hijacked airplanes had trained at small airports in Florida and Arizona. Consequently, new security procedures were put into effect for foreign students seeking flight training—procedures that hopefully will

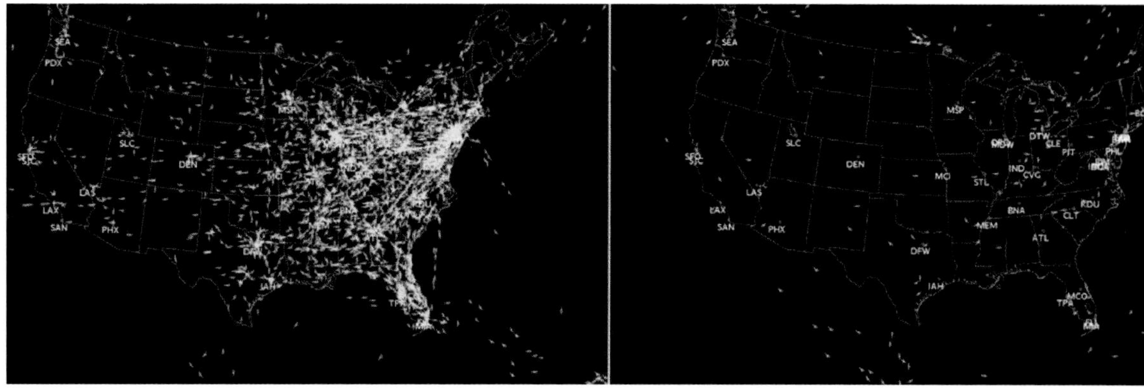

prove their worth as future deterrents. The measures include verifying a foreign student's nationality, and having the student undergo a criminal background check.

In spite of general aviation's enthusiastic cooperation in national security matters, 9/11 seemed to somehow leave a smear of suspicion. This became apparent in the tone by which a couple of isolated incidents were covered by the general press. Three examples are illustrative.

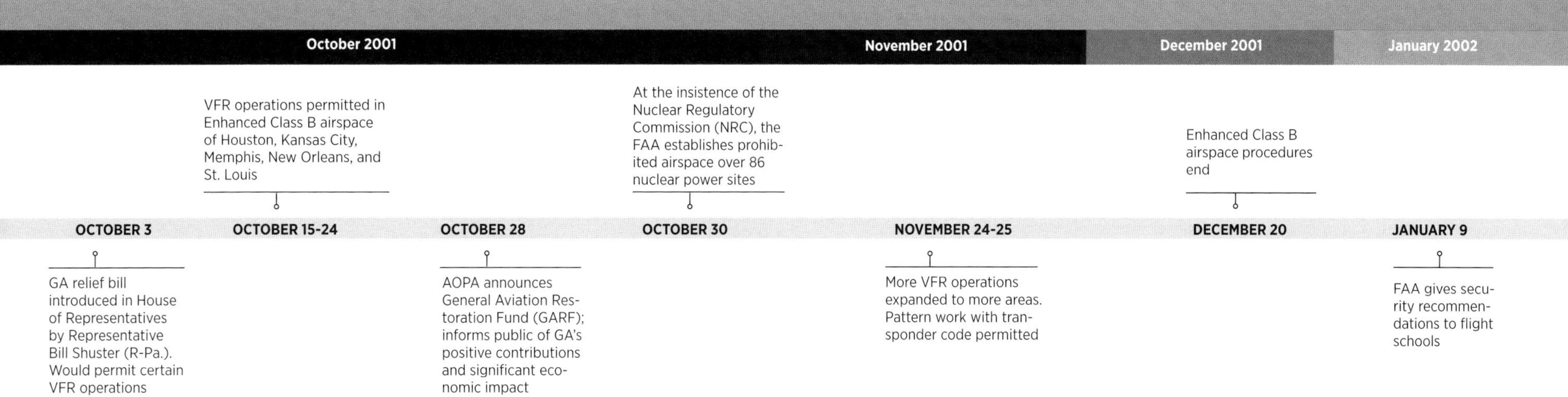
October 2001
November 2001
December 2001
January 2002
OCTOBER 3
GA relief bill introduced in House of Representatives by Representative Bill Shuster (R-Pa.). Would permit certain VFR operations
OCTOBER 15-24
VFR operations permitted in Enhanced Class B airspace of Houston, Kansas City, Memphis, New Orleans, and St. Louis
OCTOBER 28
AOPA announces General Aviation Restoration Fund (GARF); informs public of GA's positive contributions and significant economic impact
OCTOBER 30
At the insistence of the Nuclear Regulatory Commission (NRC), the FAA establishes prohibited airspace over 86 nuclear power sites
NOVEMBER 24-25
More VFR operations expanded to more areas. Pattern work with transponder code permitted
DECEMBER 20
Enhanced Class B airspace procedures end
JANUARY 9
FAA gives security recommendations to flight schools

BOOTS ON THE GROUND

Inside AOPA's 9/11 response

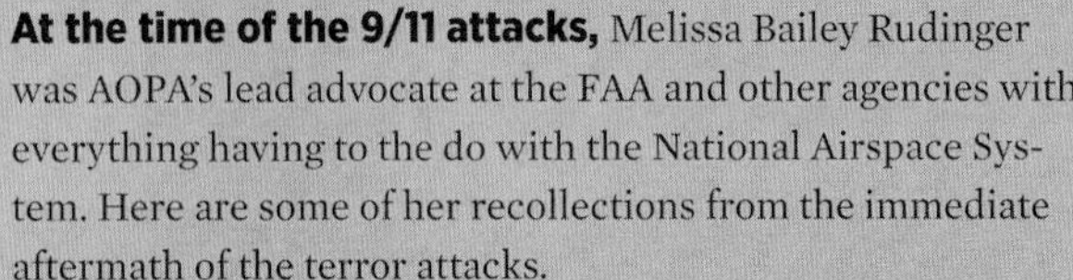

At the time of the 9/11 attacks, Melissa Bailey Rudinger was AOPA's lead advocate at the FAA and other agencies with everything having to the do with the National Airspace System. Here are some of her recollections from the immediate aftermath of the terror attacks.

What were you doing when the attacks occurred?
I was in my office at AOPA headquarters and heard some commotion and talk of a crash into a building in New York. Some said it was caused by a small airplane, so a bunch of us went to the television in the conference room to watch CNN. You couldn't really see the full extent of the damage yet. But then the second plane hit, and everyone then knew that this wasn't a "typical" accident. It looked like a coordinated attack, and from my standpoint I knew this was a tragedy for aviation.

What happened next?
After the second plane hit, I called my contact at the FAA Command Center in Herndon, Virginia, Linda Schuessler, to find out what was up. This is a facility that handles nationwide air traffic flow control, ground stops—anything to do with high-level air traffic management decisions. I could hear talking in the background, some of it frantic, having to do with looking for another plane. Then I heard that the entire airspace system was about to be shut down within an hour. I couldn't wrap my head around the concept of closing down the entire system and making everyone land. I called the Pilot Information Center in Frederick, which handles all the calls on the 800 line, to let them know what was about to happen. A lot of GA pilots were about to get stranded, and we knew there would be a lot of questions.

How did you get the assignment to work with the FAA?
The next day, [AOPA President] Phil Boyer, who is pretty direct, told me to grab my laptop, pack some things, go to the FAA, and don't come back until we were flying again. So I did. I had a badge—a contractor's badge, because I was on an air traffic procedures advisory committee. That allowed me in FAA headquarters, so when I got there I went to the situation room. Inside, there were FAA staff, like the deputy administrator, the vice president of air traffic, controllers, and others in the administrative area. But there were also people from the security community—FBI, DOD, Secret Service, and so on. I had a good working relationship with many of the FAA people, and one of them in the room was Nancy Kalinowski, the head of systems operations—Sysops—which is the working group where I spent most of my time. Sysops is mainly concerned with the day-to-day operations of the air traffic system. Because I'd worked with the FAA many times before, and had that badge, the people on the security side—whose main job was security, not moving traffic—assumed that I was with the FAA. Of course, my priority was to get stranded general aviation pilots flying home in their own airplanes.

Were there conflicts with the security side?
Yes, and sometimes it got tense. Airliners were flying within three days, but GA wasn't. We had all these pilots grounded, and it took a lot for me to convince them of the need to get the pilots moving. The FAA understood this, but the security establishment didn't. They didn't know much of anything about general aviation. Meanwhile, we were being flooded by calls from pilots wanting to know how soon they could get flying. Some of them weren't located near the East Coast, so they didn't have the same sense of seriousness about the order to remain grounded. But we were able to convince the DOD and other security elements in the room that we could devise a scheme that would give us the control they wanted, and a plan to allow limited VFR flying.

What was the plan?
We'd take calls from AOPA's hotline and take down each pilot's name and other information. As the calls came in, I'd batch the information and send it along to security. Then they'd individually approve each pilot to fly. They were vetted, then given a PIN number to use on their flight plans, and granted a one-time waiver to fly on a direct route to their home airport. It took a long time. I worked 20-hour days, and stayed at a Holiday Inn near the FAA building. Some nights I'd just sleep on a couch in someone's office.

What were the main frustrations?
Well, it wasn't until September 19 that we got limited VFR flights going without the waiver. It took that long because the DOD didn't want to have any VFR flying ever again. So we compromised. The power shifted back and forth, and they finally agreed to our invention of the idea of enhanced Class B operations. ECB airspace went from the surface to infinity, and

out to the lateral limits of Class B airspace. To fly in ECB you needed to be on an IFR flight plan, and of course be in contact with ATC, have permission to enter, and have a discrete transponder code. It was sort of a precursor to the ADIZ and then the SFRA that's over Washington, D.C., right now.

Then, when the FAA established a ban on flying within a 10-nautical-mile radius of each nuclear power plant in the U.S., there was another security problem. About 100 public-use airports were within that airspace, which was prohibited airspace, by the way. So the pilots there were grounded, period. The latitude and longitude of each powerplant were in the notams listing the power plants, but the airspace wasn't charted so pilots couldn't see its dimensions visually, which made it very difficult to locate—and would make it easy for anyone to fly into that airspace by mistake, with the risk of being intercepted by a fighter, or worse.

So AOPA staffers, plotting by hand, did charting of their own, and then put the charts online so you could see the location and extent of the power plant no-fly sites. That only lasted a little while because the Secret Service demanded that we take down the website showing the charted power plant airspace. They were worried that terrorists could locate the plants, and not so much worried that general aviation pilots might stray into the airspace. We reached a compromise, which was that there would be a notam and another advisory posted that would give pilots notice not to loiter or circle near a nuclear power plant. That came on November 6, so from October 30 to November 6 we were doing all these charts and then taking them down.

Then there was this push to get me out. The DOD and other security people didn't much like me by then, especially after they discovered I was with a user group and not the FAA. They wanted me out on national security grounds, even though I wasn't in on the threat assessment side of things, which required a security clearance. That was in a different office altogether, behind closed doors. But the FAA leadership felt that it was important for general aviation to be represented, so they stuck up for me. And so did I.

"PHIL BOYER, WHO IS PRETTY DIRECT, TOLD ME TO GRAB MY LAPTOP, PACK SOME THINGS, GO TO THE FAA, AND DON'T COME BACK UNTIL WE WERE FLYING AGAIN." —MELISSA BAILEY RUDINGER

Looking back, it must have one of the biggest achievements of your career, right?
You bet. I was AOPA's—and general aviation's—boots on the ground. I was even part of the signoff process on the notams. It felt like I was part of the FAA at times. And remember I was the only non-government worker in the place, the only general aviation pilot and, many times, the only pilot in the room! Sure, there were adversaries, and there was conflict and compromise, but we collaborated and formed bonds. Now I have deep contacts and many friends within the FAA bureaucracy. I, together with many others in AOPA, did our best in that critical time, and I'd challenge anyone who says otherwise.

In January 2002 a high school student who was a student pilot stole a Cessna 172 and flew it into a building in Tampa, Florida. Although he claimed to have contact with al-Qaida, investigations ruled that out and said the crash was a suicide.

In May 2005, a student pilot and an instructor without recent flight experience inadvertently flew their Cessna 150 into the Flight Restricted Zone—the central area of Washington, D.C., airspace, where the White House and many federal offices are located. They exited the airspace and were soon intercepted and made to land, coincidentally, at the Frederick, Maryland, Municipal Airport, where AOPA's headquarters are located. Both pilots were taken into custody and then released after it became clear that bad judgment and a lack of proficiency—not terrorist intentions—were to blame. The lapsed pilot's certificate was revoked, and AOPA launched renewed measures designed to educate pilots about security-sensitive airspace and intercept procedures.

In an October 2006 incident, a Cirrus SR20 flown by New York Yankees pitcher Cory Lidle and his flight instructor crashed into an apartment building near New York's East River VFR flight corridor. Again, poor piloting skills were blamed. Lidle was turning within the corridor and strong easterly winds aloft blew the airplane west of the intended flight path, and into the building. Although it raised alarms because of its proximity to the World Trade Center, the FBI quickly determined it was no act of terrorism.

Sweeping restrictions on aviation after 9/11 left airplanes stranded and businesses languishing in the immediate aftermath of 9/11. Particularly affected were airports in the Washington, D.C., area, such as Montgomery County Airpark in Gaithersburg, Maryland.

It's worth mentioning that in none of these cases was anyone killed, other than the pilots who flew into the buildings. AOPA drove home the message that most general aviation airplanes lack the speed and mass to create very much damage, and that suicide by airplane is an extremely rare occurrence. But never say never. The entire aviation community remains on alert for any sign of future terrorist activity.

Meigs Field

As we've seen, Chicago Mayor Richard Daley had always had his sights set on closing Chicago's Merrill C. Meigs Field. He even ordered the airport closed at one point, after the Chicago Park District—now the owner of the property—refused to renew its lease to the city. Daley then re-opened it under terms of an agreement in February 1997 following pressure from AOPA, the state of Illinois, and the Friends of Meigs Field interest group. That five-year agreement was to expire in 2002, but Meigs got another reprieve in December 2001, when Illinois Governor George Ryan and Daley signed another agreement. The new agreement was to keep Meigs open until 2026, as part of a larger plan to distribute air traffic among an expanded

“MAYOR DALEY HAS NO HONOR AND HIS WORD HAS NO VALUE. THE SNEAKY WAY HE DID THIS SHOWS THAT HE KNOWS IT WAS WRONG. WE’RE NOT GOING TO ALLOW THE MAYOR TO HIDE BEHIND THE FICTION OF HOMELAND SECURITY FOR HIS REPREHENSIBLE ACTION.”

—Former AOPA President Phil Boyer on the late-night destruction of Chicago’s Meigs Field

Steve Fossett was an adventure-seeker who strove to conquer aviation's most impressive records. Balloons, gliders, and airplanes, Fossett tackled them all. Despite his dangerous pursuits, Fossett was killed on a normal day of flying a Decathlon near Yosemite National Park in California.

RECORDS GALORE

Speed, altitude, and more

Setting new records has long been a centerpiece of aviation—and there's never been a more prolific record-setter than Steve Fossett.

He set new speed and altitude marks in jets, gliders, and balloons, as well as other pursuits such as sailing, swimming, and mountaineering. Even Fossett's death in 2007 at age 63 in an airplane accident set a world record: It was the largest search ever conducted by the Civil Air Patrol, with more than two dozen airplanes and volunteer pilots scanning the eastern Sierra Nevada.

The aerial search came up empty. However, one year after Fossett's disappearance in an American Champion Super Decathlon, a hiker found ID cards belonging to the missing adventurer, and the airplane wreckage was later located nearby.

The former commodities trader set more than 100 world records in five sports, and 60 of them still stood at the time of his death.

Fossett said he had little aptitude for team sports but discovered as a young teen that he excelled at individual enterprises based on persistence and endurance. He's perhaps best known for a solo circumnavigation of the Earth in a balloon in 2002, on his sixth attempt.

In 2005, he flew the single-engine jet *GlobalFlyer* around the world, the first solo, nonrefueled, fixed-wing circumnavigation. The trip began and ended in Salina, Kansas, and took 67 flight hours. When *GlobalFlyer* left the ground, jet fuel accounted for 83 percent of its total weight. (The one-of-a-kind airplane was designed by Burt Rutan's Scaled Composites.)

A year later, Fossett flew the same airplane around the world starting at Kennedy Space Center in Cape Canaveral, Florida, then crossed the Atlantic a second time and landed in England to set the longest total flight distance mark for any airplane (25,766 statute miles). That nonstop flight lasted 76 hours and 45 minutes. *GlobalFlyer* is now on display at the Smithsonian's Udvar-Hazy Center in Virginia.

Fossett set 91 aviation world records, and his marks in gliders included the highest altitude (50,720 feet over Argentina). Others included point-to-point speed dashes in a Cessna Citation X.

He also climbed the Matterhorn and Mount Kilimanjaro, finished the Iditarod dogsled race in Alaska, swam the English Channel, completed an Ironman triathlon in Hawaii, and drove at the famed 24 hours of Le Mans and Dakar rally.

At the time of his death, Fossett held an airline transport pilot, single- and multiengine land and sea ratings, and was certificated in helicopters and balloons. He had logged 6,731 total flight hours. His final flight was meant to be a "Sunday drive" when he took off alone from a private airstrip in western Nevada, overflew the spine of the Sierras, then went down in jagged terrain about 10 miles east of Yosemite National Park at an elevation of about 10,000 feet.

An NTSB investigation said downdrafts on the lee side of the mountain range likely exceeded the 180-horsepower Decathlon's ability to climb at a density altitude estimated to be more than 13,000 feet.

O'Hare International and a new airport to be built in Peotone, Illinois.

But Daley's true intentions became apparent in the middle of the night on March 30, 2003, when he ordered crews to use bulldozers to gouge large Xs in Meigs' single runway, rendering it unusable. The entire aviation community was appalled. Daley said this was done to protect public safety, as Meigs is so close to downtown Chicago. But as AOPA President Phil Boyer said, it was really an example of contempt for due process, a defiance of open government and democracy itself. AOPA filed a complaint with the FAA, citing the fact that Daley had failed to provide the required 90-day advance notice of any demolition work affecting an airport (the city paid a $33,000 fine for this). Another complaint was lodged with the state of Illinois, citing Daley's failure to obtain the state's approval of the demolition.

AOPA's airport advocacy went deeper into overdrive when it filed an injunction to prevent further destruction, took out full-page ads in the *Chicago Tribune* and *Chicago Sun-Times* containing an open letter to Daley and city residents explaining the outrage of all pilots. AOPA's Legal Services Plan lawyers developed additional legal arguments pleading the rights of 16 stranded pilots, and Daley's neglecting to coordinate the destruction with the Department of Homeland Security. Boyer launched another warning: AOPA would oppose any attempts to let state or federal funds be used for the development of a $27 million park slated to replace Meigs, and would seek emergency legislation to allow the state of Illinois to buy the airport.

The fallout reached Congress. House Transportation Committee Chairman John Mica (R-Fla.), during a session dealing with FAA funding, said, "It's pretty difficult for me to sit up here and listen to requests for additional infrastructure when destruction like this happens." Meanwhile, polling revealed that two-thirds of Chicago residents disapproved of the airport's destruction, and that 70 percent believed Meigs did not represent a terrorist threat to the city.

By June 2003, AOPA was nearing the end of its legal options to preserve Meigs. Boyer even announced AOPA was pursuing a $41 million buyout program that would let the FAA grant the city of Chicago federal AIP funds to buy the airport from the Park District. If this happened, FAA grant assurances would yield a 20-year guarantee that the airport would remain open. This concept had the support of Senator James Inhofe and DOT Secretary Sam Skinner.

But Daley held fast, saying that the proposed park belonged to the people of Chicago, and that "the people wanted a park." So, without FAA financing—which Chicago had once accepted, then repaid—there could be no grant assurances, and no way to be sure that Meigs would survive. It became clear that the idea of even expecting grant assurances would not happen under the Daley administration. In a final blow, Judge James Moran, the U.S. District judge for the Northern District of Illinois, said that he'd rule against any lawsuit asking for a federal buyout of the airport.

To many, Meigs' closure was illegal in the first place. But courts affirmed that Daley had the right to do it. "We won the PR battle, but lost the war to save the airport," Boyer said. It was a bitter defeat for general aviation, one that stood in stark contrast to the many successful airport-access and other airport-related advocacy efforts AOPA pursued in the past, and continues to pursue.

Some examples from the early 2000s include the Airport Support Network's efforts to reject—twice—the building permit for a three-story apartment complex near the Lee's Summit, Missouri, Municipal Airport, and the ASN's 2003 role in supporting the St. Petersburg, Florida, voters' 3-1 rejection of proposal to close the Albert Whitted Airport and turn it into parkland. AOPA spent more than $100,000 and sent senior staffers to help local supporters in this fight.

The Concord, California, county supervisors voted 5-0 in 2003 to close Concord's Buchanan Field and use it for other purposes. Turns out federal grant acceptances required the field to remain an airport for 19 more years. Another factor: In 1946 the federal government gave the airport to the county on the condition it be operated as an airport forever.

The city council of Rialto, California, wanted to close, downsize, or relocate the Rialto Airport (where 250 aircraft were based) so that a residential development could take its place. Once again, AOPA had to remind the council that FAA grants worth $9 million had been spent so that Rialto could expand. That meant it had to remain an airport.

Grant obligations from the FAA's AIP funds also guaranteed the future of California's Contra Costa,

Active U.S. Pilots in 2004 | **618,930** ▼

THE SIMPLE LIFE

LSAs took aim at entry-level fliers

The sport pilot category was meant to make flying simpler, less expensive, and more fun.

The Experimental Aircraft Association led the aviation industry in a 10-year effort that culminated in 2004 with new FAA rules that created both sport pilots and the Light Sport aircraft category. Like glider and balloon pilots, sport pilots don't need FAA medical exams, and they can fly in day, VFR conditions using small, mechanically simple aircraft.

Students can become sport pilots in as few as 20 flight hours—half the time required for private pilots—and there are no night flying or towered airport requirements. Established aircraft manufacturers like Cessna, and dozens of new firms, created new designs to serve the sport pilot market.

But that market never fully materialized. Light Sport aircraft were limited to a maximum takeoff weight of 1,320 pounds and a top speed of 120 knots, and new designs typically came with prices well in excess of $100,000. Only 6,097 people had become sport pilots by the end of 2017, a figure dwarfed by the number of private pilots (162,455). (The FAA does not track the number of pilots with higher certificates operating under sport pilot privileges.)

A reckoning also took place among Light Sport aircraft manufacturers, many of whom ceased production or went out of business a decade after the sport pilot rules were adopted. Cessna stopped selling Skycatchers (right) in 2014 after delivering 192 aircraft, and the company scrapped its remaining inventory. Cirrus and Piper cancelled their own plans to license and sell Light Sport airplanes.

Light Sport aircraft suffered another setback in 2017 when AOPA and other aviation organizations successfully lobbied the FAA to reform pilot medical requirements. Under the new and simpler BasicMed standards, pilots can fly aircraft weighing up to 6,000 pounds, in visual or instrument conditions, after an exam by their personal physician rather than an FAA doctor—not just Light Sport aircraft.

The sport pilot certificate remains an attractive gateway to aviation, and the hours flown as a sport pilot count toward future ratings.

A few manufacturers, such as CubCrafters with its 180-horsepower Carbon Cub (which consistently was both the highest priced and best-selling Light Sport aircraft), and Van's Aircraft (with both factory- and kit-built RV-12s), have thrived under the 2004 rules.

But the severe weight, performance, and payload limits for Light Sport aircraft—as well as their relatively high prices compared to used airplanes—have hamstrung the sport pilot category and kept it from realizing its full potential.

With hundreds of manufacturers soon after it was enacted, the Light Sport aircraft movement was bound to see some shake out of the market. Few anticipated it would be the well-funded and successful manufacturers such as Cessna. The Skycatcher, first built in China, found some fans but never caught on, and the project—and unsold airplanes—were scrapped.

Oceanside, Bakersfield, and Sacramento airports. Memo to local governments and developers: Better check to see if an airport has accepted federal AIP funds before you decide to draw up your plans for a shopping center or housing development.

Ignorance, or failure to comply with FAA obstruction-clearance guidelines, also came to the rescue. In 2006, the Sunroad Centrum high-rise building was proposed for construction near San Diego's Montgomery Field (now Montgomery-Gibbs Executive Airport). This would be an air navigation hazard and cause circling minimums to rise, said then-AOPA Vice President of Airports Bill Dunn and Airport Support Network volunteer Rich Beach. What followed was a compliance study to see if the building project would meet obstruction evaluation standards. Result: The top 20 feet had to go.

Or how about the Fullerton, California, airport? Until December 2004, there was a 760-foot-tall radio tower 1.5 miles from the airport. That's when an airplane in VFR conditions hit the tower, killing the two occupants—and knocking down the tower. This was the second time since 1947 that an airplane had flown into the tower. In 2007 the owner of the tower site wanted to rebuild it—at the same site. After pressure from AOPA, the tower owner consulted FAA authorities and the tower height was reduced.

User fees, again

We've mentioned some aspects of previous FAA funding battles in the recent past, with the emphasis on two facts. One is uplifting: User fees have been avoided to date. The other, not so reassuring: The issue keeps popping up during every budget cycle.

So it was with the 2008 budgeting cycle. The budget was set to expire in September 2007, and the government had been funding the FAA under a series of annual extensions. This time, the FAA was again insistent on having more money. It cited that ATC modernization, which had begun in 1981, was at one time expected to take 10 years to complete and cost $11 billion. By early 2007 the modernization effort had instead taken 25 years and was expected to cost $45 billion, thanks to the technological leaps forward represented by GPS navigation and research on Automatic Dependent Surveillance-Broadcast (ADS-B). Without a hefty increase from the government's general fund, user fees would have to make up the difference. Meanwhile, the Bush administration wanted to cut funding levels, and saw a privatized ATC system as a way to move forward.

Once more, AOPA and other user groups stepped forward to oppose privatization and user fees. "There's no funding shortfall," Boyer said before congressional committees. "The aviation trust fund could have a $4.2 billion surplus by 2011—and may well reach $9.3 billion."

Other forces seemed to agree. The Reason Foundation, which once advocated user fees, now said it saw no reason for assessing them on VFR flights. The Air Transport Association of America (now Airlines for America)—which represents airline interests—at one point said it wouldn't seek fees for general aviation piston aircraft. And Representative James Oberstar (D-Minn.), the new chairman of the House Transportation and Infrastructure Committee, also was against user fees, and said "the idea of a cash register in the sky is not appealing to me, to general aviation, or to regional aviation."

"DON'T BUY THE RHETORIC OF THOSE WHO WOULD TURN OVER OUR NATION'S AVIATION DOMINANCE FROM GOVERNMENT CONTROL TO THE HIGHEST PRIVATE BIDDER." —PHIL BOYER

Meanwhile, the administration and the airlines wanted to take the FAA "off budget," which would free it of budget limitations—and also free it to charge user fees. Advocates argued that a privatized FAA would be consistent with these aims. AOPA argued that the FAA didn't conduct proper accounting the way it was currently structured, so how could it run the ATC system like a business? Boyer even said that a corporatized FAA might well be in violation of 2002's Sarbanes-Oxley Act governing enhanced standards for all public companies and accounting firms.

The administration's budget proposal didn't mention privatization, but it did rely on increased fees. Avgas taxes would be raised to 50 cents per gallon, up from 19.4 cents. Jet fuel taxes would jump from 21.8 cents to 70.1 cents per gallon. And, there would be a $1 billion cut in AIP funding, and a "congestion fee" for aircraft flying in Class B airspace. In all, it was estimated that piston aircraft would pay $100 million more than under the current funding arrangement—344 percent more. On the other hand, estimates put the airlines' payments to the Airport and Airway Trust Fund at $1.7 billion, or 27 percent less than before.

The FAA also wanted some new fees: $130 to register an aircraft, $42 for a medical certificate, $25 for a replacement airman certificate, among other fees. AOPA secured more than 50,000 signatures on a petition opposing the FAA's proposal.

Next, it was Congress' turn to offer up their ideas for FAA funding in 2008. The House Aviation Subcommittee, under Chairman Jerry Costello (D-Ill.), proposed $13 billion for ATC modernization ($1 billion more than the FAA proposal), $15.8 billion for AIP funding ($4 billion more than the FAA proposal), and modest increases in fuel taxes—to 24.1 cents per gallon for avgas, and 30.7 cents per gallon for jet fuel. There would be fees for registration and certificate issuances—but no new user fees.

The Senate Aviation Subcommittee offered up its bill, and it too seemed to respond to some of AOPA's concerns. Avgas taxes would remain the same, for example, and AIP funding would rise slightly. The congestion fee was

AOPA launched the Let's Go Flying initiative in 2008 with a mission of identifying and engaging more student pilots, reversing the student pilot attrition rate, and growing the general aviation pilot population.

included and a $25-per-flight ATC modernization fee was proposed, as was an increase in jet fuel taxes to 49 cents per gallon.

AOPA endorsed the House bill, which was a compromise on the fuel tax and registration and issuances fee increases, but a win on no per-flight user fees.

As things progressed in the runup to the budget deadline, another Senate funding bill emerged, one from the Senate Finance Committee. Its provisions included a 65-percent hike in jet fuel taxes but no new user fees. However, the two Senate bills couldn't be reconciled because of disagreement over nonaviation riders.

It all came down to this: The FAA proposal died from a lack of support, the House bill stood alone, and without any consensus from the Senate side there could be no markup or conference committee—where the final wheeling and dealing is done—to tailor a final bill, and so no bill could be passed along for signing by President George W. Bush.

All of which is to explain that instead of passing a new funding bill, there was another extension of the existing FAA funding legislation—to September 30, 2008. This would be the sixth such extension. Another extension—to March 31, 2009—would come later in 2008.

It's no way to do government business, but FAA funding extensions have increasingly become the norm in recent years. Senate Aviation Subcommittee Chairman John D. Rockefeller (D-W.Va.) said there wouldn't be an FAA funding bill in 2008 "based on the general aviation community's inability to compromise."

AOPA and the rest of general aviation look at it somewhat differently. By avoiding—yet again—the threat of user fees, Boyer said, "we've won the battle for now...but the issue starts all over again next year, when both the House and Senate have to start drafting new legislation to determine how the FAA will be funded and what its budget will be." Which is as true then as it is now.

NextGen

We tend to forget the aura of urgency that surrounded the funding tensions of the 2000s. But it's worthwhile to remember the stakes at hand. The extra funding was needed for no less than a complete overhaul in how we'd fly in the decades to come. New, GPS-based Automatic Dependent Surveillance-Broadcast (ADS-B) technology was to become the future means of separating air traffic. Datalinked GPS location information allows controller and pilots alike to see the positions, tracks, and altitudes of nearby traffic, avoiding conflicts and enabling more direct routings. Weather information could be broadcast via the same datalink concept. This is the core of the FAA's Next Generation Air Transportation System, or NextGen. For this to happen, however, a network of ground stations had to be built to relay the position reports and feed information to the cockpit. Pilots would have to buy avionics that supported ADS-B, and buy them in time to meet the January 2020 deadline in order to fly in designated airspace. And tests would have to prove that the technology would be robust and reliable enough to earn regulatory endorsement. All of this would require substantial funding, as would the commissioning of GPS approaches to eventually replace many of the VOR and ILS instrument approach procedures that pilots had been relying on since the 1950s.

ADS-B testing began in Alaska in the late 1990s. AOPA President Phil Boyer and senior AOPA staffers visited Alaska in July 2000 to view a demonstration of what was called the Capstone project. This localized test of prototype NextGen capabilities used a captive fleet of airplanes, among them Cessna 206s, Piper Navajos, and Cessna Caravans. Building on the Capstone results, the FAA issued a contract worth $1.8 billion through 2025 to design and install a network of ADS-B ground stations—666 currently are in service—and announced the January 2020 equipage mandate.

The shift to a satellite-based system also meant pilots would be able to fly approaches to many more runways using Wide Area Augmentation System (WAAS)-enhanced GPS. By mid-2003 the first 25 WAAS stations were turned on. These stations refine GPS signals and make the position information much more accurate, allowing GPS approaches to airports that previously had no instrument approaches. GPS approaches were phased in gradually; first they were flown as overlays to existing VHF-based approaches. But by the late 2004, stand-alone GPS approaches with vertical guidance—such as LNAV/VNAV (lateral navigation and vertical navigation) and LPV (localizer performance with vertical guidance) began to be certified in earnest. LPV approaches were especially beneficial, as they often allowed decision altitudes and decision heights that rivaled those of ILS approaches. AOPA fought for a decade for these approaches—and frankly didn't expect LPV approach approvals until late 2005. Now they're widespread and allow access to more and more airports around the United States.

Flight service of the future

Another big funding priority was bringing the existing flight service station concept into the modern era. The then-current system was a creature of the 1970s, and didn't take advantage of the sort of high-speed, centralized transmission of weather information that the internet offered. It relied heavily on phone-in pilot requests for weather and flight plan filing, had many walk-in facilities at airports large and small, and the system was overloaded. It was costing $600 million per year to operate, and analysts worked out that each phone call to a flight service station cost $25.

Since 1989, computer-savvy pilots could obtain their weather information online, through the government-contracted Direct User Access Terminal System (DUATS) programs—web services that offered weather briefing, flight planning, and flight plan filing services. In many ways it became flight service's competitor, as it was fairly high-tech in its day. Boyer was fond of saying "Thank goodness for DUATS, because that system is there to take the load as the FSS system started collapsing."

The Office of Management and Budget wondered, in its Circular A-76, if commercial services could provide information more efficiently than a government-run system. AOPA and others provided their input to the study, and the decision was made to keep a government-funded flight service system, outsource its functions to private providers, and keep a close eye on the new system's progress. The first bidders were Lockheed Martin, Northrop Grumman, and Raytheon.

Lockheed Martin won the flight service contract—called FS21 (Flight Service for the Twenty-First Century) in February 2004. It was for $1.9 billion over 10 years, and would give us modern computers, monitors, and connectivity through three hub stations and a network of upgraded outlying stations. AOPA learned of many instances of system outages, dropped calls, and poor briefings by newly hired specialists unfamiliar with the local areas under their responsibility. More training—and bringing back seasoned briefers to work with the new hires—helped solve that problem. And once again, FAA DUATS was there to take up the slack. But DUATS and its offshoots would continue to morph over the years, even as FS21 experienced its teething problems. And those who feel most comfort-

Phil Boyer, AOPA president 1991-2008

A VISIT WITH PHIL BOYER

Hangar talk with AOPA's fourth president

You spent decades in the television industry before becoming AOPA's president. Were there any big surprises in the first months after making the transition?
Yes, I spent 32 years in broadcasting, and though most pilots know me from the *ABC Wide World of Flying* videos, my main positions were in management. I ran ventures with annual revenues five times those of AOPA. So the surprise for me was that AOPA was a business—not just a big flying club. I thought I was leaving what I'd been doing, but here I was doing the same thing as I was before in television. But the neat thing was that it had to do with flying, my passion, not the changing world of broadcasting. You know, there are a lot of similarities between broadcasting and running AOPA, so there weren't too many real surprises. I mean, in broadcasting you have ratings. Well, we have membership numbers. You want people to come back next week to watch a program. Well, we have membership renewals. You want to know what an audience wants. AOPA wants to know what the members want. Broadcasting has to have advertising revenue, and so does *AOPA Pilot* magazine. We had to deal with the Federal Communications Commission, AOPA has to deal with the FAA.

What was your biggest achievement as president?
It boils down to two things: getting new members and renewing existing members. I'd go to bed every night thinking, *What did I do today to address those two issues?* It could be getting

GPS approaches, or keeping an airport open—both of which would appeal to members. I think reaching the 415,000-member level was the product of me executing that strategy over all those 18 years.

What was your worst experience?
It was 9/11. A lot of people think it would have been losing the battle to keep Meigs Field open, but we expected that to happen. We didn't have the FAA law on our side. Then the FAA grant obligations expired. But we did extend Meigs for five years beyond what we expected. It was a shock the way it [the runway destruction and closure] happened. I think of it when I fly past it, which is often. You know, they haven't really developed the land.

But 9/11 was not expected, and it changed aviation in ways we could never anticipate. General aviation was impacted a lot less because of what AOPA did, but all of aviation was changed, probably forever.

What's general aviation's biggest challenge now?
The dwindling number of pilots. I beat my head against the wall with the Project Pilot and Let's Go Flying game plans, and we made a dent, but the numbers still kept going down. It still concerns me. Costs of flying will continue to increase with a low volume of pilots.

What's the reason for the drop in the pilot population?
I wish I had the answer. I just think it's too expensive. In the last two decades the economics and demographics are such that younger couples need to have both spouses working in order to meet expenses, so both have a say in how the money will be spent. Kids coming out of high school or college have a hard time making enough money to fly, so there's not a lot of them. If you look at flight schools you'll see that most students not seeking an aviation career are something like 40 to 55 years old. They have the money and the time, but there's not enough of them to make a difference either.

It's the one thing I'll go to my deathbed saying I never got accomplished. We never could figure out what could be done to enhance the pilot population. And America's not alone. I really applaud the current You Can Fly effort. It's a really good program, but I don't think it alone will bring us back to the numbers we had back in the 1970s. Again, it's all about the new and renewing member metric, applied to flying in general. It's a lot easier to get an already-certificated pilot back in the cockpit than it is to start flying from scratch. That's why the Rusty Pilots seminars are doing so well. The Rusty Pilots are already sold on flying.

SAFETY ON THE WEB

ASI expands online education offerings

With AOPA's Air Safety Foundation Executive Director Bruce Landsberg at the helm, ASF's accident research and analysis continued the important work of pinpointing weak areas and gaps in general aviation pilots' flight proficiency. As it does today, this analysis also served as the backbone for ASF's aviation safety education development from its popular in-person seminars and weekend ground schools to numerous online programs. 2001 marked an important milestone in ASF history with the tenth anniversary of the its *Joseph T. Nall Report*, which by now had expanded from an eight-page pocket booklet to a more robust 20-page document, setting the stage for it to become the most widely accepted source for in-depth, factual reporting of general aviation accidents and accident trend analysis in the United States.

Another remarkable first happened in June 2001, when the Air Safety Foundation—teaming up with Jeppesen, which had created a popular online refresher course for flight instructors—launched the ASF Jeppesen Online Flight Instructor Refresher Course. That year, the course won a regional award for distinction by the Society for Technical Communication.

Building on its successes during the 1990s, the AOPA Air Safety Foundation immersed itself into developing more powerful, informative, and entertaining online safety education. ASF's first interactive online course, *IFR Adventures: Rules to Live By*, incorporated real-world instrument flight and decision-making scenarios, from flight planning to an instrument flight. The course taker's progress was monitored throughout, and answering enough questions correctly would render a certificate at the end of the course. That approach found its way in numerous courses that followed.

By the end of the decade, the Air Safety Foundation had developed and launched more than two dozen interactive online courses, along with other programs such as Pilot Safety Announcement, Accident Case Study, and Real Pilot Stories videos.

In 2009, Landsberg was named president of the AOPA Air Safety Foundation. One year later, the AOPA Foundation—which had been formed in 2007—merged with the AOPA Air Safety Foundation to become the single-entity AOPA Foundation, headed up by Landsberg as its president.

By then, ASF had reached hundreds of thousands of pilots annually through its online education programs. The AOPA Air Safety Institute continues its educational mission.

ASF's first interactive online course, *IFR Adventures: Rules to Live By*, launched in 2002. The idea was that an interactive discussion of instrument flight operation regulations would make the course intriguing and memorable despite the conceivably "boring" discussion of IFR rules.

“EVERY DAY IN AMERICA, SMALL PLANES ARE SERVING OUR COUNTRY. FROM NORTH DAKOTA AND WEST VIRGINIA TO CALIFORNIA AND FLORIDA, GENERAL AVIATION PLAYS A VITAL ROLE IN KEEPING OUR ECONOMY STRONG.” —HARRISON FORD, GA SERVES AMERICA SPOKESMAN

able talking on the phone with a real, live, human briefer will be reassured to know that this option is still there.

Looking to the future

In 2006, Erik Lindbergh, Charles Lindbergh's grandson, had signed on as AOPA Project Pilot spokesman; by 2008, more than 6,000 new student pilots had joined Project Pilot, motivated by some 5,200 Project Pilot Mentor participants. AOPA's Let's Go Flying program, meant to reach out to nonpilots, inspire potential student pilots, promote flight training, and encourage the growth of flying clubs, launched in late 2008.

To support these and other efforts, AOPA formed a new fundraising arm under Boyer's leadership—the AOPA Foundation, a 501(c)(3) organization. The foundation's goals were to preserve airports, improve general aviation's image, boost pilot safety through educational efforts, and grow the pilot population. The general aviation community responded, and within a year of its establishment, $26 million of its target $58 million had been raised.

After almost 18 years at AOPA's helm, Boyer retired in December 2008. Under his tenure, he became known as general aviation's foremost advocate, savvy in his persuasiveness before Congress, ubiquitous in his grassroots airport appearances at an average of 28 Pilot Town Meetings per year, and infectious in his enthusiasm for technology. His accomplishments were many, but his highest priority—reversing the decline of the pilot population—established a legacy of programs that continue today. Last but certainly not least, under Boyer, AOPA membership grew by 40 percent—to an unprecedented 415,000 members—in spite of a pilot population that continued a stubborn and slow overall decline.

A changing of the guard

AOPA's board of trustees selected Craig Fuller as the association's fifth president. Fuller, like those who preceded him, had a long background flying general aviation airplanes. He first soloed in 1967, at Concord, California's Buchanan Field, but it was a seaplane ride in Oregon that really hooked him on flying. Although he had a busy career in public affairs, he took time off with his father in 1980 to make a memorable trip to Wichita, where he took delivery of a brand-new Cessna Cutlass RG. After the return trip to Santa Monica, Fuller made another memorable trip in 1981—all the way to Washington, D.C. He had been hired to work for the newly elected Reagan administration, where he rose to become the chief of staff for Vice President George H.W. Bush.

After leaving the White House in 1989 Fuller put his considerable Washington background to work as a public policy consultant and manager of a health-care association. It was then that he bought a Beechcraft Bonanza A36 and flew it some 200 hours per year for business and pleasure.

Fuller's 35 years' worth of Washington expertise would come in handy. The economic downturn of 2007-2009 was in full swing and the federal government was looking for ways to trim the cost of government. In an interview with *AOPA Pilot* magazine, Fuller said, "The Obama administration is faced with getting the economy going. Some of the solutions presented to him will be the same ones presented to President [George W.] Bush, such as implementing user fees as a means of reducing the cost of the ATC system. We're going to have to be vigilant in making sure that they don't attempt to reduce federal expenditures on the backs of general aviation."

Budget extensions had by now become the norm. But the current extension would expire on March 31, 2009, and the Obama administration was proposing "direct user charges" (which Fuller called "another name for user fees") of $7 billion by 2011. AOPA and many others still supported the budget provisions enacted in 2007 (which had no new user fees), and as luck would have it, this budget was extended once more as the March 2009 deadline came and went. This time, the new extension would expire in September 2009.

Then what? The White House proposed a new budget with even higher user fees—worth $9.6 billion, up from the previous $7 billion, and increasing to $11 billion by 2011. The GA Caucus in Congress—which AOPA was instrumental in forming—came together to object to this idea; 100 members of Congress sent a message to Obama that user fees would be a non-starter in the next budget cycle.

That came just three months later, and then yet another three-month extension—the eighth since 2007. It would expire in March 2010. On and on it went like this until 2011, when federal spending caps, lasting until 2021, were put in place across most government agencies. The caps were invoked so that the federal debt ceiling wouldn't be exceeded. If spending went above the caps, then sequestration—mandatory, automatic budget cuts—would kick in to cut $1.2 trillion from the federal deficit.

Sequestration went into effect in May 2013. For the FAA, this meant a budget cut of 5 percent, or about $500 million. It also meant that 149 FAA-contracted control towers were closed, and that furloughs and other measures were taken to reduce FAA staffing costs. In the end, the debt ceiling was raised, ending sequestration. The good news for general aviation is that user fees haven't been enacted to offset debt or manage the FAA's budget to this day. But we'd be foolish to ignore future threats.

On the offensive

The massive economic collapse of 2007 and 2008 spared no one, and general aviation was hit particularly hard. Aircraft deliveries, student pilot starts, and the pilot population all saw a marked decline, unfortunately coming just as aviation was starting to recover from 9/11. As the industry was squeezed more and more, under Fuller's direction AOPA went on the offensive. To spread the word about general aviation's role in the economy, in 2009 Fuller pushed for AOPA to establish an initiative called GA Serves America. The goal of this program was to block user fees and promote a better understanding of general aviation. Fuller recruited actors Harrison Ford, Morgan Freeman—both pilots—and Cuba Gooding Jr., who played a fighter pilot in the movie *Red Tails*, to serve as spokesmen at events around the United States, including at some well-attended congressional testimony, and at AOPA's annual conventions, now renamed "Summits." Articles in *AOPA Pilot* magazine and on the GA Serves America website profiled key examples of general aviation's many contributions. One magazine profile highlighted a police helicopter unit at work in Virginia Beach, Virginia. Another covered general aviation airplanes surveying the Deepwater Horizon oil-spill damage in the Gulf of Mexico. Thanks to this sort of publicity, the GA Caucus swelled to 116 members in the House and 29 members in the Senate.

AOPA pursued other ways to engage the pilot community, including video. *AOPA Live* started as a live broadcast from the exhibit hall floor at the 2009 AOPA Summit in Tampa. IN 2012, Fuller backed the start of *AOPA Live This Week*, a popular 15- to 20-minute show highlighting the week's general aviation news, events, and entertainment, and it continues today. A free daily email—*Aviation eBrief,* a clipping-service-style compilation of industry and pilot community news—complemented AOPA's weekly *ePilot* offerings.

Spreading the word, convincing Congress, and educating the general population was one thing: cultivating new pilots was something quite different. The downward trend in both student pilot starts and pilot activity continued at an alarming rate. One 2011 study revealed that 70 percent of student pilots did not go on to earn their private pilot certificates.

Under Fuller, the Let's Go Flying initiative gave way to a new unit within AOPA: The Center to Advance the Pilot Community, or CAPCOM for short. This multipronged effort produced flight training field guides for students and instructors and began annual Flight Training Excellence Awards, given to exemplary flight instructors and schools. The CAPCOM staff also began to study flying clubs as an avenue to access flying at a reasonable cost. This slew of new programs was the first time AOPA attacked the pilot population slump as a coordinated effort, rather than just trying to get new students in the door. Hard data, rather than hunches and personal experience, were the basis for the programs, and form the foundation of today's pilot population efforts.

Unified voice

Fuller realized that a collaborative approach would be the only way to address many of general aviation's needs. In the past, some general aviation manufacturers, interest groups, user groups, press vehicles, and other advocates too often seemed pitted against each other. With all of general

Who would think a carbonated energy drink could raise awareness of aviation? The Red Bull Air Race Championship began in 2002. The series of races is just one of many Red Bull-sponsored events throughout the world promoting the brand through extreme sports.

Craig Fuller, AOPA president 2009-2013

WORKING TOGETHER

Hangar talk with AOPA's fifth president

A longtime Washington insider, you became president of AOPA at the beginning of the Obama administration. Did you see that as a challenge or an opportunity?
We knew it would be a challenge when right out of the box, he announced his plans to implement a large user fee. We knew we would have to confront that. We had strong supporters in Congress, but we knew we would need more to fend off a user fee.

Was that the genesis of the GA Caucus effort?
The House side asked if we—the general aviation associations—would help build support for a caucus. Caucuses are a creature of each chamber. They have to be formed from within, but they wanted us to encourage participation by other members of Congress. It was a great opportunity for the GA associations to work together. And we did. There was a wonderful outcome of Congressional support—even without the immediate threat of user fees. So once the threat actually came, we were prepared. The majority of members of Congress were on board and a letter to the administration gave a clear indication that any future such proposals [for user fees] would not be accepted.

It seems like that theme of working together was an important one to you.
It was. Among the things I'm proudest of is the dedicated team of people who worked together to greatly strengthen our ability to win. It's all about more productive relationships with the airlines, for example, rather than drawing battle lines. Part of telling the story of those wins is great communication, and I'm proud of what we did to strengthen communications at AOPA, including video and social media and *Aviation eBrief.* Video, especially, has proven to be a powerful way to communicate with and influence people.

What surprised you when you got to AOPA?
As a member since 1973, I felt like I knew the organization through the magazine and understood its influence in Washington. I was not so aware of the extent or volume of the issues worked at the state and local levels. The breadth and reach of the organization is very impressive. I was surprised, though, by the extent to which Congress and staff didn't understand the value of general aviation. The GA Caucus helped with some of that but it

seemed the biggest threat was a lack of appreciation for what GA contributes. That's where we came up with the GA Serves America campaign idea—to educate the public and Congress about the value of GA and especially of small, rural airports. You need a campaign for these sorts of things and the AOPA board agreed to support it. Harrison Ford signed up to help. He really wanted us to tell the stories of pilots and airports and the contributions they make to the country. It was very successful. We ran ads and brought Harrison to Capitol Hill for meetings. It helped them understand us, again supporting that idea that if you have influencers on your side, you can survive future issues that crop up.

AOPA presidents before and after you wrestled with the declining pilot population issue and the challenges of flight training. What can be done to make a difference?
That question dogged me when I was there and still does. There's always a percentage of people who will learn to fly for the pleasure of it. I hope it doesn't just become something for those of higher means. The challenge is improving the access to training and helping people understand how to use GA airplanes. The flight training survey work we did showed ways to improve the flight training experience and those results are showing up now in the great work AOPA is doing in the You Can Fly program. Flying clubs are such an important part of it because they give access to different types of aircraft and families can get involved. The work AOPA is doing is absolutely vital here. The entire community has learned a lot about what it takes to teach people to fly and it's paying off. As the co-chair of Redbird [Flight Simulations] we now know how simulators can help with training—it reduces the time and cost. I'm also involved with [the Bye Aerospace] Sun Flyer. Electricity, I think, can have a big impact on training. Hunting, fishing, golf, sailing, scuba—they're all facing challenges getting people involved. But when they do get involved, they have a great time. We need to make sure when people give aviation a try they have a great experience. Surveys show millions have an interest in piloting an airplane. We need to get a better handle on the flight training experience. What they see in the airplane is important, too. Technology appeals to a lot of them. They're using apps, and iPhones, and tablet computers elsewhere in their life. They need to experience that when they get into aviation.

Although the method of delivery has evolved, the mission has not. Communicating to members is a core mission of AOPA, however they happen to consume the information. New products, such as the enhanced digital editions of *AOPA Pilot* and *Flight Training*, seek to serve members' needs for information and entertainment in myriad ways.

aviation's serious challenges, competition and name-calling only served to alienate pilots from each other, dilute central messages, and serve as opportunities for those seeking to exploit any perceived divisions.

"My approach is not a partisan approach. There's nothing partisan about general aviation," Fuller often said. With this spirit in mind, AOPA senior executives traveled to the headquarters of the Experimental Aircraft Association in Oshkosh, Wisconsin, to meet with then-President Tom Poberezny. For too long there were open beliefs that AOPA and EAA worked at odds with each other and sought to promote opposing ends. The visit to Oshkosh put an end to that. AOPA's GA Serves America, Let's Go Flying, and CAPCOM programs and EAA's Young Eagles programs had similar goals—to up awareness and grow the pilot population—so both organizations vowed to fully endorse each other's programs.

Future such meetings would result in unified endorsements of successful proposals to expand the recreational pilot certificate holders' 50-nautical-mile limit for cross-country flight, as long as the pilot received additional training and a signoff, seek an additional $2 million in the FAA budget to support the development of an alternative to leaded avgas, and allow automobile drivers' licenses to serve as a self-certifying means of medical certification. Under the latter proposal, pilots would be allowed to fly single-engine, fixed-gear airplanes of no more than 180 horsepower—as long as the airplanes had no more than four seats and the pilot carried no more than one passenger. While this particular proposal didn't come to fruition, it served as an important precedent for future self-assessment-based medical standards.

Airport advocacy

In the airport-advocacy arena, AOPA saw signs of hope during Fuller's presidency. The Lorain County, Ohio, government wanted to close the Lorain County Regional Airport in 2010, but alas, it had received federal

Active U.S. Pilots in 2010 | **627,588** ▲
Student pilot certificates went from a duration of 36 months to 60 months for those under 40 years old in 2010

Garmin may have racked up more sales, but Avidyne was first to the party. The Entegra integrated avionics system launched on the Cirrus SR20 and SR22 in 2003 (right). It used third-party navigation and communication equipment to display a moving map on a large multifunction display, and an air data and heading reference system to display the parameters of the six flight instruments on the primary flight display. Garmin delivered the first G1000 system a year later, launching on Cessna and Diamond models.

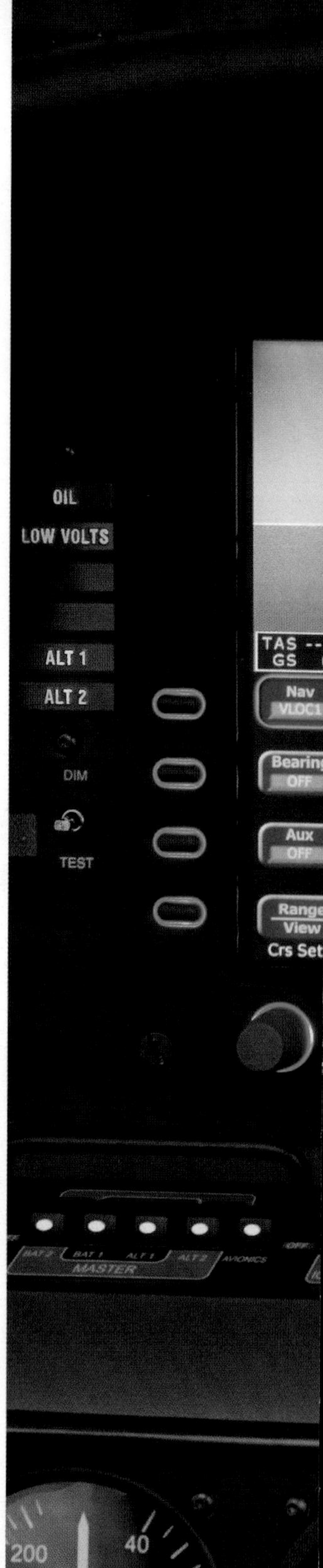

funding. And by now we know what that means: The airport must continue as an airport. The FAA told it so, but Lorain County said it was moving ahead with the closure. The FAA responded, threatening a court order to keep it open. Guess who won that one?

Also in 2010, Watsonville, California, was all set to violate state law by planning to eliminate runway safety zones around the Watsonville Municipal Airport so that the area could be developed. By this time, AOPA's Airport Support Network had grown by another 300 volunteers, but this time the ASN wasn't needed. The Watsonville Pilots Association, the Friends of Buena Vista, and the Sierra Club joined to file suit in the California Court of Appeals. The court ruled that cities and counties cannot ignore safety provisions the state had already put in place. Chalk up another airport victory.

There were other general aviation victories at the state level. Among the more noteworthy was Florida Governor Charlie Crist's tax exemption for visiting out-of-state aircraft. Before the tax break, visitors staying more than 21 days in Florida could be charged a "use tax" of 6 percent of the value of the aircraft. Out-of-staters buying an aircraft in Florida could be similarly taxed within six months of the purchase date. Ditto anyone from outside Florida having any maintenance, modifications, or training. Some states still have taxes like these, and they could learn a lot from the increase in business revenues that come from their elimination.

Fuller wrapped up his five-year term as AOPA president with more examples of his knack for outreach. To better address the needs of a more savvy audience, the first digital editions of *AOPA Pilot* and *Flight Training* were offered. AOPA media expansion in a down market was because of Fuller's mantra to "Meet the members where they are." And as with EAA, Fuller forged a bond with the Recreational Aviation Foundation (RAF), and made a number of backcountry flights to RAF events on both coasts of the United States—this time in his newly purchased Aviat Husky. The economy was gradually recovering from the recession; more WAAS and GPS RNAV approaches were being commissioned; favorable outcomes to airport threats in Venice, Florida, and Palmyra, Wisconsin—among others—were secured; overall FAA tax cuts had saved general aviation pilots from spending $100 million in proposed user fees; and AOPA Foundation donations continued to rise.

But one dominant, existential challenge remained: the decline in the pilot population. Since 1980, the number of pilots had dropped by roughly 200,000. And everything that had been tried had so far failed to significantly reverse the trend. The current generation's leadership would be judged on how it dealt with this issue.

4000 FT
30.20"
226
Hdg Bug 052°
Alt Bug 4000 FT
VSI Bug 0 FPM
Baro Set 30.20"
Hdg-Sync
UTC 20:08:47
ABV 11
ERROR
NXR 3min
Traffic ABOVE
Lightning ERROR
Clear Strikes
Wx Rprts SIGMET
Emerg. Checklist
Map TAWS Chart Trip Nrst Chklst Setup Engine
KRDU
View CENTER
Declutter
BaseMap TERRAIN
Wx Ovly NEXRAD
Range
EXTERIOR LIGHTS
INTERIOR LIGHTS
GARMIN
PILOT
COPILOT
KRDU

9. ON THE THRESHOLD

Today's initiatives for tomorrow's pilots

It would fall to Mark Baker, AOPA's current president, to galvanize support against the critical, and increasing, number of challenges to general aviation. Baker—no relation to former president John L. Baker—came from a background different than those of his predecessors. His first job was working for $2 an hour at a lumberyard; he began flying as a teenager attending the University of Minnesota; and he then went on to serve as an executive with Home Depot, outdoor outfitter Gander Mountain, Scott's Miracle-Gro Company, and Orchard Supply Hardware, a West Coast home-improvement chain. Along the way, he has managed to own and fly a wide variety of airplanes, among them Beechcraft Bonanzas, Barons, and a Twin Beech on floats; Cessna piston twins; and even a TBM 700 and Cessna Citation jets. For all that, Baker likes his 1953 Piper Super Cub on floats the best. He may have bought and sold a small armada of lightplanes, but says he'll keep the Super Cub. With an informal, congenial persona, Baker would need his positive attitude for the many tasks ahead. In his first five years AOPA would launch an unprecedented number of efforts to advance general aviation's cause, fend off its opponents, and nullify adverse trends.

The 'driver's license medical'

Soon after his first days on the job in September 2013, Baker and AOPA's senior executives reviewed a two-year-old AOPA/EAA proposal that had the potential to make it easier for pilots to begin flying, or return to flying if sidelined. This was what came to be called the "driver's license medical" certificate. The idea, dating back to the 1980s, was to offer an alternative to the third class medical certificate requirement by essentially having pilots self-certify before flying certain light general aviation airplanes (fixed-gear piston singles of 180 horsepower or less, with no more than four seats, flown under VFR noncommercially, and carrying no more than one passenger). In this sense, the driver's license method would mimic the longstanding medical rules governing those who fly gliders. Pilots could fly their existing airplanes, and not have to buy a new, increasingly expensive airplane in the Light Sport aircraft (LSA) class, which already relied on self-certification. Although more than 16,000 comments favoring this proposal were filed with the FAA, the proposal did not progress out of the FAA's parent agency, the Department of Transportation. The will for change persisted, but it would take time, and much more effort, for this sort of medical certificate reform to come about.

Customs and border protection stops

The first reports began surfacing in late summer 2013. By October, AOPA had learned of 42 cases where general aviation airplanes on domestic flights were arbitrarily stopped and searched after landing by U.S. Customs and Border Protection (CBP) or Immigration and Customs Enforcement (ICE) agents, or a local police force acting on CBP's behalf, sometimes with weapons drawn. Access panels were often removed, and occupants were separately questioned and detained—for up to three hours—before being released. One such stop in the Chicago area involved 40 law enforcement personnel and 25 vehicles stopping a couple after they left their parked airplane, having tagged them as suspicious.

"This doesn't look like the work of a few misguided agents," said AOPA General Counsel Ken Mead.

Why were they stopped? The answers were vague. Agents would say that the airplanes were "flying erratically," or too slow, or air-filing flight plans, or landing in states where marijuana sales were legal.

AOPA, saying that the agents had no authority to stop and search the affected airplanes, filed a Freedom of Information Act (FOIA) request and learned that even internal CBP memos called these actions "zero-suspicion seizures." In the Senate GA Caucus, eight senators wrote to the head of the Department of Homeland Security (which controls both the CBP and ICE), demanding the records of all such stops since 2009.

The number of these sorts of stops and searches climbed to more than 50 by early 2014, and AOPA President Baker sent Gil Kerlikowske, the new CBP commissioner, a letter asking for a review of zero-suspicion activity. Baker met with Kerlikowske to talk over the problem, and our stalwart allies on Capitol Hill—Representative Sam Graves (R-Mo.) and Senator Pat Roberts (R-Kan.)—were instrumental in applying more pressure. The result was a CBP promise of better training and procedures. This included a tracking system to log all contacts with general aviation airplanes, and to refrain from using local law enforcement officers unfamiliar with general aviation to make stops. So far, this deal seems to have held up.

Even so, AOPA created a kneeboard-format set of guidelines titled "What to do if stopped by law enforcement," and made it available to all on AOPA's website.

Third class medical reform

With the "driver's license medical" lost in a bureaucratic wilderness, AOPA changed course and methods. The regulatory pathway was going nowhere. Baker decided it was time for a legislative solution to third class medical

PILOT IN COMMAND

Hangar talk with AOPA's current president

Here on the fifth anniversary of you taking the left seat at AOPA, what do you think of your role and where the organization is right now?
First of all, let me say that it is a special role, one that I wouldn't trade for anything. I can't imagine a better way to give back to aviation, which has been wonderful to me—personally and professionally. I couldn't have done what I did in my career in retail without general aviation. I am hopeful that my time here in some way helps to repay that debt that I have to this community and all it has done for me.

Given the threats facing general aviation, it would be easy to predict GA's best days are behind it. What do you see for the future?
I'm more optimistic now than I was five years ago—more optimistic than ever. There are good jobs in aviation right now; the pay is better than ever. We have a little bit of a tailwind. AOPA's work in educating young people about the opportunities in aviation, our fly-ins, the work we're doing with flying clubs—I'm bullish. There are those who say that people aren't interested in aviation anymore. That's not true. There's lots of interest. We just need to continue to knock down the hurdles that keep cropping up, and that's what this organization is really good at.

Among the challenges you've taken on is addressing the issues related to the aging fleet. Why is that so important?
With the industry only turning out about 1,000 new piston airplanes a year, we're never going to refresh the fleet. The good news is that we can make a difference in other ways. The aluminum on those old airplanes is still good. They fly just fine. We just need to modernize them and do so cost-effectively. That's why we have focused so much on the efforts to remanufacture older airframes and to bring non-TSOed equipment into the fleet. It's remarkable what you can do to an existing airplane, improving its safety, reliability, and utility. And then you look at the new propulsion systems coming along—electric and hybrids. They can lower costs, reduce noise. Add in the possibility of autonomous or semi-autonomous aircraft—light touch, we call them—that's going to lead to more companies and more people using aircraft, using airports. That's good for all of us. It's pretty darned exciting.

You've placed a lot of emphasis on the You Can Fly initiatives, particularly around growing the pilot population. That seems like a different role for AOPA.
It is. For decades, AOPA has mostly played defense, but we need to play offense, too. Some in the industry have had trouble accepting AOPA as an entity that is actively working to grow the pilot population. They want to pigeonhole us as just an advocacy organization, but looking at 30 years of declining pilot population we need to look forward, not just backward, and no organization is better positioned to do that than AOPA. Our mission has always been to protect the freedom to fly, and now a part of that is assuring that we have enough pilots and aircraft to keep general aviation viable. There is no silver bullet, but over time the You Can Fly initiatives can make a difference. And just as we have been with advocacy, we're in it for the long haul. AOPA is all about making the aviator safer, the aircraft better, and the airport accessible for all. That's what we do.

What advice would you give to whoever the president of AOPA might be on its 100th anniversary?
We should always celebrate the freedom to fly. Never give that up. I'm still excited about it; still fired up about it. The device and machine may change—and I hope it does. But there will always be people who enjoy defying gravity. This organization needs to be there for them. And I know it will be because of the strength of our membership, the expertise of our staff, and the dedication of this entire community.

certificate reform. Thus came about a measure signed into law on July 15, 2016, by President Barack Obama. It was a long time coming, since the first efforts to unburden third class medical requirements dated back to the 1980s, when the recreational pilot certificate was authorized.

The 2016 victory for medical reform was preceded by numerous stalled attempts. In 2011 Senator James Inhofe (R-Okla.) introduced a bill known as the Pilot's Bill of Rights that provided for an appeals process that would allow pilots facing FAA enforcement actions to bring their cases directly to U.S. district courts. It contained language that called for a committee to review medical certification, but the provisions were nonspecific.

Then came a bill called the General Aviation Pilot Protection Act. Introduced in late 2013, the bill had language that would have allowed those without third class medical certificates to fly airplanes with expanded performance envelopes, compared to the earlier driver's license proposal. The airplanes could be capable of flying no more than 250 knots up to 14,000 feet msl, have 6,000-pound maximum takeoff weights, and up to six seats. There was no mention of engine power, and airplanes with retractable landing gear were included.

The breakthrough came when medical reforms from the Pilot's Bill of Rights 2 passed as part of an FAA authorization extension. This was after AOPA members had sent some 220,000 letters to Congress supporting the measure. It was a major victory for general aviation. Pilots, not bureaucrats, would be responsible for their fitness to fly. Any pilot who held a valid medical certificate in the decade before July 15, 2016, may not need to take another FAA medical exam—and that includes regular medical certificates as well as special-issuance medicals. Those whose most recent medical certificate was revoked, denied, suspended, or withdrawn have to obtain a new FAA medical before being eligible for flying under the reforms. But those who have never held an FAA medical will only have to go through the process one time.

How does it work? Pilots visit any state-licensed physician every four years, at which time the pilot gives the doctor an FAA checklist to fill out, certifying that the pilot is safe to fly. The pilot makes a note of the visit and places his or her copy of the checklist in their pilot logbook. Every two years, the pilot takes a free online training course in aeromedical factors, keeping a completion certificate in his or her logbook. AOPA had a version of the online course ready when the FAA process became effective May, 1, 2017. If the pilot develops a disqualifying condition, he or she must obtain an FAA

"GOVERNMENT-APPOINTED MEDICS...CLAIM THEY HAVE SOMETHING THE FAMILY PHYSICIAN LACKS WHEN IT COMES TO PASSING A CANDIDATE MEDICALLY FOR A PILOT'S TICKET. WE ARE CURIOUS TO KNOW EXACTLY WHAT THAT 'SOMETHING' IS.

—"LET'S SIMPLIFY MEDICAL EXAMS," "AOPA SECTION," FEBRUARY 1945

THE LOWDOWN ON BASICMED

Reform was decades in the making

AOPA has submitted third class medical reform petitions to the FAA since the 1970s. With the exception of the sport pilot driver's license medical standard in 2004, the petitions fell on deaf ears. The sport pilot standard has now been in place for more than a decade—but despite its success, there was not enough support to expand it so more pilots could take a passenger and go for a ride on a Sunday afternoon in a Cessna 172 or Piper Cherokee.

So while BasicMed is a bit more complicated than a driver's license standard, it also allows for many more types of operations than previous proposals. BasicMed allows pilots to fly aircraft up to 6,000 pounds, up to 250 knots indicated airspeed, with five passengers, day, night, VFR, IFR, and at altitudes up to 18,000 feet msl.

Medical Reform Timeline

1942 The third class medical standard is introduced.

1960 The FAA "outlaws" use of family physicians for student and private medical certificates, and requires pilots to visit "designated examiners."

1979 AOPA submits a regulatory petition to extend the duration of third class medical certificates.

July 27, 2004 The FAA publishes a new rule allowing pilots to exercise the privileges of the sport pilot certificate without an FAA medical certificate.

March 20, 2012 In response to the FAA's request for changes to outdated or unnecessary regulations, AOPA submits a petition to strike the third class medical requirement and replace it with a driver's license standard.

April 2, 2014 The FAA announces it is beginning rulemaking aimed at easing third class medical requirements.

February 25, 2015 AOPA champions a legislative solution and works with lawmakers in the House and Senate, who introduce the Pilot's Bill of Rights 2, which includes third class medical reform language.

December 15, 2015 The Senate passes PBR 2.

April 19, 2016 The Senate passes PBR 2 language as part of a new FAA reauthorization.

June 14, 2016 The Senate passes PBR 2 language in the National Defense Authorization Act.

July 11, 2016 The House of Representatives passes H.R.636, an FAA extension that includes third class medical reform language.

July 13, 2016 The Senate adopts H.R.636 by voice vote.

July 15, 2016 President Barack Obama signs H.R.636.

May 1, 2017 BasicMed goes into effect.

special issuance and start the process over again to seek the new certification, now called simply BasicMed.

For most, BasicMed meant not seeing an aviation medical examiner ever again. Best of all, compared to earlier proposals, BasicMed further expands the performance envelopes and privileges of eligible airplanes. BasicMed pilots can fly singles and twins (there are no limitations on engine power), with fixed or retractable gear, at altitudes up to 18,000 feet msl, day or night, under either visual or instrument flight rules, and carrying up to five passengers in an airplane with no more than six seats. The 6,000-pound maximum takeoff weight and 250-knot speed limitations, plus the caveats regarding no compensation or for hire, remain.

The significance of BasicMed can't be overstated. Before, pilots with medical issues had to wait long periods of time and undergo repeated testing after even routine procedures. Many such pilots were told they couldn't fly—even though they'd been successfully treated. This discouraged many from even trying, and almost certainly tempted others to not reveal or treat a medical condition out of fear of FAA reprisal. By one year in, more than 30,000 pilots had qualified to fly under BasicMed.

Regional Fly-Ins

BasicMed was but one of the initiatives with the potential to build the pilot population. "We need more openness, and a welcoming spirit, to make general aviation airports more attractive to the general public, especially younger people," Baker is fond of saying, "and not have it look like a maximum-security prison." This was the key thought behind the plan to offer multiple regional fly-ins each year, rather than a single national convention. By making

AOPA's wings and other insignia carried essentially the same look since the beginning in 1939. The wings and other graphics were updated as part of a 2016 rebranding move aimed at modernizing AOPA's public face.

LIGHT SPORT

The Icon A5's futuristic looks promised an uplifting jolt to the Light Sport airplane market. But a series of setbacks—manufacturing delays, price hikes, and a pair of fatal accidents—marred its reputation among many pilots. Some suggest that Icon's demonstration flights, involving aggressive low-altitude maneuvering, set the stage for fatal accidents.

ICON A5

Singular sensation

Icon Aircraft created a sensation with its sleek A5 amphibian. Folding wings, carbon fiber material, exquisite design—and a bold marketing message that rejected the traditional, business-oriented general aviation sales pitch—made the Icon A5 stand out since its first flight in 2008.

This Light Sport airplane is all about fun, excitement, and good times on the lake with friends. The company downplayed traditional aircraft measures of speed, range, and payload, and it created dynamic videos that showed off the airplane's attributes: visibility, maneuverability, comfort, and safety.

Icon filled its order book with more than 1,800 aircraft deposits, and the California firm announced ambitious plans to quickly become the biggest single-engine airplane manufacturer in the world by producing hundreds of airplanes annually. It successfully lobbied the FAA for an exemption to Light Sport aircraft weight limits that allowed the company to incorporate "anti-spin" features that made the A5 highly resistant to stalls and spins.

Initial reviews of the A5 and its flying qualities have been universally glowing. But more recently Icon has had to endure some punishing and unexpected blows.

In May 2017, Icon's designer Jon Karkow and engineer Cagri Sever were killed in an A5 crash at Lake Berryessa near the company's Napa Valley, California, home base. An NTSB report showed that Karkow, the pilot, made a navigational error and mistakenly turned into a dead-end canyon. The loss was a gut punch to Icon, which had recruited the highly respected designer, only to lose him and another promising engineer in a tragic, fluke accident.

Icon also faced production delays and cost overruns, and those led to price increases that caused some depositors to seek refunds. Understandable, since the original price target was about $140,000, but prices upon delivery were mostly in the neighborhood of $400,000. Instead of high-rate production that drives unit costs down, the company was building airplanes slowly, and that drove unit costs sharply up. Icon shifted composite parts production to Mexico in an effort to speed production of labor-intensive components, but that move caused even more delays.

Icon delivered its first production A5 to former baseball great Roy Halladay in late 2017, and tragedy struck again. Halladay, an experienced pilot with an instrument rating, was killed while flying solo near his home on Florida's Gulf Coast. The accident investigation turned up evidence that Halladay had mood-altering drugs in his bloodstream, as well as eyewitness reports and video that he was maneuvering aggressively at dangerously low altitude in the minutes leading up to the crash.

Icon has established flight schools in California and Florida that teach both new and experienced pilots to fly the A5, and the company plans to open more of them in Texas and elsewhere. Icon also started a fractional ownership program that sells membership to Icon clubs around the country in an effort to create a distinct community and lower ownership costs.

It's unclear whether Icon will ever be able to live up to its brash goal of reinventing and vastly expanding general aviation by attracting youthful, adventure-oriented pilots. But the A5 is an airplane with broad and deep appeal.

N550AD
N185CX
N8516M
WWW.BONANZA.ORG

Like all of AOPA's regional fly-ins, the ramp scene at AOPA's fly-in at Camarillo, California, in 2017 drew crowds, including many young families who wouldn't otherwise have the chance to see airplanes up close.

them free of charge to anyone; locating them at airports across the nation; and exposing a younger, family-oriented crowd to regional fly-ins, the spirit and fun of general aviation flying could go a long way to building rapport with more pilots—and, especially, nonpilots.

Previously, AOPA held annual conventions, beginning with the Plantation Parties, then conventions and expos, then summits. "But the conventions and summits didn't make sense," Baker said. "A lot of members and others said they were too far away, too time-consuming, and too expensive. We needed to get to thousands of others."

In their first year, seven fly-ins attracted 16,000 attendees. Subsequent years saw four and five fly-ins per year, equally well-attended, with all of them featuring large static displays, live music, and parties at the end of the day. By 2016, when the fly-ins switched to two-day events, the total number of attendees (many of them young families) reached 43,760, along with 6,026 aircraft that flew in for the events. By 2018, more than 80,000 people and 8,000 aircraft had participated.

THE DRONE REVOLUTION

Great ideas from university dorm rooms

This is an open question to the next generation: What are you doing in your dorm rooms? We all know Facebook mogul Mark Zuckerberg started his little enterprise in his college dorm room and, guess what? The largest drone manufacturer in the world started his business in his dorm room, too! Frank Wang, founder of DJI, which as of summer 2018 controlled 70 percent of the world drone market, was granted $2,300 from the Hong Kong University of Science and Technology to develop an unmanned aerial vehicle. He created his first drone in his dorm room in 2006. DJI—Da Jiang Innovations—is currently the market leader in commercial drone production; its Phantom line, now on its fourth generation, is the leader in easy-to-fly, camera-mounted, commercial and recreational drones. The quadcopter style is also the most popular. DJI is located in Shenzhen, China's "Silicon Valley." At 37, Wang became Asia's youngest tech billionaire in 2017. The FAA estimates there are 110,000 commercial drones in use as of summer 2018 and projects there will be 450,000 by 2022—with the model UAS fleet growing from 1.1 million in 2017 to 2.4 million in 2022. The agency also believes there will be 300,000 registered remote pilots (holding Part 107 certificates) by 2022.

Active U.S. Pilots in 2014 | **593,499** ▼

MEET-UPS

An event by any other name

Associations love meetings. Getting the membership together in one form or another is a central objective of most associations. Over the years, AOPA's meetings have ranged from social to formal, and today they've come full circle.

AOPA's first member meetings took place in 1940, soon after the organization was founded. These "breakfast flights" were not unlike the pancake breakfasts of today. AOPA executives would join a group of pilots at a destination and engage in social activities. Many of those early events celebrated pilots' shared love of flying, and didn't dwell on becoming a better pilot or buying new gear, although some were clinics focused on skills. They were held in beach towns, near cities, and other tourist-friendly spots.

In the late 1950s, the flavor of the events changed and they became somewhat more formalized. This era of Plantation Parties (so-called because they tended to be held in the South) were high-end affairs that were party first, business second.

Over the years the events became more academic, and more businesslike. Plantation Parties gave way to an annual meeting, and shortly after Phil Boyer became president of AOPA, the annual expo. This change created a more typical annual trade show, complete with vendors, seminars, evening events, and more. President Craig Fuller changed the name of the event to AOPA Aviation Summit, with the goal of creating an event that also showcased ideas and big thinkers.

President Mark Baker believed the organization needed a new direction, one that turns out to be as old as AOPA itself. The regional fly-ins now mirror the original events, with social gatherings, free admission, and diverse locations.

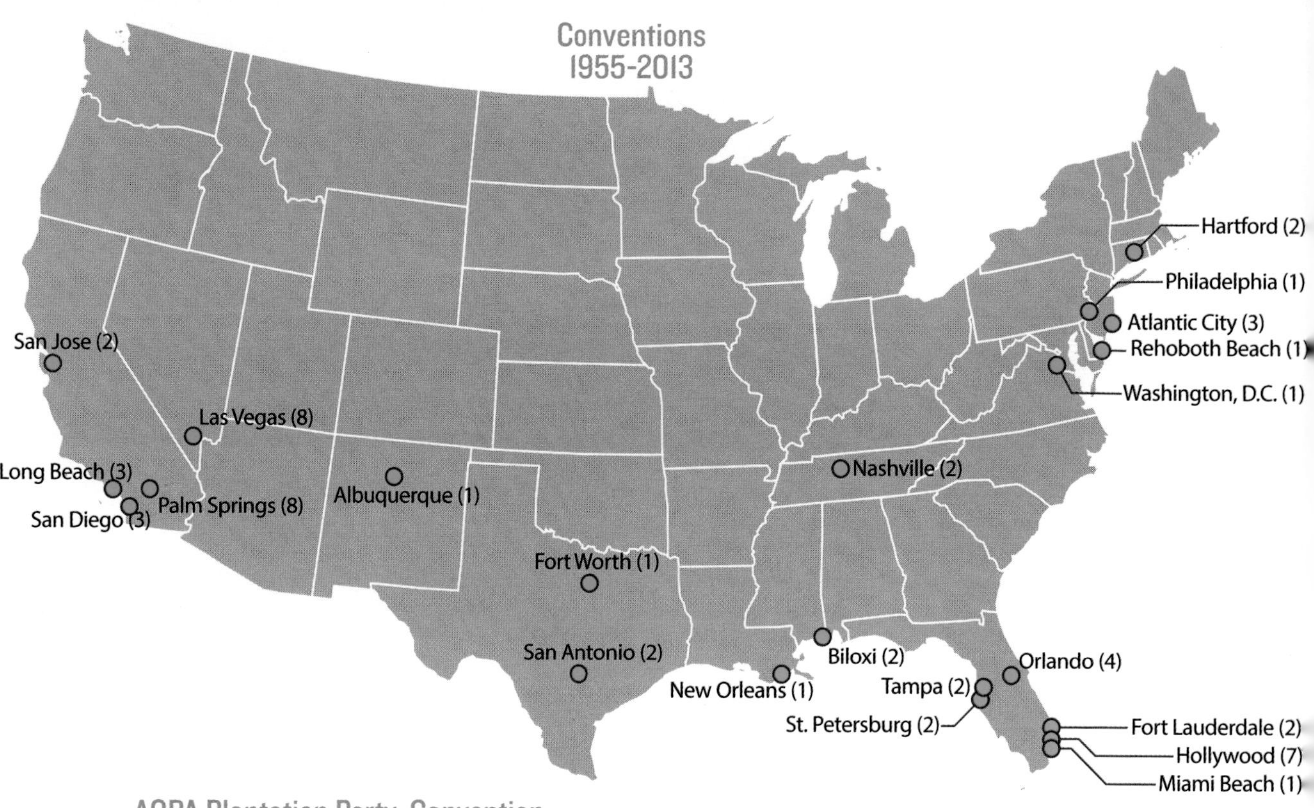

AOPA Plantation Party, Convention, Expo, and Summit Locations

Plantation Party	1955	Rehoboth Beach, Delaware (not officially labeled)
	1956	Edgewater Park, Mississippi (Biloxi) ("Plantation Party" was a Saturday-night event)
	1957	Edgewater Park, Mississippi (at the same hotel, reportedly because of attendee demand)
	1958	St. Petersburg, Florida
	1959	Fort Lauderdale, Florida
	1960	Las Vegas, Nevada
	1961	St. Petersburg, Florida
	1962	Miami Beach, Florida
	1963	Palm Springs, California
	1964	Hollywood, Florida
	1965	Las Vegas, Nevada
	1966	Palm Springs, California
	1967	Hollywood, Florida
	1968	Las Vegas, Nevada
	1969	Atlantic City, New Jersey
	1970	Hollywood, Florida
	1971	Las Vegas, Nevada
	1972	Hollywood, Florida
	1973	San Diego, California
	1974	Hollywood, Florida
	1975	San Diego, California
	1976	San Antonio, Texas
	1977	Hollywood, Florida
	1978	Las Vegas, Nevada
	1979	Hollywood, Florida
Convention	1980	San Diego, California
	1981	Orlando, Florida
	1982	Las Vegas, Nevada
	1983	Albuquerque, New Mexico
	1984	Nashville, Tennessee
	1985	Washington, D.C.
	1986	San Antonio, Texas
	1987	Las Vegas, Nevada
	1988	Nashville, Tennessee
	1989	Orlando, Florida
	1990	Palm Springs, California

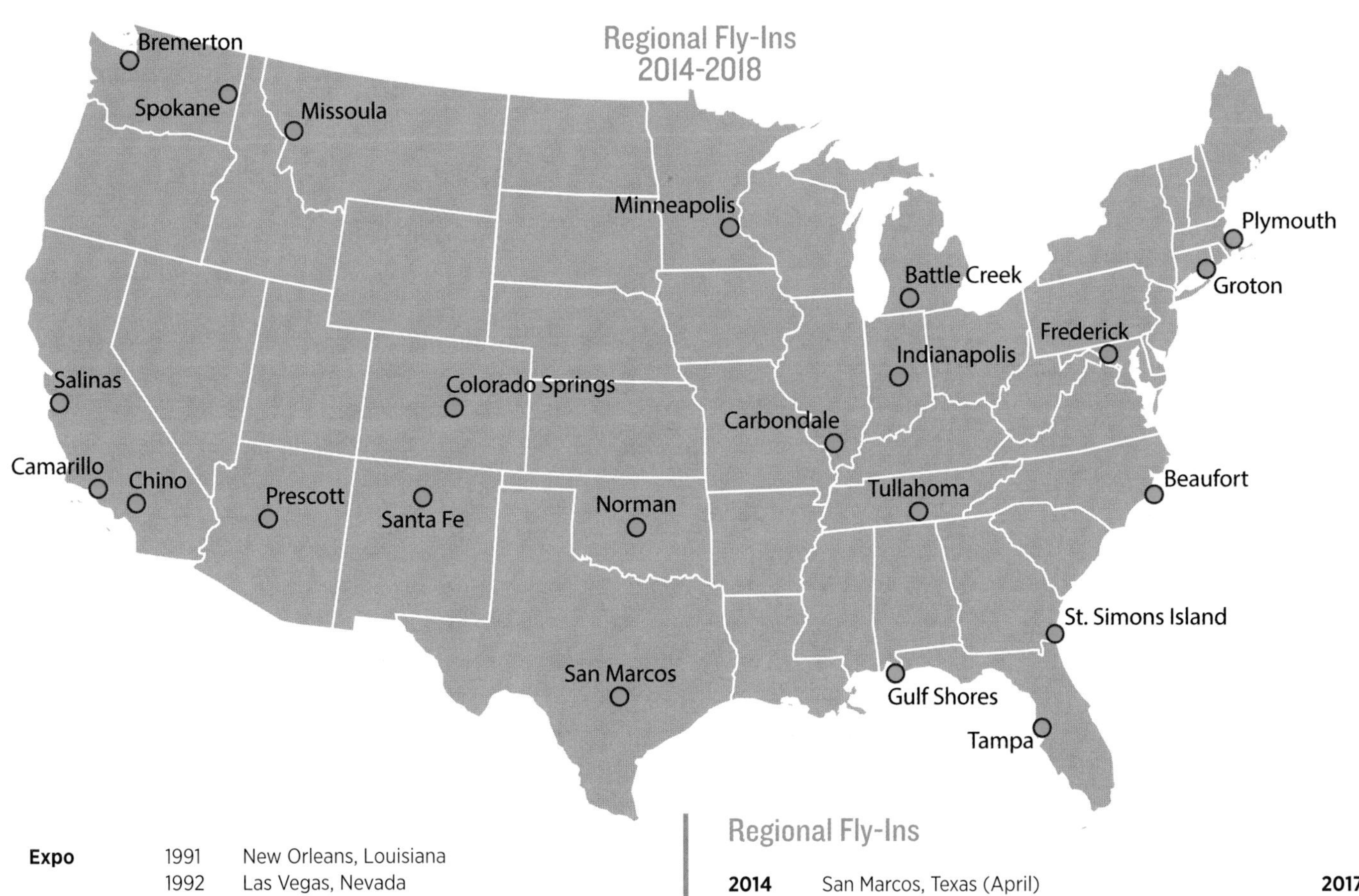

AOPA's Plantation Parties, Conventions, Expos, and Summits returned often to the same popular locations (facing page). That left large areas of the country beyond practical flying distance, so the AOPA Fly-Ins (this page) have been strategically located to reach as many members as possible where they fly.

Expo	1991	New Orleans, Louisiana
	1992	Las Vegas, Nevada
	1993	Orlando, Florida
	1994	Palm Springs, California
	1995	Atlantic City, New Jersey
	1996	San Jose, California
	1997	Orlando, Florida
	1998	Palm Springs, California
	1999	Atlantic City, New Jersey
	2000	Long Beach, California
	2001	Fort Lauderdale, Florida
	2002	Palm Springs, California
	2003	Philadelphia, Pennsylvania
	2004	Long Beach, California
	2005	Tampa, Florida
	2006	Palm Springs, California
	2007	Hartford, Connecticut
	2008	San Jose, California
Summit	2009	Tampa, Florida
	2010	Long Beach, California
	2011	Hartford, Connecticut
	2012	Palm Springs, California
	2013	Fort Worth, Texas

Regional Fly-Ins

2014
San Marcos, Texas (April)
Indianapolis, Indiana (May)
Plymouth, Massachusetts (July)
Spokane, Washington (August)
Chino, California (September)
Frederick, Maryland (October)
St. Simons Island, Georgia (November)

2015
Salinas, California (May)
Frederick, Maryland (June)
Tullahoma, Tennessee (October)
Minneapolis, Minnesota (August)
Colorado Springs, Colorado (September)

2016
Beaufort, North Carolina (May)
Bremerton, Washington (August)
Battle Creek, Michigan (September)
Prescott, Arizona (October)

2017
Camarillo, California (April)
Norman, Oklahoma (September)
Groton, Connecticut (October)
Tampa, Florida (October)

2018
Missoula, Montana (June)
Santa Fe, New Mexico (September)
Carbondale, Illinois (October)
Gulf Shores, Alabama (October)

FUELING AVIATION'S FUTURE

Donations to the AOPA Foundation support general aviation

Established in 2007, the AOPA Foundation is a 501(c)(3) nonprofit organization that accepts tax-deductible contributions to fund efforts, which help pilots fly safer and strengthen our pilot community. Although AOPA membership dues cover advocacy, publications, and many other member services, enerous donors' contributions to the AOPA Foundation support the important work of the AOPA Air Safety Institute and the You Can Fly program.

AOPA Air Safety Institute
The AOPA Air Safety Institute (ASI) creates safety education programs that are available free to all pilots thanks to donations to the AOPA Foundation. In 2017, ASI's seminars, videos, podcasts, and publications were utilized more than 3.6 million times. Since 1950, ASI's goal has been to make general aviation safer—and it's working. The general aviation accident rate reached an all-time low of 0.84 per 100,000 flight hours in 2017.

You Can Fly program
The AOPA Foundation funds the You Can Fly program to get—and keep—more pilots flying. The You Can Fly program comprises four initiatives: High School, Flight Training, Flying Clubs, and Rusty Pilots.

The High School initiative offers comprehensive STEM-based aviation curriculum to high school students nationwide. Through the program, AOPA is opening the door to aviation careers for thousands of teens. The courses are designed to capture the imagination and give students from diverse backgrounds the tools to pursue advanced education and careers in aviation fields. The initiative includes the STEM-based curriculum, flight training scholarships, and an annual symposium for educators.

The Flight Training initiative is developing resources to make the flight training experience easier and more enjoyable for students and training providers alike. The initiative also presents the annual Flight Training Experience Awards, which recognize outstanding flight schools and instructors, as identified by their customers.

The Flying Clubs initiative focuses on building and growing flying clubs so more pilots can enjoy the benefits of shared ownership and community, making flying more affordable and enjoyable. The initiative has launched nearly 100 new clubs and holds "Maximum Fun, Minimum Cost" seminars throughout the country to expose pilots to the benefits of flying club membership.

The Rusty Pilots initiative supports those pilots who stopped flying and who now want to return to the air. Rusty Pilots seminars, held nationwide, make it easy for lapsed pilots to regain currency. Nearly 6,000 of them have gone on to successfully complete a flight review. The course is also available online.

The AOPA Foundation offers several ways to contribute, and donors can select the best fit for their financial situation. Visit aopafoundation.org/donate to make a one-time gift or set up monthly contributions. For information on other ways to give, including wire transfers, gifts of stock, IRA rollovers, and endowments, visit aopafoundation.org/ways. Donors who contribute up to $999 are recognized as Friends of General Aviation. Members of the Hat in the Ring Society contribute $1,000 to $9,999 in the "meet any challenge" spirit of the 94th Aero Squadron that fought in World War I. Inclusion in additional recognition groups is available for contributions of more than $10,000. Visit aopafoundation.org/legacy to learn more about joining the Legacy Society and recognition in Legacy Court (below) at AOPA headquarters in Frederick, Maryland.

You Can Fly

While the regional fly-ins are outreach programs with a long-term objective aimed at bringing the public and general aviation together, AOPA had long since identified a more pressing crisis. We've already addressed the declining pilot population, and by 2015, things had only become worse. General aviation lightplane manufacturing hit its peak in the late 1970s, followed by a breathtaking plunge. The pilot population was surging at the same time, with 827,071 active pilots in 1980. Then came a slow but steady downward trajectory to 590,038 pilots in 2015—a drop of more than 28 percent in 35 years. As for new private pilot certificate issuances in the same period, there was a stunning 67-percent decline, from 1980's 50,458 to 2015's 16,473. Something had to be done—again. We've already seen how programs such as Project Pilot, Project Pilot Mentor, and the Center to Advance the Pilot Community tried to turn the trend around.

In 2014, AOPA built on those efforts and answered with renewed energy by establishing You Can Fly, a multi-faceted program with the goal of building the pilot community. Headed up by AOPA Senior Vice President of Aviation Strategy and Programs Katie Pribyl, and with funding from donations to the AOPA Foundation, You Can Fly started out by offering its Rusty Pilots seminars. These free seminars target lapsed pilots with a desire to get back in the game. In its first year, 58 classes teaching 1,750 pilots were held; some were conducted as part of the regional fly-ins. By late 2018, tens of thousands of rusty pilots had attended the seminar and more than 5,800 were back flying again.

The Flying Clubs initiative offers guidance and expertise on how to form a flying club, a network of flying clubs that offers communication through a *Club Connector* newsletter, and a Flying Club Finder to locate a flying club near you. AOPA Ambassadors travel within their regions to set up meetings, help start flying clubs, conduct Rusty Pilots seminars, and bring AOPA resources to the grassroots level. Ambassadors fly distinctive yellow "Reimagined" Cessna 152s and 172s on their travels as a way of showing how fully refurbished older airplanes can serve as an inexpensive and capable means of recreational flying.

A High School initiative provides a curriculum for science, technology, engineering, and mathematics (STEM) courses geared to aviation, plus an annual educator's symposium designed to "teach the teachers" and foster an exchange of information and strategy.

The Flight Training program provides information, training, resources, and *Flight School Business* newsletters to those in the industry. This program also gives out annual Flight Training Experience Awards to CFIs and schools voted the best in a nationwide survey. The effort built upon a program Fuller had begun that was modeled on similar award programs in the healthcare and restaurant industries. By highlighting the great work of other institutions, the awards seek to raise the standard for everyone in flight training. In a separate show of support for flight training, AOPA gives out dozens of scholarships each year ranging from $2,500 to $12,000 each to use toward a private pilot certificate or advanced training. All of these scholarships are made possible by funding from the AOPA Foundation.

At last count, You Can Fly has a lot to be proud of. The flying club network has surpassed 800 participating clubs—including nearly 100 new clubs started under the program; more

The Flight Training initiative in AOPA's You Can Fly program helps flight schools leverage resources such as new-generation, lower-cost simulators to provide a positive, effective training experience for students.

WINGS AND WHEELS >

Since the beginning of powered flight, automobile companies have tinkered in aviation, some more seriously than others. Ford, of course, was serious about the Trimotor and a few other, lesser-known models. Around the globe on both sides of the Allied/Axis line, automobile companies played significant roles in World War II manufacturing. BMW once built aircraft engines. Mercedes automobile engines are the backbone of several GA diesel engines. Similarly, Renault was a partner in development of the SMA diesel engine. In the 1990s, Toyota certified an aviation variant of its Lexus engine, but never put it into production. The company also designed two four-place piston singles and flew a proof of concept of one of them before shelving the project. Nissan engines powered the ill-fated Pond Racer in the early 1990s. But only Honda with its unusual HondaJet (right) has stuck it out all the way through design, development, and now full-fledged production. The 20-year project has paid off, with the light jet finding a niche among individual owners and charter operators. Designed and shepherded by Honda Aircraft President and CEO Michimasa Fujino, the jet features a cockpit shape designed to maintain laminar flow and over-the-wing pylon-mounted engines, also meant to reduce drag. The result is an airplane that leads its class in speed, fuel economy, and cabin space. And Honda didn't stop at just aircraft design. It teamed with GE to create the new generation of engines that power the HondaJet.

N420EX
HONDA

LEAPING FROM THE STRATOSPHERE

Alan Eustace and Felix Baumgartner pushed limits

They seem an unlikely pair to have something in common—Alan Eustace is a computer scientist who could have been featured in a remake of *Revenge of the Nerds,* and Felix Baumgartner (right) is an Austrian skydiver who dates supermodels. But both achieved the same thing—and Eustace did it better (nerd revenge!). Eustace, a pilot, holds the record for highest-altitude freefall stratospheric parachute jump, but Baumgartner did it first. Baumgartner jumped to Earth from a helium balloon on October 14, 2012. He ascended in the balloon for nearly 90 minutes, reaching just more than 24 miles above Earth. He then jumped and his parachute deployed three minutes and 48 seconds later. Eustace climbed to 26 miles in a gas-powered balloon, which he hung tethered below on October 24, 2014. An explosive separated him from his balloon, and his freefall lasted 15 minutes. Because Eustace used a drogue parachute (more elongated, producing less drag) the two jumpers' vertical speed and freefall distance records are in different world record categories.

than 80 high schools are offering aviation-related STEM classes to more than 2,000 students in its first year; more than 5,000 pilots are flying again, thanks to Rusty Pilots seminars; and more than $100,000 in flight training scholarships have been awarded.

ADS-B compliance

Of course, a sagging pilot population isn't the only news affecting general aviation. On the technology front, plenty has been afoot. One is an industry/government effort to eliminate lead from avgas; representatives from AOPA, EAA, GAMA, NBAA, and NATA serve on the steering committee for the FAA's Piston Aviation Fuels Initiative (PAFI). The FAA's quest for an unleaded fuel replacement for 100LL avgas began in earnest in 2013, supported by $6 million in federal funds. By July 1, 2014, the agency closed the window for companies to submit their alternative fuels for testing. Initially, nine fuels from five fuel companies were submitted. Top contenders Swift Fuels submitted samples of two of its fuels, and Shell and Total each submitted one sample. The first phase of testing—which required 100 gallons of fuel—examined the fuels' impacts on the existing fleet of avgas-powered aircraft, the fuels' production and distribution infrastructure, any environmental or toxic effects, and the operational costs of using biofuels. Phase 2 would require 10,000 gallons for full-scale engine testing. Testing is taking place at the FAA's William J. Hughes Technical Center in Atlantic City, New Jersey. The FAA hoped to complete testing by the end of 2019, at which time any compliant fuels will have earned ASTM (formerly American Society of Testing and Materials) product specification approval. After that, the FAA can authorize the use of these fuels in the general aviation fleet.

Swift Fuels and Shell were selected for Phase 2 evaluations in static engine tests and in-flight trials in April 2016, including those for low- and high-temperature operations, carburetor icing, detonation, and particulate emissions, among many others. Swift Fuels, however, has dropped out of the PAFI trials in favor of an alternative fuel certification path.

Hanging over many pilots' heads is the mandate to comply with the rule to equip their airplanes with Automatic Dependent Surveillance-Broadcast (ADS-B) Out transceivers. Without ADS-B Out in your cockpit, you won't be able to fly in airspace where a Mode C transponder is required. This ambitious new technology, a central part of the NextGen ATC system of the future, uses GPS satellites, ground-based stations, and cockpit equipment to give both pilots and controllers more accurate position information, collision-avoidance guidance, and enhanced point-to-point GPS navigation and approaches. Another aspect of ADS-B technology is its ability, via a datalinked ADS-B In receive-only functionality, to provide pilots with in-flight graphic and text weather, plus ground-based Doppler weather radar imagery and nearby traffic information—free of charge.

But first you must buy and install ADS-B Out (ADS-B In is not mandatory) by a hard deadline: January 1, 2020. And this had been a problem, because, in many cases, buying and installing ADS-B Out equipment for a certified aircraft runs from $5,000 to $6,000 at a minimum. AOPA did some research and learned that 43 percent of registered fixed-gear piston singles were valued at $40,000 or less in 2014, so it's no wonder tens of thousands of pilots and owners were unable or reluctant to invest in avionics worth nearly one-fourth the value of the airplane.

By 2015, only 10,000 aircraft owners had complied with the ADS-B Out mandate. That's a slow response, since the final rule was published in 2010. An FAA-industry task force was formed to address barriers to ADS-B implementation, and AOPA was a member. In the end, the private sector did what the task force couldn't, with some avionics manufacturers introducing innovative and simple new products that halve purchase prices and reduce installation times. But as the 2020 deadline drew nearer, owners were still reluctant. So much so that in a June 6, 2016, meeting of the Wichita Aero Club, FAA Administrator Michael Heurta announced a twelve-month FAA program that pledged rebates of $500 to the next 20,000 single-engine

TIP OF THE NEXTGEN ICEBERG

ADS-B is key to future capabilities

By 2015, talk among aircraft owners increasingly included ADS-B. Automatic Dependent Surveillance-Broadcast, a key technology behind the FAA's Next Generation Air Transportation System, uses satellites instead of ground-based radar to determine aircraft location. The FAA mandated installation of ADS-B Out equipment for flights after January 1, 2020, in airspace where only a Mode C transponder was previously required.

Think of ADS-B as a datalink, broadcasting the aircraft's position—determined by a very accurate GPS receiver—every second. Optional equipment allows the pilot to receive and view weather and other flight information, as well as nearby traffic, on a panel-mounted display or tablet. Ground network of 666 radio stations receive ADS-B position broadcasts and forward them to ATC facilities, where the ADS-B data is fused with radar returns and displayed to controllers. ADS-B will replace some FAA ground-based radars, especially en route radars, which are slow to update and expensive to maintain. Ground stations also relay traffic information as needed, and transmit graphical and textual weather data and other flight information to properly equipped aircraft.

But ADS-B was hardly new in 2015. The technology was validated during the Capstone demonstration program in Alaska during the late 1990s. Capstone had a broader focus that included prevention of controlled flight into terrain accidents and midair collisions, and featured large (for the time), color moving map displays in the cockpit in addition to an early ADS-B datalink. Enhanced displays and electronically aided terrain avoidance soon made their way into general aviation cockpits through increasingly sophisticated GPS navigators. In May 2010, the FAA published a final rule mandating airspace-based ADS-B equipage by 2020.

The FAA characterizes its modernization of the U.S. air transportation system—with the goal of increasing safety, efficiency, and capacity—as one of the most ambitious infrastructure projects in U.S. history. NextGen seeks to benefit pilots, commercial operators, and air traffic controllers with better information and tools that help aircraft reach their destinations more quickly, using less fuel and producing fewer emissions. Initial estimates put the cost of ADS-B compliance as high as $10,000 to $15,000 for even the most basic general aviation aircraft. However, determined efforts by AOPA, combined with innovations from some avionics manufacturers, resulted in the availability of compliant hardware for less than $2,000, exclusive of installation.

The first NextGen improvements rolled out in 2007, and all major components are targeted to be in place by 2025. Many new capabilities, such as optimized profile descent, are designed to address air carrier issues. But new automation and other support for air traffic controllers can benefit all pilots. And many general aviation aircraft owners have benefitted from performance-based navigation, which uses Wide Area Augmentation System-enhanced GPS signals to enable more than 14,000 instrument approaches. New LPV procedures provide ILS-like minimums to thousands of airports—many of which never had a precision instrument approach. As AOPA enters its eighth decade, however, it's clear that NextGen's greatest benefit to general aviation has been the incredible pilot situational awareness made possible by in-cockpit display of datalinked traffic and near-real-time weather information.

N16196

Like Chicago's Meigs Field before it, Santa Monica, California's general aviation airport faces harassment and threats of closure. Its runway has been shortened, and barriers to airplane-watchers have been erected. An agreement between the FAA and the city of Santa Monica allowed the runway to be shortened to 3,500 feet in exchange for the city's keeping the airport open until the end of 2028.

piston owners who equip with ADS-B Out. Huerta said the fleet needed to be equipping at a rate of 23,000 to 25,000 aircraft per year. But at the time, Aircraft Electronics Association (AEA) President Paula Derks said that the installation rate was less than half that, even though avionics shops could handle the expanded workload.

AOPA applauded other technology innovations and regulatory reform. A remote-tower experiment involving the use of airports equipped with cameras, dedicated communications facilities, and air traffic- and weather-radar overlays was conducted at Leesburg, Virginia's Executive Airport. The program uses remotely located tower personnel and has shown promise in increasing controller efficiency while improving traffic flow. As of April 2016, a hike in the training credit for using an advanced aviation training device (AATD) toward the instrument flight time requirement for the instrument rating went from 10 to 20 hours. Students in FAR Part 141 schools now receive up to 14 hours of credit in an AATD, up from 3.5 hours. And changes that took effect in 2018 allow commercial pilot applicants to train in technically advanced aircraft in lieu of complex airplanes.

The association also backed the movement to allow non-TSOed avionics and other equipment to be installed in FAR Part 23 airplanes. New aircraft sales may have been relatively flat for decades, but shops were full as owners increasingly took advantage of full-featured, advanced avionics with impressive displays. Why limit them to use in Experimental-category airplanes when they've demonstrated their usefulness and reliability well enough for certified airplanes? AOPA, EAA, and others continue to argue that performance-based metrics should be developed so that non-TSOed equipment can be included in any future Part 23 airplanes.

Santa Monica Airport

As always, challenges at the state level also consumed much of the general aviation stage. AOPA joined the Colorado Pilots Association to reverse a ban on seaplane operations on state waters. The association helped defeat an effort by the state of Ohio to divert $6 million in airport funding to nonaviation-related economic programs. New Jersey's Solberg-Hunterdon Airport, a 75-year-old, family-owned, public use airport, badgered by the local township with threats of seizure by eminent domain, has its future back after a judge ruled in favor of the family.

But if the early 2000s had its Meigs Field, today we face similarly daunting problems with the actions the Santa Monica city council continues to pursue in hopes of eliminating California's historic Santa Monica Airport. And as with Meigs, the goal is to replace it with housing or other development.

Santa Monica Airport has been in existence since 1919, and was home to the Douglas Aircraft Company's factory. The federal government leased the airport from the city of Santa Monica during World War II. Afterward, it relinquished its leasehold and the city resumed operation of the airport. It grew as Douglas built its DC–4s, –6s, and –7s there, and as more and more general aviation air traffic used Santa Monica in the economic boom of the 1950s and 1960s. Total operations reached a high of 365,000 per year—or about 975 takeoffs and landings per day. Noise became an issue, even though everyone living near it knew an airport was close by. The first jet curfew came in 1968. When Douglas began building its four-engine DC–8 jet airliners, the city objected, so Douglas set up its factory at Long Beach, California.

In 1979, the Santa Monica city council enacted its first ban on larger jets, including larger corporate jets. Another jet ban came in 2008, but this time the FAA objected, and a U.S. District Court agreed and issued a restraining order, which the city appealed. AOPA filed an *amicus curiae* (friend of the court) brief. And the court upheld the FAA side of the argument. Why? Because in the 1980s the city council voted to close the airport, giving all tenants 30 days to clear out. The FAA and the city reached an agreement specifying how the airport was to be run over the next 30 years. A federal Airport Improvement Program grant in the 1990s assured that the airport would be open until August 2023.

But that didn't stop the harassment. In 2011, a Santa Monica "visionary project" was formed to discuss the airport's potential as something other than an airport. In 2013 the city talked about ending fuel sales and not renewing leases. The city even filed a lawsuit against the FAA seeking control of the airport property. In 2014, AOPA and NBAA filed another *amicus curiae* brief in another city lawsuit seeking land control, which was rejected.

At this point AOPA supported a ballot initiative that would give voters a say in the airport's future. However, a controversial January 2017 weekend, backdoor agreement between the FAA and the city of Santa Monica resulted in the city's shortening the single runway (from 4,973 feet to 3,500 feet) in exchange for keeping it open until at least December 31, 2028. Then it becomes the city's choice as to whether to keep it open or not. "We're not going to stop fighting for Santa Monica," said Baker. "Now we have time to change minds and make sure that this airport continues to operate as it should." That will be a big job, but as usual, we'll have NBAA's help in matters affecting airport access.

The city's harassment of FBOs, hangar tenants, and pilots shows the commitment of both government and local protest groups. Aircraft owners have been subject to "security inspections." Plexiglass barriers between observation and movement areas have been built to discourage airplane watching. The city at one point threatened to refuse any lease extensions. City officials have openly discussed other, similar measures to discourage airport use. In one bold move, the city sent eviction notices to FBO Atlantic Aviation and flight school American Flyers. The FAA countered with cease and desist orders. FAA Administrator Michael Huerta said the city was "obligated to allow tenants to provide services."

If Santa Monica is further minimized, or closed, 175 businesses, 1,500 jobs, and $275 million in economic output would be lost. The 102,000 annual operations would have to shift to other airports in the Los Angeles basin. And surveys have shown that nearby residents don't want the airport closed. They would rather see the local government deal with automobile traffic problems, improve schools, and provide more parking. A 2011 survey of Santa Monica residents showed that the airport ranked sixteenth out of 17 issues of concern, that 53 percent want the airport to stay open, and that 54 percent feel it benefits the county.

For now, Santa Monica remains open. Of the latest FAA rulings, Baker said, "It's a reprieve, not a rout." Until the end of 2028, Santa Monica will remain open, and AOPA will remain vigilant—both before and after that date.

Electric aircraft

BEFORE ITS TIME

Electric technology outpaces certification

Cars are going all-electric or hybrid. Boats are going electric. Solar panels adorn house after house across the nation's suburbs. It seems like it's time for aviation to see some electric innovation as well.

Decisions on which powerplant to use in a vehicle are driven more by economics or performance than environmental considerations. Which is why aircraft manufacturers in the United States haven't been enthusiastic about electric propulsion. While the motor technology has long been suitable, heavy batteries and relatively cheap avgas take away incentives for innovation.

That's why it's not surprising that the first practical all-electric airplane hailed from Europe. In a place where avgas is extremely expensive and noise is a major concern, electric power can be more competitive. But Slovenian manufacturer Pipistrel's Alpha Electro (right) has proved that electric can be suitable everywhere.

Based on Pipistrel's Light Sport Alpha trainer, the Electro is an all-electric two-seat training aircraft with a one-hour endurance. The Alpha was created to fit under the Light Sport rules, and the Electro does as well with one key exception—initial adoption of the LSA standards didn't have a provision for electric propulsion.

The initial aircraft in the United States were given Experimental Exhibition certificates awaiting approval of an electric standard. Meanwhile, other manufacturers, such as Bye Aerospace, planned to go the route of a traditionally certificated aircraft under FAR Part 23.

Despite the certification hassles, the future of electric aircraft looks promising. Electric offers a lower operating cost, less noise, simpler operation, and many other advantages. Pipistrel recognized this early and became a pioneer in the process.

PIPISTREL
I-XD38

The classic Piper Cub's enduring appeal has spawned a number of more recent look-alikes. Above, from left to right, are the Aviat Husky A-1C, American Legend's Super Legend Cub, and CubCrafters' Top Cub.

SUPER SUPER CUBS

Contemporary designs improve on the theme

Increased demand to carry more payload—farther, and often into unimproved landing sites—pushed the evolution of Piper Aircraft's iconic J-3 through the PA-11 Cub Special to its pinnacle, the PA-18 Super Cub.

The original PA-18 weighed just 781 pounds empty and was powered by a 90-horsepower Continental engine. Eventually Piper would almost double that to 160 horsepower; the company certified and produced Super Cubs with engines ranging from the original Continental C-90 through the Lycoming O-235, O-290, and O-320. The Super Cub also gained flaps and saw tweaks to the vertical tail, control surfaces, and other details.

Piper built more than 10,000 PA-18s in Lock Haven, Pennsylvania, between November 1949 and November 1982, when the Super Cub was dropped from Piper's catalog. Fast forward to the summer of 1988, when M. Stuart Millar bought Piper from private equity firm Forstmann Little; he returned the Super Cub into production in Vero Beach, Florida. Only 44 were built in Florida before production ended in December 1994.

Demand remained high in Alaska and other backcountry environments for aircraft with the PA-18's performance, however, and several companies began to market Cub- and Super Cub-like airframes. Several Cub clones are available as kits, and some meet Light Sport aircraft certification rules. Three factory-built Super Cub variants dominate the market segment today. With higher gross weights, better performance, and increased payloads, it can be argued that they have raised the Super Cub to a new level.

American Legend Super Legend

American Legend Aircraft Company was founded specifically to build the Legend Cub, a certified Light Sport iteration of the J-3. Incorporating the same basic airframe design, the company made the cabin three inches wider, moved the fuel tank into the wings—adding capacity and allowing solo flight from either tandem seat—and introduced an electrical system as well as an opening left-side window and door, among other enhancements.

The follow-on Super Legend, with a 115-horsepower Lycoming, offers the same power-to-weight ratio as a 150-horsepower PA-18. The design has continued to evolve into the Super Legend HP and XP—which sport a four-cylinder engine producing more than 180 horsepower, while weighing less than a larger Lycoming O-360.

Aviat Husky

Frank Christensen of Christen Industries began designing what would become the Aviat Husky in 1985. Designed to fill the void left by the end of Super Cub production, this new, computer-aided design clearly was influenced by its inspiration. It was certified in 1987.

The Husky boasts a 975-pound useful load and pilot-friendly center-of-gravity envelope. Today's Husky A-1C is powered by a 180- or 200-horsepower Lycoming engine; a reversible MT Propeller prop can be installed for better control on the water during floatplane operations.

In 2018 Aviat enhanced the Husky further, replacing the legacy bungee trim system with an elevator trim tab; making the rear seat and rear stick easily removable; and, optionally, extending the landing gear forward, down, and wider—increasing both propeller clearance and angle of attack. And optional electrically heated seats were added. What would Bill Piper think?

CubCrafters Top Cub

Jim Richmond founded CubCrafters in 1980 to repair and restore Piper Cubs, and in 1999 the company began building "new" Cubs from surplus parts. The FAR Part 23-certified Top Cub followed in 2004; it was based on the Piper Super Cub and incorporated the most popular supplemental type certificated modifications. In 2006, CubCrafters introduced the Sport Cub, a clean-sheet Light Sport design that brought new thinking to conventional-gear, backcountry aircraft.

Then in 2016, the company launched the XCub, another Part 23 design with a useful load of 1,084 pounds and a cruise speed of 145 mph. Combined with increased range, improved cockpit ergonomics, and well-balanced flight controls, this model exceeds its Super Cub inspiration.

ATC privatization

User fees seem to have been removed—at least explicitly—from FAA funding agendas of late. Perhaps general aviation's accumulated resistance to this concept has produced a learning curve over the years. However, another tactic appears to have taken its place, one that would give a privatized ATC system greater authority to levy fees and enact measures contrary to general aviation's interests. It's no secret that the Trump administration favors ATC "privatization"—handing control of a government-run function to a private-sector, nonprofit corporation. This corporation would turn jurisdiction of more than $14 billion in air transportation taxes to a private board, which could then determine policies and procedures as it saw fit. And it would all happen apart from the FAA's authority and congressional oversight. True, the annual FAA funding process can be cumbersome and repetitive. But the move would come at the expense of federal control over the nation's airspace system.

AOPA and other general aviation interest groups oppose the corporatization concept. As proposed by a 2017 House bill, a privatized ATC would be run by a 13-member board of directors. Only one of the board members would represent general aviation; the rest would come from the airlines, airports, unions, and ATC officials. As it would be independent from government oversight, the board's public accountability would be negligible, and congressional influence severely curtailed. This leaves the airline-dominated board free to act as a sort of monopoly, with strong airline favoritism. To use a popular analogy, it would be like handing over the interstate highway system to six major trucking companies and trusting them to look out for the interests of those driving cars.

Those favoring privatization, believing that the private sector can always function more efficiently than government, face some strong arguments. Most air traffic delays are caused by the airlines, which schedule arrivals and departures around rush hours, using airports without enough runway capacity to

YOU CAN FLY

OUR AIRPORT HOME

AOPA's headquarters at Frederick Municipal Airport in Maryland

Believing that the world's largest aviation organization ought to be located on a general aviation airport rather than in an urban office building, the AOPA board entertained offers from several communities in the Washington, D.C., area to build a new headquarters. The city of Frederick, Maryland, won the negotiations. AOPA moved into its new building at Frederick Municipal Airport in 1983, about the same time that Avemco Insurance Company moved into its own nearly identical office building next door. The two entities were previously housed together in the Air Rights Building in Bethesda, Maryland. AOPA's business relationship with Avemco dissolved in the mid-1980s. When Avemco downsized its office needs in the early 2000s, AOPA bought that building. In 2017, AOPA remodeled the first floor of the former insurance building and turned it into the You Can Fly Academy, which houses classrooms, an auditorium, flight simulators, and an online learning studio to educate flight school owners and managers and flight instructors in best practices. The building also houses the AOPA Live studios, AOPA Insurance Agency, AOPA Air Safety Institute, and numerous other businesses. Between the two buildings is the AOPA Legacy Court, with its distinctive vertical wing sculpture and Legacy Founders Wall. The names of those who include the AOPA Foundation in their estates are engraved on the wall.

A NEW NAME, A NEW ERA HERALD THE FUTURE

AOPA's safety arm looks ahead

As the AOPA Air Safety Foundation and the AOPA Foundation merged in 2010, more changes were in store. The safety arm took a new name—the AOPA Air Safety Institute (ASI)—and wasted no time upholding its legacy of being the leading-edge educator in aviation safety—whether in person or online.

On July 1, 2013, ASI launched a new online Flight Instructor Refresher Course (eFIRC) for desktop and mobile devices. The eFIRC is the only flight instructor refresher course that puts all its net revenue back into developing safety programs for all pilots. ASI also modernized its vast arsenal of interactive online courses to make them compatible with new platforms, including mobile phones and tablets, and overhauled numerous publications and quizzes. Of note was the transformation of the popular printed *InstructoReport* to the *CFI to CFI* electronic publication.

ASI's focus on increasing its video library meant the launch of six new safety videos and more than a half dozen new video series. The AOPA Air Safety Institute also launched nine new online courses, and delved into novel ways to engage and educate pilots. A new podcast series, *There I was...* debuted in 2017.

The AOPA Air Safety Institute's proven record in writing and developing interactive online programs also led it to produce courses in support of industry initiatives, including the first FAA-approved BasicMed course.

In 2017, the AOPA Air Safety Institute split from the AOPA Foundation and became a division of AOPA, allowing the foundation to focus on fundraising.

The AOPA Air Safety Institute's vision asks us to imagine a year without a single fatal accident in general aviation: lives saved, aircraft preserved, and general aviation's reputation as a safe, reliable form of travel and recreation at an all-time high—and climbing. Aspirational? Sure, but not altogether out of reach.

GA accident trends show a 50-percent reduction in the fatal accident rate since 1994. That's promising, but the AOPA Air Safety Institute is determined to do more.

AOPA Air Safety Institute Executive Director Richard McSpadden, former commander and flight leader of the U.S. Air Force Thunderbirds flight demonstration team and an active general aviation pilot, leads ASI's efforts to reduce general aviation mishaps through research, education, and collaboration (facing page).

handle the crunch. Then there's this: In nations where ATC is removed from direct government oversight, there have been declines in general aviation activity. In a Yahoo News interview, Capt. Chesley "Sully" Sullenberger, famous for flying an Airbus to a successful January 2009 ditching in New York's Hudson River after bird strikes caused a dual-engine flameout, said, "In most countries it's either too restrictive or too expensive for an average person to fly, and the only way you can go is to fly on an airliner. Freedom to fly is something we need to protect and preserve. So why in the world would we give the keys to the kingdom to the largest airlines? Because they definitely have their own agenda."

"EXCLUSIVE AVIATION SALES MONOPOLIES ARE THREATENING THE EXISTENCE OF FREE AIRPORTS....THE AIRPORT IS NO EXCEPTION TO THE RULE THAT GOOD BUSINESS IS BUILT THROUGH COMPETITION."
—EDITORIAL, AUGUST 1947 "THE AOPA PILOT"

The jury is still out on ATC privatization, but it's certain to come up in future budget and funding authorization cycles. When it does, AOPA and its allies will provide their own oversight of the deliberations.

The bite

Back in the late 1940s, the AOPA section of *Flying* magazine ran cartoons showing examples of pilots being subjected to high avgas prices and generally lousy treatment. Others showed exemplary service. Price gouging back then was called getting "the bite." And AOPA members who ran into it were encouraged to send in their AOPA-issued postcards identifying both bad actors and good. Guess what? AOPA is still at it today. Since 2017, AOPA has received word of a small number of airports with large FBOs levying gas prices two and three dollars above market rate, $100-plus ramp and/or parking fees (even if no services are used), and examples of restrictive access to public spaces. Signature Flight Support—the largest FBO chain, born of mergers—comes up as the top offender. So, $200 for a TBM pilot to pick up a passenger? Even a $2,500 charge for the 15 minutes it took for a Gulfstream to pick up a passenger. AOPA filed complaints with the FAA against three airports with particularly egregious FBOs and put others on notice; the association has seen some progress with "self-help" airports taking steps to protect pilots from access restrictions and unreasonable fees. So it is that AOPA's mission to serve the interests of general aviation pilots has not wavered in its 80 years.

In this particular issue, AOPA often presented itself as a lone actor in its advocacy. But those days are over. With the increased pace and intensity of today's discriminatory policies—whether at the local, state, federal, or corporate level—increased collaboration and consensus building is necessary among as many of the general aviation alphabet groups as possible: the Experimental Aircraft Association, National Business Aviation Association, General Aviation Manufacturers Association, National Air Transportation Association, Helicopter Association International, and Aircraft Electronics Association among them.

Still, it's safe to say that without AOPA's public voice, and the force of its 350,000 members, many outcomes would have worked to our detriment. General aviation would not have survived as we know it. Think of a pursuit that has been more beset than general aviation. Then think what would have happened if AOPA hadn't spoken up. After the September 11 terrorist attacks in 2001, there would have been no more VFR flying, with Class B and other airspace turned into no-fly zones. After FAA funding fights there would have been user fees and $100-per-flight ATC charges. After developer pressure on airports, there would have been more encroachments on airport land, runways, and runway clear zones; more obstructions; and more outright airport closures. After airports were tempted to cave in to developer pressure, there would have been no one to point out that FAA grant assurances prohibit such closures. After zero-suspicion stops and searches by U.S. Custom and Border Protection agents, no one to persuade the CBP commissioner to stop this practice. And for pilots with well-managed medical conditions, no BasicMed to obviate a pilot's medical grounding.

And AOPA will continue to fight for all of this—and more—for all of general aviation.

Active U.S. Pilots in 2017 | **609,306**

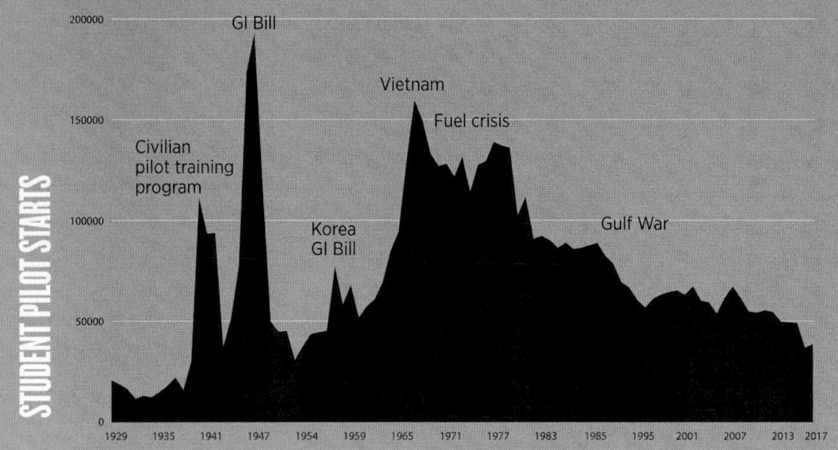

PILOTS, BY THE NUMBERS

Creating more pilots

More than aircraft deliveries or fuel sales, the number of active pilots is aviation's best indication of the industry's health. Policy makers and industry leaders obsess over the number, and for good reason. To thrive, the community needs more pilots.

Despite some admirable efforts over the years there's little to suggest the size of the pilot population has been driven from within the aviation industry. Instead, outside factors such as the economy, war, and government-funded training have at various times helped to raise the number significantly.

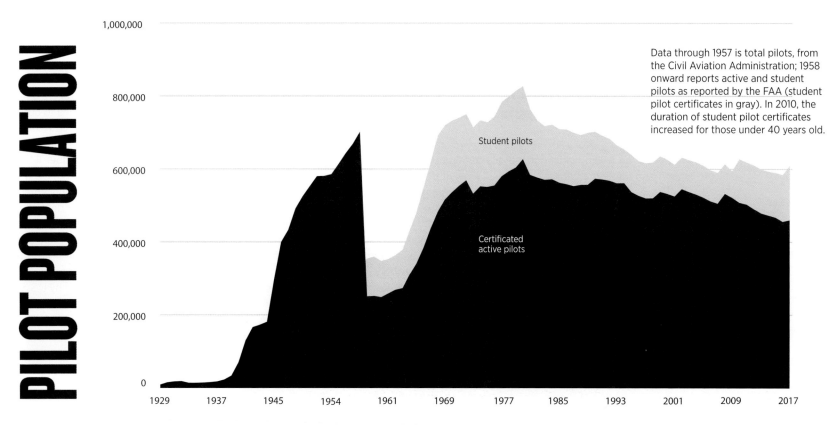

PILOT POPULATION

1,000,000
800,000
600,000
400,000
200,000
0

Data through 1957 is total pilots, from the Civil Aviation Administration; 1958 onward reports active and student pilots as reported by the FAA (student pilot certificates in gray). In 2010, the duration of student pilot certificates increased for those under 40 years old.

Student pilots

Certificated active pilots

1929 1937 1945 1954 1961 1969 1977 1985 1993 2001 2009 2017

Since at least the 1950s, pilots have been worrying about where the next generation will come from. An editorial in the July 1953 issue of "The AOPA Pilot" insert of *Flying* magazine discussed the lack of kids hanging out at airports. The editorial concludes that's because airplanes are now commonplace, and accepted. That sentiment—that aviation was in trouble because future generations don't care—has persisted.

History has shown that the most robust pilot numbers were yet to come. The number of pilots peaked in 1980 at around 825,000. Many factors came together to drive the growth, including relatively inexpensive airplanes, excess income, and government-funded flight training.

Government involvement, both direct and indirect, has been the single biggest factor in driving pilot growth. A portion of the hundreds of thousands of pilots trained for World War II, Korea, and Vietnam came back and flew for fun or a career. Thousands more used government benefits, including the GI Bill, to fund their training. The first GI Bill, passed in 1944, was a boon for post-secondary and vocational training providers after the war. It makes sense that it also drove new pilot starts in that era, and in fact, the highest number of student pilot starts was in 1947. That year, nearly 193,000 pilots began training, more even than at the height of the civilian pilot training program a few years earlier.

The number of new students peaked again in 1967 when roughly 150,000 people started learning to fly. Congress passed the Cold War GI Bill the year prior. Vietnam veterans took advantage of bill benefits at a higher rate than even their World War II counterparts. More than 8 million people benefited from the education payments between 1966 and 1989, and based on the number of new student pilots, many used it for flight training.

Given the relatively low numbers of pilots coming from the military in the past few decades, there have also been fewer new civilian pilots, despite strong commercial pilot opportunities. As the demographics of the country change and disposable income becomes more competitive, we shouldn't expect a massive change in the student number anytime soon.

MEMBERSHIP

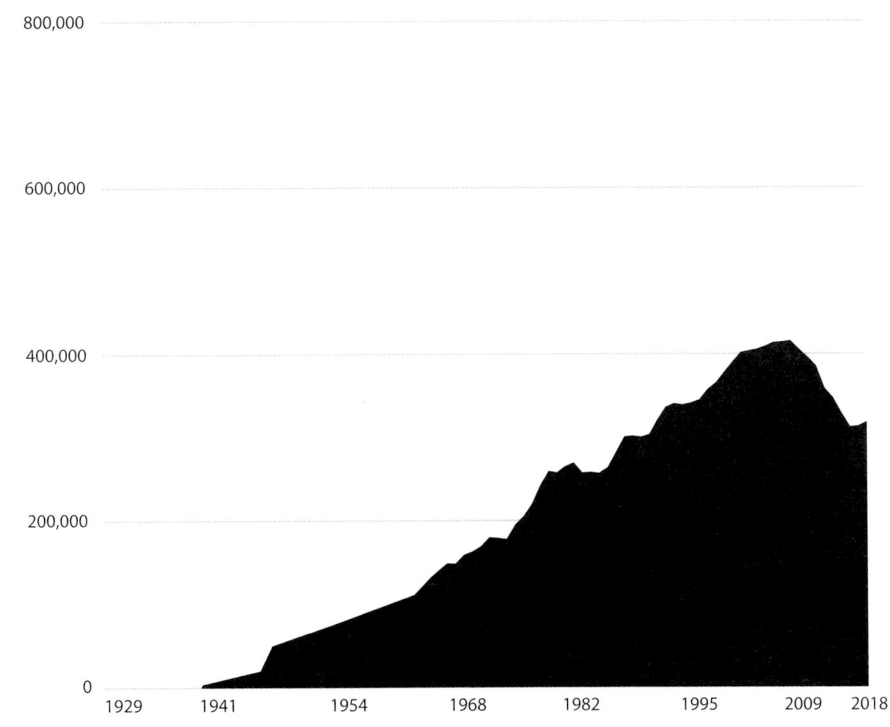

MEMBERS THROUGH THE YEARS

AOPA membership climbed steadily through the early 2000s, despite the ups and downs of the overall pilot population. Following the recession that began in 2008, membership began another uptick in 2017. Overall pilot numbers surged in postwar America, when returning service members converted military certificates and took advantage of GI Bill benefits for flight training. The coming-of-age of baby boomers and a 10-percent investment tax credit that incentivized aircraft purchases contributed to the flying boom of the 1970s, but a look at student starts over the years shows a strong correlation between new pilots and federal dollars.

EPILOGUE /

LOOKING TO THE FUTURE

BY THOMAS B. HAINES

AOPA Editor in Chief Tom Haines has worked at AOPA for more than 30 years.

Preparing for aviation's next 80 years

Buffing the spinner of a Beechcraft Bonanza A36, one can't help but wonder what is in store for this old girl, built during the Nixon administration. At 46, she's just about the average age of an airplane in the GA fleet. Did those designers back in the mid-1940s when the Bonanza was conceived—and the production-line workers in late 1971 who hand-built Serial Number E-292—ever believe that this aircraft would still be flying nearly a half century later? Now on her third engine, second paint job and interior, and after several panel upgrades, she is as sporting as ever and as capable as anything rolling out of Wichita, or anywhere else. There is no reason she can't still be flying in the mid-twenty-first century and beyond—certainly beyond AOPA's 100th anniversary in 2039.

The fact that this old Bonanza is about as good as it gets all these decades later is either really cool, if you're a nostalgist, or terribly sad if you're a futurist. Putting avionics and instrument panels aside for a moment, general aviation has looked pretty much the same for the past few decades. But, futurist, fear not, as change is afoot—or shall we say, aflight?

Always in aviation, engines drive airframe development. Nowadays, though, we should say that "propulsion" drives airframe development, as we are beginning to see the impact of electric motors on airframe designs. As with early automobile development, much of what we see today likely will be relegated to the history books in a couple of decades, but for now we are fascinated with projects such as the Bye Aerospace Sun Flyer 2, a two-place electrically powered trainer that is nearing certification. A four-place variant is also in development. Pipistrel is delivering its two-place Alpha Electro, an electric aircraft certified elsewhere in the world, but hopefully approved as a Light Sport aircraft in the United States—flying at the moment under a special exemption, as the FAA regulations and Light Sport ASTM standards don't yet

In spite of other activities and expenditures competing for disposable income, the dream of flight endures. The future of general aviation depends on the next generation of pilots carrying the torch.

recognize electric motors as a means of propulsion. History will undoubtedly look back and ask, "Why?"

The idea of ending a flight by plugging your airplane into the wall rather than calling the fuel truck is intriguing, especially with projections of hourly "fuel" costs of between $3 and $7. The cost of 100LL avgas averages $5.07 a gallon at the moment, with many locations charging $6 to $8. Converting the existing fleet to electric is unlikely, although hybrid electric may become an option for some.

Converting existing airplanes to diesel engines may be more practical, but diesel development has languished. Diamond Aircraft offshoot Austro and Continental Motors have had some success with diesel engines. However, companies such as EPS—Engineered Propulsion Systems—and DeltaHawk have had various diesel engine models in development for years, always seemingly close to certification, but not quite there. Even then, it is unclear how likely pilots will be to accept an all-new engine, despite frequent complaints about the ancient air-cooled, horizontally opposed engines powering airplanes today, including my old Bonanza. Capable of burning jet fuel, which is widely available around the globe, the diesel-cycle engines offer a lot of promise, but the conversion costs will be high. And with barely 1,000 new piston-powered airplanes being manufactured a year, the new-airframe market isn't all that lucrative, either.

Removing the lead from avgas would simplify distribution, eliminate the constant threat from environmental groups, and clarify the future for many piston-engine owners. But the development of an unleaded fuel has languished. Regardless, the use of fossil fuels is falling out of favor.

While the fuels effort has proven to be cumbersome, a characteristic of many FAA projects, there have been regulatory wins that may spur some general aviation revitalization. For example, the FAA has seen the light when it comes to allowing proven, modern safety-enhancing equipment to be more easily installed in the legacy fleet.

Part 23 of the federal aviation regulations outlines the requirements a manufacturer must meet to certify a new airplane. AOPA, the General Aviation Manufacturers Association, and other organizations worked with the FAA on a decade-long project to rewrite the onerous regulations into ones that are less prescriptive and more appropriate to the type of flying a particular airplane model is designed for. In other words, moving away from a one-size-fits-all approach into a certification environment that allows manufacturers to demonstrate in simpler and novel ways that the product meets the regulations. The goal is not a lower level of safety. To the contrary, such moves increase the likelihood that companies will develop new, affordable products that take advantage of modern materials and standards, which, in the long run will improve the safety, reliability, and utility of the fleet. The Part 23 rewrite was fully recognized by the FAA in late 2017. The general aviation world is in a wait-

and-see mode to understand what the future might bring as a result. The perspective from 2039 will be interesting indeed.

Meanwhile, the European regulatory agencies—a traditional bastion of mercurial regulatory overbearingness—have seen the light and begun to wind down the onerous maintenance and certification laws they once demanded for light general aviation airplanes across the pond. The European Aviation Safety Agency at one point made the FAA look fleet and not at all domineering. However, starting around 2015 EASA recognized that general aviation was all but gone from the continent and that no one was being served well by its Draconian oversight. As a result it began to back off on its regulations and began encouraging general aviation activity and manufacturing. The result are a number of new high-performance light airplanes. Unfortunately none of them fit into useful FAA categories, so they are a bit handicapped if imported into the United States. But it's another sign that general aviation's future is bright, as companies develop fast, efficient new designs—most of which, by the way, don't require leaded fuel or 100 octane.

The regulatory burden for general aviation around the world is still a significant deterrent to growth, but recent positive trends in safety have helped regulators understand that GA can be safe and that recreational flying and even light business transportation need to be treated differently than airline flight. If the trend continues, we can look forward to more opportunities to fly in more parts of the world and perhaps to fly in new, modern designs.

In fact, we've seen Europe as a hotbed of new designs for the past decade or more. It's as if Wichita went to sleep. Meanwhile, Tecnam, Pipistrel, Flight Design, Diamond, and other European brands have become the Cessna, Beechcraft, Piper, and Mooney of the twenty-first century. The number of deliveries is small compared to the American Big Four in the 1970s, but the innovation is huge. Tecnam, for example, has created a complete product line of airplanes from Light Sport aircraft—trainers and travelers—to a fixed-gear cruiser and a light workhorse of a twin, with more plans in the works. Pipistrel too has an interesting lineup of ultralights, powered gliders, Light Sports—including the Alpha Electro electric LSA—and the sleek Panthera, a high-performance single still in development and designed for a variety of powerplants, including electric and hybrid diesel-electric. Flight Design has designed a light four-place airplane that may benefit from the Part 23 rewrite's regulatory changes.

Several advances in recent years have led to this new generation of airplanes: composite manufacturing, lightweight avionics, and the Rotax engine. While Fiberglas has been in use in gliders and Experimental airplanes for decades, Cirrus Aircraft really brought composite manufacturing to the forefront for general aviation in the early 2000s. Modern materials—especially carbon fiber—and manufacturing techniques have further reduced weight and decreased manufacturing time. Meanwhile, modern avionics have allowed the lightest of airplanes and especially LSAs to come equipped with an entire suite of capabilities blended into one screen that may be 10 inches diagonal but only three inches deep and weighing just a few pounds. No longer do you need a six-pack full of heavy and cumbersome mechanical instruments to equip your light airplane. A single Dynon display, for example, includes your primary flight display—with synthetic vision; a moving map; an engine management and monitoring system; and a two-axis autopilot. If it fails, swap it out with two connectors. Breathtaking situational awareness in an LSA—features not available at any price 20 years earlier. Now, buy the whole thing for around $5,000.

The Rotax 912 in particular has had a significant impact on how we fly here in the first part of the twenty-first century. Its small frontal area; lightweight, liquid-cooled cylinder heads; and amazing fuel specifics allow its 100 horsepower

THE FACT THAT THIS OLD BONANZA IS ABOUT AS GOOD AS IT GETS ALL THESE DECADES LATER IS EITHER REALLY COOL, IF YOU'RE A NOSTALGIST, OR TERRIBLY SAD IF YOU'RE A FUTURIST. BUT, FUTURIST, FEAR NOT, AS CHANGE IS AFOOT.

What's old is new again. From Molt Taylor's Aerocar to the modern Terrafugia Transition, flying cars—or roadable airplanes—have remained a dream. New vertical-lift technology may finally make the intended point-to-point transportation possible. Terrafugia has joined the flock of start-ups and established companies exploring automated vertical-takeoff designs with its TF-2, shown here as a tiltrotor.

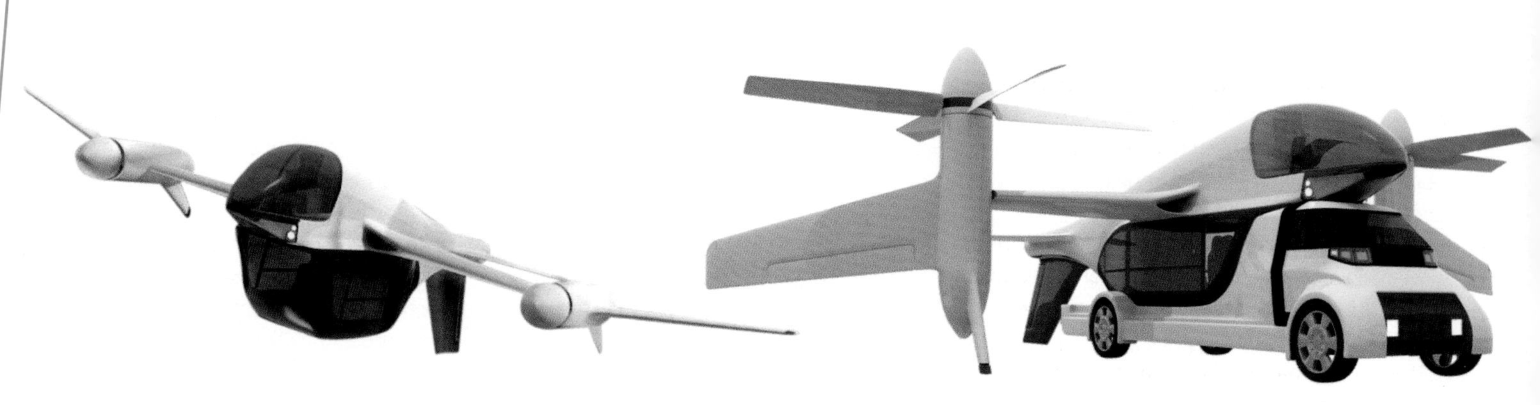

to propel well-designed LSAs at 120 knots true airspeed on about 3.8 gallons per hour. And while Rotax has been in the aviation business for a couple of decades, only recently have pilots begun to recognize its significance. Meanwhile, the company is working on the 915 iS, a 135-horsepower fuel-injected turbocharged version. Many industry observers believe it will drive a whole new generation of airframes built from scratch to take advantage of its performance. The challenge for Rotax is developing the knowledge base among mechanics to make service as ubiquitous as it is for a Lycoming or Continental.

Those new airframe development programs may benefit from another new technology that can fast-track product development: additive manufacturing, *aka* 3-D printing. Airframe manufacturers large and small are already using additive manufacturing to make one-off parts for modeling and prototyping. The process can dramatically reduce turnaround times and costs for small numbers of parts that are needed in product development. With the technology developing quickly, it's only a matter of time before GA manufacturers routinely manufacture finished parts for production aircraft using 3-D printing. After all, at current rates of production, all GA manufacturing is small-run.

It is those small numbers that continue to dog general aviation costs, though. At such small runs, manufacturers struggle to make a profit and provide long-term support without charging eye-watering prices for even the most basic of airplanes. Unfortunately, there is no manufacturing technique, material development, or other change on the horizon that will have a significant impact on cost.

Still, there are ways to begin experiencing aviation at a low cost. Most recently drones have become the cheap way into aviation. For only a few hundred dollars, a person can get a highly capable drone—unmanned aircraft system (UAS), if you prefer. Carrying a lightweight point-of-view camera, your drone can amaze your friends and neighbors with high-resolution images of their house—and perhaps your dog as you chase it around the yard. And although "real pilots" often dismiss drone pilots as not being the real deal, there is no doubt that drones are here to stay. Everything from home construction to disaster relief is benefiting from the burgeoning eyes in the sky, often flown by people with minimal traditional aviation training. A few irresponsible drone pilots have given the rest a bad name, too often flying close to airports and airliners and endangering others.

The FAA is cracking down on such operators and has created Part 107 to certify drone pilots. In addition, the agency requires drones weigh more than 0.55 pounds to be registered like any other aircraft. This, too, has been controversial, with some hobbyist drone operators challenging the registration requirement in court—and winning. Congress later reinstated the requirement. As of 2018, just more than 1 million drones have been registered—about eight out of 10 flown by hobbyists, the rest by commercial operators and public service groups.

Like other entities in this dynamic drone environment, AOPA has sought to find a way to fit in. While others have profit motives, AOPA's role is first and foremost to protect the safety of its members flying manned aircraft. To that end, AOPA created a biweekly email newsletter and dedicated web properties to provide safety and other information to drone pilots. It has also partnered with drone training organizations to provide discounted training programs.

Perhaps some of these millions of new entrants will decide that rather than standing on the ground looking at a bird's-eye view on their iPhone app, they would like to experience flight for themselves, looking at that real-world moving map scrolling by below. If so, those new pilots will help solve a challenging pilot shortage.

In 2018, Boeing estimated a need for some 635,000 additional commercial pilots, 96,000 business aviation pilots, and 59,000 helicopter pilots around the world by 2037—that's about 40,000 new pilots a year on average, and assuming no retirements or dropouts along the way. The majority of global aviation training occurs in the United States and in 2017, the FAA issued only about 17,700 private pilot certificates, the traditional entry point to those headed to an airline cockpit. That's well less than half the number needed, and doesn't account for the fact that most people who learn to fly do so for recreational purposes, not because they want to fly an airliner.

The bottom line is that the flight training industry is seriously unprepared to meet the demands of the coming decades. On top of that, word is slow getting out to young people that aviation offers a promising career. For years, airline travel has been marginalized by both the passengers and the airlines themselves. Pilot pay has been flat, at best, and downright awful at the regional airlines. The pay issue has begun to turn around and business at flight schools is picking up. But too many flight schools still teach the way they did in the 1970s—at a time when millennials consume most of their information online.

Noting the pilot population decline, the need for new pilots, and the lack of sophistication at many flight schools, AOPA developed a group of programs to help and branded them You Can Fly.

Supported entirely by donations to the AOPA Foundation, You Can Fly introduces youth to aviation through a new science, technology, engineering, and math (STEM) curriculum for grades nine through 12 via two tracks: pilot and drones. Modern curriculum and business solutions for flight schools is another You Can Fly initiative. Keeping new pilots involved through flying clubs is another. Returning lapsed pilots via the Rusty Pilots program is another part of You Can Fly.

Looking at an improving global regulatory environment that may allow for creative new aircraft, new propulsion possibilities, and advanced lower-cost avionics—and a current demand for commercial

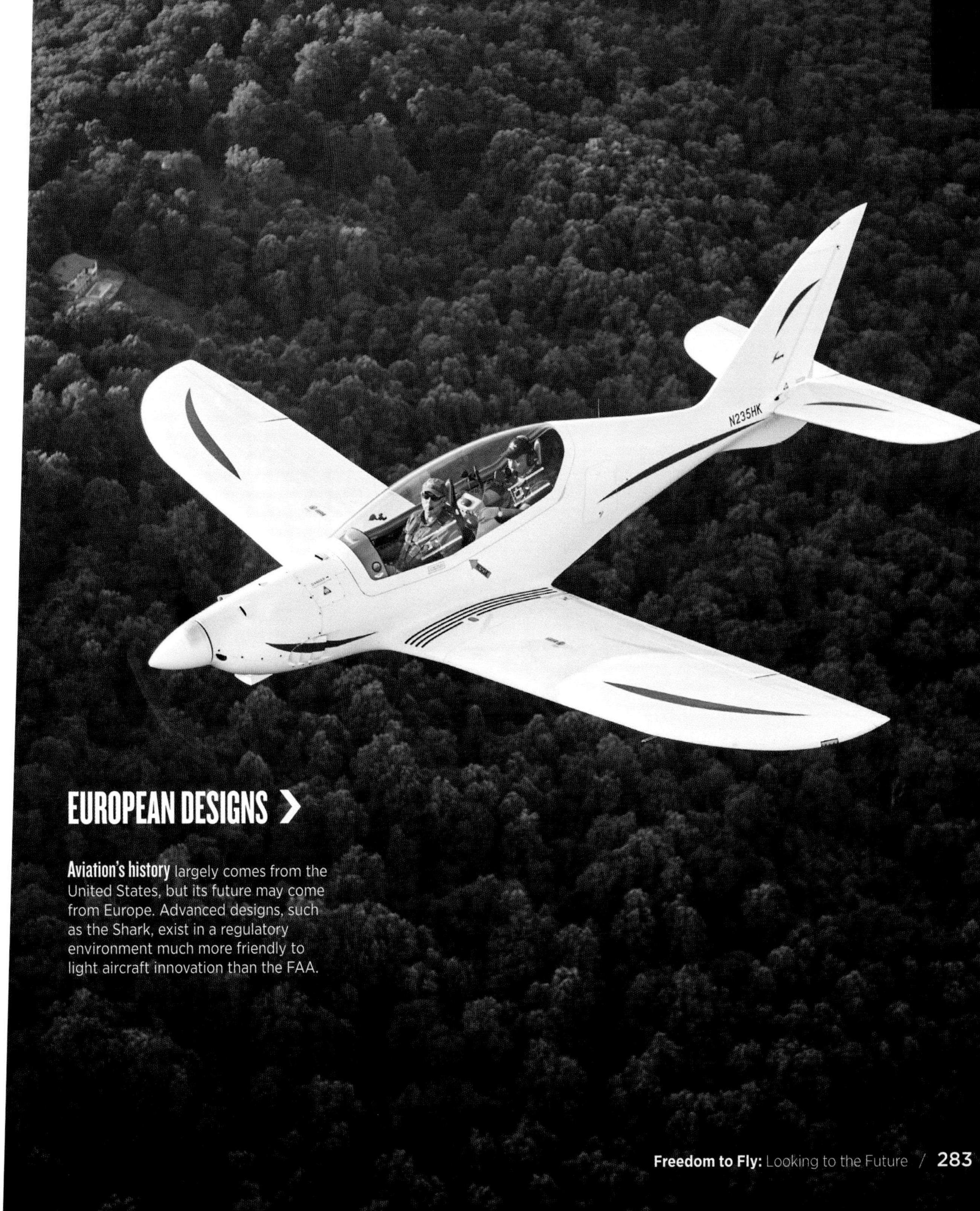

EUROPEAN DESIGNS ❯

Aviation's history largely comes from the United States, but its future may come from Europe. Advanced designs, such as the Shark, exist in a regulatory environment much more friendly to light aircraft innovation than the FAA.

pilots—one could assume that the future for general aviation is bright. But the trends mask a severe erosion of the underpinnings of our system. The decline of the pilot population is real and continuing, and no one has a solid reason why, nor a highly sure-fire plan to fight it.

Nothing has flummoxed AOPA presidents and their leadership teams—as well as manufacturers and the FAA—more than the continuing decline in the pilot population. Countless programs have been launched by all parties to try to make a difference. A few have had small impacts and undoubtedly over time the You Can Fly programs will, too. But none of them can address the larger societal changes occurring around us that impact interest in GA—and many other leisure activities, such as golf, sailing, scuba, skiing, and motorcycling. These activities are all struggling to attract new audiences.

E.M. Beck, a professor emeritus and pilot at the University of Georgia, briefed the AOPA leadership team on his findings in 2015 about the effects of socio-economic changes in the United States in the early twenty-first century. The baby boomer generation is aging out; their impact on leisure activities is waning. The U.S. fertility rate is at 1.86; 2.11 is needed just to sustain the current population. In other words, our society is aging. And while the economy at this time is strong, not everyone has benefited. Disposable

With Europe's high fuel prices and strict noise regulations, creative design is flourishing. Pipistrel has developed a range of appealing aircraft that are fast, efficient, and fun to fly. The Panthera is designed to be powerplant-flexible. Avionics advancements have also accelerated, thanks to better and cheaper technology, and a focus on performance-based regulations.

THE IDEA OF ENDING A FLIGHT BY PLUGGING YOUR AIRPLANE INTO THE WALL RATHER THAN CALLING THE FUEL TRUCK IS INTRIGUING, ESPECIALLY WITH PROJECTIONS OF HOURLY "FUEL" COSTS OF BETWEEN $3 AND $7.

income for middle-class families is flat at best and people choose to spend their income on things that weren't popular or even an option a generation ago. Most families spend hundreds of dollars a month on wireless data plans, cellphones, and cable television bills—none of them an issue for earlier generations. Families today want four- and five-bedroom homes with about that many bathrooms and probably a three-car garage to house all their cars, whereas earlier, families lived in three-bedroom homes with one or two bathrooms and drove one or two cars. The cost of higher education is taking a great deal more discretionary income than it did for earlier generations.

The idea of buying a new or nearly new airplane was feasible for a middle-income family in the 1970s. Today, that is almost unheard of. At best, a 2018 family might buy a 1970s airplane—one now 45 years old.

While it's hard to quantify, some believe younger generations are more risk averse and seek the sort of immediate gratification that learning to fly can't deliver. Are helicopter parents to blame? Is it an effect of youth growing up with handheld devices where they can immediately and constantly—but virtually—interact with friends and instantly find any fact? Has curiosity been stifled when you don't have to comb through a newspaper or set of encyclopedias to find what you're looking for?

Aviation is a lot like those other activities also in decline. You'll never play the perfect golf game or sail the perfect sortie, just like you'll never fly the perfect flight. These are activities we can never completely master, and yet we strive to get better. We are challenged by the experience, knowing we will never completely reach the goal.

Undoubtedly, some in our younger generations possess that same yearning today's pilots have—the desire to master flight, propel themselves in three dimensions across breathtaking landscapes toward shimmering sunsets. The difference is they have so many more ways to spend their leisure time and dollars.

It's important to keep in mind, though, that we don't need hundreds of thousands of new pilots; tens of thousands can have a significant impact on the pilot population. That many more pilots would infuse new activity into the aircraft market, result in the sale of more fuel and maintenance services, all helpful in keeping GA vibrant.

If that now-very-shiny Bonanza spinner is our crystal ball, the future for general aviation holds promise on AOPA's eightieth anniversary. The regulatory environment is more welcoming than at any time in decades, which may lead to compelling new designs; powerplant options are emerging for the first time in many years; the demand for pilots is strong, which will help revitalize the flight training industry; and the pace of progress regarding new avionics and systems is breathtaking. This upgraded old Bonanza sports avionics capabilities its builders could not have imagined—and it's already a generation out of date.

The current avionics capabilities are just a few software updates short of autonomous or semi-autonomous flight, which undoubtedly will be a thing in the future. But for those of us for whom the journey is the best part of the trip, hands-on flying will endure for decades to come. From our perspective, there is no human pursuit more satisfying than the challenge of flying a personal aircraft—and doing it well. The turning of a calendar page is not going to change that.

Acknowledgements

Editorial

Special thanks to the writers who contributed to the creation of this book. Thomas A. Horne's extensive contributions, including researching, writing, and editing the main chapters, helped guide the content, tone, structure, and overall focus. In addition, the staff of *AOPA Pilot* and others contributed stories highlighted throughout the book. Writers are listed below, along with the page number(s) of their editorial contributions.

Mark R. Baker....11
Mike Collins....18, 32, 48, 106, 211, 220, 265, 270
Stephen Coonts....7
Sarah Deener....35
Thomas B. Haines....104, 244, 250, 273, 278
Dave Hirschman....25, 36, 46, 49, 96, 102, 114, 156, 168, 172, 232, 234, 254
Sylvia Schneider Horne....11, 130
Thomas A. Horne....22, 62, 67, 68, 124, 126, 132, 142, 146, 152, 154, 162, 164, 167, 176, 184, 196, 208, 210, 228, 238,
David Jack Kenny....30, 40, 58, 84, 108, 112, 116, 118, 120
Kristy O'Malley....72
Machteld Smith....240, 274
Jill W. Tallman....34, 38, 82, 98, 128, 140
Ian J. Twombly....28, 44, 135, 138, 150, 160, 166, 170, 174, 186, 190, 198, 204, 222, 258, 268, 276
Julie Summers Walker....20, 26, 39, 100, 111, 182, 188, 257, 260, 264
Text on the following pages was adapted from *AOPA Pilot* and *Flight Training* archives:....74, 90, 94, 121, 134, 161, 192, 195, 221, 252

Images

AOPA would like to thank the following people and organizations for supplying the photographs and images featured in this book.

Alamy Stock Photo/Aviation History Collection....38
Alamy Stock Photo/Hum Images....158
Alamy Stock Photo/Christine Osborne....167
Alamy Stock Photo/Trinity Mirror/Mirrorpix....170
AOPA Archives....16, 50, 52, 53, 54, 67, 70, 80, 81, 86, 88, 98, 101, 104, 110, 114, 115, 118, 121, 127, 128, 134, 135, 142, 146, 147, 149, 152, 153, 154, 160, 162, 163, 164, 169, 171, 174, 176, 182, 184, 188, 192, 195, 196, 202, 207, 210, 211, 213, 214, 220, 221, 230, 236, 240, 245, 253
AOPA Archives, Hagley Museum and Library....52, 55, 56, 57, 58, 60, 61, 62, 64, 65, 66, 67, 68, 69, 71, 72, 73, 77, 78, 79, 80, 85, 89, 92, 93, 97, 98, 99, 111, 121, 122, 123, 125, 131, 132, 136, 148
Archives American Art....42
Associated Press....181, 183
Avidyne....206
Daniel Berek....29
Cirrus....222
Mike Collins....18, 22, 30, 198, 218, 272, 278, 279
Elton Eddy....160
Edwards Air Force Base....101
Experimental Aircraft Association....93
Federal Aviation Administration....181
Mike Fizer....8, 12, 13, 14, 24, 74, 91, 94, 96, 97, 108, 112, 116, 118, 120, 138, 178, 186, 191, 194, 203, 204, 207, 208, 215, 216, 217, 234, 247, 257, 261, 266, 270, 271, 274, 280, 283, 287
Charles Floyd....258, 259
Garmin....206
Getty Images....26, 48, 82, 83, 131, 145, 151, 168, 224, 232
Elise Grenier....43
Historic Images Outlet....111
Historical Society of Dauphin County....166
Steve Karp....276, 277
Bill Larkins....33
Library of Congress....7, 19, 40, 47
National Aeronautics and Space Administration....35, 106
The Paragon Agency....27
Chris Rose....1, 4, 11, 21, 32, 44 ,45, 140, 157, 173, 174, 187, 200, 223, 228, 239, 250, 251, 254, 260, 262, 269, 284, 288
Mark Schaible....230
Smithsonian National Air and Space Museum....35, 49, 146, 147
Smithsonian National Air and Space Museum (NASM 80-12371)....20
Smithsonian National Air and Space Museum (NASM A-48532-L)....21
Smithsonian National Air and Space Museum (NASM 94-7993)....21
Smithsonian National Air and Space Museum (NASM A-672)....36
Smithsonian National Air and Space Museum (NASM 9A06449)....36
Smithsonian National Air and Space Museum (NASM 86-533)....39
Smithsonian National Air and Space Museum (NASM 79-3161)....39
Smithsonian National Air and Space Museum (NASM 84-11902)....48
Smithsonian National Air and Space Museum (NASM 81-16962)....48
Smithsonian National Air and Space Museum (NASM 2008-1213)....84
Smithsonian National Air and Space Museum (NASM 2003-35026)....90
Smithsonian National Air and Space Museum (NASM 00049679)....95
Smithsonian National Air and Space Museum (NASM 83-12597)....106
Sporty's Pilot Shop....153
Lonna Tucker....197
David Tulis....244, 248, 256
U.S. Air Force....36, 76
Phil Vabre....25
Dave Walton....103